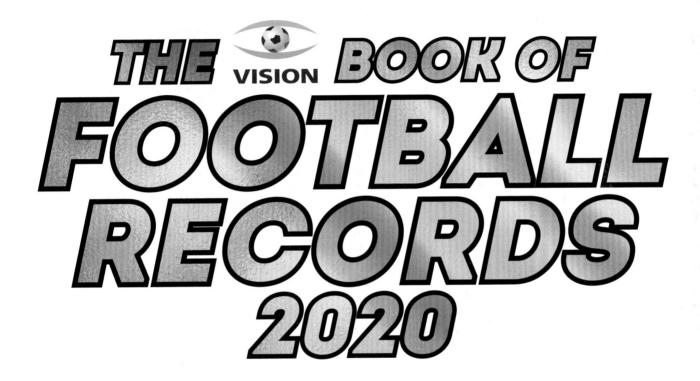

THE VISION BOOK OF FOOTBALL RECORDS 2020

BY CLIVE BATTY

Published by Vision Sports Publishing in 2019

Vision Sports Publishing
19-23 High Street
Kingston upon Thames
Surrey
KT1 1LL

www.visionsp.co.uk

© Clive Batty

ISBN: 978-1909534-95-7

Editors: Ed Davis and Jim Drewett
Design: Neal Cobourne
Proof reader: Xander Chevallier
Kit images: David Moor, www.historicalkits.co.uk
All pictures: Getty Images

Printed and bound in Slovakia by Neografia
A CIP catalogue record for this book is available from the British Library

FSC® C020353
MIX
Paper from responsible sources
www.fsc.org

All statistics in the *Vision Book of Football Records 2020* are correct up until the start of the 2019/20 season

Welcome to the 2020 edition of the *Vision Book of Football Records*. Incredibly, a full decade has now passed since this book first appeared on the shelves – a period during which the football world has evolved at bewildering speed. Players have come and gone, managers have switched clubs almost as often as they change their socks and, just occasionally – think Leicester City winning the Premier League in 2015/16 or England reaching the World Cup semi-finals three years later – something so remarkable has happened that even those strange folk who don't much like football have had to sit up and take some notice.

Meanwhile, video technology has transformed the role of the officials. Of course, this season sees the introduction of 'VAR' to the Premier League for the first time, and it will be interesting to see how successful it proves in the long run. Clearly, it's vital that the referee makes the right call over a disputed goal or debatable penalty decision, but nobody wants to hang around for ages on a cold February night in Newcastle or Norwich while the 'video assistants' endlessly study a potential offside or handball. So, c'mon guys, get a move on!

Away from the pitch, the sums of money swirling around the game have grown ever more mind-boggling in the last 10 years. Back in 2010 Cristiano Ronaldo's £80 million move from Manchester United to Real Madrid the previous summer had smashed the world transfer record, but now a similar fee might only land your club a non-scoring defensive midfielder with a dodgy disciplinary record. Inevitably, perhaps, the decade has also seen the cash-rich clubs dominate their respective leagues like never before, leaving slim pickings for the rest.

The 2018/19 season was a case in point, with very familiar names sweeping up the main prizes across Europe. For the first time ever, the winners of the continent's five main leagues had also lifted the title the previous year: Manchester City retained their Premier League crown after an exciting two-horse race with Champions League winners Liverpool, and then went on to clinch an unprecedented 'Treble'; in Italy, Juventus won Serie A for a staggering eighth season on the trot; in Spain, Barcelona again got the better of arch rivals Real Madrid; in Germany, Bayern Munich claimed a seventh consecutive Bundesliga title; and in France, few were surprised to see Paris Saint-Germain top the table for the fifth time in six years.

All a bit too predictable, some might say. However, while the big guns were grabbing most of the silverware they were also setting numerous records along the way. As you'd expect, these have all been included in this latest edition along with loads of other changes, revisions and amendments. There are also many new entries for players who came to the fore in the 2018/19 campaign, including promising youngsters like Phil Foden, Callum Hudson-Odoi and Jadon Sancho. Alongside them are entries for all the top players and managers, based both in Britain and beyond, as well as for the 92 English league clubs (plus poor old Notts County, who dropped out of League Two in 2019), the 12 Scottish Premiership clubs, the leading lights in European football and the top international nations. There are also more entries than ever before covering the women's game, which is very much on a roll after this summer's fantastic World Cup in France.

There's much more, too, including entries on all the major domestic, European and international competitions, plus individual aspects of the game such as free-kicks, headers and penalty shoot-outs. In addition, you'll find a ton of 'Wild card' entries on subjects as diverse as 'Animals' (read about the playful black dog who saved a certain goal in Argentina), 'Size' (any idea who the shortest player is in the Premier League?) and 'Twitter' (guess which player has the most followers worldwide).

Actually, the answer to that last one is easy: it's our old friend Cristiano Ronaldo. Which just goes to prove that while much has changed in football over the last decade, some things – like the undimmed brilliance of the Juventus superstar and his old adversary, Lionel Messi – remain the same. May they both continue to entertain us for many more years to come. Enjoy the book!

CLIVE BATTY

ABANDONED MATCHES

Since the Premier League was formed in 1992, only six matches have had to be abandoned. The most recent was on 30th December 2006 when Watford's game with Wigan Athletic was called off after 56 minutes due to a waterlogged pitch. The score at the time was 1-1, as it was when the match was replayed later in the season.

• **The shortest ever Football League game took place in 1894, when a raging blizzard caused the match between Stoke and Wolves at the Victoria Ground to be called off after just three minutes. Only 400 hardy fans had braved the elements, and even they must have been secretly relieved when the referee, Mr Helme, called the game off.**

• The most significant Football League match to be abandoned was in November 1904 when Woolwich Arsenal's home game with Everton was called off after 76 minutes due to fog with the Merseysiders leading 3-1. When the match was replayed later in the season the Toffees lost 2-1 – if they had managed to win they would have been league champions, rather than finishing second behind Newcastle.

• **The Brazilian league match between Vitoria and Bahia on 18th February 2018 was abandoned after 79 minutes when the home side were reduced to just six men – one fewer than the minimum allowed by the rules – after having a fifth player sent off. Opponents Bahia also had four men dismissed by the referee in a tempestuous affair.**

• The Women's Championship match on 13th January 2019 between Charlton Athletic and Manchester United was abandoned after just 11 minutes when Addicks defender Charlotte Kerr was injured and had to be taken to hospital in an ambulance. Happily, Kerr was not seriously hurt but the referee decided that the home side's failure to provide her with oxygen was sufficient reason to call off the match.

ABERDEEN

Year founded: 1903
Ground: Pittodrie Stadium (20,866)
Nickname: The Dons
Biggest win: 13-0 v Peterhead (1923)
Heaviest defeat: 0-9 v Celtic (2010)

Aberdeen were founded in 1903, following the amalgamation of three city clubs, Aberdeen, Orion and Victoria United. The following year the club joined the Scottish Second Division, and in 1905 the Dons were elected to an expanded First Division. Aberdeen have remained in the top flight ever since, a record shared with just Celtic.

• **The club was originally known as the Whites and later as the Wasps or the Black and Golds after their early strips, but in 1913 became known as the Dons. This nickname is sometimes said to derive from the involvement of professors at Aberdeen University in the foundation of the club, but is more likely to be a contraction of the word 'Aberdonians', the term used to describe people from Aberdeen.**

• Aberdeen first won the Scottish title in 1955, and later enjoyed a trio of championship successes in the 1980s under manager Alex Ferguson. Before he moved on to even greater triumphs with Manchester United, Fergie also led the Dons to four victories in five years in the Scottish Cup, which included a record run of 20 cup games without defeat between 1982 and 1985.

• **The club's finest hour, though, came in 1983 when the Dons became only the second Scottish club (after Rangers in 1972) to win the European Cup Winners' Cup, beating Real Madrid 2-1 in the final. Later that year Aberdeen defeated Hamburg over two legs to claim the European Super Cup and remain the only Scottish side to win two European trophies.**

• In 1984 Aberdeen became the first club outside the 'Old Firm' to win the Double, after finishing seven points clear at the top of the league and beating Celtic 2-1 in the Scottish Cup final.

• **Aberdeen's record of 16 appearances in the Scottish Cup final (including seven wins) is only bettered by Celtic and Rangers.**

• Scottish international defender Willie Miller has made more appearances for the club than any other player, an impressive 560 games between 1973 and 1990. Hotshot striker Joe Harper is the Dons' record goalscorer, with 199 during two spells at Pittodrie (1969-72 and 1976-81).

• **Ginger-haired central defender Alex McLeish made a club record 77 appearances for Scotland between 1980 and 1993.**

• On 12th May 2017 midfielder Dean Campbell became Aberdeen's youngest ever player when he made his debut as a sub in a home defeat against Celtic aged 16 and 51 days. Earlier the same day the teenager had sat an English exam at his school, Hazlehead Academy.

HONOURS
Premier Division champions 1980, 1984, 1985
Division 1 champions 1955
Scottish Cup 1947, 1970, 1982, 1983, 1984, 1986, 1990
League Cup 1956, 1977, 1986, 1990, 1996, 2014
Double 1984
European Cup Winners' Cup 1983
European Super Cup 1983

Jon Gallagher in action for Aberdeen

AC Milan goalkeeper Gianluigi Donnarumma is an expensive shirt-name choice!

AC MILAN

Year founded: 1899
Ground: San Siro (80,018)
Nickname: Rossoneri
League titles: 18
Domestic cups: 5
European cups: 14
International cups: 4

One of the giants of European football, the club was founded by British expatriates as the Milan Cricket and Football Club in 1899. Apart from a period during the fascist dictatorship of Benito Mussolini, the club has always been known as 'Milan' rather than the Italian 'Milano'.

• Milan were the first Italian side to win the European Cup, beating Benfica in the final at Wembley in 1963, and have gone on to win the trophy seven times – a record surpassed only by Real Madrid, with 13 victories.

• In 1986 the club was acquired by the businessman and future Italian President Silvio Berlusconi, who invested in star players like Marco van Basten, Ruud Gullit and Frank Rijkaard. Milan went on to enjoy a golden era under coaches Arrigo Sacchi and Fabio Capello, winning three European Cups and four Serie A titles between 1988 and 1994. Incredibly, the club were undefeated for 58 league games between 1991 and 1993, a record run in Italian football.

• Another star of that AC Milan team was legendary defender Paolo Maldini, who made a record 647 appearances in Serie A between 1985 and 2009.

• AC Milan's all-time leading scorer is Gunnar Nordahl, with an impressive tally of 210 goals in just 257 games. The legendary Swedish striker was top scorer in Serie A on a record five occasions during the 1950s.

> HONOURS
> *Italian champions* 1901, 1906, 1907, 1951, 1955, 1957, 1959, 1962, 1968, 1979, 1988, 1992, 1993, 1994, 1996, 1999, 2004, 2011
> *Italian Cup* 1967, 1972, 1973, 1977, 2003
> *European Cup/Champions League* 1963, 1969, 1989, 1990, 1994, 2003, 2007
> *European Cup Winners' Cup* 1968, 1973
> *European Super Cup* 1989, 1990, 1994, 2003, 2007
> *Club World Cup/Intercontinental Cup* 1969, 1989, 1990, 2007

ACCRINGTON STANLEY

Year founded: 1968
Ground: Crown Ground (5,450)
Nickname: The Stans
Biggest win: 10-1 v Lincoln United (1999)
Heaviest defeat: 2-8 v Peterborough (2008)

Accrington Stanley were founded at a meeting in a working men's club in Accrington in 1968, as a successor to the former Football League club of the same name which had folded two years earlier.

• **Conference champions in 2006, Stanley were promoted to the Football League in place of relegated Oxford United. After more than a decade in League Two the club finally went up to the third tier as champions in 2018, setting new club records for games won (29) and points accumulated (93).**

• The original town club, Accrington, were one of the 12 founder members of the Football League in 1888, but resigned from the league after just five years.

• **In 2019 the Stans came close to reaching the fifth round of the FA Cup for the first time in their history, but were beaten 1-0 by Derby County in front of a record crowd of 5,397 at the Crown Ground.**

• Midfielder Romauld Boco, the scorer of the Stans' first ever league goal, made a club record 17 appearances for Benin between 2005 and 2008.

> HONOURS
> *League Two champions* 2018
> *Conference champions* 2006

AFC WIMBLEDON

Year founded: 2002
Ground: Kingsmeadow (4,850)
Nickname: The Dons
Biggest win: 9-0 v Chessington United (2004) and Slough Town (2007)
Heaviest defeat: 0-5 v York City (2010)

AFC Wimbledon were founded in 2002 by supporters of the former Premier

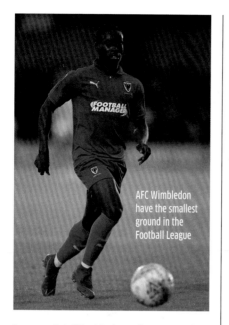

AFC Wimbledon have the smallest ground in the Football League

League club Wimbledon, who opposed the decision of the FA to sanction the 'franchising' of their club when they allowed it to move 56 miles north from their south London base to Milton Keynes in Buckinghamshire (the club later becoming the MK Dons).

• In October 2006 an agreement was reached with the MK Dons that the honours won by the old Wimbledon would return to the London Borough of Merton. This was an important victory for the AFC fans, who view their club as the true successors to Wimbledon FC.

• In their former incarnation as Wimbledon the club won the FA Cup in 1988, beating hot favourites Liverpool 1-0 at Wembley. Incredibly, the Dons had only been elected to the Football League just 12 years earlier, but enjoyed a remarkable rise through the divisions, winning promotion to the top flight in 1986. Dubbed the 'Crazy Gang' for their direct, physical approach on the pitch and hard-living, madcap antics off it, Wimbledon remained in the Premier League until 2000.

• In 2011 the Dons gained promotion to League Two after beating Luton Town on penalties in the Conference play-off final. Then, in 2016, AFC became the first club formed in the 21st century to play in the Football League play-offs and delighted their fans by beating Plymouth Argyle 2-0 in the League Two final at Wembley.

• With a capacity of just 4,850, the club's tiny Kingsmeadow Stadium is the smallest in the Football League.

• Defender Barry Fuller made a club record 205 league appearances for the Dons between 2013 and 2018. The club's record scorer is Montserrat international striker Lyle Taylor who notched 44 league goals before he moved on to Charlton in the summer of 2018.

HONOURS
Division 4 champions 1983 *(as Wimbledon FC)*
FA Cup 1988 *(as Wimbledon FC)*
FA Amateur Cup 1963 *(as Wimbledon FC)*

AFRICA CUP OF NATIONS

The Africa Cup of Nations was founded in 1957. The first tournament was a decidedly small affair consisting of just three competing teams (Egypt, Ethiopia and hosts Sudan) after South Africa's invitation was withdrawn when they refused to send a multi-racial squad to the finals. Egypt were the first winners, comfortably beating Ethiopia 4-0 in the final in Khartoum. The current holders are Algeria, who beat Senegal 1-0 in the 2019 final in Cairo.

• With seven victories, Egypt are the most successful side in the history of the competition. The north Africans have also won more matches (54) and scored more goals (159) than any other country at the finals.

• Ghana striker Asamoah Gyan appeared at the finals for an eighth time in 2019, equalling a record previously set by Cameroon's Rigobert Song and Egypt's Ahmed Hassan.

• The top scorer in the history of the competition is Cameroon striker Samuel Eto'o, who hit a total of 18 goals in the tournament between 2000 and 2010. Pierre Ndaye Mulamba of Zaire holds the record for the most goals in a single tournament, with nine in 1974.

• Egypt have hosted the finals on a record five occasions, most recently in 2019.

AFRICAN FOOTBALLER OF THE YEAR

The African Footballer of the Year award was established by the Confederation of African Football in 1992. The 2018 winner was Liverpool and Egypt striker Mohamed Salah for a second consecutive year, who topped the poll ahead of his team-mate, Senegal forward Sadio Mane.

• Ivory Coast midfielder Yaya Toure enjoyed a record four wins on the trot between 2011 and 2014. Legendary Cameroon striker Samuel Eto'o also won the award four times, including a hat-trick between 2003 and 2005.

• The first Premier League-based player to win the award was Arsenal's Nigerian striker Kanu in 1999. Altogether, players at English clubs have won the award a record 12 times.

• Former Chelsea striker Didier Drogba figured in the poll's top three a record nine times, winning the award in both 2006 and 2009.

AGE

The youngest player to appear in the Premier League is Fulham midfielder Harvey Elliott, who was aged 16 and 30

Algeria's 2019 Africa Cup of Nations win was definitely a 'selfie' moment!

days when he came on as a sub for the Cottagers against Wolves on 4th May 2019. Elliott also holds the record for the youngest player to play in the League Cup, making his debut in the competition against Millwall on 25th September 2018 when he was aged just 15 and 174 days.

• Striker Jordan Allan became the youngest player ever in British football history when he came on as a sub for Airdrie United against Livingston in April 2014 aged 14 and 189 days. At the time he was still a pupil at the Calderside Academy in South Lanarkshire.

• The oldest player in the history of English league football is Neil McBain, the then New Brighton manager, who had to go in goal for his side's Division Three (North) match against Hartlepool aged 51 and 120 days during an injury crisis in 1947. Goalkeeper John Burridge holds the Premier League record, turning out aged 43 and 162 days for Manchester City against QPR in May 1995.

• The oldest player to play for a FIFA-affiliated nation is former World Player of the Year George Weah, the President of Liberia, who was aged 51 and 345 days when he started for his country in a specially arranged friendly against Nigeria held to 'retire' his number 14 shirt on 11th September 2018. The youngest player to appear in international football

Another goal for Sergio Aguero, Manchester City's all-time top scorer

is Lucas Knecht, who turned out for the Northern Mariana Islands against Guam two days after his 14th birthday in 2007.

• The youngest player to score in international football is Aung Kyaw Tun of Myanmar, who found the net in a 3-1 defeat against Thailand in November 2000 aged 14 and 93 days.

• The oldest professional footballer to score a goal is former Japan international Kazuyoshi Miura, who slotted home from inside the six-yard box for Yokohama FC against Thespa Kusatsu in the J2 League (Japanese second division) on 12th March 2017, aged 50 and 14 days.

• Roy Hodgson became the oldest man to manage in the Premier League when he led Crystal Palace to an impressive 4-1 victory at Leicester City on 23rd February 2019 aged 71 and 198 days.

SERGIO AGUERO

Born: Quilmes, Argentina, 2nd June 1988
Position: Striker
Club career:
2003-06 Independiente 54 (23)
2006-11 Atletico Madrid 175 (74)
2011- Manchester City 239 (164)
International record:
2006- Argentina 96 (40)

Manchester City's all-time top scorer with 231 goals in all competitions, Sergio Aguero is also the highest-scoring non-European in Premier League history with 164 goals, and one of just two players (along with Arsenal legend Thierry Henry) to hit 20 or more goals in five consecutive Premier League

seasons, achieving this feat with 21 in 2018/19 to help City win a fourth title in his eight years at the Etihad. In the same season he equalled Alan Shearer's record of 11 Premier League hat-tricks when he banged in a treble in City's 6-0 mauling of Chelsea at the Etihad on 10th February 2019.

• Known as 'El Kun' because of his resemblance to a Japanese cartoon character, Aguero became the youngest ever player to appear in Argentina's top flight when he made his debut for Independiente in 2003 aged just 15 years and 35 days. The previous record was set by the legendary Diego Maradona, Aguero's former father-in-law.

• Aguero moved on to Atletico Madrid in 2006 aged 17, helping the Spanish club win the inaugural Europa League in 2010. The following year he joined Manchester City for £38 million, becoming the second most expensive player in British football history at the time.

• The fee proved to be a bargain as Aguero banged in 23 Premier League goals – including a dramatic title-clinching winner against QPR on the last day of the season – as City topped the table for the first time since 1968. Two years later he contributed another 17 goals as City won the title again, and in 2015 he became the first Manchester City player to win the Premier League Golden Boot outright after topping the scoring charts with an impressive total of 26 goals. The following season he became only the fifth player in Premier League history to score five goals in a game, doing so in record time – just 23 minutes and 34 seconds – during a 6-1 hammering of Newcastle.

TOP 10

YOUNGEST ENGLAND PLAYERS

1.	Theo Walcott	17 years and 74 days (2006)
2.	Wayne Rooney	17 years and 110 days (2003)
3.	James Prinsep	17 years and 251 days (1879)
4.	Tot Rostron	17 years and 311 days (1881)
5.	Raheem Sterling	17 years and 341 days (2012)
6.	Clement Mitchell	18 years and 23 days (1880)
7.	Michael Owen	18 years and 59 days (1998)
8.	Callum Hudson-Odoi	18 years and 134 days (2019)
9.	Micah Richards	18 years and 143 days (2006)
10.	Duncan Edwards	18 years and 182 days (1955)

A quicksilver attacker who possesses excellent close control, Aguero made his international debut for Argentina in a 2006 friendly against Brazil at Arsenal's Emirates Stadium. In 2008 he was a key figure in the Argentina team that won gold at the Beijing Olympics, and he is now third on his country's list of all-time top scorers with 40 goals.

AIR CRASHES

On 21st January 2019 a light aircraft carrying Cardiff City's record signing Emiliano Sala crashed into the English Channel, killing both the Argentinean striker and the pilot, Dave Ibbotson.

• **Leicester City owner Vichai Srivaddhanaprabha was among five people killed when their helicopter crashed just outside the King Power Stadium shortly after taking off from the pitch following the Foxes' home match with West Ham United on 27th October 2018.**

• On 6th February 1958 eight members of the Manchester United 'Busby Babes' team, including England internationals Roger Byrne, Duncan Edwards and Tommy Taylor, were killed in the Munich Air Crash. Their plane crashed while attempting to take off in a snowstorm at Munich Airport, where it had stopped to refuel after a European Cup tie in Belgrade. In total, 23 people died in the incident, although manager Matt Busby and Bobby Charlton were among the survivors. Amazingly, United still managed to reach the FA Cup final that year, but lost at Wembley to Bolton Wanderers.

• **The entire first team of Torino, the strongest Italian club at the time, were wiped out in an air disaster on 4th May 1949. Returning from a testimonial match in Portugal, the team's plane crashed into the Basilica of Superga outside Turin. Among the 31 dead were 10 members of the Italian national side and the club's English manager, Leslie Lievesley. Torino fielded their youth team in their four remaining fixtures and, with their opponents each doing the same as a mark of respect, won a joint-record fifth consecutive league title at the end of the season.**

AJAX

Year founded: 1900
Ground: Johan Cruyff Arena (54,990)
Nickname: De Godenzonen (the sons of the Gods)
League titles: 34
Domestic cups: 19
European cups: 8
International cups: 2

Founded in 1900 in Amsterdam, Ajax are named after the Greek mythological hero. Reigning Eredivisie champions and Champions League semi-finalists in 2019, Ajax are the most successful club in Holland, having won the league a record 34 times and the Dutch Cup a record 19 times.

• **Ajax's most glorious decade was in the 1970s when, with a team featuring legends like Johan Cruyff, Johan Neeskens and Johnny Rep, the Amsterdam outfit won the European Cup three times on the trot, playing a fluid system known as 'Total Football'. In 1995 a young Ajax team won the trophy for a fourth time, Patrick Kluivert scoring the winner in the final against AC Milan.**

• When Ajax beat Torino in the final of the UEFA Cup in 1992 they became

Noussair Mazraoui crosses the ball for Ajax, who have won the Dutch league a record 34 times

only the second team, after Juventus, to win all three major European trophies. In 2017 Ajax reached their first European final for two decades, but lost 2-0 in the Europa League final to Manchester United.

• Ajax recorded the biggest ever win in the UEFA Cup/Europa League when they hammered Luxembourg minnows Red Boys Differdange 14-0 in 1984.

• In 2018 Ajax's home, the largest stadium in the Netherlands, was renamed the Johan Cruyff Arena in recognition of their greatest ever player, who died in March 2016

HONOURS

Dutch champions *1918, 1919, 1931, 1932, 1934, 1937, 1939, 1947, 1957, 1960, 1966, 1967, 1968, 1970, 1972, 1973, 1977, 1979, 1980, 1982, 1983, 1985, 1990, 1994, 1995, 1996, 1998, 2002, 2004, 2011, 2012, 2013, 2014, 2019*

Dutch Cup *1917, 1943, 1961, 1967, 1970, 1971, 1972, 1979, 1983, 1986, 1987, 1993, 1998, 1999, 2002, 2006, 2007, 2010, 2019*

European Cup/Champions League *1971, 1972, 1973, 1995*

UEFA Cup *1992*

European Cup Winners' Cup *1987*

European Super Cup *1973, 1995*

Intercontinental Cup *1972, 1995*

TRENT ALEXANDER-ARNOLD

Born: Liverpool, 7th June 199
Position: Defender
Club career:
2016- Liverpool 55 (2)
International record:
2018- England 6 (1)

In the 2018/19 season Liverpool right-back Trent Alexander-Arnold set a new record for Premier League assists by a defender with 12, earning himself a place in the PFA Team of the Year. He then topped a superb campaign by helping Liverpool win the Champions League in Madrid, to become the youngest ever player to start in consecutive finals of the competition.

• Alexander-Arnold was just six years old when he joined the Liverpool academy, progressing through the ranks to skipper the club at Under-16 and Under-18 level before making his first-team debut in a 2-1 victory

"Great stuff, Trent, I reckon you're the world's best number 66!"

against Tottenham in the League Cup fourth round in October 2016.

• When he rifled in a free-kick against Hoffenheim in a Champions League play-off round in August 2017 Alexander-Arnold became the third youngest Liverpool player to score on his European debut and when he played in the Reds' 3-1 defeat to Real Madrid in Kiev he was the youngest player in the club's history to start a Champions League final. At the end of the 2017/18 season he was nominated for the Golden Boy award for the best young European player, but lost out to Ajax defender Matthijs de Ligt.

• **After representing England from Under-16 level onwards, Alexander-Arnold made his senior debut against Costa Rica at Elland Road in June 2018. When he played for England at the World Cup in Russia against Belgium he was only the fourth teenager to feature for the Three Lions at the finals.**

ALISSON

Born: Novo Hamburgo, Brazil, 2nd October 1992
Position: Goalkeeper
Club career:
2013-16 Internacional 44
2016-18 Roma 37
2018- Liverpool 38
International record:
2015- Brazil 42

Brazil international Alisson enjoyed a tremendous first season with Liverpool in 2018/19, claiming the Golden Glove award after totalling an impressive 21 clean sheets in the Premier League. Even better, he helped the Reds win the Champions League, keeping a clean sheet in the final against Tottenham in Madrid.

• **A tall and commanding goalkeeper who is adept with his feet, Alisson started out as back-up to his brother, Muriel, at Internacional, a club based in Porto Alegre in southern Brazil.**

After breaking into the first team he won four consecutive regional titles before moving to Roma for around £6 million in 2016.

• Alisson spent his first season in the Italian capital as understudy to Wojciech Szczesny and had to wait until the Polish international joined Juventus before making his Serie A debut on the opening day of the 2017/18 campaign in a 1-0 win against Atalanta. After an excellent season with 'I Lupi' Alisson joined Liverpool in July 2018 for a staggering £66.8 million, at the time a world record transfer fee for a goalkeeper.

• Alisson made his debut for Brazil in a 3-1 defeat of Venezuela in 2015 and has since held off the challenge of Manchester City's Ederson to become his country's first-choice No 1. In 2019 he helped Brazil win the Copa America on home soil, conceding just one goal in six matches to claim the tournament's Best Goalkeeper award.

DELE ALLI

Born: Milton Keynes, 11th April 1996
Position: Midfielder
Club career:
2011-15 Milton Keynes Dons 62 (18)
2015- Tottenham Hotspur 131 (42)
2015 Milton Keynes Dons (loan) 12 (4)
International record:
2015- England 37 (3)

An attacking midfielder who loves making runs into the opposition box, Dele Alli helped Tottenham reach the Champions League final for the first time in the club's history in 2019, setting up team-mate Lucas Moura for the winning goal in Spurs' dramatic semi-final victory against Ajax. However, he finished on the losing side in the final, as the north Londoners lost 2-0 to Liverpool in Madrid.

• Alli joined his local club MK Dons as an 11-year-old, making his first-team debut aged just 16 in November 2012

against Cambridge City in the FA Cup. After helping the Dons win promotion to the Championship in 2015 he was voted the Football League Young Player of the Year.

• Alli moved to Tottenham for a bargain £5 million during the 2015 winter transfer window, but was loaned back to MK Dons for the rest of the season. He eventually made his Spurs debut in August 2015 and later that season scored with a brilliant effort against Crystal Palace at Selhurst Park that was voted the BBC's Goal of the Season. At the end of the 2015/16 campaign he was voted PFA Young Player of the Year and he topped the poll again the following season to become only the fourth player to win the award twice.

• First capped by England at Under-17 level, Alli's eye-catching displays for Tottenham soon earned him a call up to the senior squad and he marked his first start for England in

Dele Alli felt a sudden urge to punch the ball very hard...

fine style with a blistering long-range strike past Spurs team-mate Hugo Lloris in a 2-0 friendly victory over France at Wembley in November 2015. A niggling thigh injury prevented him from showing his best form at the 2018 World Cup in Russia, but he still managed to get on the scoresheet in the 2-0 quarter-final defeat of Sweden with a well-taken header.

FELIPE ANDERSON

Born: Santa Maria, Brazil, 15th April 1993
Position: Winger
Club career:
2010-13 Santos 61 (7)
2013-18 Lazio 137 (25)
2018- West Ham United 36 (9)
International record:
2015- Brazil 2 (0)

Tricky winger Felipe Anderson became West Ham's record signing in July 2018 when he moved to east London from Lazio for £36 million, although he has since lost top spot to new Hammers striker Sebastien Haller. The Brazilian enjoyed an excellent first season at the London Stadium, chipping in with nine Premier League goals and impressing with his immaculate close control and mazy dribbling skills.

• Anderson started out with Santos in his native Brazil, playing alongside a young Neymar. In January 2013 he moved to Lazio for around £6.5 million, where his eye-catching performances soon saw him linked with the likes of Manchester United and Chelsea.

• Anderson enjoyed his best season with the Roman club in 2014/15, firing in 10 league goals and helping Lazio reach the final of the Coppa Italia, which they lost 2-1 to Double winners Juventus.

• After earning his first cap for Brazil in 2015, Anderson played for his country at the 2016 Olympics and picked up a gold medal after the South Americans beat Germany on penalties in the final in Rio de Janeiro.

ANIMALS

Fans at the Argentinian third-tier match between Juventud Unida and Defensores de Belgrano on 2nd December 2018 witnessed an incredible incident when an effort from a home player appeared to be dribbling into an empty net only for a black dog to appear from nowhere and nod the ball off the line! However, Belgrano failed to match the mutt's 'dogged defending' and slumped to a 3-0 defeat.

• The most famous dog in football, Pickles, never appeared on the pitch but, to the relief of fans around the globe, discovered the World Cup trophy which was stolen while on display at an exhibition in Central Hall, Westminster, on 20th March 1966. A black and white mongrel, Pickles found the trophy under a bush while out for a walk on Beulah Hill in south London with his owner. He was hailed as a national hero but, sadly, later that same year he was strangled by his lead while chasing after a cat.

• The Uruguayan first division match between Fenix and Racing in March 2018 was briefly halted when two chickens painted in the green and white colours of the visitors were let loose on the pitch by protesting fans. Fenix director Gaston Alegari reacted angrily, booting one of the chickens off the turf to land himself in hot water with animal rights groups.

• The Premier League match between Everton and Wolves on 2nd February 2019 was held up for four minutes when a black cat ran onto the Goodison pitch and evaded the combined efforts of the players and stewards to catch him.

• Fans at the League Cup tie between Manchester City and Wolves on 24th October 2017 were amused to spot a grey squirrel scampering about the pitch before the little fellow was caught by a member of the Etihad groundstaff minutes before the kick-off.

APPEARANCES

Goalkeeping legend Peter Shilton holds the record for the most Football League appearances, playing 1,005 games between 1966 and 1997. His total was made up as follows: Leicester City (286 games), Stoke City (110), Nottingham Forest (202), Southampton (188), Derby County (175), Plymouth (34), Bolton (1) and Leyton Orient (9). Shilton is followed in the all-time list by Tony Ford (931 appearances, 1975-2001), who holds the record for an outfield player.

• Shilton also holds the world record for first-class appearances in all competitions for his various clubs

and England, with an incredible total of 1,390.

• Swindon Town stalwart John Trollope holds the record for the most league appearances for a single club, with 770 between 1960 and 1980. Manchester United legend Ryan Giggs appeared in 672 league games for the Red Devils between 1991 and 2014, a record for the same club in the top flight.

• Well-travelled former England utility player Gareth Barry made a record total of 653 Premier League appearances for Aston Villa, Manchester City, Everton and West Brom between 1998 and 2018.

• Spain goalkeeper Iker Casillas holds the record for the most appearances in the Champions League with 177 for Real Madrid and Porto from 1999. Inter Milan defender Giuseppe Bergomi made a record 96 appearances in the UEFA Cup, now the Europa League, between 1980 and 1998.

ARGENTINA

First international: Uruguay 2 Argentina 3, 1901
Most capped player: Javier Mascherano, 147 caps (2003-18)
Leading goalscorer: Lionel Messi, 68 goals (2005-)
First World Cup appearance: Argentina 1 France 0, 1930
Biggest win: Argentina 12 Ecuador 0, 1942
Heaviest defeat: Argentina 1 Czechoslovakia 6 (1958) and Argentina 1 Bolivia 6 (2009)

Outside Britain, Argentina is the oldest football nation on the planet. The roots of the game in this football-obsessed country go back to 1865, when the

Nicolas Otamendi providing further proof that Argentinian footballers favour a flash hairdo...

Buenos Aires Football Club was founded by British residents in the Argentine capital. Six clubs formed the first league in 1891, making it the oldest anywhere in the world outside Britain.

• **Losing finalists in the first World Cup in 1930, Argentina had to wait until 1978 before winning the competition for the first time, defeating Holland 3-1 on home soil. Another success, inspired by brilliant captain Diego Maradona, followed in 1986 and Argentina came close to retaining their trophy four years later, losing 1-0 in the final to West Germany. After a 24-year wait they reached the final again in 2014, but narrowly lost to Germany.**

• Argentina's oldest rivals are neighbours Uruguay. The two countries first met in 1901, in the first official international to be played outside Britain, with Argentina winning 3-2 in Montevideo. In the ensuing years the two sides have played each other 188 times, making the Argentina-Uruguay fixture the most played in the history of international football.

• **With 14 victories to their name, Argentina have the second best record in the Copa America. In 2015 and 2016 Messi and co. had a great chance to equal Uruguay's record of 15 wins but frustratingly lost both finals to Chile on penalties.**

• With 147 caps to his name, former Argentina captain Javier Mascherano is the second-highest capped South American in history behind Ecuador defender Ivan Hurtado (168 caps).

> ## HONOURS
> **World Cup winners** *1978, 1986*
> **Copa America winners** *1921, 1925, 1927, 1929, 1937, 1941, 1945, 1946, 1947, 1955, 1957, 1959, 1991, 1993*
> **World Cup Record**
> *1930 Runners-up*
> *1934 Round 1*
> *1938 Did not enter*
> *1950 Did not enter*
> *1954 Did not enter*
> *1958 Round 1*
> *1962 Round 1*
> *1966 Quarter-finals*
> *1970 Did not qualify*
> *1974 Round 2*
> *1978 Winners*
> *1982 Round 2*
> *1986 Winners*
> *1990 Runners-up*
> *1994 Round 2*
> *1998 Quarter-finals*

> *2002 Round 1*
> *2006 Quarter-finals*
> *2010 Quarter-finals*
> *2014 Runners-up*
> *2018 Round 2*

KEPA ARRIZABALAGA

> **Born:** Ondarroa, Spain, 3rd October 1994
> **Position:** Goalkeeper
> **Club career:**
> 2012-13 Basconia 31
> 2013-16 Bilbao Athletic 50
> 2015 Ponferradina (loan) 20
> 2015-16 Valladolid (loan) 39
> 2016-18 Athletic Bilbao 53
> 2018- Chelsea 36
> **International record:**
> 2017- Spain 6

Following his transfer from Athletic Bilbao to Chelsea for £71.6 million, a world record fee for a goalkeeper, Spain international Kepa Arrizabalaga experienced a dramatic first season at Stamford Bridge. He hit the headlines after refusing to be substituted in the Blues' League Cup final defeat by Manchester City, but was instrumental in helping the Londoners win the Europa League, saving two penalties in the dramatic semi-final shoot-out against Eintracht Frankfurt.

• **A tall goalkeeper who commands his box with authority, Arrizabalaga joined the Athletic Bilbao youth set-up aged 10, progressing to make his debut for the Basque outfit's feeder club, Basconia, in January 2012 when still a teenager. The following year he moved up to the reserve side, Bilbao Athletic. After successful loan spells at two second-tier clubs, Ponferradina and Valladolid, the young goalie finally made his debut for Bilbao in a 1-0 away win at Deportivo la Coruna in September 2016.**

• After playing for Spain at Under-18 level, Arrizabalaga was a key member of the Spanish team which won the Under-19 European Championships in Estonia in 2012. His stand-out performance came in the semi-final against France when he saved two penalties in a penalty shoot-out.

• **Arrizabalaga made his senior debut for Spain in a 5-0 hammering of Costa Rica in Malaga in November 2017. He was picked for his country's World Cup** squad the following year but spent the entire tournament in Russia on the bench as back-up to David de Gea.

ARSENAL

> **Year founded:** 1886
> **Ground:** Emirates Stadium (60,432)
> **Previous name:** Dial Square, Royal Arsenal, Woolwich Arsenal
> **Nickname:** The Gunners
> **Biggest win:** 12-0 v Ashford United (1893) and Loughborough Town (1900)
> **Heaviest defeat:** 0-8 v Loughborough Town (1896)

Founded as Dial Square in 1886 by workers at the Royal Arsenal in Woolwich, the club was renamed Royal Arsenal soon afterwards. Another name change, to Woolwich Arsenal, followed in 1891 when the club turned professional. Then, a year after moving north of the river to the Arsenal Stadium in 1913, the club became simply 'Arsenal'.

• **One of the most successful clubs in the history of English football, Arsenal enjoyed a first golden period in the 1930s under innovative manager Herbert Chapman. The Gunners won the FA Cup for the first time in 1930 and later in the decade became only the second club to win three league titles on the trot. The first was the club Chapman managed in the 1920s, Huddersfield Town.**

• Arsenal were the first club from London to win the league, topping the table in 1931 after scoring an incredible 60 goals in 21 away matches – an all-time record for the Football League.

• **Arsenal are the most successful club in the history of the FA Cup with 13 victories to their name, the most recent coming in 2017 when the Gunners beat London rivals Chelsea 2-1 in the final at Wembley. Seven of those cup triumphs were achieved during the long reign of former boss Arsène Wenger, the best haul of any manager in FA Cup history. Wenger also led the Gunners to the Double in both 1998 and 2002, and their total of three Doubles (including an earlier triumph in 1971) is only matched by Manchester United.**

• Wenger's greatest achievement, though, came in the 2003/04 season when his team were crowned Premier League champions after going through the entire campaign undefeated. Only Preston North End had previously matched this feat, way back in 1888/89, but they had only played 22 league games compared to the 38 of Wenger's 'Invincibles'.

• The following season Arsenal extended their unbeaten run to 49 matches – setting an English league record in the process – before crashing to a bad-tempered 2-0 defeat against Manchester United at Old Trafford on 24th October 2004.

• One of the stars of that great Arsenal side was striker Thierry Henry, who is the Gunners' all-time leading scorer with 228 goals in all competitions in two spells at the club between 1999 and 2012. His total includes 42 goals in European competition, another club record. The former fans' favourite is also the most capped Arsenal player, appearing 81 times for France during his time with the club.

• In 1989 Arsenal won the closest ever title race by beating Liverpool 2-0 at Anfield in the final match of the season to pip the Reds to the championship on goals scored (the two sides had the same goal difference). But for a last-minute goal by Gunners midfielder Michael Thomas, after Alan Smith had scored with a second-half header, the title would have stayed on Merseyside.

• Irish international defender David O'Leary made a club record 722 first-team appearances for Arsenal between 1975 and 1993.

• Arsenal endured a nightmare season in 1912/13, finishing bottom of Division One and winning just one home game during the campaign – an all-time record. However, the Gunners returned to the top flight in 1919 and have stayed there ever since – the longest unbroken run in the top tier.

• Arsenal tube station on the Piccadilly Line is the only train station in Britain to be named after a football club. It used to be called Gillespie Road, until Herbert Chapman successfully lobbied for the name change in 1932.

• Three years later, on 14th December 1935, Arsenal thrashed Aston Villa 7-1 at Villa Park. Incredibly, centre-forward Ted Drake grabbed all seven of the Gunners' goals to set a top-flight record that still stands to this day. The previous season Drake scored a club best 44 goals, including 42 in the league.

• Arsenal appeared in the group stages of the Champions League for 19 consecutive seasons from 1998/99 to 2016/17 – a record for an English club and one which is only bettered by Real Madrid. On their way to the Champions League final in 2006, which they lost to Barcelona, the Gunners kept 10 consecutive clean sheets to set a new record for the competition.

• Arsenal's most expensive signing is Ivory Coast winger Nicolas Pepe, who cost the Gunners £72 million when he joined them from Lille in August 2019. The club's record sale is Alex Oxlade-Chamberlain, who boosted the Gunners' coffers by £35 million when he signed for Liverpool in 2017.

• In winning the title in 2002 Arsenal became the first club to score in every Premier League fixture in a season.

• In 2019 Arsenal met Chelsea in Baku in the Europa League final, the first ever European final between two English sides from the same city. However, the Gunners went down to a dispiriting 4-1 defeat, their fourth consecutive loss in European finals dating back to 1995.

HONOURS
Premier League champions 1998, 2002, 2004
Division 1 champions 1931, 1933, 1934, 1935, 1948, 1953, 1971, 1989, 1991
FA Cup 1930, 1936, 1950, 1971, 1979, 1993, 1998, 2002, 2003, 2005, 2014, 2015, 2017
League Cup 1987, 1993
Double 1971, 1998, 2002
Fairs Cup 1970
European Cup Winners' Cup 1994

Arsenal's players love a good cuddle!

ASTON VILLA

Year founded: 1874
Ground: Villa Park (42,660)
Nickname: The Villans
Biggest win: 13-0 v Wednesbury Old Athletic (1886)
Heaviest defeat: 0-8 v Chelsea (2012)

One of England's most famous and distinguished clubs, Aston Villa were founded in 1874 by members of the Villa Cross Wesleyan Chapel in Aston, Birmingham. The club were founder members of the Football League in 1888, winning their first title six years later.

• The most successful team of the Victorian era, Villa became only the second club to win the league and FA Cup Double in 1897 (Preston North End were the first in 1889). Villa's manager at the time was the legendary George Ramsay, who went on to guide the Villans to six league titles and six FA Cups – a trophy haul which has only been surpassed by the iconic duo of Liverpool's Bob Paisley and former Manchester United boss Sir Alex Ferguson.

• Ramsay is also the second longest serving manager in the history of English football, taking charge of the Villans for an incredible 42 years between 1884 and 1926. Only West Brom's Fred Everiss has managed a club for longer, racking up 46 years' service at the Hawthorns.

• Although they slipped as low as the old Third Division in the early 1970s, Villa have spent more time in the top flight than any other club apart from Everton (106 seasons compared to the Toffees' 117). The two clubs have played each other 202 times to date, making Aston Villa v Everton the most played fixture in the entire history of league football.

• Villa won the last of their seven league titles in 1980/81, when manager Ron Saunders used just 14 players throughout the whole campaign – equalling Liverpool's record set in 1965/66. The following season Villa became only the fourth English club to win the European Cup when they beat Bayern Munich 1-0 in the final in Rotterdam.

• **In 1961 Villa won the League Cup in the competition's inaugural season, beating Rotherham 3-2 in a two-legged final. The Villans are the joint-third most successful side in the tournament behind Liverpool and Manchester City with five triumphs, their most recent success coming in 1996 against Leeds.**

• Villa's most capped international is former Republic of Ireland defender Steve Staunton, who played 64 times for his country while at Villa Park between 1991 and 1998. His team-mate Gareth Southgate, now England manager, played a club record 42 times for the Three Lions between 1995 and 2001.

• **Stalwart defender Charlie Aitken made more appearances for the club than any other player, turning out in 657 games between 1959 and 1976. Villa's all-time top goalscorer is Billy Walker, who found the back of the net** an incredible 244 times between 1919 and 1933.

• Walker helped Villa bang in 128 league goals in the 1930/31 season, a record for the top flight which is unlikely ever to be broken. In the same campaign, Tom 'Pongo' Waring scored a club record 49 league goals.

• **After going on a club record 10-game winning run in the league, Villa reached the 2019 Championship play-offs and were promoted back to the Premier League after a three-year absence thanks to a 2-1 victory against Derby County in the final at Wembley.**

HONOURS
Division 1 champions 1894, 1896, 1897, 1899, 1900, 1910, 1981
Division 2 champions 1938, 1960
Division 3 champions 1972
FA Cup 1887, 1895, 1897, 1905, 1913, 1920, 1957
Double 1897
League Cup 1961, 1975, 1977, 1994, 1996
European Cup 1982
European Super Cup 1982

ATLETICO MADRID

Year founded: 1903
Ground: Wanda Metropolitano (67,703)
Previous names: Athletic Club de Madrid, Athletic Aviacion de Madrid
Nickname: El Atleti
League titles: 10
Domestic cups: 10
European cups: 7
International cups: 1

The club was founded in 1903 by breakaway members of Madrid FC (later Real Madrid). In 1939, following a merger with the Spanish air force team, the club became known as Athletic Aviacion de Madrid before becoming plain Atletico Madrid eight years later.

• **Atletico are the third most successful club in Spanish football history with 10 La Liga triumphs under their belt. The most recent of these came in 2014 when Atleti drew 1-1 at runners-up Barcelona on the last day of the season to become the only club in the last 15 years to break the usual Barca/Real Madrid duopoly.**

Atletico Madrid like to keep things close to their chest

• Atletico have enjoyed great success in Europe in recent years, winning the inaugural Europa League in 2010 after a 2-1 win against Fulham in the final in Hamburg. Another triumph followed in 2012 and in 2018 Atleti became only the second club to win the new competition three times following a 3-0 thrashing of Marseille in the final in Lyon. Less impressively, Atletico are the only club to reach three finals of the European Cup/Champions League and lose them all.

• **In September 2017 Atletico moved to their new near 68,000-capacity Wanda Metropolitano stadium, the venue for the 2019 Champions League final between Liverpool and Tottenham Hotspur.**

HONOURS
Spanish champions 1940, 1941, 1950, 1951, 1966, 1970, 1973, 1977, 1996, 2014
Spanish Cup 1960, 1961, 1965, 1972, 1976, 1985, 1991, 1992, 1996, 2013
Europa League 2010, 2012, 2018
European Cup Winners' Cup 1962
European Super Cup 2010, 2012, 2018
Intercontinental Cup 1974

TOP 10

PREMIER LEAGUE AVERAGE ATTENDANCES 2018/19

1.	Manchester United	74,498
2.	Arsenal	59,899
3.	West Ham United	58,336
4.	Tottenham Hotspur	54,216
5.	Manchester City	54,130
6.	Liverpool	52,983
7.	Newcastle United	51,121
8.	Chelsea	40,437
9.	Everton	38,780
10.	Leicester City	31,851

ATTENDANCES

The Maracana Stadium in Rio de Janeiro holds the world record for a football match attendance, 199,854 spectators having watched the final match of the 1950 World Cup between Brazil and Uruguay. Most of the fans, though, went home in tears after Uruguay came from behind to win 2-1 and claim the trophy for a second time.

• **The biggest crowd at a match in Britain was probably for the first ever FA Cup final at Wembley in 1923. The official attendance for the match between Bolton and West Ham was 126,047, although, with thousands more fans gaining entry without paying, the actual crowd was estimated at 150,000-200,000. The record official attendance for a match in Britain is 149,547, set in 1937 for Scotland's 3-1 victory over England in the Home International Championship at Hampden Park.**

• In 1948 a crowd of 83,260 watched Manchester United entertain Arsenal at Maine Road (United's temporary home in the post-war years after Old Trafford suffered bomb damage), a record for the Football League. However, the biggest attendance ever for an English club's home fixture is 85,512, set on 2nd November 2016 for Tottenham's Champions League group game with Bayer Leverkusen at Wembley.

• **On 15th April 1970 the biggest crowd ever to watch a European Cup tie, 135,826, crammed into Hampden Park in Glasgow to see Celtic beat Leeds United 2-1 in the semi-final second leg.**

• A record Premier League crowd of 83,222 watched Tottenham beat Arsenal 1-0 in the north London derby at Wembley on 10th February 2018. Less impressively, Wimbledon against Everton at Selhurst Park on 26th January 1993 drew the lowest Premier League attendance ever, just 3,039.

• **On 17th March 2019 a crowd of 60,739 watched Atletico Madrid take on Barcelona at the Wanda Metropolitano in the Spanish 'Liga Feminina' – a record for a women's club match.**

PIERRE-EMERICK AUBAMEYANG

Born: Laval, France 18th June 1989
Position: Striker
Club career:
2008-11 AC Milan 0 (0)
2008-09 Dijon (loan) 34 (8)
2009-10 Lille (loan) 14 (2)
2010-11 Monaco (loan) 19 (2)
2011 Saint-Etienne (loan) 33 (8)
2011-13 Saint-Etienne 54 (29)
2013-18 Borussia Dortmund 144 (98)
2018- Arsenal 49 (22)
International record:
2009- Gabon 59 (24)

African Player of the Year in 2015, Pierre-Emerick Aubameyang became Arsenal's record signing at the time when he joined the Gunners from Borussia Dortmund in a £55 million deal in January 2018. The Gabonese striker has subsequently proven his worth, topping the Premier League scoring charts in 2018/19 with 22 goals, a tally matched by the Liverpool duo Sadio Mane and Mohamed Salah. He was also joint-third top scorer in the Europa League with eight goals, helping Arsenal reach the final where they lost to London rivals Chelsea in Baku.

• **Born in France, Aubameyang began his career with AC Milan but was subsequently loaned out to four French clubs before making a permanent move to Saint-Etienne with whom he won the French League Cup in 2013. In the same year he was voted into the Ligue 1 Team of the Season after coming second in the goalscoring charts.**

• He joined Borussia Dortmund in 2013, and two years later scored in 10 straight Bundesliga matches to equal a record set by Cologne's Klaus Allofs 34 years earlier. Aubameyang enjoyed a golden season in 2016/17 when he was top scorer in the Bundesliga with 31 goals and scored the winning goal in the German Cup final from the penalty spot in Dortmund's 2-1 victory against Eintracht Frankfurt.

• **Aubameyang played for the French Under-21 side in a friendly against Tunisia in February 2009 but the following month committed his international future to Gabon, for whom his father, Pierre, had previously played. He is now his country's captain and all-time leading scorer with 24 goals.**

Pierre-Emerick Aubameyang takes an unusual view of the Emirates stadium

BADGES

Rye United of the Sussex County League claim to have the world's oldest club crest, dating back to the 13th century. Their badge features the three lions which appeared on the coat of arms of the Confederation of the Cinque Ports – which provided for the defence of the realm before the formation of a permanent navy – and was established by Royal Charter in 1155.

• **Juventus were the first club to add a star to their badge, representing their achievement in winning a then record tenth Italian title in 1958. Other clubs and nations have followed suit, a famous example being the five stars above Brazil's badge to represent their five World Cup triumphs.**

• In January 2018 Leeds United were forced to scrap plans for a new badge after 77,000 unhappy fans signed a petition condemning the unpopular design, which featured a nondescript figure giving the 'Leeds salute'.

• **In September 2018 football magazine FourFourTwo rated Ajax's badge as the world's best. Birmingham City's badge came seventh in the list, the highest placing of any British club.**

GARETH BALE

Born: Cardiff, 16th July 1989
Position: Winger/striker
Club career:
2006-07 Southampton 40 (5)
2007-13 Tottenham Hotspur 146 (22)
2013- Real Madrid 155 (78)
International record:
2006- Wales 77 (31)

In 2018 Gareth Bale became only the second British player (after Liverpool defender Phil Neal) to win the European Cup/Champions League four times, when he scored twice in Real Madrid's 3-1 defeat of Liverpool in the final in Kiev.

Gareth Bale could make a fortune as a human statue

He also equalled Neal's British record of scoring in two finals, having previously netted in Real's 4-1 defeat of Atletico Madrid in 2014. For good measure, Bale also scored in Real's shoot-out victory against their city rivals in the 2016 final.

• **Bale began his career at Southampton, where he became the second youngest player to debut for the club (behind Theo Walcott) when he appeared in a 2-0 win against Millwall in the Championship in April 2006. The following season his superb displays for the Saints earned him the Football League Young Player of the Year award.**

• In the summer of 2007 Bale joined Tottenham for an initial fee of £5 million and was soon being hailed as one of the most exciting talents in the game. He enjoyed an outstanding season with Spurs in 2010/11 and at the end of the campaign he was named PFA Player of the Year – only the fourth Welshman to receive this honour. He was also the only Premier League player to be voted into the UEFA Team of the Year for 2011. He had an even better season in 2012/13, picking up both Player of the Year gongs and the PFA Young Player of the Year award –

only the second player, after Cristiano Ronaldo, to collect this individual treble.

• **Bale joined Real for a then world record fee of £86 million in August 2013 and has scored more goals in La Liga, 78, than any other British player. However, his future with the club looked uncertain at the start of the 2019/20 season when he was made available for transfer by boss Zinedine Zidane.**

• When Bale scored his first international goal, in a 5-1 home defeat by Slovakia in 2006, he became his country's youngest ever scorer aged 17 and 35 days. He starred for Wales on their unlikely run to the semi-finals of Euro 2016 and in March 2018 became his country's all-time top scorer when he banged in a hat-trick in a 6-0 rout of China.

BALL BOYS

Ball boys developed from a gimmick employed by Chelsea in the 1905/06 season. To emphasise the extraordinary bulk of the team's 23-stone goalkeeper, William 'Fatty' Foulke, two young boys would stand behind his goal. They soon proved themselves useful in retrieving the ball when it went out of play, and so the concept of the ball boy was born.

• **Amazingly, a ball boy scored a goal in a match between Santacruzense and Atletico Sorocaba in Brazil in 2006. Santacruzense were trailing 1-0 when one of their players fired wide in the last minute. Instead of handing the ball back to the Atletico goalkeeper, the ball boy kicked it into the net and the goal was awarded by the female referee despite the angry protests of the Atletico players.**

• Seventeen-year-old Swansea ball boy Charlie Morgan helped his side reach

IS THAT A FACT?
Liverpool ball boy Oakley Cannonier, 14, was hailed as a hero by Reds fans after the Champions League semi-final with Barcelona at Anfield. Taking advantage of the multi-ball system, the youngster quickly threw a ball to Trent Alexander-Arnold and the full back's sharply-taken corner was converted by Divock Origi for the home side's winning goal.

the League Cup final in 2013 by falling on top of the ball when Chelsea's Eden Hazard wanted to take a corner kick. Frustrated at the lad's refusal to return the ball quickly, Hazard kicked it out from under him and was promptly shown a red card that pretty much ended Chelsea's chances of overhauling a two-goal deficit from the first leg.

• **Watford striker Isaac Success was shown a yellow card after attempting to retrieve the ball from a dawdling ball boy in stoppage time of the Hornets' 2-1 defeat against Tottenham at Wembley on 30th January 2019.**

• Adelaide United defender Michael Marrone sparked a mass melee involving players, coaches and eventually the police during his side's 2-1 defeat by Sydney FC in the 2017 FFA Cup final when he knocked over a time-wasting ball boy in his frustration. Marrone was shown a red card and later hit with a four-match suspension.

The days of the all-white ball are long gone...

BALLS

The laws of football specify that the ball must be an air-filled sphere with a circumference of 68-70cm and a weight before the start of the game of 410-450g. Before the first plastic footballs appeared in the 1950s, balls were made from leather and in wet conditions would become progressively heavier, sometimes actually doubling in weight.

• **Most modern footballs are made in Pakistan, especially in the city of Sialkot, and are usually stitched from 32 panels of waterproofed leather or plastic. In the past child labour was**

often used in the production of the balls but, following pressure from UNICEF and the International Labour Organisation, manufacturers agreed in 1997 not to employ underage workers.

• Adidas have supplied the official ball for the World Cup since the iconic black-and-white Telstar in 1970. The ball for the 2018 tournament in Russia, the Adidas Telstar 18, featured six textured panels seamlessly glued together and was produced by Forward Sports in Sialkot. Adidas also supplied the official match ball, the Conext 19, for the 2019 Women's World Cup in France.

• **Nike are the official supplier of balls for the Premier League, taking over the role from Mitre in 2000. A winter 'Hi-Vis' yellow ball has been used in the league since the 2004/05 season.**

• In 2018 Mitre replaced Nike as the official suppliers of the ball for FA Cup matches. The Mitre Dell Max is also used for Women's FA Cup matches and those in the Women's Super League.

• In a remarkable incident, a shot by Sunderland striker Darren Bent struck a red beach ball thrown on the pitch by a Liverpool fan and deflected into the net for the Black Cats' winning goal against the Reds at the Stadium of Light on 17th October 2009.

BARCELONA

Year founded: 1899
Ground: Nou Camp (99,354)
Nickname: Barça
League titles: 26
Domestic cups: 30
European cups: 17
International cups: 3

One of the most famous and popular clubs in the world, Barcelona were founded in 1899 by bank worker Joan Gamper, a former captain of Swiss club Basel. The club were founder members and first winners of the Spanish championship, La Liga, in 1928 and have remained in the top flight of Spanish football ever since.

• **For the people of Catalonia, Barcelona is more like a national team than a mere club. As former manager Bobby Robson once succinctly put it, "Catalonia is a country and FC Barcelona is their army." The hierarchy of the club and many of its fans are strong supporters of Catalan independence, demonstrating their backing for the cause on the day of**

Jordi Alba explains how many times better Barcelona are than most teams they play

the 2017 referendum on the issue by playing their La Liga match against Las Palmas behind closed doors.

• With a capacity of 99,354 Barcelona's Nou Camp stadium is the largest in Europe. Among the stadium's many facilities are a museum which attracts over one million visitors a year, mini training pitches and even a chapel for the players.

• **For many years Barcelona played second fiddle to bitter rivals Real Madrid. Finally, in the 1990s, under former player-turned-coach Johan Cruyff, Barça turned the tables on the team from the Spanish capital by winning four La Liga titles on the trot between 1991 and 1994. Cruyff also led the Catalans to a first taste of glory in the European Cup, Barcelona beating Sampdoria at Wembley in 1992. The club have since won the Champions League on four more occasions, most recently beating Juventus 3-1 in the 2015 final to become the first European club to win the Treble twice (the first occasion was in 2009).**

• Reigning Spanish champions, Barcelona were unbeaten for a La Liga record 43 consecutive league games between 15th April 2017 and 9th May 2018.

HONOURS
Spanish champions *1929, 1945, 1948, 1949, 1952, 1953, 1959, 1960, 1974, 1985, 1991, 1992, 1993, 1994, 1998, 1999, 2005, 2006, 2009, 2010, 2011, 2013, 2015, 2016, 2018, 2019*
Spanish Cup *1910, 1912, 1913, 1920, 1922, 1925, 1926, 1928, 1942, 1951,1952, 1953, 1957, 1959, 1963, 1968, 1971, 1978, 1981, 1983, 1988, 1990, 1997, 1998, 2009, 2012, 2015, 2016, 2017, 2018*
European Cup/Champions League *1992, 2006, 2009, 2011, 2015*
Fairs Cup *1958, 1960, 1961*
European Cup Winners' Cup *1979, 1982, 1989, 1997*
European Super Cup *1992, 1997, 2009, 2011, 2015*
Club World Cup *2009, 2011, 2015*

Karen Bardsley was in great form for England at the 2019 World Cup

KAREN BARDSLEY

Born: Santa Monica, USA, 14th October 1984
Position: Goalkeeper
Club career:
2007 Ajax America Women
2008 Pali Blues 5
2009-11 Sky Blue FC 17
2011-12 Linkopings FC 3
2013 Lincoln Ladies 14
2014- Manchester City 52
International record:
2005- England 81

Born in California to parents from Greater Manchester, Karen Bardsley opted to play for England rather than the USA and she has been a fixture between the posts for the Lionesses for a number of years, representing her country at three World Cups.

• **The tall shot-stopper came through the college system in America to play for clubs on both the west and east coast before moving to Sweden and then on to England, signing first for Lincoln Ladies and then, in November 2013, for Manchester City.**

• Bardsley won the Women's Super League with City in 2016 and the Women's FA Cup the following year, after a crushing 4-1 defeat of Birmingham City in the final at Wembley. In 2019 she saved two penalties in the shoot-out against Arsenal to help City win the Women's League Cup and she was also in the City side that thumped West Ham 3-0 in the Women's FA Cup final.

• **England's number one since the 2011 World Cup, Bardsley has had some bad luck playing for the Lionesses in recent years. At the 2015 World Cup she had to be subbed off in the quarter-final against hosts Canada after suffering a mysterious eye inflammation and two years later she broke her leg against France at the same stage of the European Championships in the Netherlands. Then, after making some great saves earlier in the tournament, she missed the semi-final defeat to the USA at the 2019 World Cup with a hamstring injury.**

ROSS BARKLEY

Born: Liverpool, 5th December 1993
Position: Midfielder
Club career:
2011-18 Everton 150 (21)
2012 Sheffield Wednesday (loan) 13 (4)
2013 Leeds United (loan) 4 (0)
2018- Chelsea 29 (3)
International record:
2013- England 29 (4)

After an injury-hit start to his Chelsea career following his £15 million move from Everton in January 2018, Ross Barkley enjoyed a decent season in 2018/19, playing a full part in the Blues' Europa League triumph.

Ross Barkley places his European Super Cup penalty through Barnsley (think about it...) and into the net

• After joining Everton as an 11-year-old, Barkley recovered from a triple leg fracture when he was 16 to make his debut against QPR in 2011, before spending most of the next season on loan at Sheffield Wednesday and Leeds United.

• A powerful player who loves to drive forward from central midfield positions, Barkley shone with the Toffees during the 2013/14 season and was shortlisted for the PFA Young Player of the Year award, although he was eventually pipped to top spot by Eden Hazard.

• Barkley played for England at all levels from Under-16 to Under-21, helping his country win the Under-17 European Championships in 2010 after a 2-1 victory over Spain in the final. Since making his full debut against Moldova in September 2013 he has struggled to pin down a starting place but came to the fore in 2019, scoring twice against Montenegro in a European Championships qualifier and converting a penalty in England's tense shoot-out victory over Switzerland at the UEFA Nations League finals in Portugal.

BARNSLEY

Year founded: 1887
Ground: Oakwell (23,009)
Previous name: Barnsley St Peter's
Nickname: The Tykes
Biggest win: 9-0 v Loughborough United (1899)
Heaviest defeat: 0-9 v Notts County (1927)

Founded as the church team Barnsley St Peter's in 1887 by the Rev. Tiverton Preedy, the club changed to their present name a year after joining the Football League in 1898.

• Promoted back to the Championship in 2019, the Tykes have spent more seasons (76) in the second tier of English football than any other club and had to wait until 1997 before they had their first taste of life in the top flight. Unfortunately for their fans, however, it lasted just one season.

• The Yorkshiremen's finest hour came in 1912 when they won the FA Cup, beating West Bromwich Albion 1-0 in a replay. The club were nicknamed 'Battling Barnsley' that season as they played a record 12 games during their cup run, including six 0-0 draws, before finally getting their hands on the trophy. Barnsley came close to repeating this feat in 2008, but were beaten in the semi-finals by fellow Championship side Cardiff City after they had sensationally knocked out Liverpool as well as cup holders Chelsea.

• **The youngest player to appear in the Football League is Barnsley striker Reuben Noble-Lazarus, who was 15 years and 45 days old when he faced Ipswich Town in September 2008. Afterwards, then Barnsley boss Simon Davey joked Noble-Lazarus would be rewarded with a pizza as he was too young to be paid!**

• Stalwart defender Barry Murphy made a club record 569 league appearances for the Tykes between 1962 and 1978. Striker Ernie Hine scored a club record 131 goals in two spells with the Tykes between 1921 and 1938.

• **The Tykes splashed a club record £1.5 million on Red Star Belgrade striker Georgi Hristov in the summer of 1997. The club's coffers were boosted by a record £5 million in August 2016 when defender Alfie Mawson moved on to Swansea City.**

HONOURS
Division 3 (North) champions 1934, 1939, 1955
FA Cup 1912
EFL Trophy 2016

Bambo Diaby has been a lynchpin of the Tykes' defence in 2019/20

Bayern Munich's goal-poaching master Thomas Muller

BAYERN MUNICH

Year founded: 1900
Ground: Allianz Arena (75,000)
Nickname: The Bavarians
League titles: 29
Domestic cups: 19
European cups: 7

The biggest and most successful club in Germany, Bayern Munich were founded in 1900 by members of a Munich gymnastics club. Incredibly, when the Bundesliga was formed in 1963, Bayern's form was so poor that they were not invited to become founder members of the league. But, thanks to the emergence in the mid-1960s of legendary players like goalkeeper Sepp Maier, sweeper Franz Beckenbauer and prolific goalscorer Gerd Muller, Bayern rapidly became the dominant force in German football. The club won the Bundesliga for the first time in 1969 and now have a record 29 German championships to their name, including a record seven on the trot between 2013 and 2019.

• **In 1974 Bayern became the first German club to win the European Cup, defeating Atletico Madrid 4-0 in the only final to go to a replay. Skippered by the imperious Beckenbauer, the club went on to complete a hat-trick of victories in the competition.**

• In winning the Bundesliga title in 2012/13, Bayern set numerous records, including highest points total (91), most wins (29) and best goal difference (+80). They then beat Borussia Dortmund 2-1 at Wembley in the first all-German Champions League final, before becoming the first ever German team to win the Treble when they beat Stuttgart 3-2 in the final of the German Cup.

• **Former French international Franck Ribery is the only foreign player to win nine Bundesliga titles, achieving this feat with Bayern between 2008 and 2019.**

• Bayern have won the domestic Double a record 12 times, most recently clinching yet another clean sweep in 2019 with a 3-0 defeat of RB Leipzig in the German Cup final.

HONOURS
German champions 1932, 1969, 1972, 1973, 1974, 1980, 1981, 1985, 1986, 1987, 1989, 1990, 1994, 1997, 1999, 2000, 2001, 2003, 2005, 2006, 2008, 2010, 2013, 2014, 2015, 2016, 2017, 2018, 2019
German Cup 1957, 1966, 1967, 1969, 1971, 1982, 1984, 1986, 1998, 2000, 2003, 2005, 2006, 2008, 2010, 2013, 2014, 2016, 2019

European Cup/Champions League 1974, 1975, 1976, 2001, 2013
UEFA Cup 1996
European Cup Winners' Cup 1967
European Super Cup 2013
Club World Cup 2013

BELGIUM

First international: Belgium 3 France 3, 1904
Most capped player: Jan Vertonghen, 114 caps (2007-)
Leading goalscorer: Romelu Lukaku, 48 goals (2010-)
First World Cup appearance: Belgium 2 Germany 5, 1934
Biggest win: Belgium 10 San Marino 1, 2001
Heaviest defeat: England amateurs 11 Belgium 2, 1909

A rising force in the world game, Belgium are yet to win a major trophy but they came mighty close in the 1980 European Championships in Italy. After topping their group ahead of Italy, England and

Eden Hazard is seemingly about to be 'haunted' by Belgium's terrifying mascot

Spain, Belgium went straight through to the final against West Germany where they were unfortunate to go down 2-1 in a close encounter.

• Belgium's best performance at the World Cup came in 2018 when, after beating Japan and Brazil in the earlier knock-out rounds, they lost 1-0 to eventual winners France in the semi-final in St Petersburg. The defeat ended the country's best ever run of 24 games without defeat, but the Belgians were soon back to winning ways, beating England 2-0 in the third place play-off match thanks to well-worked goals by wing-back Thomas Meunier, who became his team's record 11th scorer at the 2018 finals, and skipper Eden Hazard.

• Belgium also reached the semi-finals in 1986 but came up against a Diego Maradona-inspired Argentina and went down 2-0 in Mexico City. After losing 4-2 in the third place match to France, Belgium had to be content with fourth place at the tournament.

• On 10th October 2016 Belgium scored the fastest ever goal in the World Cup, when Christian Benteke netted after just 8.1 seconds in a qualifier against Gibraltar.

World Cup Record
1930 Round 1
1934 Round 1
1938 Round 1
1950 Withdrew
1954 Round 1
1958 Did not qualify
1962 Did not qualify
1966 Did not qualify
1970 Round 1
1974 Did not qualify
1978 Did not qualify
1982 Round 2
1986 Fourth place
1990 Round 2
1994 Round 2
1998 Round 1
2002 Round 2
2006 Did not qualify
2010 Did not qualify
2014 Quarter-finals
2018 Third place

TOP 10

BELGIUM GOALSCORERS

1. Romelu Lukaku (2010-)		45
2. Eden Hazard (2008-)		30
Paul Van Himst (1960-74)		30
Bernard Voorhoof (1928-40)		30
5. Joseph Mermans (1945-56)		28
Marc Wilmots (1990-2002)		28
7. Robert De Veen (1906-13)		26
8. Wesley Sonck (2001-10)		24
9. Ray Braine (1925-39)		23
Marc Degryse (1984-96)		23

BENFICA

Year founded: 1904
Ground: Estadio Da Luz, Lisbon (64,642)
Nickname: The Eagles
League titles: 37
Domestic cups: 29
European cups: 2

Portugal's most successful club, Benfica were founded in 1904 at a meeting of 24 football enthusiasts in south Lisbon. The club were founder members of the Portuguese league in 1933 and have since won the title a record 37 times, most recently in 2019.

• Inspired by legendary striker Eusebio, Benfica enjoyed a golden era in the 1960s when the club won eight domestic championships. In 1961 Benfica became the first team to break Real Madrid's dominance in the European Cup when they beat Barcelona 3-2 in the final. The following year, the trophy stayed in Lisbon after the Eagles sensationally beat star-studded Real 5-3 in the final in Amsterdam.

• In 1972/73 Benfica went the whole season undefeated – the first Portuguese team to achieve this feat – winning a staggering 28 and drawing just two of their 30 league matches. Along the way, Benfica set a still unbroken European record by winning 29 consecutive domestic league matches.

• In 2015/16 Benfica won the Portuguese league with a record 88 points. The club also hold the record for the longest ever unbeaten run in the league, an incredible 56 matches between 24th October 1976 and 1st September 1978.

• Benfica hold the record for the biggest ever aggregate win in the European Cup/ Champions League with an astonishing 18-0 thrashing of Luxembourg minnows Stade Dudelange in 1965.

HONOURS
Portuguese champions *1936, 1937, 1938, 1942, 1943, 1945, 1950, 1955, 1957, 1960, 1961, 1963, 1964, 1965, 1967, 1968, 1969, 1971, 1972, 1973, 1975, 1976, 1977, 1981, 1983, 1984, 1987, 1989, 1991, 1994, 2005, 2010, 2014, 2015, 2016, 2017, 2019*
Portuguese Cup *1930, 1931, 1935, 1940, 1943, 1944, 1949, 1951, 1952, 1953, 1955, 1957, 1959, 1962, 1964, 1969, 1970, 1972, 1980, 1981, 1983, 1985, 1986, 1987, 1993, 1996, 2004, 2014, 2017*
European Cup *1961, 1962*

BIRMINGHAM CITY

Year founded: 1875
Ground: St Andrew's (29,409)
Previous name: Small Heath Alliance, Small Heath, Birmingham
Nickname: The Blues
Biggest win: 12-0 v Nottingham Forest (1899), Walsall Town Swifts (1892) and Doncaster Rovers (1903)
Heaviest defeat: 1-9 v Blackburn Rovers (1895) and Sheffield Wednesday (1930)

Founded in 1875 as Small Heath Alliance, the club were founder members and the first champions of the Second Division in 1892. Unfortunately, Small Heath were undone at the 'test match' stage (a 19th-century version of the play-offs) and failed to gain promotion to the top flight.

• The club had to wait until 2011 for the greatest day in their history, when the Blues beat hot favourites Arsenal 2-1 in the League Cup final at Wembley, on-loan striker Obafemi Martins grabbing the winner in the final minutes to spark ecstatic celebrations among Birmingham's long-suffering fans. City had previously won the competition back in 1963 after getting the better of arch rivals Aston Villa over a two-legged final, although that achievement was hardly comparable as half the top-flight clubs hadn't even bothered to enter.

Birmingham hope to be heading up in 2019/20

• England international Joe Bradford scored a club record 249 league goals for the Blues between 1920 and 1935.
• Long-serving goalkeeper Maik Taylor made a club record 58 appearances for Northern Ireland while with the Brummies between 2003 and 2011.

HONOURS
Division 2 champions 1893, 1921, 1948, 1955
Second Division champions 1995
League Cup 1963, 2011
EFL Trophy 1991, 1995

BLACKBURN ROVERS

Year founded: 1875
Ground: Ewood Park (31,367)
Nickname: Rovers
Biggest win: 11-0 v Rossendale United (1884)
Heaviest defeat: 0-8 v Arsenal (1933) and Lincoln City (1953)

Founded in 1875 by a group of wealthy local residents and ex-public school boys, Blackburn Rovers joined the Football League as founder members in 1888. Two years later the club moved to a permanent home at Ewood Park, where they have remained ever since.
• **Blackburn were a force to be reckoned with from the start, winning the FA Cup five times in the 1880s and 1890s. Of all league clubs Rovers were the first to win the trophy, beating Scottish side Queen's Park 2-1 in the final at Kennington Oval in 1884. The Lancashire side went on to win the cup in the two following years as well, remaining undefeated in a record 23 consecutive games in the competition between 1884 and 1886.**

IS THAT A FACT?
When Blackburn Rovers beat West Brom 2-0 at the Racecourse Ground, Derby, to win the FA Cup for a third consecutive year in 1886 it was the first time the final had been played outside London.

• Rovers won the cup again in 1890, 1891 and 1928 to make a total of six triumphs in the competition. In the first of these victories they thrashed Sheffield Wednesday 6-1 in the final, with left winger William Townley scoring three times to become the first player to hit a hat-trick in the final.
• **The club have won the league title three times: in 1912, 1914 and, most memorably, in 1995 when, funded by the millions of popular local steel magnate Jack Walker and powered by the deadly 'SAS' strikeforce of Alan Shearer and Chris Sutton, Rovers pipped reigning champions Manchester United to the Premiership title.**
• Derek Fazackerley made the most appearances for Blackburn, turning out in 596 games between 1970 and 1986. The club's all-time leading scorer is Simon Garner, with 168 league goals between 1978 and 1992, although England striker Alan Shearer's incredible record of 122 goals in just 138 games for the club is arguably more impressive.
• **Nineteenth-century striker Jack Southworth scored a record 13 hat-tricks for Rovers, including a seasonal best of five in 1890/91.**
• Defender Henning Berg played in a club record 58 international matches for Norway in two spells at Ewood Park between 1993 and 2003.

HONOURS
Premier League champions 1995
Division 1 champions 1912, 1914
Division 2 champions 1975
FA Cup 1884, 1885, 1886, 1890, 1891, 1928
League Cup 2002

BLACKPOOL

Year founded: 1887
Ground: Bloomfield Road (17,338)
Nickname: The Seasiders
Biggest win: 10-0 v Lanerossi Vincenza (1972)
Heaviest defeat: 1-10 v Small Heath (1901)

Founded in 1887 by old boys of St John's School, Blackpool joined the Second Division of the Football League in 1896. The club merged with South Shore in

• However, on the final day of the 2010/11 season Birmingham were relegated from the Premier League. It was the 12th time in their history that the Blues had fallen through the top-flight trapdoor, a record of misery unmatched by any other club. More positively, Birmingham have been promoted to the top tier a record 12 times.
• **Stalwart defender Frank Womack made a club record 491 league appearances for the Blues between 1908 and 1928. Incredibly, Womack played a total of 510 league games without once getting on the scoresheet – a Football League record for an outfield player.**
• On 15th May 1955 Birmingham became the first English club to compete in Europe when they drew 0-0 away to Inter Milan in the inaugural competition of the Fairs Cup. Five years later in the same tournament, Brum became the first British club to reach a European final but were beaten 4-1 on aggregate by Barcelona.

Happily, Blackpool's groundsman is an expert at walking in straight lines...

1899, the same year in which Blackpool narrowly lost their league status for a single season.

• Blackpool's heyday was in the late 1940s and early 1950s when the club reached three FA Cup finals in five years. The Seasiders lost in the finals of 1948 and 1951 but lifted the cup in 1953 after defeating Lancashire rivals Bolton 4-3 in one of the most exciting Wembley matches ever. Although centre-forward Stan Mortensen scored a hat-trick, the match was dubbed the 'Matthews Final' after veteran winger Stanley Matthews, who finally won a winner's medal at the grand old age of 38.

• An apprentice at the time of the 'Matthews Final', long-serving right-back Jimmy Armfield holds the record for league appearances for Blackpool, with 569 between 1952 and 1971. Armfield is also Blackpool's most capped player, having played for England 43 times. In 2011 a 9ft-high statue of the Seasiders legend was unveiled outside Bloomfield Road.

• Blackpool's record scorer is Jimmy Hampson, who hit 248 league goals between 1927 and 1938, including a season best 45 in the club's 1929/30 Second Division championship-winning campaign.

• Blackpool were the first club to gain promotion from three different divisions via the play-offs. In total the Seasiders have played in a record seven play-off finals and with five wins they have the best record of any club in the finals.

• The Seasiders splashed out a club record £1.25 million on Leicester striker DJ Campbell in 2010. The following year they sold goalscoring midfielder Charlie Adam to Liverpool for a record £6.75 million.

HONOURS
Division 2 champions 1930
FA Cup 1953
EFL Trophy 2002, 2004

BOLTON WANDERERS

Year founded: 1874
Ground: University of Bolton Stadium (28,723)
Previous name: Christ Church
Nickname: The Trotters
Biggest win: 13-0 v Sheffield United (1890)
Heaviest defeat: 1-9 v Preston North End (1887)

The club was founded in 1874 as Christ Church, but three years later broke away from the church after a disagreement with the vicar and adopted their present name (the 'Wanderers' part stemmed from the fact that the club had no permanent home until moving to their former stadium, Burnden Park, in 1895).

• Bolton were founder members of the Football League in 1888, finishing fifth at the end of the campaign. The Trotters have since gone on to play more seasons in the top flight without ever winning the title, 73, than any other club.

• The club, though, have had better luck in the FA Cup. After defeats in the final in 1894 and 1904, Bolton won the cup for the first time in 1923 after beating West Ham 2-0 in the first Wembley final. In the same match, Bolton centre-forward David Jack enjoyed the distinction of becoming the first player to score a goal at the new stadium. The Trotters went on to win the competition again in 1926 and 1929.

• In 1953 Bolton became the first team to score three goals in the FA Cup final yet finish as losers, going down 4-3 to a Stanley Matthews-inspired Blackpool. In 1958 Bolton won the cup for a fourth time, beating Manchester United 2-0 in the final at Wembley.

• Bolton have twice reached the League Cup final but lost on both occasions, beaten 2-1 by Liverpool in 1995 and Middlesbrough in 2004.

• Bolton's top scorer is legendary centre-forward Nat Lofthouse, who notched 285 goals in all competitions between 1946 and 1960.

• After a calamitous season ended in relegation from the Championship in 2019 Bolton's squad refused to play their penultimate fixture at home against Brentford in protest at not being paid. The Bees were awarded a 1-0 victory by the EFL while Bolton were hit with a 12-point deduction to take into the 2019/20 league campaign after falling into administration.

• Worse was to follow when the Trotters' financial woes saw them threatened with expulsion from the EFL before they were saved by a buy-out by Football Ventures in August 2019.

HONOURS
First Division champions 1997
Division 2 champions 1909, 1978
Division 3 champions 1973
FA Cup 1923, 1926, 1929, 1958
EFL Trophy 1989

BOOTS

The first record of a pair of football boots goes back to 1526 when Henry VIII, then aged 35, ordered "45 velvet pairs and one leather pair for football" from the Great Wardrobe. Whether he actually donned the boots for a royal kick-around in Hampton Court or Windsor Castle is not known.

• Early leather boots were very different to the synthetic ones worn by modern players, having hard toe-caps and protection around the ankles. Studs were originally

By the looks of it, these boots belong to a certain Mesut Ozil!

prohibited, but were sanctioned after a change in the rules in 1891. Lighter boots without ankle protection were first worn in South America, but did not become the norm in Britain until the 1950s, following the example of England international Stanley Matthews who had a bespoke lightweight pair of boots made for him by a Yorkshire company.

• Herbert Chapman, later Arsenal's manager, is believed to be the first player to wear coloured boots, sporting a yellow pair in the 1900s. White boots first became fashionable in the 1970s and in 1996 Liverpool's John Barnes was the first player to wear them in an FA Cup final, but failed to dazzle in his side's 1-0 defeat to Manchester United.

• **In 2005 then Manchester United manager Sir Alex Ferguson banned his players from wearing boots with bladed studs which he angrily condemned as 'dangerous'.**

• Cristiano Ronaldo's incredible £1 billion lifetime sponsorship deal with boot manufacturers Nike is easily the biggest in the history of the game.

BORUSSIA DORTMUND

Year founded: 1909
Ground: Signal Iduna Park (81,365)
Nickname: The Borussians
League titles: 8
Domestic cups: 4
European cups: 2
International cups: 1

Borussia Dortmund were founded by members of a church team in 1909 who formed their own club without the involvement of a strict local priest. They chose the name 'Borussia', which means 'Prussia' in Latin, after a nearby brewery.

• **In 1966 Dortmund became the first German club to win a European trophy when they beat Liverpool 2-1 in the final of the Cup Winners' Cup in Brussels. The greatest day in the club's history, though, came in 1997 when they defeated favourites Juventus 3-1 in the Champions League**

final. Later that year they lifted the Intercontinental Cup after beating Brazilian side Cruzeiro.

• The club's Signal Iduna Park (previously known as Westfalenstadion) is the largest in Germany, with a capacity of 81,365. The imposing south terrace, nicknamed 'the Yellow Wall', is the largest terrace for standing in European football, with space for 24,454 fans.

• **Bundesliga runners-up in 2019, Dortmund won their only domestic Double under then manager Jurgen Klopp in 2012. The following year they faced arch rivals Bayern Munich in the Champions League final at Wembley, but ended up losing 2-1.**

• In 2016 Dortmund were involved in the highest-scoring Champions League match ever, thrashing Legia Warsaw 8-4 at home in a group game.

> HONOURS
> *German champions 1956, 1957, 1963, 1995, 1996, 2002, 2011, 2012*
> *German Cup 1965, 1989, 2012, 2017*
> *Champions League 1997*
> *European Cup Winners' Cup 1966*
> *Intercontinental Cup 1997*

BOURNEMOUTH

Year founded: 1899
Ground: Vitality Stadium (11,329)
Previous name: Boscombe, Bournemouth and Boscombe Athletic
Nickname: The Cherries
Biggest win: 11-0 v Margate (1970)
Heaviest defeat: 0-9 v Lincoln City (1982)

The Cherries were founded as Boscombe FC in 1899, having their origins in the Boscombe St John's club, which was formed in 1890. The club's name changed to Bournemouth and Boscombe FC in 1923 and then to AFC Bournemouth in 1971, when the team's colours were altered to red-and-black stripes in imitation of AC Milan.

• **Any similarity to the Italian giants was not obvious, though, until the 2014/15 season when the Cherries won promotion to the top flight for the first time in their history, clinching the Championship title in**

Life's a bowl of Cherries for Bournemouth's Chris Mepham

on Levante's Colombian international midfielder Jefferson Lerma, while two years earlier the Cherries received a record £12 million when winger Matt Ritchie joined Newcastle.

- **Striker Joshua King is Bournemouth's most-capped player, having turned out 23 times for Norway since signing from Blackburn in 2015.**
- Appointed Bournemouth manager for a second time in October 2012, Cherries boss Eddie Howe is now the longest-serving in the Premier League.
- **In March 2018 midfielder Lewis Cook became the first current Bournemouth player to play for England, when he came on as a sub in a 1-1 draw against Italy at Wembley. His cameo appearance was especially good news for his grandfather who won £17,000 after betting £500 that Cook would represent the Three Lions while he was starting out in the Leeds reserve team.**

HONOURS
Championship champions 2015
Division 3 champions 1987
EFL Trophy 1984

BRADFORD CITY

Year founded: 1903
Ground: Valley Parade (25,136)
Nickname: The Bantams
Biggest win: 11-1 v Rotherham United (1928)
Heaviest defeat: 1-9 v Colchester United (1961)

some style with a 3-0 victory at Charlton on the final day of the campaign.
- The Cherries' attack-minded team set a new record for the second tier by scoring 50 goals on their travels. They also set a new club record for goals scored in a season, with 115 in total in all competitions.

IS THAT A FACT?
With a capacity of just 11,360 Bournemouth's Vitality Stadium is the smallest of the 59 grounds to have staged Premier League football.

- **The club recorded their biggest ever win in the FA Cup, smashing fellow seasiders Margate 11-0 at Dean Court in 1970. Cherries striker Ted MacDougall scored nine of the goals, an all-time record for an individual player in the competition. In the same season the prolific Scot scored a club record 42 league goals.**
- Bournemouth enjoyed their best ever FA Cup run as a third-tier side in 1957, knocking out Tottenham in the fifth round before losing 2-1 at home to mighty Manchester United in the quarter-finals in front of a club record attendance of 28,799.
- **The club's record scorer is Ron Eyre (202 goals between 1924 and 1933), while striker Steve Fletcher pulled on the Cherries' jersey an amazing 628 times in two spells at Dean Court between 1992 and 2013.**
- In August 2018 Bournemouth splashed out a club record £25 million

Bradford City were founded in 1903 when a local rugby league side, Manningham FC, decided to switch codes. The club was elected to Division Two in the same year before they had played a single match – a swift ascent into the Football League which is only matched by Chelsea.

- **City's finest hour was in 1911 when they won the FA Cup for the only time in the club's history, beating Newcastle 1-0 in a replayed final at Old Trafford. There were more celebrations in Bradford in 1929 when City won the Third Division (North), scoring 128 goals in the process – a record for the third tier.**

- In 2013 Bradford City became the first club from the fourth tier of English football to reach a major final at Wembley, losing 5-0 to Swansea City in the League Cup. Two years later the Bantams pulled off possibly the biggest FA Cup shock ever, coming back from 2-0 down to beat Chelsea 4-2 in the fourth round at Stamford Bridge.
- **Sadly, City will forever be associated with the fire that broke out in the club's main stand on 11th May 1985 and killed 56 supporters. The official inquiry into the tragedy found that the inferno had probably been caused by a discarded cigarette butt which set fire to litter under the stand. As a permanent memorial to those who died, Bradford added black trimming to their shirt collars and sleeves.**
- Relegated from League One in 2019, the Bantams made their record signing in 2000, splashing out £2.5 million on Leeds winger David Hopkin.

HONOURS
Division 2 champions 1908
Division 3 champions 1985
Division 3 (North) champions 1929
FA Cup 1911

BRAZIL

First international: Argentina 3 Brazil 0, 1914
Most capped player: Cafu, 142 caps (1990-2006)
Leading goalscorer: Pelé, 77 goals (1957-71)
First World Cup appearance: Brazil 1 Yugoslavia 2, 1930
Biggest win: Brazil 14 Nicaragua 0, 1975
Heaviest defeat: Brazil 1 Germany 7, 2014

The most successful country in the history of international football, Brazil are renowned for an exciting, flamboyant style of play which delights both their legions of drum-beating fans and neutrals alike.
- **Brazil are the only country to have won the World Cup five times. The South Americans first lifted the trophy in 1958 (beating hosts Sweden 5-2 in the final) and retained the prize four**

Brazil's 2019 Copa America triumph was very much a family affair

years later in Chile. In 1970, a great Brazilian side featuring legends such as Pelé, Jairzinho, Gerson and Rivelino thrashed Italy 4-1 to win the Jules Rimet trophy for a third time. Further triumphs followed in 1994 (3-2 on penalties against Italy after a dour 0-0 draw) and in 2002 (after beating Germany 2-0 in the final).
- Brazil are the only country to have appeared at every World Cup (a total of 21) since the tournament began in 1930. The South Americans have also recorded the most wins (73) at the finals and scored the most goals (229). Less impressively, Brazil suffered the heaviest ever defeat by a host nation when they were trounced 7-1 by Germany in the semi-finals of the 2014 tournament.
- **Between February 1993 and January 1996 Brazil set a new world record when they were undefeated for 35 consecutive internationals.**
- With nine wins to their name, Brazil are the third most successful side in the history of the Copa America (behind Uruguay and Argentina, who have won the trophy 15 and 14 times respectively). The South Americans are the current holders of the title after beating Peru 3-1 in the 2019 final on home soil in Rio de Janeiro.
- **Brazil have the best record of any nation in the Confederations Cup, winning the trophy four times – most**

recently in 2013, when they beat Spain 3-0 in the final in Rio de Janeiro.

HONOURS
World Cup winners 1958, 1962, 1970, 1994, 2002
Copa America winners 1919, 1922, 1949, 1989, 1997, 1999, 2004, 2007, 2019
Confederations Cup winners 1997, 2005, 2009, 2013
World Cup Record
1930 Round 1
1934 Round 1
1938 Semi-finals
1950 Runners-up
1954 Quarter-finals
1958 Winners
1962 Winners
1966 Round 1
1970 Winners
1974 Fourth place
1978 Third place
1982 Round 2
1986 Quarter-finals
1990 Round 2
1994 Winners
1998 Runners-up
2002 Winners
2006 Quarter-finals
2010 Quarter-finals
2014 Fourth place
2018 Quarter-finals

TOP 10

BRAZILIAN PREMIER LEAGUE GOALSCORERS

1.	Roberto Firmino (2015-)	48
2.	Philippe Coutinho (2013-18)	41
3.	Juninho (1995-2004)	29
4.	Willian (2013-)	28
5.	Gabriel Jesus (2017-)	27
6.	Oscar (2012-17)	21
7.	Richarlison (2017-)	18
	Fernandinho (2013-)	18
9.	Gilberto Silva (2002-08)	17
	Ramires (2010-16)	17

BRENTFORD

Year founded: 1889
Ground: Griffin Park (12,763)
Nickname: The Bees
Biggest win: 9-0 v Wrexham (1963)
Heaviest defeat: 0-7 v Swansea Town (1926), Walsall (1957) and Peterborough (2007)

Brentford were founded in 1889 by members of a local rowing club and, after playing at a number of different venues, the club settled at Griffin Park in 1904.

• **The club enjoyed its heyday in the decade before the Second World War.** In 1929/30 Brentford won all 21 of their home games in the Third Division (South) to set a record which remains to this day. Promoted to the First Division in 1935, the Bees finished in the top six in the next three seasons before being relegated in the first post-war campaign. After plunging into the Fourth Division in 1962, Brentford became the first team to have played all the other 91 clubs in the Football League.

• Defender Ken Coote played in a club record 514 league games for the Bees between 1949 and 1964, while his team-mate Jim Towers scored a record 153 league goals.

• **The Bees paid out a club record £5.5 million when they signed Leeds defender Pontus Jansson in July 2019. The west Londoners received a record £20 million the following month when French striker Neal Maupay joined Brighton.**

• In the 1974/75 season goalkeeper Steve Sherwood became the first ever on-loan player to be ever-present in a league campaign when he spent a year away from his parent club Chelsea at Griffin Park.

• **Defender John Buttigieg played in a club record 20 internationals for Malta between 1988 and 1991.**

• In a League Cup first round tie against AFC Wimbledon in August 2017 Brentford's Justin Shaibu became the first ever fourth substitute to score a competitive goal.

HONOURS

Division 2 champions 1935
Division 3 (South) champions 1933
League Two champions 2009
Third Division champions 1999
Division 4 champions 1963

The Bees' Kamohelo Mokotjo packs a bit of a sting!

BRIGHTON AND HOVE ALBION

Year founded: 1900
Ground: AMEX Stadium (30,750)
Previous name: Brighton and Hove Rangers
Nickname: The Seagulls
Biggest win: 14-2 v Brighton Amateurs (1902)
Heaviest defeat: 0-9 v Middlesbrough (1958)

Founded originally as Brighton and Hove Rangers in 1900, the club changed to its present name the following year. In 1920 Brighton joined Division Three as founder members, but had to wait another 38 years before gaining promotion to a higher level.

• **Brighton enjoyed the greatest achievement in their history in 2017 when, under manager Chris Hughton, they were promoted to the Premier League for the first time, finishing just one point behind Championship title winners Newcastle.**

• The club reached the final of the FA Cup for the only time in their history in 1983, holding favourites Manchester United to a 2-2 draw at Wembley. The Seagulls were unable to repeat their heroics in the replay, however, and crashed to a 4-0 defeat. In 2019 Brighton came close to reaching the FA Cup final again, but were beaten 1-0 by Manchester City in the semi-final at Wembley.

• **In the 1973/74 season the Seagulls were briefly managed by the legendary Brian Clough. His time in charge of the club, though, was not a successful one and included an 8-2 thrashing by Bristol Rovers – the worst home defeat in Brighton's history.**

• Brighton's record scorer is 1920s striker Tommy Cook, with 114 league goals. Cult hero Peter Ward, though, enjoyed the most prolific season in front of goal for the club, notching 32 times as the Seagulls gained promotion from the old Third Division in 1976/77. Ernie 'Tug' Wilson made the most appearances for the south coast outfit, with 509 between 1922 and 1936.

• **The Seagulls' most expensive signing is central defender Adam Webster, who cost £20 million from Bristol City in August 2019. Argentinian striker**

Leonardo Ulloa boosted Brighton's coffers by a club record £8 million when he joined Leicester City in 2014.

• Brighton are the only club to have won the Charity Shield without ever winning the league title or FA Cup. In 1910 the Seagulls, then reigning Southern League champions, lifted the shield after beating title winners Aston Villa 1-0 at Stamford Bridge.

• **For the second season running, Brighton defender Shane Duffy made more clearances (243) than any other Premier League player during the 2018/19 campaign.**

HONOURS
League One champions 2011
Second Division champions 2002
Division 3 (South) champions 1958
Third Division champions 2001
Division 4 champions 1965

BRISTOL CITY

Year founded: 1894
Ground: Ashton Gate (27,000)
Previous name: Bristol South End
Nickname: The Robins
Biggest win: 11-0 v Chichester City (1960)
Heaviest defeat: 0-9 v Coventry City (1934)

Founded as Bristol South End in 1894, the club took its present name when it turned professional three years later.

In 1900 City merged with Bedminster, whose ground at Ashton Gate became the club's permanent home in 1904.

• **The Robins enjoyed a golden decade in the 1900s, winning promotion to the top flight for the first time in 1906 after a campaign in which they won a club record 14 consecutive games. The following season City finished second, and in 1909 they reached the FA Cup final for the first and only time in their history, losing 1-0 to Manchester United at Crystal Palace.**

• Since then the followers of Bristol's biggest club have had to endure more downs than ups. The Robins returned to the top flight after a 65-year absence in 1976, but financial difficulties led to three consecutive relegations in the early 1980s (City being the first club ever to suffer this awful fate).

• **City's strikers were on fire in 1962/63 as the Robins scored 100 goals in Division Three. Sadly for their fans, however, City could only finish 14th in the league – the lowest place ever by a club hitting three figures.**

• England international striker John Atyeo is the Robins' top scorer with 315 goals between 1951 and 1966. In the history of league football only Dixie Dean (Everton) and George Camsell (Middlesbrough) scored more goals for the same club. Defender Louis Carey made a record 646 appearances for the club in two spells at Ashton Gate between 1995 and 2014.

• **Much-loved defender Billy 'Fatty' Wedlock won a club record 26 caps for England while with Bristol City between 1907 and 1914.**

• The Robins are the only club to have lifted the EFL Trophy three times, winning finals against Bolton (1986), Carlisle United (2003) and Walsall (2015).

HONOURS
Division 2 champions 1906
League One champions 2015
Division 3 (South) champions 1923, 1927, 1955
EFL Trophy 1986, 2003, 2015
Welsh Cup 1934

BRISTOL ROVERS

Year founded: 1893
Ground: Memorial Stadium (12,296)
Previous name: Black Arabs, Eastville Rovers, Bristol Eastville Rovers
Nickname: The Pirates
Biggest win: 15-1 v Weymouth (1900)
Heaviest defeat: 0-12 v Luton Town (1936)

Bristol Rovers can trace their history back to 1883 when the Black Arabs club was founded at the Eastville Restaurant in Bristol. The club was renamed Eastville Rovers the following year in an attempt to attract more support from the local area, later adding 'Bristol' to their name before finally settling on plain old 'Bristol Rovers' in 1898.

• **Rovers have lived up to their name by playing at no fewer than nine different grounds. Having spent much of their history at Eastville Stadium, they have been based at the Memorial Stadium since 1996.**

• The only Rovers player to have appeared for England while with the Pirates, Geoff Bradford, is the club's record scorer, netting 242 times in the league between 1949 and 1964.

Bristol City's lonely defender Tomas Kalas wondered if he'd got the matchday wrong!

IS THAT A FACT?
In 1989 Bristol Rovers recorded the biggest away win in the play-offs, thrashing Fulham 4-0 at Craven Cottage in the Third Division semi-final to complete a 5-0 aggregate victory.

The club's record appearance maker is central defender Stuart Taylor, who turned out in 546 league games between 1966 and 1980.

• Rovers' Ronnie Dix is the youngest player ever to score in the Football League, notching against Norwich in 1928 when he was aged just 15 years and 180 days.

• Latvia striker Vitaly Astafjevs won a club record 20 of his national record 167 caps while with Rovers between 1999 and 2003.

HONOURS
Division 3 champions 1990
Division 3 (South)
champions 1953

LUCY BRONZE

Born: Berwick-upon-Tweed, 28th October 1991
Position: Defender
Club career:
2007-10 Sunderland Ladies 23 (5)
2009 North Carolina Tar Heels 24 (3)
2010-12 Everton Ladies 24 (3)
2012-14 Liverpool Ladies 28 (3)
2014-17 Manchester City Women 34 (5)
2017- Olympique Lyon Feminine 35 (3)
International record:
2013- England 73 (8)

An attacking right-back who often chips in with important goals, Lucy Bronze was hailed by England manager Phil Neville as 'the best player in the world' for her performances at the 2019 Women's World Cup in France, and was named UEFA Women's Player of the Year in August 2019.

• In 2018 Bronze became the first British player to win the Women's Champion League with a foreign club, when she

Lucy sadly just missed out on 'Bronze' at the 2019 World Cup

played for Lyon in their 4-1 defeat of Wolfsburg in the final in Kiev. A year later she helped the French club retain the trophy following a 4-1 rout of Barcelona in Budapest.

• After starting out with Sunderland, Bronze spent a year in the USA at the University of Carolina. She returned to England to play for Everton Ladies, before joining local rivals Liverpool in 2012. She won the Women's Super League title with the Reds in both 2013 and 2014, before moving on to Manchester City with whom she won the league in 2016 and the FA Women's Cup in 2017. Bronze is the only player to win the PFA Women's Player of the Year award twice, topping the poll in both 2014 and 2017.

• Bronze was part of the England Under-19 side that won the European championship in 2009. She made her full England debut in 2013 and two years later starred at the 2015 World Cup, scoring vital goals in the last 16 against Norway and in the quarter-final against hosts Canada.

KEVIN DE BRUYNE

Born: Drongen, Belgium, 28th June 1991
Position: Midfielder
Club career:
2008-12 Genk 84 (14)
2012-14 Chelsea 3 (0)
2012 Genk (loan) 13 (2)
2012-13 Werder Bremen (loan) 33 (10)
2014-15 Wolfsburg 51 (13)
2015- Manchester City 117 (23)
International record:
2010- Belgium 70 (16)

Despite suffering an injury-hit season in 2018/19, Kevin De Bruyne still managed to help Manchester City claim an historic Treble, coming off the bench to score in the Citizens' 6-0 hammering of Watford in the FA Cup final at Wembley. His lively cameo also won him the Man of the Match award, even though he was only on the pitch for 35 minutes.

• An attacking midfielder who passes the ball well and loves to strike from

THIS IS OUR CITY

Football is as easy as ABC for Manchester City's KDB

distance, De Bruyne moved from Wolfsburg to Manchester City in August 2015 for a then club record £55 million, making him the second most expensive player in British football history at the time. He has since won a host of honours with City, and in both 2016/17 and 2017/18 he topped the Premier League assists chart.

• Before his move to Manchester, De Bruyne contributed a Bundesliga record 21 assists as Wolfsburg finished second in the league in 2014/15, and scored in his side's 3-1 German Cup final victory over Borussia Dortmund. After an outstanding campaign, De Bruyne was named German Footballer of the Year in 2015, the first Belgian to win this award.

• **First capped in a friendly against Finland in 2010, De Bruyne was part of the Belgian team that came a best ever third at the 2018 World Cup in Russia, scoring a screamer in his country's 2-1 defeat of Brazil in the quarter-final and earning a place in the FIFA World Cup Dream Team.**

BURNLEY

Year founded: 1882
Ground: Turf Moor (21,401)
Nickname: The Clarets
Biggest win: 9-0 v Darwen (1892), New Brighton (1957) and Penrith (1984)
Heaviest defeat: 0-11 v Darwen (1885)

One of England's most famous old clubs, Burnley were founded in 1882 when the Burnley Rovers rugby team decided to switch to the round ball game. The club was a founder member of the Football League in 1888 and has since won all four divisions of the league – a feat matched only by four other clubs.

• Burnley have twice won the league championship, in 1921 and 1960. The first of these triumphs saw the Clarets go on a 30-match unbeaten run, the longest in a single season until Arsenal

went through the whole of 2003/04 undefeated. In its own way, Burnley's 1960 title win was just as remarkable, as the Clarets only ever topped the league on the last day of the season after a 2-1 win at Manchester City.

• The club's only FA Cup triumph came in 1914 when they defeated Liverpool 1-0. After the final whistle Burnley's captain Tommy Boyle became the first man to receive the cup from a reigning monarch, King George V.

• **On 16th April 2011 Burnley defender Graham Alexander became only the second outfield player in the history of English football to make 1,000 professional appearances when he came on as a sub in the Clarets' 2-1 win over Swansea City. Alexander is also the most successful penalty taker ever in the domestic game, with a clinical 78 goals in 86 attempts from the spot.**

• Burnley broke their transfer record in August 2017, signing New Zealand international striker Chris Wood from Leeds for £15 million. The Clarets made their record sale in July 2017 when England international defender Michael Keane moved to Everton for £25 million.

• **Club legend Jimmy McIlroy made a record 51 appearances for Northern Ireland between 1951 and 1962.**

• Burnley are the last club to have scored a century of goals in consecutive top-flight campaigns, hitting the back of the net 102 times in 1960/61 and 101 in 1961/62.

• **England international goalkeeper Jerry Dawson made a club record 552**

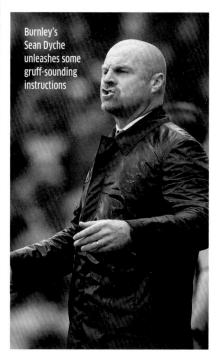

Burnley's Sean Dyche unleashes some gruff-sounding instructions

appearances for Burnley between 1907 and 1928. The club's record scorer is George Beel with 178 goals between 1923 and 1932.

• Led superbly by their gravel-voiced manager Sean Dyche, Burnley achieved their best-ever Premier League finish, seventh, in the 2017/18 campaign. As a result, the Clarets qualified for Europe for the first time since 1966, but they were eliminated from the Europa League before the group stage.

HONOURS
Division 1 champions 1921, 1960
Championship champions 2016
Division 2 champions 1898, 1973
Division 3 champions 1982
Division 4 champions 1992
FA Cup 1914

BURTON ALBION

Year founded: 1950
Ground: Pirelli Stadium (6,912)
Nickname: The Brewers
Biggest win: 12-1 v Coalville Town (1954)
Heaviest defeat: 0-10 v Barnet (1970)

Burton Albion were founded at a public meeting at the Town Hall in 1950. The town had previously supported two Football League clubs, Burton Swifts and Burton Wanderers, who merged to form Burton United in 1901 before folding nine years later.

• The Brewers gained promotion to the Football League for the first time in 2009, going up as Conference champions. In 2015, managed by former Chelsea striker Jimmy Floyd Hasselbaink, Burton gained promotion to the third tier for the first time after

There's a metal band missing a bassist when John Brayford plays for Burton!

winning the League Two title with a club record 94 points.

• The following season, Burton earned another promotion as Nigel Clough, returning for a second spell at the Pirelli Stadium, took the Brewers into the Championship but their two-year sojourn in the second-tier ended in 2018.

• In the 2018/19 season Burton enjoyed their best ever cup run, reaching the semi-finals of the League Cup. However, there was no happy ending as the Brewers were massacred 10-0 on aggregate by eventual winners Manchester City, the heaviest defeat ever suffered by a club at that late stage of the competition.

• Brewers winger Lucas Akins has played in a club record 205 league games and scored a record 44 goals since 2014.

• In June 2017 the Brewers splashed out a club record £500,000 on Ross County's Northern Ireland international striker Liam Boyce. Two months later Burton cashed a record cheque for £2 million when Australian midfielder Jackson Irvine joined Hull City.

HONOURS
League Two champions 2015
Conference champions 2009

BURY

Year founded: 1885
Ground: Gigg Lane (12,500)
Nickname: The Shakers
Biggest win: 12-1 v Stockton (1897)
Heaviest defeat: 0-10 v Blackburn Rovers (1887) and West Ham (1982)

The club with the shortest name in the Football League, Bury were founded in 1885 at a meeting at the Old White Horse Hotel in Bury, as successors to two other teams in the town, the Bury Unitarians and the Bury Wesleyans. Bury were founder members of the Lancashire League in 1889, joining the Football League five years later. Tragically for their fans, the club were expelled from the EFL in August 2019 after an ongoing financial crisis meant they were unable to start the 2019/20 season on time.

• Bury have won the FA Cup on two occasions. In 1900 the Shakers beat Southern League outfit Southampton 4-0 at Crystal Palace, and then three years later they thrashed Derby County 6-0 at the same venue to record the biggest ever victory in an FA Cup final.

• On 27th August 2005 Bury became the first club to score 1,000 goals in all four tiers of the Football League when Brian Barry-Murphy netted in a 2-2 draw with Wrexham in a League Two fixture.

• Bury became the first club to be thrown out of the FA Cup in 2006 for fielding an ineligible player – Stephen Turnbull, a loan signing from Hartlepool United.

• Dual international defender Bill Gorman made a club record 11 appearances for Northern Ireland and the Republic of Ireland. Rather bizarrely, in September 1946 he represented both countries against England within just three days.

• In 1999 Bury became the first European club to sign an Indian player when they bought Bhaichung Bhutia from East Bengal. He spent five years at Gigg Lane before returning to India in 2004.

HONOURS
Division 2 champions 1895
Second Division champions 1997
Division 3 champions 1961
FA Cup 1900, 1903

CAMBRIDGE UNITED

Year founded: 1912
Ground: Abbey Stadium (8,127)
Previous name: Abbey United
Nickname: The U's
Biggest win: 7-0 v Morecambe (2016)
Heaviest defeat: 0-7 v Sunderland (2002) and Luton Town (2017)

Cambridge United were founded as Abbey United in 1912 before taking their current name two years after turning professional in 1949.

• The club was elected to the Football League in 1970 and rose to the second tier a decade later. However, the U's soon returned to the basement division after being relegated in 1984 (setting a then league record of 31 consecutive games without a win) and in 1985 (losing 33 matches to equal the then league record).

• Midfielder Steve Spriggs played in a record 416 league games for Cambridge between 1975 and 1987. The club's all-time top scorer is John Taylor with 86

goals in two spells at the Abbey Stadium between 1988 and 2004.

• Aged 16 and two months, midfielder Ben Worman became Cambridge's youngest ever player when he came on as a sub in an EFL Trophy tie against Peterborough United on 7th November 2017.

• In 1990 the U's became the last club from the fourth tier to reach the FA Cup sixth round, but they were beaten 1-0 by eventual finalists Crystal Palace.

HONOURS
Division 3 champions
1991
Division 4 champions
1977

CAPS

Legendary goalkeeper Peter Shilton has won more international caps than any other British player. 'Shilts' played for England 125 times between 1970 and 1990 and would have won many more caps if he had not faced stiff competition for the No. 1 shirt from his great rival Ray Clemence, who won 61 caps during the same period. In women's football, midfielder Fara Williams has won a record 170 caps for England since making her debut in 2001.

• The first international caps were awarded by England in 1886, following a proposal put forward by the founder of the Corinthians, N.L. Jackson. To this day players actually receive a handmade

Fara Williams, England's highest-capped women's player

'cap' to mark the achievement of playing for their country. England caps are made by a Bedworth-based company called Toye, Kenning & Spencer, who also provide regalia for the Freemasons.

• The most capped player in the history of the game is Egypt midfielder Ahmed Hassan, who played an astonishing 184 times for his country between 1995 and 2012. The women's record is held by Kristine Lilly, who made 354 appearances for the USA between 1987 and 2010.

• The first player in the world to reach a century of caps was England skipper Billy Wright when he played in a 1-0 defeat of Scotland at Wembley on 11th April 1959.

Cambridge's Wes Hoolahan has definitely had a career to shout about

TOP 10

HIGHEST CAPPED ENGLAND PLAYERS

1.	Peter Shilton (1970-90)	125
2.	Wayne Rooney (2003-18)	120
3.	David Beckham (1996-2009)	115
4.	Steven Gerrard (2000-14)	114
5.	Bobby Moore (1962-73)	108
6.	Ashley Cole (2001-14)	107
7.	Bobby Charlton (1958-70)	106
8.	Frank Lampard (1999-2014)	105
	Billy Wright (1946-59)	105
10.	Bryan Robson (1980-91)	90

CARDIFF CITY

Year founded: 1899
Ground: Cardiff City Stadium (33,316)
Previous name: Riverside
Nickname: The Bluebirds
Biggest win: 16-0 v Knighton Town (1961)
Heaviest defeat: 2-11 v Sheffield United (1926)

Founded as the football branch of the Riverside Cricket Club, the club changed to its present name in 1908, three years after Cardiff was awarded city status.

• Cardiff are the only non-English club to have won the FA Cup, lifting the trophy in 1927 after a 1-0 victory over Arsenal at Wembley. Three years earlier the Bluebirds were pipped to the league title by Huddersfield on goal average, but if all-time leading scorer Len Davies had successfully converted a penalty in a 0-0 draw at Birmingham on the final day of the season the trophy would have gone to Wales.

• On 7th April 1947 a massive crowd of 51,621 squeezed into Cardiff's old Ninian Park Stadium for the club's match against Bristol City – an all-time record attendance for the third tier of English football.

• Cardiff have won the Welsh Cup 22 times, just one short of Wrexham's record. The Bluebirds' domination of the tournament in the 1960s and 1970s earned them regular qualification for the European Cup Winners' Cup and in 1968 they reached the semi-finals of the competition before losing 4-3 on aggregate to Hamburg.

• Cardiff's record appearance maker is midfielder Billy Hardy, who turned out 497 times for the club between 1911 and 1931.

• **In the 2002/03 season Bluebirds striker Robert Earnshaw scored a club record 31 league goals. Earnshaw is the only player ever to have scored a hat-trick in the Premier League, all three divisions of the Football League, the FA Cup, the League Cup and an international match, achieving the bulk of these feats while with Cardiff between 1998 and 2004.**

• Defender Alf Sherwood won a club record 39 caps for Wales while with Cardiff between 1946 and 1956.

• **Relegated from the Premier League in 2019, Cardiff made their record signing in January of that year when they bought Argentinian striker Emiliano Sala from Nantes for £15 million. Tragically, just two days after putting pen to paper, Sala died in a plane crash in the English Channel.**

> HONOURS
> *Championship champions* 1913
> *Division 3 (South) champions* 1947
> *Third Division champions* 1993
> *FA Cup* 1927
> *Welsh Cup* 1912, 1920, 1922, 1923, 1927, 1928, 1930, 1956, 1959, 1964, 1965, 1967, 1968, 1969, 1970, 1971, 1973, 1974, 1976, 1988, 1992, 1993

Junior Hoilett and his Cardiff City teammates seem to be big fans of grass!

CARLISLE UNITED

Year founded: 1903
Ground: Brunton Park (18,202)
Nickname: The Blues
Biggest win: 8-0 v Hartlepool (1928) and Scunthorpe (1952)
Heaviest defeat: 1-11 v Hull City (1939)

Carlisle United were formed in 1903 following the merger of two local clubs, Shaddongate United and Carlisle Red Rose. The Blues joined the Third Division (North) in 1928 and were long-term residents of the bottom two divisions until 1965, when they won promotion to the second tier for the first time.

• **The club's greatest moment came in 1974 when, in their one season in the top flight, they sat on top of the old First Division after the opening three games. The Cumbrians, though, were quickly knocked off their lofty perch and ended the campaign rock bottom of the table.**

• By 2004 they had dropped out of the Football League and become the first club ever to play in each of the top five divisions in English football.

• **Scottish goalkeeper Allan Ross made a club record 466 appearances for the Blues between 1963 and 1979. Striker Jimmy McConnell scored a record 142 league goals for the club, including a seasonal best 42 in 1928/29.**

• Carlisle have appeared in the EFL Trophy final on a record six occasions, and in 1995 became the first and only team to lose an English trophy on the 'golden goal' rule when they conceded in extra-time in the final against Birmingham City.

• **Midfielder Reggie Lambe made a club record five international appearances for Bermuda in 2017 and 2018.**

• In the 2015/16 season Carlisle travelled a record total of 15,748 miles to away matches in all domestic competitions, including three 'home' games they played at other grounds after Brunton Park was flooded.

> HONOURS
> *Division 3 champions* 1965
> *League Two champions* 2006
> *Third Division champions* 1995
> *EFL Trophy* 1997, 2011

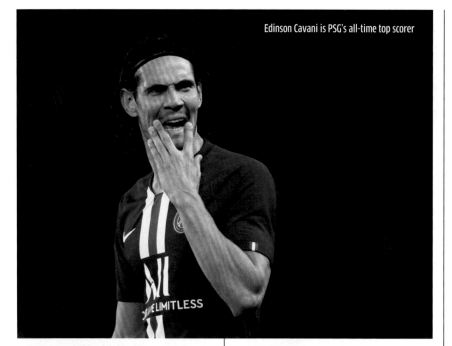

Edinson Cavani is PSG's all-time top scorer

EDINSON CAVANI

Born: Salto, Uruguay, 14th February 1987
Position: Striker
Club career:
2005-07 Danubio 25 (9)
2007-10 Palermo 109 (34)
2010-13 Napoli 104 (78)
2013- Paris St-Germain 186 (134)
International record:
2008- Uruguay 114 (48)

Long-haired Uruguayan striker Edinson Cavani is the all-time top scorer for Paris Saint-Germain with 193 goals in all competitions and only the second player – after his former PSG team-mate Zlatan Ibrahimovic – to notch 100 goals in both the Italian and French leagues.

• In six seasons with PSG Cavani has helped the club from the French capital win five Ligue 1 titles and four French Cups, his most prolific season coming in 2016/17 when he topped the scoring charts with 35 goals and was named Ligue 1 Player of the Year.

• Now a 32-year-old veteran, Cavani had to wait until 2012 before winning his first silverware, the Coppa Italia with Napoli. The following season he was top scorer in Serie A with 29 goals before joining PSG for a then French record £55 million.

• Cavani scored against Colombia on his international debut in 2008 and three years later was a key figure in the Uruguay team which won the Copa America. He is now his country's second highest scorer of all time – behind Luis Suarez – with 48 goals.

CELTIC

Year founded: 1888
Ground: Celtic Park (60,411)
Nickname: The Bhoys
Biggest win: 11-0 v Dundee (1895)
Heaviest defeat: 0-8 v Motherwell (1937)

The first British team to win the European Cup, Celtic were founded by an Irish priest in 1887 with the aim of raising funds for poor children in Glasgow's East End slums. The club were founder members of the Scottish League in 1890, and have gone on to spend a record 124 seasons in the top flight.

• Celtic have won the Scottish Cup more times than any other club, with 39 victories. The Bhoys most recently won the cup in 2019, defeating Hearts 2-1 in the final at Hampden Park.

• Under legendary manager Jock Stein Celtic won the Scottish league for nine consecutive seasons in the 1960s and 1970s, with a side featuring great names like Billy McNeill, Jimmy Johnstone, Bobby Lennox and Tommy Gemmell. This extraordinary run of success equalled a world record established by MTK Budapest of Hungary in the 1920s but, painfully for Celtic fans, was later matched by bitter rivals Rangers in the 1990s.

• The greatest ever Celtic side, managed by Stein and dubbed the 'Lisbon Lions', became the first British club to win the European Cup

when they beat Inter Milan 2-1 in the Portuguese capital in 1967. Stein was central to the team's triumph, scoring an early point by sitting in Inter manager Helenio Herrera's seat and refusing to budge, and then urging his players forward after they went a goal down to the defensive-minded Italians. Sticking to their attacking game plan, Celtic fought back with goals by Gemmell and Steve Chalmers to spark jubilant celebrations at the end among the travelling fans. Remarkably, all the 'Lisbon Lions' were born and bred within a 30-mile radius of Celtic Park.

• That 1966/67 season was the most successful in the club's history as they won every competition they entered: the Scottish league, Scottish Cup and Scottish League Cup, as well as the European Cup. To this day, no other British side has won a similar 'Quadruple'.

• The skipper of the 'Lisbon Lions' was Billy McNeill, who went on to play in a record 790 games for Celtic in all competitions between 1957 and 1975. He later managed the club, leading Celtic to the Double in their centenary season in 1987/88. The club's most capped player is goalkeeper Pat Bonner, who made 80 appearances for the Republic of Ireland between 1981 and 1996.

• Jimmy McGrory, who played for the club between 1922 and 1938, scored a staggering 396 league goals for Celtic – a British record by a player for a single club. In 1932 he hit eight goals in a 9-0 thrashing of Dunfermline, the biggest haul ever by a player in the top flight in Britain.

• In 1957 Celtic won the Scottish League Cup for the first time, demolishing Rangers 7-1 in the final at Hampden Park. The victory stands as the biggest by either side in an Old Firm match and is also a record for a major Scottish cup final. Celtic went on to enjoy more success in the League Cup, appearing in a world record 14 consecutive finals (winning six) between 1964 and 1978.

• In 2016/17 Celtic went through the entire league campaign unbeaten, only the third time this had happened in the Scottish top flight and the first time in a 38-game season. The Bhoys won the title with a record 106 points and finished an incredible 30 points clear of second-placed Aberdeen – just one point less than PSG's European record margin set a year earlier. In addition, Brendan Rodgers' 'Invincibles' were unbeaten in nine

Celtic players like Hatem Elhamed are aiming for 'nine in a row' in 2020

Premiership champions 2014, 2015, 2016, 2017, 2018, 2019
SPL champions 2001, 2002, 2004, 2006, 2007, 2008, 2012, 2013
Premier Division champions 1977, 1979, 1981, 1982, 1986, 1988, 1998
Division 1 champions 1893, 1884, 1896, 1898, 1905, 1906, 1907, 1908, 1909, 1910, 1914, 1915, 1916, 1917, 1919, 1922, 1926, 1936, 1938, 1954, 1966, 1967, 1968, 1969, 1970, 1971, 1972, 1973, 1974
Scottish Cup 1892, 1899, 1900, 1904, 1907, 1908, 1911, 1912, 1914, 1923, 1925, 1927, 1931, 1933, 1937, 1951, 1954, 1965, 1967, 1969, 1971, 1972, 1974, 1975, 1977, 1980, 1985, 1988, 1989, 1995, 2001, 2004, 2005, 2007, 2011, 2013, 2017, 2018, 2019
League Cup 1957, 1958, 1966, 1967, 1968, 1969, 1970, 1975, 1983, 1998, 2000, 2001, 2006, 2015, 2017, 2018, 2019
Double 1907, 1908, 1914, 1954, 1971, 1972, 1974, 1977, 1988, 2004, 2007, 2013
Treble 1967, 1969, 2001, 2017, 2018, 2019
European Cup 1967

CHAMPIONS LEAGUE

The most prestigious competition in club football, the Champions League replaced the old European Cup in 1992. Previously a competition for domestic league champions only, runners-up from the main European nations were first admitted in 1997 and the tournament has subsequently expanded to include up to four entrants per country. In 2015 a new rule saw the Europa League winners qualify for the Champions League, with Manchester United becoming the first English club to take this route into the competition two years later.

• Spanish giants Real Madrid won the first European Cup in 1956, defeating French side Reims 4-3 in the final in Paris. Real went on to win the competition the next four years as well, thanks largely to the brilliance of their star players Alfredo Di Stefano and Ferenc Puskas. With six wins in the European Cup and another seven in the Champions League, Real have won the competition a record 13 times.

• The first British club to win the European Cup was Celtic, who famously beat Inter Milan in the final in Lisbon in 1967.

Scottish domestic cup matches as they clinched their third ever Treble.

• The following season Celtic extended their unbeaten run to a British record 69 matches before they lost 4-0 at Hearts in December 2017. Nevertheless, the Bhoys went on to win the Treble for a second consecutive campaign, and they made it a hat-trick a year later to become the first British club ever to land a 'Treble Treble'.

• Celtic manager Willie Maley was in charge of the club for an incredible 43 years between 1897 and 1940 – a record of longevity only surpassed in European football by Guy Roux's 44-year tenure at Auxerre between 1961 and 2005 and Fred Everiss' 46-year reign at West Brom between 1902 and 1948.

• French striker Odsonne Edouard is Celtic's record signing, joining the club from Paris Saint-Germain for £9 million in June 2018. In August 2019 Celtic full-back Kieran Tierney was sold to Arsenal for £25 million – a record fee for the Scottish league.

TOP 10

SCOTTISH TOP-FLIGHT GOALS

1.	Celtic	9,173
2.	Rangers	8,987
3.	Hearts	6,825
4.	Aberdeen	6,124
5.	Hibernian	5,990
6.	Motherwell	5,656
7.	Dundee	5,083
8.	Kilmarnock	4,680
9.	St Mirren	4,597
10.	Partick Thistle	4,426

Liverpool's Roberto Firmino was happy enough to share his seat with the Champions League trophy

The following year Manchester United became the first English club to triumph, beating Benfica 4-1 at Wembley. The most successful British club in the tournament, though, are Liverpool, with six wins in 1977, 1978, 1981, 1984, 2005 and 2019, followed by Manchester United with three (1968, 1999 and 2008). Three other English clubs, Nottingham Forest (in 1979 and 1980), Aston Villa (in 1982) and Chelsea (in 2012) have also won the tournament, making England the only country to boast five different winners.

• Portuguese superstar Cristiano Ronaldo is the leading scorer in the history of the competition with 126 goals (including a record 17 in the 2013/14 season for Real Madrid), and has been the tournament's leading scorer in a record seven seasons. Meanwhile, Real Madrid and Porto goalkeeper Iker Casillas has appeared in a record 177 games in the tournament, keeping a record 59 clean sheets.

• Real Madrid winger Francisco Gento is the most successful player in the history of the competition with six winner's medals (1956-60 and 1966) while Cristiano Ronaldo is the only player to win the Champions League five times.

• In 2018 Real Madrid became the first club to win the trophy three times on the trot in the Champions League era, after defeating Liverpool 3-1 in the final in Kiev.

• Real also hold the record for the most consecutive appearances in the Champions League, with 23 between 1997 and 2019.

• Feyenoord recorded the biggest win in the competition in 1969 when they thrashed KR Reykjavik 12-2 in the first round. In the Champions League era Liverpool and Real Madrid jointly hold the record with ruthless 8-0 tonkings of Besiktas (2007) and Malmo (2015) respectively.

• Real legend Alfredo Di Stefano scored in a record five finals between 1956 and 1960, while Cristiano Ronaldo is the only player to have scored in three Champions League finals (2008, 2014 and 2017).

• In the 2017/18 season Paris Saint-Germain scored a record 25 goals in the group stage of the Champions League. Less impressively, BATE Borisov (2014/15) and Legia Warsaw (2016/17) conceded 24 goals each in their six group games.

• In the greatest comeback in Champions League history Barcelona beat Paris Saint-Germain 6-1 in 2017 after losing the first leg of their last 16 tie 4-0 in the French capital.

CHANTS

The loudest recorded noise created by a football crowd is 131.76 decibels by Galatasaray fans during their home derby against Istanbul rivals Fenerbahce on 18th March 2011. Despite the raucous atmosphere created by the home fans, visitors Fenerbahce won the match 2-1.

• Manchester City players were widely criticised after a video emerged of them singing a song about Liverpool fans being 'battered in the street' after they celebrated their 2019 Premier League title triumph on a plane back from their final game of the campaign at Brighton.

IS THAT A FACT?
In June 2016 'You'll Never Walk Alone' was rated the best terrace chant ever by football magazine FourFourTwo, topping its list of the 50 greatest fan songs worldwide.

• Possibly the oldest football chant is 'Who ate all the pies?', which researchers at Oxford University have discovered dates back to 1894 when it was playfully directed by Sheffield United fans at their 22-stone goalkeeper William 'Fatty' Foulke. The chant stemmed from an incident when the tubby custodian got up early at the team hotel, sneaked down into the dining room and somehow munched his way through all the players' breakfast pies.

• In a bizarre incident, Leipzig striker Timo Werner asked to be substituted after 32 minutes of his side's 2-0 defeat away to Besiktas in the Champions League in September 2017 because the chants and shrill whistles of the Turkish fans were making him feel dizzy.

CHARLTON ATHLETIC

Year founded: 1905
Ground: The Valley (27,111)
Nickname: The Addicks
Biggest win: 8-1 v Middlesbrough (1953)
Heaviest defeat: 1-11 v Aston Villa (1959)

Charlton Athletic were founded in 1905 when a number of youth clubs in the south-east London area, including East Street Mission and Blundell Mission, decided to merge. The club, whose nickname 'the Addicks' stemmed from the haddock served by a local chippy, graduated from minor leagues to join the Third Division (South) in 1921.

• Charlton's heyday was shortly before and just after the Second World War. After becoming the first club to win successive promotions from the Third to First Division in 1935/36, the Addicks finished runners-up, just three points behind league champions Manchester City, in 1937. After losing in the 1946 FA Cup final to Derby County, Charlton returned to Wembley the following year and this time lifted the cup thanks to a 1-0 victory over Burnley in the final.

• Charlton's home ground, The Valley, used to be one of the biggest in English football with a capacity of around 75,000. In 1985, though, financial problems forced Charlton to leave The Valley and the Addicks spent seven years as tenants of West Ham and Crystal Palace before making an emotional return to their ancestral home in 1992.

• Sam Bartram, who was known as 'the finest keeper England never had', played a record 623 games for the club between 1934 and 1956. Striker Derek Hales is Charlton's record goalscorer, notching 168 in two spells at the club in the 1970s and 1980s.

• Midfielder Mark Kinsella won a club record 33 caps for the Republic of Ireland between 1998 and 2002.

• Promoted to the Championship in 2019 after beating Sunderland 2-1 in the League One play-off final, Charlton made their record signing in July 2001 when striker Jason Euell moved from Wimbledon for £4.75 million. The Addicks' record sale saw striker Darren Bent join Tottenham for £16.5 million in June 2007.

> **HONOURS**
> **First Division champions** 2000
> **League One champions** 2012
> **Division 3 (South) champions** 1929, 1935
> **FA Cup** 1947

CHEATING

The most notorious instance of on-pitch cheating occurred at the 1986 World Cup in Mexico when Argentina's Diego Maradona punched the ball into the net to open the scoring in his side's quarter-final victory over England. Maradona was unrepentant afterwards, claiming the goal was scored by "the hand of God, and the head of Diego".

• In a similar incident in 2009 France captain Thierry Henry clearly handled the ball before crossing for William Gallas to score the decisive goal in a World Cup play-off against Ireland. "I will be honest, it was a handball – but I'm not the ref," a sheepish Henry admitted after the match.

Charlton's wall just couldn't decide which way to face...

Mateo Kovacic on the attack for Chelsea

• In October 2017 Carlisle striker Shaun Miller became the first player to be retrospectively punished for diving, his fall in a match against Wycombe Wanderers earning his side a penalty which was converted. He was given a two-match ban by the FA.

• During the 2012/13 season Tottenham's Gareth Bale was booked a record seven times in all competitions for 'simulation' – more commonly known simply as 'diving'.

• The Brazilian Serie D play-off between Tupi and Aparecidense in 2013 ended in bizarre fashion when a Tupi striker rounded the goalkeeper and looked certain to score... until Aparecidense masseur Romildo da Silva ran onto the pitch and hoofed the ball clear. He may have saved a goal, but his club were thrown out of the league as a punishment.

• A 2011 study by researchers at Wake Forest University in North Carolina found that players in the men's game faked injuries almost twice as often as players in the women's game.

CHELSEA

Year founded: 1905
Ground: Stamford Bridge (41,631)
Nickname: The Blues
Biggest win: 13-0 v Jeunesse Hautcharage (1971)
Heaviest defeat: 1-8 v Wolves (1953)

Founded in 1905 by local businessmen Gus and Joseph Mears, Chelsea were elected to the Football League in that very same year. At the time of their election, the club had not played a single match – only Bradford City can claim a similarly swift ascent into league football.

• Thanks to the staggering wealth of their Russian owner, Roman Abramovich, Chelsea are now one of the richest clubs in the world. Since taking over the Londoners in 2003, Abramovich has pumped hundreds of millions into the club and has been rewarded with 16 major trophies, including five Premier League titles, five FA Cups and the Double in 2010. After watching his team come agonisingly close on numerous occasions, Abramovich finally saw Chelsea win the Champions League in 2012 when, led by caretaker manager Roberto di Matteo, the Blues beat favourites Bayern Munich on penalties in the final.

• The following year Chelsea won the Europa League after defeating Benfica 2-1 in the final in Amsterdam. That victory meant the Blues became the first British club to win all three historic UEFA trophies, as they had previously won the European Cup Winners' Cup in both 1971 and 1998. In 2019 the Blues won the Europa League again, easily thrashing London rivals Arsenal 4-1 in Baku to become the first English club to win the competition twice.

• The Blues' recent success is in marked contrast to their early history. For the first 50 years of their existence Chelsea won precisely nothing, finally breaking their duck by winning the league championship in 1955. After a succession of near misses, the club won the FA Cup for the first time in 1970, beating Leeds 2-1 at Old Trafford in the first post-war final to go to a replay. Flamboyant striker Peter Osgood scored in every round of the cup run and remains the last player to achieve this feat.

• The club's fortunes declined sharply in the late 1970s and 1980s, the Blues spending much of the period in the Second Division while saddled with large debts. However, an influx of veteran foreign stars in the mid-1990s, including Gianfranco Zola, Ruud Gullit and Gianluca Vialli, sparked an exciting revival capped when the Blues won the FA Cup in 1997, their first major trophy for 26 years.

• On 26th December 1999 Chelsea became the very first English club to field an entirely foreign line-up for their Premier League fixture at Southampton.

• Chelsea's arrival as one of England's top clubs was finally confirmed when charismatic manager Jose Mourinho led the Blues to the Premier League title in 2005. A second title followed in 2006, and Mourinho claimed another in 2015 in his second spell at the Bridge. When the club first won the championship way back in 1955, they did so with a record low of just 52 points.

• In 2007 Chelsea won the first ever FA Cup final at the new Wembley, Ivorian striker Didier Drogba scoring the only goal against Manchester United. In the same year the Blues won the League Cup, making them just the third English team after Arsenal (1993) and Liverpool (2001) to claim a domestic cup double. The Blues also won the FA Cup in 2009, 2010, 2012 and 2018, to give them the best record of any club in the competition at the new stadium.

• Hardman defender Ron 'Chopper' Harris is Chelsea's record appearance maker, turning out an incredible 795 times for the club between 1962 and 1980. Midfielder Frank Lampard, a key figure in the club's successes in the first decade of Abramovich's reign, scored a record 211 goals in all competitions between 2001 and 2014. Legendary striker Jimmy Greaves scored the most goals in a single season, with 41 in 1960/61.

• Between 2004 and 2008 the Blues were unbeaten in 86 consecutive home league matches, a record for both the Premier League and the Football League. The impressive run was eventually ended by Liverpool, who won 1-0 at Stamford Bridge on 26th October 2008.

• Club legend and current boss Frank Lampard is Chelsea's most-capped international, making 104 appearances for England while at Stamford Bridge between 2001 and 2014.

• The club's most expensive signing is Kepa Arrizabalaga, who moved to west London from Athletic Bilbao in August 2018 for £71.6 million – a world record fee for a goalkeeper. In June 2019 Chelsea sold attacking midfielder Eden Hazard to Real Madrid for an initial fee of £89 million, a club record which could eventually rise to £150 million.

CHELTENHAM TOWN

Year founded: 1892
Ground: Whaddon Road (7,066)
Nickname: The Robins
Biggest win: 12-0 v Chippenham Rovers (1935)
Heaviest defeat: 1-10 v Merthyr Tydfil (1952)

Cheltenham Town were founded in 1892 but had to wait over a century to join the Football League, eventually making their bow in 1999 after winning the Conference title. The Robins dropped out of the league in 2015, but bounced back the following year as the first winners of the National League.

• The Robins have twice gained promotion to the third tier via the play-offs, defeating Rushden 3-1 in the final at the Millennium Stadium in 2002 and Grimsby 1-0 four years later at the same venue, but they missed out on a hat-trick when they lost 2-0 to Crewe in the 2012 final at Wembley.

• Midfielder Dave Bird made a record 289 league appearances for the Robins between 2002 and 2012.

• In the 2017/18 season Sudan-born striker Mo Eisa banged in a club record 23 league goals for Cheltenham, prompting Bristol City to buy him for £1.4 million – a record sale for the Robins.

STEVE CLARKE

Born: Saltcoats, 29th August 1963
Managerial career:
2012-13 West Bromwich Albion
2014-15 Reading
2017-19 Kilmarnock
2019- Scotland

Appointed Scotland manager in May 2019 as successor to Alex McLeish, Steve Clarke came into the job on the back of a tremendous season with Kilmarnock, having guided the club to third in the Premiership – an achievement which saw him awarded both the PFA Scotland and SFWA Manager of the Year awards.

• After spells as assistant manager at Newcastle, Chelsea, West Ham and Liverpool, Clarke became manager of West Brom in June 2012. In his first season in charge of the Baggies he guided them to a best ever eighth-place in the Premier League, but a slump in results saw him sacked in November 2013.

• A year later Clarke took over at Reading and led the Royals to their first FA Cup semi-final for 88 years. However, a 2-1 defeat to Arsenal at Wembley ended their hopes of lifting silverware and he was dismissed in December 2015.

• A calm and steady right back in his playing career, Clarke started out with St Mirren before signing for Chelsea in 1987. At the tail-end of a decade-long stay at Stamford Bridge he helped the Blues win the FA Cup, League Cup and, in his last game for the club before hanging up his boots, the European Cup Winners' Cup after a 1-0 victory against Stuttgart in Stockholm. He also won six caps for Scotland.

Will Scotland's fortunes revive under new boss Steve Clarke?

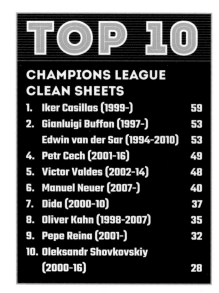

TOP 10

CHAMPIONS LEAGUE CLEAN SHEETS

1.	Iker Casillas (1999-)	59
2.	Gianluigi Buffon (1997-)	53
	Edwin van der Sar (1994-2010)	53
4.	Petr Cech (2001-16)	49
5.	Victor Valdes (2002-14)	48
6.	Manuel Neuer (2007-)	40
7.	Dida (2000-10)	37
8.	Oliver Kahn (1998-2007)	35
9.	Pepe Reina (2001-)	32
10.	Oleksandr Shovkovskiy (2000-16)	28

CLEAN SHEETS

Petr Cech holds the Premier League clean sheet record with 202 for Chelsea and Arsenal between 2004 and 2019. Of these, 162 came with the Blues – a record by a goalkeeper with a single club. Cech also kept a Premier League record 24 clean sheets for the west Londoners in the 2004/05 season.

• The world record for consecutive clean sheets is held by Brazilian goalkeeper Mazaropi of Vasco de Gama, who went 1,816 minutes without conceding in 1977/78.

• Italy's long-serving goalkeeper Dino Zoff holds the international record, going 1,142 minutes without having to pick the ball out of his net between September 1972 and June 1974. Another Italian goalkeeper, Walter Zenga, holds the record for clean sheets at the World Cup, with a run of 517 minutes at the 1990 tournament. However, New Zealand's Richard Wilson did even better during the qualifying rounds for the 1982 tournament, going 921 minutes without conceding.

• **England's Peter Shilton (1982-90) and France's Fabien Barthez (1998-2006) jointly hold the record for clean sheets at the World Cup with 10 each. The USA's Briana Scurry also kept a record 10 clean sheets at the Women's World Cup between 1995 and 2007.**

• Former Manchester United goalkeeper Edwin van der Sar holds the British record for consecutive league clean sheets, keeping the ball out of his net for 14 Premier League games and a total of 1,311 minutes in the 2008/09 season. He was finally beaten on 4th March 2009 by Newcastle's Peter Lovenkrands in the visitors' 2-1 victory at St James' Park.

CLUB WORLD CUP

A competition contested between the champion clubs of all six continental confederations of FIFA, the Club World Cup was first played in Brazil in 2000 but has only been an annual tournament since 2005 when it replaced the old Intercontinental Cup.

• **Manchester United's participation in the first Club World Cup led to the Red Devils pulling out of the FA Cup in 2000, a tournament they had won the previous season. United's decision attracted a lot of criticism at the time, not least from many of their own fans.**

• Real Madrid have the best record in the competition with four triumphs, most recently beating Al-Ain of host nation United Arab Emirates 4-1 in the 2018 final.

• **Manchester United became the first British winners of the tournament when a goal by Wayne Rooney saw off Ecuadorian side Quito in the 2008 final in Yokohama.**

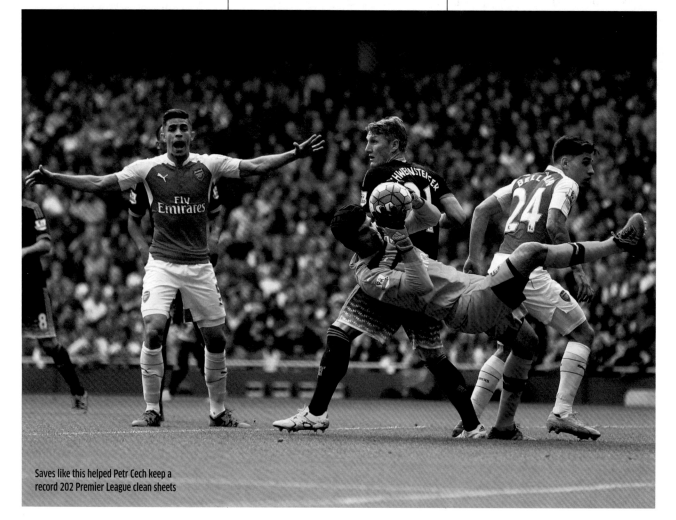

Saves like this helped Petr Cech keep a record 202 Premier League clean sheets

Sergio Ramos knows exactly how many times Real Madrid have won the Club World Cup

• Cristiano Ronaldo is the competition's top scorer with seven goals, followed by his former Real Madrid team-mate Gareth Bale with six goals. Barcelona's Luis Suarez scored a record five goals at the 2015 tournament in Japan.

COLCHESTER UNITED

Year founded: 1937
Ground: The Colchester Community Stadium (10,105)
Nickname: The U's
Biggest win: 9-1 v Bradford City (1961) and Leamington (2005)
Heaviest defeat: 0-8 v Leyton Orient (1989)

Founded as the successors to amateur club Colchester Town in 1937, Colchester United joined the Football League in 1950. The club lost its league status in 1990, but regained it just two years later after topping the Conference.

• **The U's enjoyed their greatest day in 1971 when they beat then-mighty Leeds United 3-2 in the fifth round of the FA Cup at their old Layer Road ground to become only the second club from the basement tier to reach the quarter-finals. However, a 5-0 thrashing at Everton ended their hopes of an unlikely cup triumph.**

• The first brothers to be sent off in the same match while playing for the same team were Colchester's Tom and Tony English against Crewe in 1986.

• **Defender Chris Coyne made a club record seven international**

appearances for Australia while with the U's between 2008 and 2009.

• Defender Micky Cook made a record 614 appearances for the U's between 1969 and 1984. Martyn King is the club's all-time top scorer with 132 league goals, including a joint-record five hat-tricks, between 1959 and 1965.

HONOURS
Conference champions 1992

COLOURS

In the 19th century, players originally wore different coloured caps, socks and armbands – but not shirts – to distinguish between the two sides. The first standardised kits were introduced in the 1870s, with many clubs opting for the colours of the schools or other sporting organisations from which they had emerged.

• **Thanks largely to the longstanding success of Arsenal, Liverpool and Manchester United, teams wearing red have won more trophies in England than those sporting any other colour. Teams wearing stripes have fared less well, their last FA Cup success coming in 1987 (Coventry City) and their last league triumph way back in 1936 (Sunderland).**

• Sheffield Wednesday manager Steve Bruce was furious that the Owls were ordered to play in their blue-and white striped home shirts for an away match at Millwall on 12th February 2019, as the hosts' dark blue shirts made it difficult to distinguish between the two sets of players. "Both teams had a colour clash with the strips, and forgot how to pass it to each other," he moaned after a drab 0-0 draw.

• **A kit clash in the Scottish League One match between Stenhousemuir and Dumbarton on 29th December 2018 led to the visitors wearing Stenny's old light blue and white striped shirts from the previous season. Appropriately, perhaps, the match ended in a 2-2 draw.**

• In the 2011/12 Premier League season Aston Villa wore a record nine different kit combinations.

The Community Shield joined every other piece of domestic silverware in the City trophy cabinet in 2018/19

COMMUNITY SHIELD

Won by Manchester City for a second consecutive year in 2019, the Community Shield was originally known as the Charity Shield and since 1928 has been an annual fixture usually played at the start of the season between the reigning league champions and the FA Cup winners. Founded in 1908 to provide funds for various charities, the Charity Shield was initially played between the Football League First Division champions and the Southern League champions, developing into a game between select teams of amateurs and professionals in the early 1920s.

• **Manchester United were the first club to win the Charity Shield, defeating QPR 4-0 in a replay at Stamford Bridge. With 17 outright wins and four shared, United are also the most successful side in the history of the competition.**

• Manchester United's Ryan Giggs is the most successful player in the history of the Shield, with nine wins in 15 appearances (another record).

• **Everton won the Shield a record four times on the trot between 1984 and**

1987, although they shared the trophy with Liverpool in 1986 after a 1-1 draw at Wembley.

• Manchester United striker Harold Halse scored a record six goals in the highest-scoring Shield match ever in 1911, when United beat Swindon Town 8-4 at Stamford Bridge. Proceeds from the match went to survivors of the HMS *Titanic* disaster the following year.

COMPUTER GAMES

FIFA 13 sold more than 4.5 million copies worldwide in the first five days after its launch in 2012, leading publishers EA to claim it was the biggest-selling sports video launch of all time. The FIFA series as a whole has sold well over 100 million copies since it launched in 1993, making it the best selling football video game of all time.

• **The first football video game was created in 1973 by Tomohiro Nishikado, who later designed Space Invaders. Called simply Soccer, the ball-and-paddle game allowed two players to each control a goalkeeper and a striker.**

• The longest ever game of Football Manager saw Lech Poznan fan Michal Leniec take charge of his club for a mind-boggling 221 seasons over two years of actual playing time. During his long reign he boasted a win rate of 76% and guided Poznan to an incredible 45 Champions League triumphs.

• **Patrick Hadler, a 19-year-old from Hannover, holds the record for the biggest win in a computer football game. Playing as Germany on FIFA 14 he crushed the Cook Islands 321-0 in**

2014, earning himself a place in *The Guinness Book of Records*.

• The first ever FIFA Interactive World Cup (now known as the FIFA eWorld Cup) was held in 2004 in Zurich and won by Thiago Carrico de Azevedo from Brazil.

CONFEDERATIONS CUP

The Confederations Cup was a competition held every four years contested by the holders of each of the six FIFA confederation championships – such as the European Championships and the Copa America – plus the World Cup holders and host nation. In March 2019 FIFA announced that the competition would be abolished and replaced with an expanded Club World Cup.

• **Between 2005 and 2017 the Confederations Cup was held in the country that hosted the following year's World Cup, acting as a dress rehearsal for the larger and more prestigious tournament.**

• Brazil have the best record in the tournament with four victories to their name: in 1997 (after a 6-0 win over Australia in the final), in 2005 (4-1 against Argentina), 2009 (3-2 against the USA) and 2013 (3-0 against Spain). The only other country to win the Confederations Cup more than once are France (in 2001 and 2003). The last winners were Germany, who beat Chile 1-0 in the 2017 final in St Petersburg.

• **Ronaldo (Brazil) and Cuauhtemoc Blanco (Mexico) are the leading scorers in the competition, with nine goals each. Brazilian striker Romario scored a record seven goals at the 1997 tournament in Saudi Arabia.**

COPA AMERICA

The oldest surviving international football tournament in the world, the Copa America was founded in 1916. The first championships were held in Argentina as part of the country's independence centenary commemorations, with Uruguay emerging as the winners from a four-team field. Originally known as the South American Championship, the tournament was renamed in 1975. Previously, the Copa America was held every two years, but in 2007 it was decided to stage future tournaments at four-year intervals.

• **Uruguay have won the tournament a record 15 times, while Argentina are**

IS THAT A FACT?

League title winners have won the Community Shield 47 times, compared to just 20 victories for the FA Cup holders. Double winners have won the trophy six times.

second in the winners' list, lifting the trophy on 14 occasions. The holders are Brazil, who won the 2019 final on home soil with a 3-1 victory against Peru.

• The all-time top scorers at the finals are Argentina's Norberto Mendez and Brazil's Zizinho with 17 goals each.

• From the next finals, to be held in Argentina and Colombia in 2020, the tournament will be held in even years instead of odd.

COPA LIBERTADORES

The Copa Libertadores is the South American equivalent of the Champions League, played annually between top clubs from all the countries in the continent (in recent years, leading clubs from Mexico have also participated). Argentine club Independiente have the best record in the competition, winning the trophy seven times, including four in a row between 1972 and 1975.

• Ecuadorian striker Albert Spencer is the leading scorer in the history of the competition with 54 goals (48 for Uruguayan club Penarol, helping them to win the first two tournaments in 1960 and 1961, and six for Ecuadorian outfit Barcelona de Guayaquil).

• Defender Francisco Sa won the competition a record six times in the 1970s – four times with Independiente and twice with Boca Juniors.

• In 1970 Uruguayan giants Penarol recorded the biggest victory in the history of the competition, thrashing

An ant's eye view of a Crystal Palace corner at Selhurst Park

River Plate were thrilled to win the Copa Libertadores in 2018

Venezuela's Valencia 11-2. Penarol also hold the record for the most emphatic aggregate win, destroying Ecuadorian minnows Everest 14-1 in 1963.

• Argentinian clubs have won the trophy a record 25 times, most recently River Plate in 2018. In a first for the competition, the second leg of River's final with local rivals Boca Juniors was played in Europe, at the Santiago Bernabeu in Madrid, after the Boca coach had been attacked outside River's stadium in Buenos Aires. Despite playing thousands of miles from home, River won the match 3-1 to claim the title 5-3 on aggregate.

CORNERS

Corner kicks were first introduced in 1872, but goals direct from a corner were not allowed until 1924. The first player to score from a corner in league football was Billy Smith of Huddersfield in the 1924/25 season. On 2nd October 1924 Argentina's Cesareo Onzari scored direct from a corner against reigning Olympic champions Uruguay in Buenos Aires, the first goal of this sort to occur in an international fixture.

• Turkish striker Sukru Gulesin holds the record for the most goals scored direct from corners with an incredible 32 between 1940 and 1954 for a

variety of clubs, including Besiktas, Lazio, Palermo and Galatasaray.

• On 21st January 2012 Coleraine's Paul Owens became the first player ever to score two goals direct from a corner in the same professional match when his wind-assisted efforts sailed over the Glenavon goalkeeper in his team's 3-1 Irish Premiership win.

• Former Blackburn winger Morten Gamst Pedersen claims to have scored an incredible six goals from corners in a Norwegian youth-team match for Idrettslaget Norild against Alta in 2000.

• Liverpool won a Premier League record 309 corners in the 2011/12 season. Tottenham midfielder Christian Eriksen took a Premier League record 195 corners in the 2016/17 season.

TOP 10 PREMIER LEAGUE CORNERS TAKEN 2018/19	
1. James Maddison (Leicester City)	163
2. Joao Moutinho (Wolves)	159
3. Luka Milivojevic (Crystal Palace)	143
4. Ryan Fraser (Bournemouth)	116
5. Jose Holebas (Watford)	115
Robert Snodgrass (West Ham)	115
7. Willian (Chelsea)	111
8. Gylfi Sigurdsson (Everton)	105
9. Matt Ritchie (Newcastle United)	102
Ashley Young (Manchester United)	102

PHILIPPE COUTINHO

Born: Rio de Janeiro, Brazil, 12th June 1992
Position: Midfielder
Club career:
2009-10 Vasco da Gama 19 (1)
2010-13 Inter Milan 28 (3)
2012 Espanyol (loan) 16 (5)
2013-18 Liverpool 152 (41)
2018- Barcelona 51 (13)
2019- Bayern Munich (loan)
International record:
2010- Brazil 55 (15)

Quicksilver midfielder Philippe Coutinho became the third most expensive footballer in the history of the game when he joined Barcelona from Liverpool for £142 million in January 2018. He didn't take long to settle in Catalonia, either, contributing eight league goals to help Barca win La Liga and scoring in his new side's 5-0 drubbing of Sevilla in the Spanish Cup final. The following season he was a mainstay of the Barca team which retained the title before joining Bayern Munich on a season-long loan in August 2019.

• Coutinho was less fortunate with Liverpool, collecting runners-up medals in the 2016 League Cup final, despite scoring against Manchester City at Wembley, and in that year's Europa League final, which the Reds lost to Sevilla.

• Coutinho moved to Italian giants Inter Milan from Vasco da Gama when he was just 18, but ultimately struggled to adapt to Serie A. A loan spell at Spanish outfit Espanyol in 2012 proved a turning point in his career and the following January he joined Liverpool in a bargain £8.5 million deal.

• A typical Brazilian number 10 who combines vision, flair and creativity in equal measure, Coutinho made his debut for his country in a 3-0 friendly win against Iran in 2010 when he was aged just 18. At Russia 2018 he was voted into the FIFA World Cup Dream Team and the following year he helped Brazil win the Copa America.

If you must move from Barcelona, Bayern Munich's not a bad place to go!

COVENTRY CITY

Year founded: 1883
Ground: Ricoh Arena (32,609)
Previous name: Singers FC
Nickname: The Sky Blues
Biggest win: 9-0 v Bristol City (1934)
Heaviest defeat: 2-11 v Berwick Rangers (1901)

Coventry were founded in 1883 by workers from the local Singer's bicycle factory and were named after the company until 1898. The club was elected to the Second Division in 1919, but their league career started unpromisingly with a 5-0 home defeat to Tottenham Hotspur.

• A club with a history of ups and downs, Coventry were the first team to play in seven different divisions: Premier, Division One, Two, Three, Four, Three (North) and Three (South). They have also played in the Championship, League One and League Two, which they escaped from via the play-offs at the end of the 2017/18 season.

• Coventry's greatest moment came in 1987 when the club won the FA Cup for the only time, beating Tottenham 3-2 in an exciting Wembley final. Two years later, though, the Sky Blues were surprisingly dumped out of the cup by non-league Sutton United.

• In July 2000 the Sky Blues made their record sale when striker Robbie Keane joined Inter Milan for £13 million. The following month Coventry forked out a club record fee of £6.5 million for Norwich striker Craig Bellamy.

• Long-serving goalkeeper Steve Ogrizovic played in a club record 504 league games, including 241 consecutively between 1984 and 1989. Sky Blues legend Clarrie Bourton scored a club record 173 league goals between 1931 and 1937, including a season's best 49 goals in 1931/32.

• Goalkeeper Magnus Hedman won a club record 44 caps for Sweden while with Coventry between 1997 and 2002.

HONOURS
Division 2 champions 1967
Division 3 champions 1964
Division 3 (South) champions 1936
FA Cup 1987
EFL Trophy 2017

CRAWLEY TOWN

Year founded: 1896
Ground: Broadfield Stadium (6,134)
Nickname: The Red Devils
Biggest win: 8-0 v Droylsden (2008)
Heaviest defeat: 0-7 v Bath City (2000)

Founded in 1896, Crawley Town started out in the West Sussex League, eventually rising to the Conference in 2004. Dubbed the 'Manchester City of non-league', Crawley splashed out more than £500,000 on new players at the start of the 2010/11 season, an investment which paid off when the club won promotion to the Football League at the end of the campaign.

• Runaway Conference champions, Crawley's haul of 105 points set a new record for the division, while they also equalled the records for fewest defeats (3) and most wins (31). The following season Crawley enjoyed a second successive promotion, after finishing third in League Two behind Swindon and Shrewsbury.

• Crawley reached the fifth round of the FA Cup for the first time in their history in 2011 after knocking out Swindon, Derby and Torquay. To their fans' delight they were then paired with Manchester United, and their team did them proud, only losing 1-0 at Old Trafford.

• Along with Accrington Stanley, Crawley are one of just two current Football League clubs never to have played at Wembley.

• 40-year-old Crawley midfielder Dannie Bulman is the oldest player in the Football League and has turned out for the Red Devils in a record 211 league games since 2011.

CREWE ALEXANDRA

Year founded: 1877
Ground: Gresty Road (10,153)
Nickname: The Railwaymen
Biggest win: 8-0 v Rotherham (1932)
Heaviest defeat: 2-13 v Tottenham Hotspur (1960)

Founded by railway workers in 1877, the Crewe Football Club added 'Alexandra' to their name in honour of Princess Alexandra, wife of the future king, Edward VII. The club were founder members of the Second Division in 1892, although they lost their league status four years later before rejoining the newly formed Third Division (North) in 1921.

• Club legend Herbert Swindells scored a record 126 goals for Crewe between 1927 and 1937. Crewe's appearance record is held by Tommy Lowry, who turned out in 437 league games between 1966 and 1977.

• Alex fans endured a miserable spell in the mid-1950s when their club failed to win away from home for a record 56 consecutive matches. The depressing run finally ended with a 1-0 win at Southport in April 1957.

• Goalkeeper Clayton Ince made a club record 31 international appearances for Trinidad and Tobago between 1999 and 2005.

• The Railwaymen made their record signing in July 1998, forking out £650,000 for Torquay United striker Rodney Jack. The club's coffers were boasted by a record £6 million when striker Nick Powell joined Manchester United in July 2012.

CRYSTAL PALACE

Year founded: 1905
Ground: Selhurst Park (26,074)
Nickname: The Eagles
Biggest win: 9-0 v Barrow (1959)
Heaviest defeat: 0-9 v Burnley (1909) and Liverpool (1989)

The club was founded in 1905 by workers at the then cup final venue at Crystal Palace, and was an entirely separate entity to the amateur club of the same name which was made up of groundkeepers at the Great Exhibition and reached the first ever semi-finals of the FA Cup in 1872.

• After spending their early years in the Southern League, Palace were founder members of the Third Division (South) in 1920. The club had a great start to their league career, going up to the Second Division as champions in their first season.

• Crystal Palace are only the second club (after Scottish outfit Queen's Park in 1885) to reach two FA Cup finals and lose on both occasions to the same club. In 1990 the Eagles held Manchester United to a thrilling 3-3 draw at Wembley before losing 1-0 in the replay. Then, in 2016, the south London club endured more agony at the hands of United when they went down to a 2-1 defeat in extra-time despite taking the lead through substitute Jason Puncheon.

• Pre-war striker Peter Simpson is the club's all-time leading scorer with 153 league goals between 1930 and 1936, including a club record six goals in a match against Exeter City in October

Veteran boss Roy Hodgson hopes to see his Eagles soar up the Premiership table

1930. Defender Jim Cannon holds the club appearance record, turning out 660 times between 1973 and 1988.

• Palace are the only club to have been promoted to the top flight four times via the play-offs, most recently in 2013. The Eagles are also the only club to have won play-off finals at four different venues: Selhurst Park (1989), old Wembley (1997), Millennium Stadium (2004) and new Wembley (2013).

• The club made their record signing in August 2016, when Belgium striker Christian Benteke signed from Liverpool for £27 million. In June 2019 the Eagles sold right-back Aaron Wan-Bissaka to Manchester United for a club record £45 million.

• A record fourth-tier crowd of 37,774 watched Palace's home match with Millwall on 31st March 1961, but it proved to be a disappointing afternoon for the Selhurst faithful as the Eagles slumped to a 2-0 defeat.

• Striker Andy Johnson scored a Premier League record 11 penalties for the Eagles in 2004/05, but his goals unfortunately could not prevent the south Londoners from being relegated.

• Goalkeeper Wayne Hennessey has won a club record 40 caps for Wales since joining Palace from Wolves in 2014.

D

DEATHS

The first recorded death as a direct result of a football match came in 1889 when William Cropper of Derbyshire side Staveley FC died of a ruptured bowel sustained in a collision with an opponent.

• In 1931 Celtic's brilliant young international goalkeeper John Thompson died in hospital after fracturing his skull in a collision with Rangers forward Sam English. Some 40,000 fans attended his funeral, many of them walking the 55 miles from Glasgow to Thompson's home village in Fife. In the same decade two other goalkeepers, Jimmy Utterson of Wolves and Sunderland's Jimmy Thorpe, also died from injuries sustained on the pitch. Their deaths led the Football Association to change the rules so that goalkeepers could not be tackled while they had the ball in their hands.

• On 1st June 2019 former Sevilla, Arsenal and Atletico Madrid winger Jose Antonio Reyes was killed in a high-speed car crash in south-west Spain. The 35-year-old's passing was marked with a moment of silence before the Champions League final later that day.

• In October 2014 Indian player Peter Biaksangzuala died after injuring his spine while performing a somersault to celebrate a goal he had scored for his club, Bethlehem Vengthlang.

IS THAT A FACT?

In a tragic incident in Rio de Janeiro, 10 youth-team players with Brazilian club Flamengo were killed in a fire at the club's training complex in February 2019. The inferno was later blamed on a short circuit in an air conditioning unit.

• Josef Sural, a Czech Republic international with 20 caps, was killed when the bus carrying him and his team-mates from Turkish outfit Alanyaspor crashed after an away match at Kayserispor on 28th April 2019.

• In July 2018 Facundo Espindola, a goalkeeper with a fourth-tier club in Argentina, was stabbed to death in a street fight in Buenos Aires. One of the men later arrested for his murder was Nahuel Oviedo, a player with Chilean side Deportes la Serena.

• On 11th November 1923 Aston Villa centre-half Tommy Ball was shot dead by his neighbour, becoming the first and last Football League player to be murdered. Ball's killer, George Stagg, was sentenced to life imprisonment and later declared to be insane.

DEBUTS

Aston Villa striker Howard Vaughton enjoyed the best England debut ever, scoring five goals in a 13-0 rout of Ireland in 1882. The last England player to score a hat-trick on his debut was Luther Blissett, who smashed three past Luxembourg in a 9-0 win at Wembley in 1982.

• One of the most remarkable international debuts was by Dieter Muller for West Germany in the 1976 European Championship semi-final against Yugoslavia. Coming on as a sub in the 79th minute, Muller scored just three minutes later and then added two more in extra-time in his side's eventual 4-2 victory.

• The worst ever international debut was by American Samoa goalkeeper Nicky Salapu against Fiji in 2001. He conceded 13 goals in that game, and then another 44 within a week in three matches against Samoa, Tonga and Australia.

• Freddy Eastwood scored the fastest goal on debut, netting after just seven seconds for Southend against Swansea in 2004.

• Italian striker Fabrizio Ravanelli is the only player to score a hat-trick on his Premier League debut, striking three times for Middlesbrough in a 3-3 draw against Liverpool on the opening day of the 1996/97 season.

• Arsenal Ladies striker Danielle Carter enjoyed a fantastic debut for England

Women in September 2015, scoring a hat-trick in an 8-0 hammering of Estonia in September 2015. For good measure, she hit another treble against the same opposition in her second international appearance the following year.

TROY DEENEY

Born: Birmingham, 29th June 1988
Position: Striker
Club career:
2006-10 Walsall 123 (27)
2006-07 Halesowen Town (loan) 10 (8)
2010- Watford 341 (114)

Fiery and abrasive Watford skipper Troy Deeney is the Hornets' all-time leading scorer in the Premier League with 37 goals, and is only the fifth player to pass a century of goals for the club. In 2019 he helped his club reach only

The Hornets' Troy Deeney is a waspish sort of player

their second FA Cup final, scoring a vital last-minute equaliser from the spot in the Hornets' exciting 3-2 win over Wolves in the semi-final. However, he barely had a kick in the final as Watford were hammered 6-0 by Treble winners Manchester City at Wembley.

• Deeney's career almost went completely off the rails in 2012 when he was sentenced to 10 months' imprisonment for his part in a brawl outside a Birmingham nightclub. After serving almost three months he was released, and returned to Watford to score 20 goals in the Championship in the 2012/13 season.

• The bustling and aggressive Deeney was equally prolific in the following two campaigns to become the first Watford player ever to score 20 or more goals in three consecutive seasons. His hot scoring streak helped Watford gain promotion to the Premier League in 2015 and earned Deeney a place in the PFA Championship Team of the Year.

• Deeney started out at Walsall, where he was named the club's Player of the Year in 2010, shortly before joining Watford in a bargain £250,000 (rising to £500,000) deal.

DERBIES

So called because they matched the popularity of the Epsom Derby horse race, 'derby' matches between local sides provoke intense passions among fans and players alike.

• Celtic v Rangers is the most played derby in world football – the two teams having met an incredible 416 times since their first encounter in the Scottish Cup in September 1890. In the 2010/11 season the two teams met a record seven times, the clashes provoking so many violent incidents in Glasgow that the frustrated chairman of the Scottish Police Federation called for future Old Firm matches to be banned.

• The biggest win in a derby match in England was Nottingham Forest's 12-0 thrashing of east Midland rivals Leicester City in the old First Division in 1909. In the Premier League era Chelsea recorded the most emphatic derby win when they smashed Arsenal 6-0 at Stamford Bridge in March 2014.

• Arsenal's prolific Thierry Henry scored a record 43 goals in 59 Premier League London derbies between 1999 and 2007.

• On three occasions a European final has also doubled as a city derby: Real Madrid getting the better of rivals Atletico Madrid in the Champions League showdown in 2014 and 2016; then, in 2019, Chelsea beat Arsenal 4-1 in the Europa League final in Baku.

DERBY COUNTY

Year founded: 1884
Ground: Pride Park (33,597)
Nickname: The Rams
Biggest win: 12-0 v Finn Harps (1976)
Heaviest defeat: 2-11 v Everton (1890)

Derby were formed in 1884 as an offshoot of Derbyshire Cricket Club and originally wore an amber, chocolate and blue strip based on the cricket club's colours. Perhaps wisely, they changed to their traditional black-and-white colours in the 1890s.

• The club were founder members of the Football League in 1888 and seven years later moved from the ground they shared with the cricketers to the Baseball Ground (so named because baseball was regularly played there in the 1890s). Derby had to oust a band of gypsies before they could move in, one of whom is said to have laid a curse on the place as he left. No doubt, then, the club was pleased to leave the Baseball Ground for Pride Park in 1997... although when Derby's first game at the new stadium had to be abandoned due to floodlight failure, there were fears that the curse had followed them!

• Runners-up in the FA Cup final in 1898, 1899 and 1903, Derby reached their last final in 1946. Before the match the club's captain, Jack Nicholas, visited a gypsy encampment and paid for the old curse to be lifted. It worked, as Derby beat Charlton 4-1 after extra-time.

• **Under charismatic manager Brian Clough, Derby took the top flight by storm after winning promotion to the First Division in 1969. Three years later they won the league in one of the closest title races ever. Having played all their fixtures ahead of their title contenders, Derby's players were actually sitting on a beach in Majorca when they heard news of their victory. The following season Derby reached the semi-finals of the European Cup and, in 1975 under the management of former skipper Dave Mackay, they won the championship again.**

• The Rams' last season in the top flight in 2007/08 was an utter disaster

Former Derby boss Brian Clough and his assistant Peter Taylor are immortalised at Pride Park

as they managed just one win in the whole campaign, equalling a Football League record set by Loughborough in 1900. Even worse, between September 2007 and September 2008 Derby went a record 36 league games without a win, including a record 32 games in the Premier League and another four more in the Championship.

• Derby made their record signing in August 2019, buying Polish defender Krystian Bielik from Arsenal for £9.5 million. in the summer of 2017 the Rams sold midfielder Tom Ince to Huddersfield Town for a club record £11.3 million.

• Derby's best ever goalscorer was one of the true greats of the game in the late 19th and early 20th centuries, Steve Bloomer. He netted an incredible 332 goals in two spells at the club between 1892 and 1914, and in 1899 became the first and only Derby player to score a double hat-trick in a match against Sheffield Wednesday.

• In 2019 Derby became the first club to get through the semi-finals of the Championship play-offs despite losing the first leg at home. However, after a sensational 4-3 aggregate win against Leeds the Rams were beaten 2-1 by Aston Villa in the final at Wembley.

> HONOURS
> *Division 1 champions* 1972, 1975
> *Division 2 champions* 1912, 1915, 1969, 1987
> *FA Cup* 1946

DISCIPLINE

Yellow and red cards were introduced into English league football on 2nd October 1976, and on the same day Blackburn's David Wagstaffe received the first red card during his side's match with Leyton Orient. Five years later cards were withdrawn by the Football Association as referees were getting 'too flashy', but the system was re-introduced in 1987.

• A stormy last 16 match between the Netherlands and Portugal in 2006 was the most ill-disciplined in the history of the World Cup. Russian referee Valentin Ivanov was the busiest man on the pitch as he pulled out his yellow card 16 times and his red one four times, with the match ending as a nine-a-side affair. In total, a record 28 players were sent off during the 2006 tournament.

TOP 10

TOTAL PREMIER LEAGUE YELLOW CARDS

1.	Chelsea	1,627
2.	Everton	1,571
3.	Arsenal	1,546
4.	Tottenham Hotspur	1,503
5.	Manchester United	1,473
6.	West Ham United	1,453
7.	Aston Villa	1,362
8.	Newcastle United	1,328
9.	Liverpool	1,301
10.	Manchester City	1,261

• Former West Brom midfielder Gareth Barry has been shown a record 123 yellow cards in the Premier League. Richard Dunne, Duncan Ferguson and Patrick Vieira share the record for receiving the most red cards in Premier League matches, with eight each.

• Former Colombian international Gerardo Bedoya was sent off a record 46 times in his playing career. In March 2016 in his first match as a coach with Independiente Santa Fe, the man dubbed 'the world's dirtiest footballer' was shown a red card in the first half.

• A record nine Sunderland players were sent off in the 2009/10 season, a total equalled by QPR in 2011/12. Sunderland also hold the record for the most yellow cards in a single campaign, with 94 in 2014/15.

• When a mass brawl erupted in the middle of the pitch during a match between Argentinian sides Victoriano Arenas and Claypole on 26th February 2011, referee Damian Rubino showed red cards to all 22 players and 14 substitutes as well as coaches and technical staff. The total of 36 players sent off set a new world record, smashing the previous 'best' of 20!

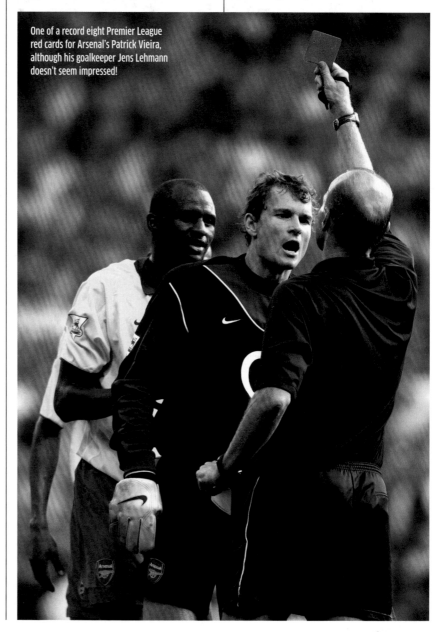

One of a record eight Premier League red cards for Arsenal's Patrick Vieira, although his goalkeeper Jens Lehmann doesn't seem impressed!

• In a comical incident in March 2018 former Arsenal striker Sanchez Watt was sent off while playing for Hemel Hempstead Town in the National League South for repeatedly saying 'Watt' when asked for his name by the referee. The official thought Watt was showing dissent by saying 'What?' and showed him the red card, before realising his mistake and bringing out the yellow card instead.

DONCASTER ROVERS

Year founded: 1879
Ground: Keepmoat Stadium (15,231)
Nickname: The Rovers
Biggest win: 10-0 v Darlington (1964)
Heaviest defeat: 0-12 v Small Heath (1903)

Founded in 1879 by Albert Jenkins, a fitter at Doncaster's Great Northern Railway works, Doncaster turned professional in 1885 and joined the Second Division of the Football League in 1901.

• **Remarkably, Doncaster hold the record for the most wins in a league season (33 in 1946/47) and for the most defeats (34 in 1997/98).**

• Midfield stalwart James Coppinger has played in a club record 553 league games since signing from Exeter City in 2004. Rovers all-time top scorer is Tom Keetley, with 180 league goals in the 1920s, including a club record six in a 7-4 win at Ashington in February 1929.

Who knew that Doncaster Rovers' Keepmoat Stadium was a natural breeding ground for footballs?

• **In 1946 Doncaster were involved in the longest ever football match, a Third Division (North) cup tie against Stockport County at Edgeley Park which the referee ruled could extend beyond extra-time in an attempt to find a winner. Eventually, the game was abandoned after 203 minutes due to poor light.**

• Beaten in the League One play-off semi-finals in 2019, Doncaster have won the third tier a joint-record four times.

• **On 26th April 2003 then Doncaster chairman John Ryan became the oldest man ever to appear in the top five flights of English football when he came on as an 89th-minute sub for Rovers against Hereford United in the Football Conference aged 52 years and 11 months.**

HONOURS
League One champions 2013
Division 3 (North) champions 1935, 1947, 1950
Third Division champions 2004
Division 4 champions 1966, 1969
EFL Trophy 2007

DOUBLES

The first club to win the Double of league championship and FA Cup were Preston North End, in the very first season of the Football League in 1888/89. The Lancashire side achieved this feat in fine style, remaining undefeated in the league and keeping a clean sheet in all their matches in the FA Cup.

• **Arsenal and Manchester United have both won the Double a record three times. The Red Devils' trio of**

Spurs were chuffed to win the Double in 1961

successes all came within a five-year period in the 1990s (1994, 1996 and 1999), with the last of their Doubles comprising two-thirds of a legendary Treble which also included the Champions League. Arsenal first won the Double in 1971, and since then the Gunners have twice repeated the feat under then manager Arsène Wenger in 1998 and 2002.

• The other English clubs to win the Double are Aston Villa (1897), Tottenham (1961), Liverpool (1986), Chelsea (2010) and Manchester City (2019), the latter also lifting the League Cup to secure English football's first ever entirely domestic Treble.

• **Linfield have won a world record 24 Doubles, the most recent coming in 2017. The Northern Ireland outfit are followed by Hong Kong's South China (22) and Rangers (18).**

• The only players to win the Double with two English clubs are Nicolas Anelka (Arsenal 1998 and Chelsea 2010) and Ashley Cole (Arsenal 2002 and Chelsea 2010).

DRAWS

Preston North End have drawn more league matches than any other club, having finished on level terms 1,275 times. Bootle FC have drawn the fewest league matches, just three in their single season in the Second Division in 1892/93.

• **The highest-scoring draw in the top division of English football was 6-6, in a match between Leicester City and Arsenal in 1930. In an incredible match in the fourth qualifying round of the FA Cup in November 1929, Dulwich Hamlet and Wealdstone drew 7-7 before Dulwich won the replay 2-1.**

• England and Italy have featured in the most draws at the World Cup, with a total of 21 apiece.

• Manchester City (1993/94), Sheffield United (1993/94) and Southampton (1994/95) jointly hold the record for the most draws in a Premier League season, with 18. At the other end of the scale, Manchester City and Tottenham both drew just two games each in 2018/19 with Spurs becoming the first side ever not to draw a single match away from home. Tottenham also set a new Premier League record by going 32 consecutive matches without drawing.

• Everton have drawn a record 1,135 top-flight matches, including a record 296 Premier League games.

• The highest-scoring ever recorded in a professional match saw German lower league sides Manzur and DJK Sparta Burgel tie 9-9 in May 2015.

TONI DUGGAN

Born: Liverpool, 25th July 1991
Position: Striker
Club career:
2007-13 Everton Ladies 40 (17)
2013-17 Manchester City Women 44 (19)
2017-19 Barcelona Femini 51 (20)
2019- Atletico Madrid Feminino
International record:
2012- England 71 (22)

In July 2017 Toni Duggan became the first English player since Gary Lineker in 1986 to sign for Barcelona when she joined the Catalan giants' women's team from Manchester City. Two years later she helped Barca reach the UEFA Women's Champions League final, which they lost to Lyon, before joining Atletico Madrid.

• Like many top female footballers, Duggan started out playing in a boys' team, Jellytots in Liverpool. She went on to play for Everton Ladies, being named the FA Women's Young Player of the Year in 2009. The following year she helped Everton win the FA Women's Cup, after a 3-2 triumph against Arsenal in the final at the Ricoh Arena, Coventry. In 2013 she moved on to Manchester City, adding the Women's Super League title (2016) and another FA Cup (2017) to her list of honours.

• A lively and energetic striker, Duggan first represented England at Under-17 level. On her 18th birthday she scored in the final of the 2009 UEFA Women's Under-19 championship, which England won against Sweden. She won her first full England cap against Croatia in September 2012, and the following year scored her first international hat-trick in a clinical 8-0 demolition of Turkey at Fratton Park.

• In 2019 Duggan was an important part of the England squad which came fourth at the Women's World Cup in France but was dropped to the bench for the 2-1 semi-final defeat by the USA.

• In April 2015 Duggan was criticised by Manchester City fans after posting a picture of herself on social media smiling with then Manchester United manager Louis van Gaal only hours after City had lost 4-2 to United in the Premier League. However, she maintained her online presence and the following year became the first female England player to reach 100,000 followers on Twitter.

"If I score here that will definitely go down well with my Twitter followers!"

EDERSON

Born: Osasco, Brazil, 17th August 1993
Position: Goalkeeper
Club career:
2011-12 Ribeirao 29
2012-15 Rio Ave 37
2015 Benfica B 4
2015-17 Benfica 37
2017- Manchester City 74
International record:
2017- Brazil 5

Heavily-tattooed Brazil international Ederson was a key member of the Manchester City side which won the domestic Treble in 2018/19, earning a place in the PFA Team of the Year after keeping 20 clean sheets – a tally only bettered by Liverpool's Alisson. He also became the first Manchester City goalkeeper to record a Premier League assist with a long goal-kick to Sergio Aguero against Huddersfield in the first month of the season, which the Argentinian striker converted in a 6-1 drubbing of the Terriers.

• A nimble goalkeeper who distributes the ball superbly with his feet, Ederson joined City from Benfica in June 2017 for £35 million, a then record amount for a Premier League goalkeeper. He paid back much of that fee by helping the Citizens win the 2018 Premier League title with a record 100 points and keeping 16 clean sheets.

• Ederson started out with Portuguese second-tier outfit Ribeirao before earning a move to the Primeira Liga with Rio Ave. His excellent performances soon caught the eye of Benfica who he joined in 2015, and two years later he won the domestic Double with the Portuguese giants.

• In May 2018 Ederson gained an entry in the *Guinness Book of Records* after setting a world record in training for the longest-ever drop kick, an impressive 75.3 metres.

EFL TROPHY

Formerly called the Football League Trophy before being rebranded in 2016, and currently known as the Leasing.com Trophy for sponsorship reasons, the EFL Trophy was first established in 1983 as a knock-out competition for the 48 League One and League Two clubs.

• The most successful team in the competition are Bristol City with three victories in the final, against Bolton in 1986, Carlisle United in 2003 and Walsall in 2015, while Carlisle have appeared in a record six finals.

• The competition was expanded in the 2016/17 season to include 16 Premier League and Championship academy teams. The following season Chelsea became the first academy side to reach the semi-finals but lost on penalties to eventual winners Lincoln City.

• However, the new format has not greatly appealed to fans with an

Portsmouth won the EFL Trophy in 2019

all-time competition low attendance of just 202 turning out for the match between Burton Albion and Middlesbrough academy at the Pirelli Stadium on 7th November 2018. Nonetheless, a record crowd of 85,021 watched the 2019 final between Portsmouth and Sunderland at Wembley.

UNAI EMERY

Born: Hondarribia, Spain, 3rd November 1971
Managerial career:
2004-06 Lorca Deportivo
2006-08 Almeria
2008-12 Valencia
2012 Spartak Moscow
2013-16 Sevilla
2016-18 Paris Saint-Germain
2018- Arsenal

Appointed Arsenal head coach on a two-year contract in May 2018, Unai Emery is the only manager to have won the Europa League three times. The Spaniard achieved this feat with Sevilla between 2014 and 2016, the last of those triumphs coming thanks to a 3-1 defeat of Liverpool in Basel. At the end of his first season with the Gunners Emery had a chance to extend that record to four Europa League triumphs, but his side were crushed 4-1 by Chelsea in the final in Baku.

• After a playing career spent mostly in the Spanish second tier, Emery started out in management with Lorca

Ederson really takes the classic bit of goalkeeping advice of 'make yourself big' seriously...

ENGLAND

First international: Scotland 0 England 0, 1872
Most capped player: Peter Shilton, 125 caps (1971-90)
Leading goalscorer: Wayne Rooney, 53 goals (2003-18)
First World Cup appearance: England 2 Chile 0, 1950
Biggest win: England 13 Ireland 0, 1882
Heaviest defeat: Hungary 7 England 1, 1954

England, along with their first opponents Scotland, are the oldest international team in world football. The two countries met in the first official international in Glasgow in 1872, with honours being shared after a 0-0 draw. The following year, William Kenyon-Slaney of Wanderers FC scored England's first ever goal in a 4-2 victory over Scotland at the Kennington Oval.

• **With a team entirely composed of players from England, Great Britain won the first Olympic Games football tournament in 1908 and again in 1912.**

• England did not lose a match on home soil against a team from outside the British Isles until 1953 when they were thrashed 6-3 by Hungary at Wembley. The following year England went down to their worst ever defeat to the same opposition, crashing 7-1 in Budapest.

• **Although Walter Winterbottom was appointed as England's first full-** time manager in 1946, the squad was picked by a committee until Alf Ramsey took over in 1963. Three years later England hosted and won the World Cup – the greatest moment in the country's football history by some considerable margin.

• There were many heroes in that 1966 team, including goalkeeper Gordon Banks, skipper Bobby Moore and striker Geoff Hurst, who scored a hat-trick in the 4-2 victory over West Germany in the final at Wembley. Ramsey, too, was hailed for his part in the success and was knighted soon afterwards.

• **Since then, however, England fans have experienced more than their fair share of disappointment. Many believed the World Cup was 'coming home' when England reached the semi-final of the tournament in 2018, but Gareth Southgate's team were beaten 2-1 by Croatia after extra-time in Moscow despite taking an early lead thanks to a magnificent Kieran Trippier free kick. England also made it through to the last four in 1990 but, agonisingly, Bobby Robson's team lost on penalties in the semi-final to the eventual winners, West Germany.**

• In 1996 England hosted the European Championship and were again knocked out on penalties by Germany at the semi-final stage, with Gareth Southgate the unfortunate player to miss the decisive spot-kick.

• **Defender Billy Wright, the first man in the world to win 100 international caps, and Bobby Moore both captained England a record 90 times. Wright also played in a record 70 consecutive England internationals between 1951 and 1959.**

Ole! Unai Emery's flamenco moves are always entertaining

Deportivo, leading the club to their first ever promotion to the Second Division in 2005. He soon moved on to Almeria, taking the southern Spanish outfit into the top flight for the first time in their history in 2007. The following year he joined Valencia, guiding 'Los Ches' to an impressive three consecutive third-place finishes between 2010 and 2012.

• After a brief and unsuccessful spell with Spartak Moscow, Emery returned to Spain with Sevilla, where he enjoyed three memorable years and was voted European Coach of the Season in 2014.

• **In 2016 Emery took over as manager of Paris Saint-Germain. He led the French giants to two French Cup triumphs and the Ligue 1 title in 2018 before succeeding the long-serving Arsene Wenger at the Emirates.**

Improving England have their eyes set on finally winning another trophy

- Frank Lampard scored a record nine penalties for England between 2005 and 2012.
- **Gary Lineker is England's top scorer at the World Cup, with a total of 10 goals in 1986 and 1990. Lineker won the Golden Boot at the first of these tournaments, a feat matched by Three Lions skipper Harry Kane in 2018.**
- Robert Green is the only goalkeeper to have been sent off while playing for England, getting his marching orders in a World Cup qualifier against Ukraine in October 2009.
- **Arsenal winger David Rocastle played in a record 14 matches for England between 1988 and 1992 without once finishing on the losing side.**

HONOURS

World Cup winners 1966

World Cup Record

1930 Did not enter
1934 Did not enter
1938 Did not enter
1950 Round 1
1954 Quarter-finals
1958 Round 1
1962 Quarter-finals
1966 Winners
1970 Quarter-finals
1974 Did not qualify
1978 Did not qualify
1982 Round 2
1986 Quarter-finals
1990 Fourth place
1994 Did not qualify
1998 Round 2
2002 Quarter-finals
2006 Quarter-finals
2010 Round 2
2014 Round 1
2018 Fourth place

After their World Cup heroics, England stars like Jill Scott are in demand for 'selfies' more than ever

ENGLAND WOMEN

First international: Scotland 2 England 3, 1972
Most capped player: Fara Williams, 170 caps (2001-)
Leading goalscorer: Kelly Smith, 46 goals (1995-2014)
First World Cup appearance: England 3 Canada 2, 1995
Biggest win: England 13 Hungary 0, 2005
Heaviest defeat: Norway 8 England 0, 2000

The England women's team played their first international against Scotland at Greenock on 18th November 1972. MIdfielder Sylvia Gore scored the Lionesses' first ever goal in a 3-2 victory.

- **Although England have never won a major trophy they have reached two finals of the European Championships, losing on penalties to Sweden in 1984 and going down 6-2 to Germany in 2009. The Lionesses' best ever showing at the World Cup was in 2015 when they came third after a Fara Williams penalty clinched a nail-biting 1-0 win against Germany in the third/fourth play-off. Four years later they were beaten by the USA in the semi-final in France and then lost 2-1 to Sweden in the battle for a bronze medal.**
- Williams is England's most decorated player, with a total of 170 caps since making her debut in 2001. The Lionesses'

all-time top scorer is ex-Arsenal Ladies striker Kelly Smith who banged in 46 goals between 1995 and 2014.
- **Former Arsenal Ladies defender Faye White is England's longest-serving captain, skippering her country for 10 years between 2002 and 2012, and wearing the armband for the vast majority of her 90 caps.**
- Ellen White has scored a record seven goals for England at the Women's World Cup, gaining global attention at the 2019 finals when her six goals made her the joint-top scorer at the tournament.

World Cup Record

1991 Did not qualify
1995 Quarter-finals
1999 Did not qualify
2003 Did not qualify
2007 Quarter-finals
2011 Quarter-finals
2015 Third place
2019 Fourth place

TOP 10

ENGLAND WOMEN GOALSCORERS

1.	Kelly Smith (1995-2015)	46
2.	Kerry Davis (1982-98)	44
3.	Karen Walker (1988-2003)	40
	Fara Williams (2001-)	40
5.	Hope Powell (1983-98)	35
	Ellen White (2010-)	35
7.	Eniola Aluko (2004-16)	33
8.	Karen Carney (2005-)	31
9.	Gillian Coultard (1981-2000)	30
10.	Marieanne Spacey (1984-2001)	28

Christian Eriksen looks to the future – but will it be with Tottenham?

CHRISTIAN ERIKSEN

Born: Middelfart, Denmark, 14th February 1992
Position: Midfielder
Club career:
2010-13 Ajax 113 (25)
2013- Tottenham Hotspur 206 (49)
International record:
2010- Denmark 89 (27)

Silky Tottenham Hotspur midfielder Christian Eriksen is the highest-scoring Danish player in Premier League history with 49 goals, passing the previous benchmark set by Arsenal striker Nicklas Bendtner when he scored in a 3-2 win at West Ham in September 2017. The following season he became only the second player – after former Manchester United star David Beckham – to record 10 or more assists in four consecutive Premier League campaigns.

• As a youth player with Odense Boldklub, Eriksen was a transfer target for numerous top European clubs, but after trials with Chelsea, Manchester United, Barcelona and Real Madrid, he decided to join Ajax as a 16-year-old in 2008. It proved to be an extremely wise move, as the youngster soon cemented a place in the Dutch giants' side and went on to win three league titles before joining Spurs for £11 million in 2013.

• When he made his international debut in 2010 against Austria, aged 18, Eriksen became the fourth youngest Danish player ever to appear for the national team. He then became the youngest Danish player ever to score in a European Championship qualifier when he netted in a 2-0 win against Iceland the following year. His total of 11 goals in the 2018 World Cup qualifying campaign was only bettered by Cristiano Ronaldo and Robert Lewandowski in Europe.

• Voted into the Premier League Team of the Year for the first time in 2018, Eriksen is only the second player (after the legendary Brian Laudrup) to be named Danish Footballer of the Year four times, collecting the award in 2013, 2014, 2015 and 2018.

EUROPA LEAGUE

Since European football's second-tier competition was rebranded as the Europa League in 2010, two clubs have won the trophy three times: Sevilla in 2014, 2015 and 2016, and Atletico Madrid in 2010, 2012 and 2018. Thanks to Sevilla's two previous triumphs in the UEFA Cup, the forerunner of the Europa League, the team from southern Spain are the most successful club in the history of the competition.

• In 2011 Porto beat Braga 1-0 in Dublin in the first ever all-Portuguese European final. Porto's match-winner was Colombian striker Radamel Falcao, whose goal in the final was his 17th in the competition that season – a record for the tournament.

• The competition is now in its third incarnation, having previously been known as the Fairs Cup (1955-71) and the UEFA Cup (1971-2009). The tournament was originally established in 1955 as a competition between cities, rather than clubs. The first winners were Barcelona, who beat London 8-2 on aggregate in a final which, bizarrely, did not take place until 1958!

• The first team to win the newly named UEFA Cup were Tottenham Hotspur in 1972, who beat Wolves 3-2 on aggregate in the first all-English European final. Following Chelsea's triumph in the 2019 Europa League final against London rivals Arsenal, English clubs have won the competition 13 times. However, Spanish teams lead the way with 17 victories.

Chelsea winger Pedro has nabbed the Europa League and he's not giving it up!

Portugal are still celebrating their shock 2016 European Championship win

• Swedish striker Henrik Larsson is the leading scorer in the history of the UEFA Cup with 40 goals for Feyenoord, Celtic and Helsingborg between 1993 and 2009.

• Liverpool are the most successful English club in the competition, with three victories in the UEFA Cup in 1973, 1976 and 2001, the last of these triumphs coming courtesy of a thrilling 5-4 victory over Alaves – the most goal-packed of all the one-off finals.

EUROPEAN CHAMPIONSHIP

Originally called the European Nations Cup, the idea for the European Championship came from Henri Delaunay, the then secretary of the French FA. The first championship in 1960 featured just 17 countries (the four British nations, Italy and West Germany were among those who declined to take part). The first winners of the tournament were the Soviet Union, who beat Yugoslavia 2-1 in the final in Paris.

• Germany have the best record in the tournament, having won the trophy three times (in 1972, 1980 and 1996) and been runners-up on a further three occasions. Spain have also won the title three times (1964, 2008 and 2012) and are the only country to retain the trophy following a 4-0 demolition of Italy in the final at Euro 2012 – the biggest win in any European Championships or World Cup final.

• Germany recorded the biggest win in the competition, smashing San Marino 13-0 in a qualifier in 2006.

• French legend Michel Platini and Portugal's Cristiano Ronaldo are the

leading scorers in the finals of the European Championship with nine goals each. Platini's goals all came in 1984, setting a record tally for a single tournament.

• Including qualifying matches, Cristiano Ronaldo is the leading scorer in the competition with 29 goals and is the only player to have scored at four finals (2004, 2008, 2012 and 2016). Ronaldo has also made a record 21 appearances at the finals.

• Italy and Spain have met a record six times at the finals, with the Italians coming out 2-0 winners in the pair's most recent meeting in the last 16 in 2016.

• Luxembourg are the least successful country in the history of the competition, having failed to qualify once for the finals in 14 attempts since 1964.

European Championship finals
1960 USSR 2 Yugoslavia 1 (Paris)
1964 Spain 2 USSR 1 (Madrid)
1968 Italy 2 Yugoslavia 0 • (Rome)
1972 West Germany 3 USSR 0 (Brussels)
1976 Czechoslovakia 2 *
West Germany 2 (Belgrade)
1980 West Germany 2 Belgium 1 (Rome)
1984 France 2 Spain 0 (Paris)
1988 Netherlands 2 USSR 0 (Munich)
1992 Denmark 2 Germany 0
(Gothenburg)
1996 Germany 2 Czech Republic 1
(London)
2000 France 2 Italy 1 (Rotterdam)
2004 Greece 1 Portugal 0 (Lisbon)
2008 Spain 1 Germany 0 (Vienna)
2012 Spain 4 Italy 0 (Kiev)
2016 Portugal 1 France 0 (Paris)
• After 1-1 draw   * Won on penalties

EURO 2020

Euro 2020 will be the first European Championships to be held in multiple countries, as a special one-off event to mark the 60th anniversary of the first tournament in 1960.

• The 12 countries which will host matches are Azerbaijan, Denmark, England, Germany, Hungary, Italy, the Netherlands, Republic of Ireland, Romania, Russia, Scotland and Spain. Wembley Stadium will host both semi-finals and the final in July 2020.

• Unlike previous tournaments, no country will qualify automatically as hosts. Instead 20 countries will come through the usual qualifying process, with the remaining four qualifying via the new UEFA Nations League.

EUROPEAN GOLDEN SHOE

Formerly known as the European Golden Boot, the European Golden Shoe has been awarded since 1968 to the leading scorer in league matches in the top division of every European league. Since 1997 the award has been based on a points system which gives greater weight to goals scored in the leading European leagues.

• Barcelona star Lionel Messi has won the award six times and most recently topped the charts in 2018/19 with 36 goals to become the first player to claim the honour three seasons on the trot. Messi also holds the record for the most goals scored by a Golden Shoe winner, with an incredible 50 in 2011/12.

• The first British winner of the award was Liverpool's Ian Rush in 1984, and the most recent was Sunderland's Kevin Phillips

Messi's invisible centipede was a big hit at parties

Liverpool painted Istanbul red after winning the 2019 European Super Cup

in 2000. Since then, Arsenal's Thierry Henry (in 2004 and 2005), Manchester United's Cristiano Ronaldo (in 2008) and Liverpool's Luis Suarez (jointly with Cristiano Ronaldo in 2014) have won the Golden Shoe after topping both the Premier League and European goalscoring charts. When Ronaldo first won the Golden Shoe with Real Madrid in 2011, he became the first player to win the award in two different countries.

• **Thanks largely to Cristiano Ronaldo's four wins, players from Portugal have lifted the award on a record eight occasions.**

EUROPEAN SUPER CUP

Founded in 1972 as a two-legged final between the winners of the European Cup and the European Cup Winners' Cup, the European Super Cup trophy is now awarded to the winners of a one-off match between the Champions League and Europa League holders.

• **AC Milan and Barcelona have won the trophy a record five times each. Liverpool are the most successful English club in the competition with four victories (in 1977, 2001, 2005 and 2019).**

• The first ever meeting between two English sides took place in 2019, with Champions League winners Liverpool taking on Europa League holders Chelsea

in Istanbul. Liverpool won 5-4 on penalties after an exciting 2-2 draw.

• **Monaco's Stade Louis II has hosted the final a record 16 times, including for 15 consecutive years between 1998 and 2012.**

• Clubs from Spain have won the trophy a record 15 times, most recently in 2018 when Atletico Madrid beat local rivals Real Madrid 4-2 in Tallinn, with Atleti striker Diego Costa scoring the fastest ever goal in the competition after just 49 seconds.

EUROPEAN WOMEN'S CHAMPIONSHIP

The first winners of the European Women's Championship were Sweden, who beat England on penalties in 1984 after the sides' two-legged final had finished 1-1 on aggregate. Since then Germany have dominated the competition, lifting the trophy an astonishing eight times (once, in 1989, as West Germany), and claiming six titles on the trot between 1995 and 2013. However, the current holders are the Netherlands, who beat Demark 4-2 in an exciting final on home soil in Enschede in 2017.

• **The German pair of Birgit Prinz and Nadine Angerer have both won the competition a record five times each. Prinz is also the joint-top scorer in the competition with 10 goals at the finals between 1995 and 2009 – a**

tally equalled by fellow German Inka Grings (2005-2009) – and has played in a record 23 matches.

• A record crowd of 41,301 watched the 2013 final between Germany and Norway in Solna, Sweden.

• **England will host the 2021 finals for a second time, having previously hosted the 2005 tournament.**

European Women's Championship finals
1984 Sweden 1* England 1 (Two-legged final)
1987 Norway 2 Sweden 1 (Norway)
1989 West Germany 4 Norway 1 (West Germany)
1991 Germany 3 Norway 1 (Denmark)
1993 Norway 1 Italy 0 (Italy)
1995 Germany 3 Sweden 2 (Germany)
1997 Germany 2 Italy 0 (Norway/ Sweden)
2001 Germany 1 Sweden 0 (Germany)
2005 Germany 3 Norway 1 (England)
2009 Germany 6 England 2 (Finland)
2013 Germany 1 Norway 0 (Sweden)
2017 Netherlands 4 Denmark 2 (Netherlands)
* Won on penalties

EVERTON

Year founded: 1878
Ground: Goodison Park (39,572)
Previous name: St Domingo
Nickname: The Toffees
Biggest win: 11-2 v Derby County (1890)
Heaviest defeat: 0-7 v Sunderland (1934), Wolves (1939) and Arsenal (2005)

The club was formed as the church team St Domingo in 1878, adopting the name Everton (after the surrounding area) the following year. In 1888 Everton joined the Football League as founder members, winning the first of nine league titles three years later.

• **One of the most famous names in English football, Everton hold the proud record of spending more seasons, 116, in the top flight than any other club. Relegated only twice, in 1930 and 1951, they have spent just four seasons in total outside the top tier.**

• The club's unusual nickname, the Toffees, stems from a local business

"Please, Lucas, you can wash your hair after the match!"

IS THAT A FACT?

Everton have played the most games in the English top flight (4,518), drawn (1,135) and lost (1,546) the most, scored the most goals (7,027) and also conceded the most (6,255).

called Ye Ancient Everton Toffee House which was situated near Goodison Park. In the early 1930s Everton's precise style of play earned the club the tag 'The School of Science', a nickname which lingers to this day.

• The club's record goalscorer is the legendary Dixie Dean, who notched an incredible total of 383 goals in all competitions between 1925 and 1937. Dean's best season for the club was in the Toffees' title-winning campaign in 1927/28 when his 60 league goals set a Football League record that is unlikely ever to be beaten. Dean's total of 349 league goals is a record for a player with the same club.

• Everton's most capped player is long-serving goalkeeper Neville Southall, who made 92 appearances for Wales in the 1980s and 1990s. He is also the club's record appearance maker, turning out in 578 league games.

• In 1931 Everton won the Second Division title, scoring 121 goals in the process. The following season the Toffees banged in 116 goals on their way to lifting the First Division title, becoming the first club to find the net 100 times in consecutive seasons.

• The club's most successful decade, though, was in the 1980s when, under manager Howard Kendall, they won the league championship (1985 and 1987), FA Cup (1984) and the European Cup Winners' Cup (in 1985, following a 3-1 win over Austria Vienna in the final). Since then Everton have had to play second fiddle to city rivals Liverpool, although the Toffees did manage to win the FA Cup for a fifth time in 1995, beating Manchester United in the final thanks to a goal by striker Paul Rideout.

• The club's record signing is Icelandic midfielder Gylfi Sigurdsson, who moved to Merseyside from Swansea City for £45 million in August 2017. A month earlier the Toffees' Belgian striker Romelu Lukaku joined Manchester United for £75 million in the most expensive transfer deal between two Premier League clubs.

• In 1893 Everton's Jack Southworth became the first player in Football League history to score six goals in a match when he fired a memorable double hat-trick in a 7-1 victory against West Bromwich Albion.

• Everton's Louis Saha scored the fastest goal in the FA Cup final, when he netted after 25 seconds against Chelsea at Wembley in 2009. However, the Toffees were unable to hold on to their lead and were eventually beaten 2-1 – one of a record eight times Everton have lost in the final.

• The oldest ground in the Premier League, Goodison Park is the only stadium in the world to have a church, St Luke the Evangelist, inside its grounds.

• **Everton were the first English league club to host the FA Cup final, Goodison Park providing the stage for Notts County's 4-1 defeat of Bolton in 1894. The famous old ground was also the venue for a World Cup semi-final in 1966, West Germany beating the Soviet Union 2-1.**

• Everton were the first club to win a penalty shoot-out in the European Cup, beating German outfit Borussia Monchengladbach 4-3 on spot-kicks after a 2-2 aggregate tie.

HONOURS
Division 1 champions 1891, 1915, 1928, 1932, 1939, 1963, 1970, 1985, 1987
Division 2 champions 1931
FA Cup 1906, 1933, 1966, 1984, 1995
European Cup Winners' Cup 1985

EXETER CITY

Year founded: 1904
Ground: St James Park (8,541)
Nickname: The Grecians
Biggest win: 14-0 v Weymouth (1908)
Heaviest defeat: 0-9 v Notts County (1948) and Northampton Town (1958)

Exeter City were founded in 1904 following the amalgamation of two local sides, Exeter United and St Sidwell's United. The club were founder members of the Third Division (South) in 1920 and remained in the two lower divisions until they were relegated to the Conference in 2003. Now owned by the Exeter City Supporters' Trust, the club rejoined the Football League in 2008.

• Club legend Arnie Mitchell played a record 516 games for Exeter between 1952 and 1966. The Grecians' record

It's 'Grecian wrestling' between Exeter and Oldham

Germany won Euro 96 thanks to a golden goal in extra-time from Oliver Bierhoff

scorer is Tony Kellow with 129 league goals in three spells at St James Park between 1976 and 1988.

• On a tour of South America in 1914 Exeter became the first club side to play the Brazilian national team. The Grecians lost 2-0 but the occasion has gone into club folklore, with Exeter fans delighting in taunting their opponents by chanting, "Have you ever, have you ever, have you ever played Brazil?"

• Exeter enjoyed their best ever FA Cup run way back in 1937, reaching the fifth round before losing 5-3 to eventual finalists Preston.

HONOURS
Division 4 champions 1990

EXTRA-TIME

Normally consisting of two halves of 15 minutes each, extra-time has been played to produce a winner in knock-out tournaments since the earliest days of football, although to begin with the playing of the additional time had to be agreed by the two captains. Extra-time was first played in an FA Cup final in 1875, Royal Engineers and the Old Etonians drawing 1-1

(Royal Engineers won the replay 2-0). In all, extra-time has been played in 20 finals, the most recent in 2016 when Manchester United beat Crystal Palace 2-1 despite being reduced to 10 men after Chris Smalling was sent off.

• The first World Cup final to go to extra-time was in 1934, when hosts Italy and Czechoslovakia were tied 1-1 at the end of 90 minutes. Seven minutes into the additional period, Angelo Schiavio scored the winner for Italy. Since then, six other finals have gone to extra-time, most recently in 2014 when Germany's Mario Gotze scored the winner against Argentina with just seven minutes left to play.

• In an attempt to encourage attacking football and reduce the number of matches settled by penalty shoot-outs, FIFA ruled in 1993 that the first goal scored in extra-time would win the match. The first major tournament to be decided by the so-called 'golden goal' rule was the 1996 European Championships, Germany defeating the Czech Republic in the final thanks to a 94th-minute strike by Oliver Bierhoff. The 2000 final of the same competition was also decided in the same manner, David Trezeguet scoring a stunning winner for France against Italy in the 103rd minute.

• Concerns that the 'golden goal' put too much pressure on referees led UEFA to replace it with the 'silver goal' in 2002. Under this rule, which was used at Euro 2004 but scrapped afterwards, only the first half of extra-time was played if either team led at the interval.

• Both Germany and Italy have played extra-time on a record 11 occasions at the World Cup.

FA CUP

The oldest knock-out competition in the world, the FA Cup dates back to 1871 when it was established under the control of the Football Association. The first round of the first FA Cup was played on 11th November 1871, Clapham Rovers' Jarvis Kenrick scoring the very first goal in the competition in a 3-0 win over Upton Park.

• The following year Wanderers beat Royal Engineers at Kennington Oval in the first ever FA Cup final. The only goal of the game was scored by Morton Peto Betts, who played under the pseudonym A.H. Chequer. Uniquely, Wanderers, as holders, were given a bye all the way through to the following year's final, and they took full advantage by beating Oxford University 2-1.

• The FA Challenge Cup – the competition's full title – has always retained the same name despite being sponsored in recent years by Littlewoods (1994-98), AXA (1998-2002), E.ON (2006-11), Budweiser (2011-14) and Emirates (2015-).

• There have, however, been five different trophies. The first trophy – known as the 'little tin idol' – was stolen from a Birmingham shop window in September 1895 where it was on display, having been won by Aston Villa a few months earlier. Sixty years later the thief revealed that the trophy was melted down and turned into counterfeit coins. A second trophy was used until 1910 when it was presented to the FA's long-serving President and former five-time cup winner, Lord Kinnaird. A new, larger trophy was commissioned by the FA from Fattorini and Sons Silversmiths in Bradford – and, by a remarkable coincidence, was won in its first year by Bradford City in 1911. This trophy was used until 1992, when it was replaced with an exact replica. In 2014 a new trophy, with an identical design to the 1911 one, was presented to that year's winners, Arsenal.

• The most successful club in the competition is Arsenal, who won the cup for a record 13th time in 2017 when they beat Chelsea 2-1 in the final. The only league team to have won the FA Cup in three consecutive years are Blackburn Rovers, who lifted the trophy in 1884, 1885 and 1886. Wanderers also won the cup three years on the trot between 1876 and 1878.

• In 1903 Bury set a record for the biggest win in the final, thrashing Derby County 6-0. Manchester City matched that feat in 2019, defeating Watford by the same score at Wembley to clinch the third part of an historic domestic Treble.

• The first FA Cup final to be decided by penalties was in 2005, Arsenal beating Manchester United 5-4 following a drab 0-0 draw at the Millennium Stadium, Cardiff. In 2007 the final returned to Wembley, Chelsea becoming the first club to lift the trophy at the new national stadium after a 1-0 victory over Manchester United.

• Tottenham Hotspur are the only non-league side to win the competition since the formation of the Football League in 1888, lifting the trophy for the first time in 1901 while members of the Southern League. West Ham were the last team from outside the top flight to win the cup, memorably beating Arsenal 1-0 in the 1980 final.

• Just three players have scored a hat-trick in the FA Cup final: Billy Townley (Blackburn Rovers, 1890), James Logan (Notts County, 1894) and Stan Mortensen (Blackpool, 1953).

• In 1887 Preston North End recorded the biggest win in the history of the competition when they utterly thrashed Hyde 26-0 in a first-round tie. In the same season, Preston's Jimmy Ross scored a record 19 goals in the competition.

• Former England defender Ashley Cole won the FA Cup a record seven times with Arsenal (in 2002, 2003 and 2005) and Chelsea (in 2007, 2009, 2010 and 2012) while Arthur Kinnaird appeared in a record nine finals for Wanderers and Old Etonians between 1873 and 1883. Ex-Arsenal boss Arsène Wenger won the cup a record seven times as a manager between 1998 and 2017.

TOP 10

FA CUP FINAL APPEARANCES

1.	Arsenal	20 (won 13, lost 7)
	Manchester United	20 (won 12, lost 8)
3.	Liverpool	14 (won 7, lost 7)
4.	Chelsea	13 (won 8, lost 5)
	Newcastle United	13 (won 6, lost 7)
	Everton	13 (won 5, lost 8)
7.	Aston Villa	11 (won 7, lost 4)
	Manchester City	11 (won 6, lost 5)
9.	West Bromwich Albion	10 (won 5, lost 5)
10.	Tottenham Hotspur	9 (won 8, lost 1)

Manchester City won the FA Cup in 2019 to clinch English football's first domestic Treble

• The leading scorer in the FA Cup is Notts County's Henry Cursham, who banged in 49 goals between 1877 and 1888. Liverpool's Ian Rush scored a record five goals in three appearances in the final in 1986, 1989 and 1992, but Chelsea's Didier Drogba is the only player to have scored in four finals (2007, 2009, 2010 and 2012).

• Bournemouth striker Ted MacDougall scored a record nine goals in his club's 11-0 demolition of Margate in the first round of the cup in 1971.

"OK, you lost, but at least we both scored!"

FAMILIES

The first brothers to win the World Cup together were West Germany's Fritz and Ottmar Walter in 1954. England's Bobby and Jack Charlton famously repeated the feat in 1966, when the Three Lions beat West Germany 4-2 in the much-celebrated final at Wembley.

• The only time two sets of brothers have played in the FA Cup final was in 1876 when the victorious Wanderers side included Frank and Hubert Heron, while losers Old Etonians' line-up featured Alfred and Edward Lyttelton.

• Two sets of fathers and sons have played together in the same Football League team: Alex and David Herd (Stockport County, 1951) and Ian and Gary Bowyer (Hereford United, 1990).

• The first time a father and son both played in the same international match was in 1996 when 17-year-old Eidur Gudjohnsen came on for his father Arnor, 34, in Iceland's 3-0 win over Estonia. At the 2010 World Cup, brothers opposed each other in an international for the first time when

Jerome Boateng (Germany) lined up against Kevin-Prince Boateng (Ghana).

• Two pairs of twins have played against each other in the Premier League: Michael (Burnley) and Will Keane (Hull City) on 10th September 2016, and Josh (Cardiff City) and Jacob Murphy (Newcastle United) on 18th August 2018. Appropriately, perhaps, both matches ended in draws.

• On 24th October 2015 Jordan Ayew (Aston Villa) and Andre Ayew (Swansea City) became the first brothers to score for different sides in the same Premier League match. Andre ended up the happier, though, as the Swans won 2-1 at Villa Park.

FIFA

FIFA, the Federation Internationale de Football Association, is the most important administrative body in world football. It is responsible for the organisation of major international tournaments, notably the World Cup, and enacts law changes in the game.

• Founded in Paris in 1904, FIFA is now based in Zurich and has 211 members, 18 more than the United Nations. The President is Gianni Infantino, who was elected in February 2016 after his long-serving predecessor, Sepp Blatter, was banned from any role in FIFA for six years for making unauthorised payments to then UEFA President Michel Platini. Infantino has since taken steps to clean up an organisation whose reputation has been badly damaged in recent years by allegations that high-ranking FIFA officials have been involved in serious criminal activity.

• Changes to the game's rules that FIFA have introduced into the World Cup include the use of substitutes (1970), penalty shoot-outs to settle drawn games (1982), three points for a group-stage win (1994) and the use of video assistant referees (VAR) (2018).

• The British football associations have twice pulled out of FIFA. First, in 1918 when they were opposed to playing matches against Germany after the end of the First World War, and in 1928 over the issue of payments to amateurs. This second dispute meant that none of the British teams were represented at the first ever World Cup in 1930.

• In 1992 FIFA decided to introduce a ranking index for all its member countries. As of September 2019 the top-ranked nation was Belgium, followed by Brazil, France and England. In the women's game USA lead the way, with Germany second and Netherlands third.

ROBERTO FIRMINO

Born: Maceio, Brazil, 2nd October 1991
Position: Midfielder/striker
Club career:
2009-10 Figueirense 38 (8)
2010-15 1899 Hoffenheim 140 (35)
2015- Liverpool 137 (48)
International record:
2014- Brazil 38 (12)

With 48 goals to his name, Roberto Firmino is the highest-scoring Brazilian in the history of the Premier League, passing the old benchmark set by former Liverpool team-mate Philippe

On his day, Roberto Firmino is definitely a hair-raising player

Coutinho when he banged in a hat-trick in a 5-1 thumping of Arsenal on 29th December 2018. Later that season, Firmino helped the Reds win the Champions League, a competition in which he had scored a joint club-best 11 goals in the previous campaign.

• An attacking midfielder who is often used as a centre forward for his pressing ability, Firmino also possesses good vision, technical skills and an eye for goal. He joined his first club, Figueirense, as a youngster after being spotted by a local football-loving dentist, and he helped Figueirense gain promotion from the Brazilian second tier in 2010, before moving to join German outfit Hoffenheim in January 2011.

• After taking a while to settle in Germany, Firmino enjoyed a sensational campaign in 2013/14 when he was named the Bundesliga's 'Breakthrough Player' after scoring 16 league goals – a total only bettered by three other players. The following year he joined Liverpool for £29 million.

• Firmino won his first cap for Brazil in November 2014 and later that month he scored his first international goal in a friendly against Austria. At the 2019 Copa America he scored in Brazil's 2-0 defeat of Argentina in the semi-final, and then collected a winner's medal after the hosts beat Peru 3-1 in the final.

FLEETWOOD TOWN

Year founded: 1997
Ground: Highbury Stadium (5,327)
Previous names: Fleetwood Wanderers, Fleetwood Freeport
Nickname: The Trawlermen
Biggest win: 13-0 v Oldham Town (1998)
Heaviest defeat: 0-9 v Bradford City (1949)

Established in 1997 as the third incarnation of a club which dates back to 1908, Fleetwood Town have enjoyed a remarkable rise in recent years. In 2012 the Trawlermen were promoted to the Football League as Conference champions, and just two years later they went up to the third tier after beating Burton Albion 1-0 in the League Two play-off final. Another promotion beckoned in 2017, until Fleetwood were narrowly beaten by Bradford City in the League One play-off semi-final.

• The Trawlermen's highest capped international is Conor McLaughlin, who won 25 caps for Northern Ireland between 2012 and 2017.

• In May 2012 Fleetwood sold prolific striker Jamie Vardy to Leicester City for £1.7 million – a record fee for a non-league club.

• After making his debut for Fleetwood in the North West Counties Football League Division One in 2003, defender Nathan Pond played for the Trawlermen in seven different divisions – a world record for a player at the same club. His grand total of 460 appearances is also a club record.

• Fleetwood came close to reaching the fourth round of the FA Cup for the first time in their history in 2019, but were beaten 3-2 at home by AFC Wimbledon.

HONOURS
Conference champions 2012

FLOODLIGHTS

The first ever floodlit match was played at Bramall Lane between two representative Sheffield sides on 14th October 1876 in front of a crowd of 10,000 people (around 8,000 of whom used the cover of darkness to get in without paying). The pitch was illuminated by four lamps, powered by dynamos driven by engines located behind the goals.

• The first game in England played under 'permanent' floodlights was between South Liverpool and a touring Nigerian XI on 28th September 1949. Watched by a record crowd of 13,007 at Holly Park, the match ended in a 2-2 draw.

The Fleetwood flag has been flying high in recent years

Without floodlights, like these at Tranmere's Prenton Park, football would literally be back in the Dark Ages

• For many years the Football Association banned floodlit football, so the first league match played under lights did not take place until 1956, when Newcastle beat Portsmouth 2-0 at Fratton Park. It wasn't the most auspicious of occasions, though, as floodlight failure meant the kick-off was delayed for 30 minutes.

• **Arsenal became the first top-flight club in England to install floodlights in 1951 – some 20 years after legendary Gunners manager Herbert Chapman had advocated their use. Chesterfield were the last Football League club to install floodlights, finally putting up a set in 1967.**

• In the winter of 1997 two Premier League games, at West Ham and Wimbledon, were abandoned because of floodlight failure. What seemed to be an unfortunate coincidence was eventually revealed to be the work of a shadowy Far Eastern betting syndicate, four members of whom were eventually arrested and sentenced to three years each in prison.

• **England first played under floodlights on 8th June 1953 in a 6-3 win against the USA at the Yankee Stadium in New York.**

IS THAT A FACT?

Norwich's home match with Derby County on 29th December 2018 was interrupted for 20 minutes late in the second half when one of the Carrow Road floodlights went out. The break suited the Rams perfectly as they stormed back from 3-2 down to win 4-3.

PHIL FODEN

Born: Stockport, 28th May 2000
Position: Midfielder
Club career:
2017- Manchester City 18 (1)

In 2018 Manchester City midfielder Phil Foden became the youngest ever player to receive a Premier League winner's medal, and he has already added another one to his collection after City's successful defence of their title in the 2018/19 season.

Phil Foden, aka 'the Stockport Iniesta', in typical pose

• **A cultured player who is known as 'the Stockport Iniesta' after the legendary Spain and Barcelona midfielder, Foden joined City as a seven-year-old and came through the ranks to make his debut as a sub against Feyenoord in the Champions League in November 2017. The following month, aged 17 and 177 days, he became the youngest ever English player to start in the competition in a 2-1 defeat against Shakhtar Donetsk.**

• When he headed a vital winning goal against Tottenham at the Etihad in April 2019 Foden became the third youngest City player – after Micah Richards and Daniel Sturridge – to score in the Premier League.

• **In 2017 Foden played and scored for England in the final of the European Under-17 Championships, although he finished on the losing side after opponents Spain won on spot-kicks. Later that year Foden scored twice in the 5-2 defeat of Spain in the final of the Under-17 World Cup in Kolkata, India and he also won the Golden Ball for best player at the tournament. Then, in December 2017, he was voted the BBC's Young Sports Personality of the Year.**

FOOTBALL ASSOCIATION

Founded in 1863 at a meeting at the Freemasons' Tavern in central London, the Football Association is the oldest football organisation in the world and the only national association with no mention of the country in its name.

• **The first secretary of the FA was Ebenezer Cobb Morley of Barnes FC, nicknamed 'The Father of Football', who went on to draft the first set of laws of the game. The most controversial of the 14 laws he suggested outlawed kicking an opponent, known as 'hacking'. The first match to be played under the new laws was between Barnes and Richmond in 1863.**

• In 1871 the then secretary of the FA, Charles Alcock, suggested playing a national knock-out tournament similar to the competition he had enjoyed as a schoolboy at Harrow School. The idea was accepted by the FA and the competition, named the FA Challenge

Cup, has been running ever since. The FA Cup, as it is usually called, has long been the most famous national club competition in world football.

• Since 1992, the FA has run the English game's top division, the Premier League, which was formed when the old First Division broke away from the then four-division Football League.

• The FA is also responsible for the appointment of the management of the England men's and women's football teams. The FA's main asset is Wembley Stadium, which it owns via its subsidiary, Wembley National Stadium Limited.

• Among the innovations the FA has fought against before finally accepting are the formation of an international tournament, the use of substitutes and the use of floodlights.

FOOTBALL LEAGUE

The Football League was founded at a meeting at the Royal Hotel, Piccadilly, Manchester in April 1888. The prime mover behind the new body was Aston Villa director William McGregor, who became the league's first President.

• The 12 founder members were Accrington, Aston Villa, Blackburn Rovers, Bolton Wanderers, Burnley, Derby County, Everton, Notts County, Preston North End, Stoke City, West Bromwich Albion and Wolverhampton Wanderers. At the end of the inaugural 1888/89 season, Preston were crowned champions.

• In 1892 a new Second Division, absorbing clubs from the rival Football Alliance, was added to the league and by 1905 the two divisions were made up of a total of 40 clubs. After the First World War, the league was expanded again to include a Third Division.

TOP 10

LEAGUE GOALS 2018/19

1.	Manchester City	95
2.	Norwich City	93
3.	Luton Town	90
4.	Liverpool	89
5.	West Bromwich Albion	87
6.	Portsmouth	83
7.	Aston Villa	82
	Bury	82
9.	Barnsley	80
	Sunderland	80

• A further expansion after 1945 took the number of clubs playing in the league to its long-time total of 92. The formation of the Premier League in 1992 reduced the Football League to three divisions – now known as the Championship, League One and League Two.

• As well as being the governing body for the three divisions, the Football League also organises two knock-out competitions: the League Cup (now the EFL Cup) and the EFL Trophy.

• Before the formation of the Premier League Liverpool won the First Division a record 18 times, while Leicester City were Second Division champions a record six times.

FOOTBALLER OF THE YEAR

Confusingly, there are two Footballer of the Year awards in England and Scotland. The Football Writers' Association award was inaugurated in 1948, and the first winner was England winger Stanley Matthews. In 1974 the Professional Footballers' Association (PFA) set up their own award, Leeds hard man Norman 'Bites Yer Legs' Hunter being the first to be honoured by his peers.

• Liverpool midfielder Terry McDermott was the first player to win both awards in the same season after helping Liverpool retain the title in 1980. A total of 19 different players have won both Footballer of the Year awards in the same season, most recently Liverpool's Mohamed Salah in 2018. Former Arsenal striker Thierry Henry won a record five awards, landing the 'double' in both 2003 and 2004, and also carrying off the Football Writers' award in 2006.

• Among overseas players those from France have won the Football Writers' Association award a record seven times and the PFA honour a record five times. Vive la France!

Football Writers' Player of the Year (Premier League era)
1993 Chris Waddle (Sheffield Wednesday)
1994 Alan Shearer (Blackburn Rovers)
1995 Jurgen Klinsmann (Tottenham)
1996 Eric Cantona (Manchester Utd)
1997 Gianfranco Zola (Chelsea)
1998 Dennis Bergkamp (Arsenal)
1999 David Ginola (Tottenham)
2000 Roy Keane (Manchester Utd)
2001 Teddy Sheringham (Manchester Utd)
2002 Robert Pires (Arsenal)
2003 Thierry Henry (Arsenal)
2004 Thierry Henry (Arsenal)
2005 Frank Lampard (Chelsea)
2006 Thierry Henry (Arsenal)
2007 Cristiano Ronaldo (Manchester Utd)
2008 Cristiano Ronaldo (Manchester Utd)
2009 Steven Gerrard (Liverpool)
2010 Wayne Rooney (Manchester Utd)
2011 Scott Parker (West Ham Utd)
2012 Robin van Persie (Arsenal)
2013 Gareth Bale (Tottenham)
2014 Luis Suarez (Liverpool)
2015 Eden Hazard (Chelsea)
2016 Jamie Vardy (Leicester City)
2017 N'Golo Kante (Chelsea)
2018 Mohamed Salah (Liverpool)
2019 Raheem Sterling (Manchester City)

PFA Footballer of the Year (Premier League era)
1993 Paul McGrath (Aston Villa)
1994 Eric Cantona (Manchester Utd)
1995 Alan Shearer (Blackburn Rovers)
1996 Les Ferdinand (Newcastle Utd)
1997 Alan Shearer (Newcastle Utd)
1998 Dennis Bergkamp (Arsenal)
1999 David Ginola (Tottenham)
2000 Roy Keane (Manchester Utd)
2001 Teddy Sheringham (Manchester Utd)
2002 Ruud van Nistelrooy (Manchester Utd)
2003 Thierry Henry (Arsenal)
2004 Thierry Henry (Arsenal)
2005 John Terry (Chelsea)
2006 Steven Gerrard (Liverpool)
2007 Cristiano Ronaldo (Manchester Utd)
2008 Cristiano Ronaldo (Manchester Utd)
2009 Ryan Giggs (Manchester Utd)
2010 Wayne Rooney (Manchester Utd)
2011 Gareth Bale (Tottenham)
2012 Robin van Persie (Arsenal)
2013 Gareth Bale (Tottenham)
2014 Luis Suarez (Liverpool)
2015 Eden Hazard (Chelsea)
2016 Riyad Mahrez (Leicester City)
2017 N'Golo Kante (Chelsea)
2018 Mohamed Salah (Liverpool)
2019 Virgil van Dijk (Liverpool)

Forest Green Rovers (dark strip) reached the League Two play-offs in 2019 but were beaten by Tranmere

FOREST GREEN ROVERS

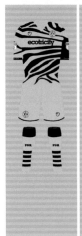

Year founded: 1889
Ground: The New Lawn (5,141)
Previous names: Forest Green, Nailsworth & Forest Green United, Stroud FC
Nickname: Rovers
Biggest win: 8-0 v Hyde (2013)
Heaviest defeat: 0-10 v Gloucester (1900)

Now owned by green energy tycoon Dale Vince, Forest Green Rovers were founded in Nailsworth, Gloucestershire by a local church minister in 1889 and five years later were founder members of the mid-Gloucestershire league. During more than a century in the non-league wilderness the club was briefly renamed Nailsworth & Forest Green United (1911) and Stroud FC (1989).

• **Rovers were finally promoted to the Football League following a 3-1 win against Tranmere Rovers in the 2017 National League play-off final at Wembley. Two years later they came close to reaching the third tier, but were beaten 2-1 on aggregate by Tranmere Rovers in the League Two play-off semi-finals.**

• In Rovers' two seasons in the Football League striker Christian Doidge has scored a club record 34 league goals, while midfielder Reece Brown has made the most league appearances with 88.

• **Powered by renewable energy, Forest Green Rovers were named as the world's very first carbon neutral football club by the United Nations in July 2018.**

• With a population of just 5,794 Nailsworth is the smallest place ever to have a Football League club.

FRANCE

First international: Belgium 3 France 3, 1904
Most capped player: Lilian Thuram, 142 caps (1994-2008)
Leading goalscorer: Thierry Henry, 51 goals (1997-2010)
First World Cup appearance: France 4 Mexico 1, 1930
Biggest win: France 10 Azerbaijan 0, 1995
Heaviest defeat: France 1 Denmark 17, 1908

The third most successful European football nation ever, France have won both the World Cup and the European championships twice. The most recent of those triumphs came in 2018 when a French side including Premier League stars like Paul Pogba, N'Golo Kante and skipper Hugo Lloris beat Croatia 4-2 in the World Cup final in the Luzhniki stadium, Moscow.

• **Twenty years earlier, France won the World Cup for the first time on home soil in 1998 with a stunning 3-0 victory over Brazil in the final in Paris. Midfield genius Zinedine Zidane was the star of the show, scoring two headed goals. The team also included Didier Deschamps, France's manager in 2018 and one of just three men (along with Brazil's Mario Zagallo and West Germany's Franz Beckenbauer) to win the World Cup as both a player and a coach.**

• In 2000 France became the first World Cup holders to go on to win the European Championship when they overcame Italy in the final in Rotterdam. This, though, was a much closer affair with the French requiring a 'golden goal' by striker David Trezeguet in extra-time to claim the trophy.

• **France had won the European Championship once before, in 1984. Inspired by the legendary Michel Platini, who scored a record nine goals in the tournament, Les Bleus beat Spain 2-0 in the final in Paris. In 2016 France had another chance to win the**

France's 2018 World Cup win put smiles on the faces of N'Golo Kante and Blaise Matuidi

trophy on home soil but surprisingly lost 1-0 in the final to Portugal after extra-time.

• French striker Just Fontaine scored an all-time record 13 goals at the 1958 World Cup finals in Sweden. His remarkable strike rate helped his country finish third in the tournament.

• Former Bordeaux defender Franck Jurietti set a record for the shortest international career ever when he came on for the last five seconds of France's 4-0 win over Cyprus in October 2005 and never played for his country again.

HONOURS
World Cup winners *1998, 2018*
European Championship winners *1984, 2000*
Confederations Cup winners *2001, 2003*
World Cup Record
1930 Round 1
1934 Round 1
1938 Round 2
1950 Did not qualify
1954 Round 1
1958 Third place
1962 Did not qualify
1966 Round 1
1970 Did not qualify
1974 Did not qualify
1978 Round 1
1982 Fourth place
1986 Third place
1990 Did not qualify
1994 Did not qualify

1998 Winners
2002 Round 1
2006 Runners-up
2010 Round 1
2014 Quarter-finals
2018 Winners

RYAN FRASER

Born: Aberdeen, 24th February 1994
Position: Winger
Club career:
2010-13 Aberdeen 21 (0)
2013- Bournemouth 155 (19)
2015-16- Ipswich Town (loan) 18 (4)
International record:
2017- Scotland 7 (1)

Hyper-active winger Ryan Fraser, taking a rare breather for Bournemouth

Industrious Bournemouth winger Ryan Fraser was his club's outstanding performer in the 2018/19 Premier League season, contributing 14 assists – a tally only bettered by Chelsea talisman Eden Hazard.

• **A tireless player whose short stature helps him squeeze past much bigger defenders, Fraser started out with his hometown club Aberdeen, making his senior debut against Hearts in October 2010 when he was aged just 16.**

• In January 2013 he moved on to Bournemouth for a bargain £400,000, immediately helping his new club gain promotion to the Championship. Two years later he was part of the Cherries' team which went up to the Premier League, but he was then loaned out to Ipswich Town for the whole of the following season.

• **Fraser made his debut for Scotland in June 2017 in an exciting 2-2 draw with England, but two years later was widely criticised after refusing to play in a Euro 2020 qualifier in Kazakhstan over fears that he might be injured on the hosts' artificial pitch.**

FREE KICKS

A method for restarting the game after an infringement, free kicks may either be direct (meaning a goal can be scored directly) or indirect (in which case a second player must touch the ball before a goal can be scored).

• Brazilian midfielder Juninho Pernambucano holds the world record for the most goals scored direct from a free kick with 76, most of them coming during his time at French club Lyon between 2001 and 2009. Incredibly, the record for the most free kicks scored by a player for just one club is held by a goalkeeper, Rogerio Ceni of Sao Paulo with 61.

• David Beckham holds the record for the most Premier League goals direct from free kicks with 15 for Manchester United between 1993 and 2003 and his total of 65 goals from dead balls outside the box is a record for a British player. Manchester United's Cristiano Ronaldo (2007/08) and Manchester City's Yaya Toure (2013/14) jointly hold the record for the most goals from free kicks in a single Premier League campaign, with four each.

• Tottenham and England goalkeeper Paul Robinson scored the longest-range free kick in Premier League history when he walloped one in from an incredible 96 yards against Watford on 17th March 2007.

• The last player to score direct from a free kick in the Champions League final was Bayern Munich's Mario Basler, who curled one around the Manchester United wall and in at the far post in his side's eventual 2-1 defeat in Barcelona in 1999.

• Vanishing spray from an aerosol can to mark the 10 yards defenders must retreat from an attacking free kick was introduced to the Premier League at the start of the 2014/15 season. The spray was first used at an international tournament in the 2011 Copa America and made its debut at the World Cup in Brazil in 2014.

FRIENDLIES

The first official international friendly took place on 30th November 1872 between Scotland and England at the West of Scotland Cricket Ground, Partick, Glasgow. The Scottish side for the match, which ended in a 0-0 draw, was made up entirely of players from the country's leading club, Queen's Park.

• England's most famous ever friendly was against Hungary at Wembley on 25th November 1953. The Three Lions were unbeaten at home in their entire history against continental opposition but crashed to a humiliating 6-3 defeat in the so-called 'Match of the Century'.

• On 6th February 2007 London played host to a record four international friendlies on the same night – and England weren't even one of the eight teams in action! At the Emirates Stadium Portugal beat Brazil 2-0, Ghana thrashed Nigeria 4-1 at Brentford's Griffin Park, South Korea beat European champions Greece 1-0 at Craven Cottage, while at Loftus Road Denmark were 3-1 winners over Australia.

• Then England manager Sven-Goran Eriksson became the first Three Lions boss to substitute all 11 starters in a 2-1 friendly defeat to Italy in 2002. However, two years later FIFA ruled that the maximum number of substitutes that could be used in an international friendly would be limited to six per team.

FULHAM

Year founded: 1879
Ground: Craven Cottage (25,700)
Previous name: Fulham St Andrew's
Nickname: The Cottagers
Biggest win: 10-1 v Ipswich Town (1963)
Heaviest defeat: 0-10 v Liverpool (1986)

London's oldest club, Fulham were founded in 1879 by two clergymen. Originally known as Fulham St Andrew's, the club adopted its present name nine years later. After winning the Southern League in two consecutive seasons Fulham were elected to the Football League in 1907.

• Before moving to Craven Cottage in 1896, Fulham had played at no fewer than 11 different grounds. Including a stay at Loftus Road from 2002-04 while the Cottage was being redeveloped, Fulham have played at 13 venues, a total only exceeded by QPR.

• The proudest moment in the club's history came in May 2010 when Fulham met Atletico Madrid in Hamburg in the first Europa League final. Sadly for their fans, the Cottagers lost 2-1 in extra-time despite putting up a spirited fight.

• In 1975 Fulham reached the FA Cup final for the first (and so far only) time, losing 2-0 to West Ham. The Cottagers have appeared in the semi-final six times, including a forgettable occasion in 1908 when they were hammered 6-0 by Newcastle, to this day the biggest ever winning margin at that stage of the competition.

• Midfield legend Johnny Haynes holds the club's appearance record, turning out in 594 league games between 1952 and 1970. 'The Maestro', as he was known to Fulham fans, is also the club's most honoured player at international level, with 56 England caps. Welsh international striker Gordon Davies is Fulham's top scorer with 159 league goals in two spells at the club between 1978 and 1991.

• Relegated from the Premier League in 2019, Fulham made their record signing when they bought Cameroon international midfielder Andre Anguissa from Marseille for £22.3 million in August 2018. Midfielder Mousa Dembele became the Cottagers' record sale when he moved to Tottenham for £18 million in August 2012.

• Fulham's biggest ever win, 10-1 against Ipswich on Boxing Day 1963, was the last time a team scored double figures in the English top flight.

• In 2013/14 Fulham used a Premier League record 39 different players, although their large squad didn't do them much good as they were relegated to the Championship at the end of the season.

HONOURS
First Division champions 2001
Division 2 champions 1949
Second Division champions 1999
Division 3 (South) champions 1932

Bobby Reid is hoping to fire the Cottagers back to the Premier League

DAVID DE GEA

Born: Madrid, 7th November 1990
Position: Goalkeeper
Club career:
2008-09 Atletico Madrid B 35
2009-11 Atletico Madrid 57
2011- Manchester United 275
International record:
2014- Spain 39

Manchester United's David de Gea has been voted into the PFA Team of the Year five times, most recently at the end of the 2017/18 season, to set a record for the Premier League era (although he has some way to go to match Peter Shilton's 10 selections in the 1970s and 1980s).

• After coming through the youth ranks at Atletico Madrid, De Gea enjoyed a great first season with Atleti, helping them win the Europa League in

"Remember – if I let a goal in, it's all your lot's fault"

2010 following a 2-1 victory against Fulham in the final in Hamburg. The next summer he moved on to Manchester United for around £18 million, then a record fee for a goalkeeper in the British game.

• Following some unconvincing early performances for United De Gea was dropped to the bench, but after winning his place back his form soon improved. In 2013 he helped United win the Premier League title and he has since added the FA Cup (2016) and League Cup (2017) to his list of honours. In 2018 he won the Golden Glove award after keeping 18 clean sheets in the Premier League but the following season his form dipped as United endured a difficult campaign.

• De Gea has won the BBC's 'Save of the Season' an incredible five times since it was introduced in 2013, easily the best record of any keeper. Manchester United's Player of the Year in 2014, 2015, 2016 and 2018, De Gea is the only player in the club's history to win this award three times on the trot.

• De Gea made his first appearance for Spain in a 2-0 friendly win against El Salvador in June 2014. He started all of Spain's four games at the 2018

World Cup but didn't enjoy the best of tournaments, conceding six goals from just seven shots on target.

GERMANY

First international:
Switzerland 5 Germany 3, 1908
Most capped player:
Lothar Matthaus, 150 caps (1980-2000)
Leading goalscorer:
Miroslav Klose, 71 goals (2001-14)
First World Cup appearance: Germany 5 Belgium 2, 1934
Biggest win: Germany 16 Russian Empire 0, 1912
Heaviest defeat: Austria 6 Germany 0, 1931

Germany (formerly West Germany) have the joint second best record in the World Cup behind Brazil, having won the tournament four times and reached the final on a record eight occasions. They have also won the European Championship a joint-record three times and been losing finalists on another three occasions.

• **The Germans recorded their fourth World Cup triumph in Brazil in 2014, when they beat Argentina 1-0 in the final thanks to Mario Gotze's extra-time goal.** Perhaps more remarkable, though, was their performance in the semi-final when they massacred the hosts 7-1 – the biggest ever win at that late stage of the competition and one of the most amazing World Cup scorelines ever. Germany's other victories came in 1954 (against Hungary), on home soil in 1974 (against the Netherlands) and at Italia 90 (against Argentina).

• Lothar Matthaus, a powerhouse in the German midfield for two decades, played in a record 25 matches at the World Cup in five tournaments between 1982 and 1998. His total of 150 caps for Germany is also a national record.

• **Germany striker Miroslav Klose is the all-time leading scorer at the World Cup with a total of 16 goals, one ahead of Brazil's Ronaldo and two better than fellow German Gerd 'the Bomber' Muller.**

• Between 10th July 2010 and 22nd June 2012 Germany won a world record 15

Germany's Miroslav Klose, scoring one of his record 16 World Cup goals, this time against Ecuador in 2006

competitive matches on the trot – a run which ended when they lost 2-1 to Italy in the semi-final of Euro 2012.

• Germany hold the record for both the biggest win in the European Championship qualifiers (13-0 against San Marino in 2006) and the UEFA section of the World Cup qualifiers (a 12-0 tonking of Cyprus in 1969).

HONOURS
World Cup winners *1954, 1974, 1990, 2014*
European Championship winners *1972, 1980, 1996*
Confederations Cup winners *2017*
World Cup Record
1930 Did not enter
1934 Third place
1938 Round 1
1950 Did not enter
1954 Winners
1958 Fourth place
1962 Quarter-finals
1966 Runners-up
1970 Third place
1974 Winners
1978 Round 2
1982 Runners-up
1986 Runners-up
1990 Winners
1994 Quarter-finals
1998 Quarter-finals
2002 Runners-up
2006 Third place
2010 Third place
2014 Winners
2018 Round 1

STEVEN GERRARD

Born: Whiston, 30th May 1980
Managerial career:
2018- Rangers

Appointed Rangers manager in June 2018 after an 18-month spell as Liverpool youth team coach, Anfield legend Steven Gerrard enjoyed a decent first season in the Ibrox hotseat, guiding his club to second place in the Scottish Premiership behind arch rivals Celtic.

• Famed for his surging runs and thunderous shooting, Gerrard is the only player to have scored in the FA Cup final, the League Cup final, the UEFA Cup final and the Champions League final. He achieved this feat between 2001 and 2006 while winning all four competitions

with the Reds (and, indeed, earning winner's medals in the FA Cup and League Cup on two occasions).

• By the time he decided to move on to LA Galaxy in 2015 he had made more than 500 Premier League appearances for the Reds, one of just three players (along with Ryan Giggs and former team-mate Jamie Carragher) to reach that milestone with one club.

• In the 2006 FA Cup final Gerrard scored two stunning goals against West Ham, including a last-minute equaliser which many rate as the best ever goal in the final. Liverpool went on to win the match on penalties and Gerrard's heroics were rewarded with the 2006 PFA Player of the Year award. Three years later he was voted Footballer of the Year by the football writers. Then, in 2014, he was voted into the PFA Team

Steven Gerrard frankly looks like he could still do a job in Rangers' midfield...

of the Year for a Premier League-era record eighth time.

• Gerrard made his international debut for England against Ukraine in 2000 and scored his first goal for his country with a superb 20-yarder in the famous 5-1 thrashing of Germany in Berlin in 2001. He captained England at the 2010 and 2014 World Cups and at the 2012 European Championships. With 114 caps, Gerrard is fourth on the list of England's all-time appearance makers behind Peter Shilton, David Beckham and fellow Liverpudlian Wayne Rooney.

GIANT-KILLING

Many of the most remarkable instances of giant-killing have occurred in the FA Cup, with teams from lower down the football pyramid beating supposedly superior opposition. The first shock of this type occurred in 1888 when non-league Warwick County beat First Division Stoke City 2-1 in the first qualifying round of the competition.

• **Only two non-league teams have beaten Premier League outfits in the FA Cup, Luton Town sensationally beating Norwich City 1-0 in the fourth round in 2013 and Lincoln City surprising Burnley by the same score in the fifth round in 2017.**

• In their non-league days Yeovil Town beat a record 20 league teams in the FA Cup. The Glovers' most famous win came in the fourth round in 1949 against First Division Sunderland, who they defeated 2-1 on their notorious sloping pitch at Huish Park.

• In the Premier League era the most notable year for giant-killings was 2007/08 when only six of the 16 teams to reach the FA Cup fifth round were from the top tier – just one short of the record of five set in 1957/58.

• Giant-killings also happen at international level. Among the shocks to

IS THAT A FACT?
National League side Barnet pulled off the biggest giant-killing act of the 2018/19 season, winning 1-0 at Championship club Sheffield United in the third round of the FA Cup.

befall the Home Nations, for instance, are England's 2-1 defeat by minnows Iceland at Euro 2016, and Scotland's unexpected 1-0 loss to underdogs Costa Rica at the 1990 World Cup.

RYAN GIGGS

> **Born:** Cardiff, 29th November 1973
> **Managerial career:**
> 2014 Manchester United (caretaker)
> 2018- Wales

He may be a novice, but Ryan Giggs has already mastered the 'glum manager' look

Appointed Wales manager in January 2018, Ryan Giggs got off to the best ever start of any Dragons boss when his side annihilated China 6-0 in his first match in charge. Since then, though, his record has been rather mixed.

• **In a glorious career with Manchester United, Ryan Giggs became the most decorated player in English football history. Between 1991 and 2014, when he announced his retirement from the game, he won 22 major honours: a record 13 Premier League titles, four FA Cups, three League Cups and two Champions League trophies. In addition, in 2009 he was voted PFA Player of the Year by his fellow professionals.**

• A one-club man who briefly filled in as caretaker manager in 2014, Giggs made a record 963 appearances for United in all competitions – 205 more than the previous record holder, Sir Bobby Charlton. His total of 632 Premier League appearances is only bettered by Gareth Barry.

• **Giggs enjoyed his best ever year in 1999 when he won the Premiership, FA Cup and Champions League with**

United. His goal against Arsenal in that season's FA Cup semi-final, when he dribbled past four defenders before smashing the ball into the roof of the net from a tight angle, was voted the best of the past 50 years by *Match of the Day* viewers in 2015.

• Once Wales' youngest ever player, Giggs previously played for England Schoolboys under the name Ryan Wilson (the surname being that of his father, a former Welsh rugby league player). However, having no English grandparents, Giggs was ineligible to play for the England national team and was proud to represent Wales on 64 occasions before retiring from international football in 2007.

GILLINGHAM

> **Year founded:** 1893
> **Ground:** Priestfield Stadium (11,582)
> **Previous name:** New Brompton
> **Nickname:** The Gills
> **Biggest win:** 12-1 v Gloucester City (1946)
> **Heaviest defeat:** 2-9 v Nottingham Forest (1950)

Founded by a group of local businessmen as New Brompton in 1893, the club changed to its present name in 1913. Seven years later Gillingham joined the new Third Division but in 1938 were voted out of the league in favour of Ipswich Town. They eventually returned in 1950.

• **Goalkeeper John Simpson played in a record 571 league games for the Gills between 1957 and 1972, while his team-mate Brian Yeo scored a club record 136 goals.**

• Midfielder Andrew Crofts won a club record 12 caps for Wales between 2005 and 2009.

• **In their 1995/96 promotion campaign Gillingham only conceded 20 goals – a record for a 46-game season in the Football League.**

• Winger Luke Freeman became the youngest ever player in the FA Cup proper when he came on as a sub for Gillingham against Barnet in 2007 aged just 15 years and 233 days.

> **HONOURS**
> *League Two champions* 2013
> *Division 4 champions* 1964

Chelsea's Olivier Giroud, top scorer in the 2018/19 Europa League with 11 goals

OLIVIER GIROUD

Born: Chambery, France, 30th September 1986
Position: Striker
Club career:
2005-08 Grenoble 23 (2)
2007-08 Istres (loan) 33 (14)
2008-10 Tours 44 (24)
2010-12 Montpellier 73 (33)
2010 Tours (loan) 17 (6)
2012-18 Arsenal 180 (73)
2018- Chelsea 40 (5)
International record:
2011- France 90 (35)

Chelsea striker Olivier Giroud was the key figure in the Blues' 2019 Europa League triumph, scoring 11 goals in total – a tally unmatched in a single European season by any other French player – including one in the final, a 4-1 thrashing of his former club Arsenal in Baku.

• **A tall, powerful striker who finishes well on the ground and in the air, Giroud first came to the fore when he was top scorer in the French second division with Tours in 2009/10, his goalscoring feats also earning him the Ligue 2 Player of the Year award.**

• A move to Montpellier followed, and in only his second season with the club Giroud helped the southern French side win the league for the first time in their history. The striker's 21 goals during the campaign made him the league's joint-top scorer and were instrumental in Montpellier's surprise success.

• **Later that summer he joined Arsenal for £9.6 million and he went on to hit double figures in all five of his complete seasons with the Gunners. He also won the FA Cup three times with the north Londoners and, after joining Chelsea for £18 million in January 2018, became only the third outfield foreign player to lift the cup four times when the Blues beat Manchester United 1-0 in the final later that year.**

• Giroud won his first cap for France in a 1-0 friendly win over the USA in 2011. In June 2017 he became the first player to score a hat-trick for his country for 17 years when he hit a treble in a 5-0 demolition of Paraguay and the following year Giroud was part of the France team that won the World Cup after a 4-2 win against Croatia in the final in Moscow.

GOAL CELEBRATIONS

Elaborate and sometimes spectacular goal celebrations have been a feature of English football since the mid-1990s when the Premier League started opening its doors to large numbers of overseas players. Middlesbrough striker Fabrizio Ravanelli, for instance, was famed for pulling his shirt over his head after scoring, and soon players were removing their shirts altogether, sometimes to reveal personal, political or religious messages written on a t-shirt.

• **In 2003 FIFA decided that things had got out of hand and ruled that any player removing his shirt would be booked. The first player to be sent off after falling foul of this new law was Everton's Tim Cahill, who was shown a second yellow against Manchester City in 2004.**

• In 2013 West Brom striker Nicolas Anelka was fined a record £80,000 by the FA and banned for five matches after celebrating a goal at West Ham by placing his arm across his chest in a gesture known as the 'quenelle' which, especially in Anelka's native France, carries anti-semitic connotations. The former France star was subsequently sacked by his club for gross misconduct.

• **Denmark striker Nicklas Bendtner was fined £80,000 by UEFA at Euro 2012 after celebrating a goal against Portugal by lowering his shorts and revealing the logo of gambling company Paddy Power branded on his underpants.**

• Brazilian striker Anderson Lopes celebrated a goal for Consadole

Will this Raheem Sterling goal celebration catch on? Time will tell...

Sapporo in their J-League match against Shimizu S-Pulse on 9th March 2019 by jumping over an advertising hoarding – only to find there was an alarmingly steep drop on the other side! After falling to the ground Lopes required medical attention but was not seriously injured.

• Wolves striker Raul Jimenez celebrated his goal in the 2019 FA Cup semi-final against Watford at Wembley by donning a gold mask emblazoned with the club crest. However, the Hornets had the last laugh as they came back from two goals down to win 3-2.

• On 6th March 2019 Luis Acuna of Guatemalan second division side Deportivo Carcha celebrated a late winner by running behind the goal, climbing a ladder and changing the scoreboard to '1-0'. The referee was distinctly unimpressed and showed him the yellow card.

GOAL OF THE SEASON

The Goal of the Season award has been awarded by the BBC's flagship football programme *Match of the Day* since 1971 (apart from the years 2001-04 when, for broadcasting rights reasons, the award was given by ITV). The 2019 winner was Manchester City captain Vincent Kompany, who topped the poll with a thunderous long-range shot against Leicester City.

• Manchester United striker Wayne Rooney is the only player to win the award three times, most recently in 2011 for an acrobatic overhead kick against local rivals Manchester City. Liverpool's John Aldridge (in 1988 and 1989) and Arsenal's Jack Wilshere (in 2014 and 2015) are the only two players to have won the award in consecutive seasons.

• Just two players have won the award while on international duty: Kenny Dalglish, playing for Scotland against Belgium in 1983 and Bryan Robson for England against Israel three years later.

• On 15 occasions FA Cup matches have produced the winning goal, most recently Steven Gerrard for a blistering shot in the 2006 final for Liverpool against West Ham at the Millennium Stadium.

GOALKEEPERS

• On 27th March 2011 Sao Paulo's Rogerio Ceni became the first goalkeeper in the history of football to score 100 career goals when he netted with a free kick in a 2-1 win against Corinthians. His unlikely century was made up of 56 free kicks and 44 penalties. By the time he retired in 2015 Ceni had taken his career goals total to 131 – better than countless outfield players!

• Just five goalkeepers have scored in the Premier League: Peter Schmeichel (Aston Villa), Brad Friedel (Blackburn Rovers), Paul Robinson (Tottenham), Tim Howard (Everton) and Asmir Begovic (Stoke City). Begovic's goal after just 13 seconds against Southampton in November 2013 is the fastest ever by a goalkeeper in English football history and was scored at a greater distance (91.9 metres) than any goal ever.

• Paraguay goalkeeper Jose Luis Chilavert scored a record eight international goals, including one from the penalty spot against Colombia in 1989. 'The Bulldog', as he was nicknamed, is also the only goalkeeper ever to score a hat-trick, finding the net three times for Argentinian side Velez Sarfield against Ferro Carril in 1999.

• In a long career for Derby County and Bradford Park Avenue between 1907 and 1925, Ernie Scattergood scored eight penalties – a record number of goals for a goalkeeper in the Football League.

• The most-capped goalkeeper in history is Mohamed Al-Deayea, who turned out 178 times for Saudi Arabia between 1993 and 2006. In the women's game, Perth-born Gemma Fay played a record 203 times in goal for Scotland between 1998 and 2017.

GOALS

Manchester City scored a Premier League record 106 goals on their way to the title in the 2017/18 season. Altogether less impressively, Derby County managed just 20 goals during the 2007/08 Premier League season. Swindon Town hold the unwanted record for the most goals conceded in a Premier League campaign, with 100 in 1993/94.

• Peterborough United hold the record for the most league goals in a season, banging in 134 in 1960/61 on their way to claiming the Fourth Division title. In 1937/38 Raith Rovers scored an incredible 142 goals in just 34 games in the Scottish Second Division to set a British record which still stands to this day.

• Aston Villa hold the top-flight record, with 128 goals in 1930/31. Despite their prolific attack, the Villans were pipped

Asmir Begovic, demonstrating the kicking power which helped him score from a record 91.9 metres in 2013

to the First Division title by Arsenal (amazingly, the Gunners managed 127 goals themselves).

• Arthur Rowley scored a record 434 Football League goals between 1946 and 1965, notching four for West Brom, 27 for Fulham, 251 for Leicester City and 152 for Shrewsbury. Former Republic of Ireland international John Aldridge is the overall leading scorer in post-war English football, with an impressive total of 476 goals in all competitions for Newport County, Oxford United, Liverpool and Tranmere between 1979 and 1998.

• Joe Payne set an English Football League record for goals in a game by scoring 10 times for Luton against Bristol Rovers on 13th April 1936. Earlier in the decade, Sheffield United striker Jimmy Dunne scored in a record 12 consecutive top-flight league games in the 1931/32 season. The Premier League record is held by Leicester City star Jamie Vardy, who scored in 11 games on the trot in 2015/16.

• In 1998 AIK Stockholm won the Swedish title despite being the lowest-scoring team in the league with a paltry 25 goals in 26 games. Incredibly, Ghana outfit Aduana Stars matched this feat in 2010, scoring just 19 goals in 30 matches.

• Sheffield United striker Billy Sharp is the leading goalscorer in the Football League in the 21st century with 227 goals for a variety of clubs, including the Blades, Doncaster Rovers and Scunthorpe United.

• Manchester City scored a total of 169 goals in all competitions in the 2018/19 season to set a new record for an English top-flight side.

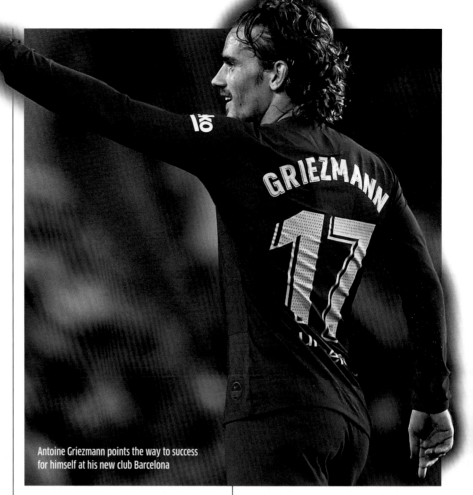

Antoine Griezmann points the way to success for himself at his new club Barcelona

ANTOINE GRIEZMANN

Born: Macon, France, 21st March 1991
Position: Striker
Club career:
2009-14 Real Sociedad 179 (46)
2014-19 Atletico Madrid 180 (94)
2019- Barcelona
International record:
2014- France 70 (29)

In July 2019 Antoine Griezmann moved from Atletico Madrid to Barcelona for £107 million in the biggest ever transfer deal between two Spanish clubs.

• After being rejected by a number of clubs in his native France for being too small, Griezmann began his career with Real Sociedad in Spain, helping the Basque outfit win the Segunda Division in his debut campaign in 2009/10. A £24 million move to Atletico followed in 2014, and in his first season in the Spanish capital Griezmann was voted into the Team of the Year after scoring 22 league goals – a record for a French player in a single La Liga campaign. Following another fine season in 2015/16 he came third in the inaugural Best FIFA Men's Player award and in 2018 he scored twice in Atleti's 3-0 defeat of Lyon in the Europa League final.

• Griezmann's total of six goals at Euro 2016 helped him win the Player of the Tournament award and was the best return for a player since fellow Frenchman Michel Platini hit a record nine goals at the 1984 tournament.

• However, the nippy forward had to be satisfied with a runners-up medal after the hosts lost in the final to Portugal, and he also finished on the losing side in the 2016 Champions League final after his club, Atletico Madrid, lost on penalties to city rivals Real – a match in which Griezmann missed from the spot in normal time. The Frenchman thus became only the second player (after Michael Ballack in 2008) to lose in both finals in the same season.

• Two years later Griezmann became the first player to score a goal in the World Cup final with the help of the video assistant referee when he converted a penalty which was eventually awarded to France in the 2018 showpiece against Croatia. After France's 4-2 win Griezmann was named Man of the Match and he also picked up the Bronze Ball for the third best player at the tournament.

GRIMSBY TOWN

Year founded: 1878
Ground: Blundell Park (9,027)
Previous name: Grimsby Pelham
Nickname: The Mariners
Biggest win: 8-0 v Darlington (1885) and Tranmere Rovers (1925)
Heaviest defeat: 1-9 v Phoenix Bessemer (1882) and Arsenal (1931)

The club was founded at the Wellington Arms in 1878 as Grimsby Pelham (the

Pelhams being a local landowning family), becoming plain Grimsby Town a year later and joining the Second Division as founder members in 1892. After losing their Football League place in 2010, the Mariners returned to League Two in 2016 after beating Forest Green Rovers 3-1 in the National League play-off final at Wembley.

• **Grimsby enjoyed a glorious decade in the 1930s, when they were promoted to the top flight and reached two FA Cup semi-finals, losing to Arsenal in 1936 and Wolves three years later.**

• In 1909 Grimsby's Walter Scott became the first goalkeeper to save three penalties in a match. However, his heroics were in vain as the Mariners still lost 2-0 to Burnley.

• Prolific striker Pat Glover scored a club record 180 league goals for the Mariners, including a seasonal best of 42 in 1933/34. He also won seven caps for Wales, and remains Grimsby's most decorated international.

HONOURS
Division 2 champions 1901, 1934
Division 3 champions 1980
Division 3 (North) champions 1926, 1956
Division 4 champions 1972
EFL Trophy 1998

PEP GUARDIOLA

Born: Santpedor, Spain, 18th January 1971
Managerial career:
2007-08 Barcelona B
2008-12 Barcelona
2013-16 Bayern Munich
2016- Manchester City

In 2019 Manchester City boss Pep Guardiola became the first manager to win the English domestic Treble, his team clinching the final leg of the trio with a record-equalling 6-0 thrashing of Watford in the FA Cup final. The Spaniard was rewarded with the Premier League Manager of the Season award, which he had also collected the previous campaign when City won the title with a record 100 points.

• **Previously, with Barcelona, Guardiola became the only coach to lead a club to six trophies in a calendar year, claiming an amazing Sextuple in 2009 when his former charges won the Spanish title, the Copa del Rey, the Champions League, the Spanish Super Cup, the UEFA Super Cup and, finally, the FIFA Club World Cup.**

• After winning 14 trophies in four years – an impressive haul unmatched by any other Barcelona manager – Guardiola quit the Catalan club in 2012, citing

"tiredness" as the main reason for his decision. A year later he took over the reins at Bayern Munich and in his first season with the German giants in 2013/14 won the league and cup Double, the FIFA Club World Cup and the European Super Cup.

• He claimed two more Bundesliga titles with Bayern before moving to Manchester in July 2016. In his first season at the Etihad he endured the worst ever run of his managerial career when his new team went six games without a win in the autumn of 2016.

• A defensive midfielder in his playing days for Barcelona and Spain, Guardiola was a key member of Johan Cruyff's attack-minded 'Dream Team' which won the Catalans' first European Cup in 1992 and four La Liga titles in the early 1990s.

"Altogether now: 'We've got Guard-i-ola, we've got Guard-i-ola...'"

HAMILTON ACADEMICAL

Year founded: 1874
Ground: New Douglas Park (6,018)
Nickname: The Accies
Biggest win: 11-1 v Chryston (1885)
Heaviest defeat: 1-11 v Hibernian (1965)

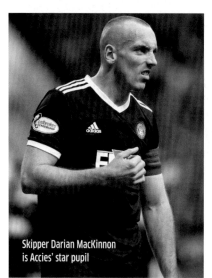

Skipper Darian MacKinnon is Accies' star pupil

Founded in 1874 by the Rector and pupils of Hamilton Academy, Hamilton Academical is the only professional club in Britain to have originated from a school team. Shortly after the start of the 1897/98 season, the Accies joined the Scottish League in place of Renton, who were forced to resign from the league for financial reasons.

• Hamilton fans have had little to cheer over the years, but the club did reach the Scottish Cup final in 1911 (losing to Celtic after a replay) and again in 1935 (losing to Rangers).

• English striker David Wilson scored a club record 246 goals for the Accies between 1928 and 1939, including a seasonal best of 34 in 1936/37.

• With a capacity of just 6,018, Hamilton's New Douglas Park ground is the smallest in the Scottish Premiership. In 2018 the Accies' artificial turf pitch was voted the worst playing surface among Scotland's 42 senior outfits, prompting the club to install a new 3G pitch at a cost of £750,000.

• Rugged defender Colin Miller won a club record 29 caps for Canada in his first of two spells at Hamilton between 1988 and 1993.

> **HONOURS**
> *First Division champions 1986, 1988, 2008*
> *Division 2 champions 1904*
> *Third Division champions 2001*

HAT-TRICKS

Geoff Hurst is the only player to have scored a hat-trick in a World Cup final, hitting three goals in England's 4-2 much-celebrated defeat of West Germany at Wembley in 1966.

• **Eighteen-year-old Tony Ross scored the fastest hat-trick in football history in 1964, taking just 90 seconds to complete a treble for Ross County in a Highland League match against Nairn County.**

• In 2004 Bournemouth's James Hayter scored the fastest hat-trick in Football League history, finding the net three times against Wrexham in just two minutes and 20 seconds. Sadio Mane holds the record for the fastest hat-trick in Premier League history, hitting a quick-fire treble for Southampton in a 6-1 rout of Aston Villa on 16th May 2015 in just two minutes and 56 seconds.

• **The legendary Dixie Dean scored a record 37 hat-tricks during his career, while his contemporary**

IS THAT A FACT?
Superstar rivals Lionel Messi and Cristiano Ronaldo are level on eight hat-tricks each in the Champions League. No other player has more than three.

George Camsell scored a record nine hat-tricks for Middlesbrough in the 1925/26 season.

• Japanese international Masashi Nakayama of Jubilo Iwata scored a world record four consecutive hat-tricks in the J League in April 1998.

• **Alan Shearer (Blackburn and Newcastle) and Sergio Aguero (Manchester City) have both scored a record 11 Premier League hat-tricks. In the whole history of the Premier League 333 hat-tricks have been scored, with players from Arsenal and Liverpool leading from the front with 39 each.**

• Just three players have scored hat-tricks in the European Cup final: Alfredo Di Stefano for Real Madrid in 1960; Ferenc Puskas, also for Real, in 1960 and 1962; and Pierino Prati for AC Milan in 1969.

• **The only player to score a hat-trick in the Women's World Cup final is Carli Lloyd, who struck three times for the USA in their 5-2 defeat of Japan in 2015.**

EDEN HAZARD

Born: Louviere, Belgium, 7th January 1991
Position: Midfielder
Club career:
2007-12 Lille 147 (36)
2012-19 Chelsea 245 (85)
2019- Real Madrid
International record:
2008- Belgium 102 (30)

A creative midfielder who possesses wonderful dribbling skills, Eden Hazard became the most expensive player in Real Madrid's history in June 2019 when he joined the Spanish giants from Chelsea for £89 million. The Belgian signed off with the Blues in some style, topping the Premier League assists chart with 15 and notching 16 goals himself before scoring twice in his side's 4-1 defeat of Arsenal in the Europa League final in Baku.

• **The son of footballers – his father played in the Belgian second tier, while his mother was a striker in the women's league – Hazard joined Lille when he was 14, making his debut for the first team just two years later. In his first full season, 2008/09, he became the first non-French player to win the Young Player of the Year award. He scooped the award again**

Eden is a real Hazard for opposition defenders!

the following season to become the first player to win it twice.

• In 2011, after completing a league and cup Double with Lille, Hazard was voted Player of the Year – aged 20, he was the youngest player to win the award. The following year he became only the second player to retain the trophy.

• After signing for Chelsea for £32 million in May 2012, Hazard collected a host of silverware with the Blues, including two Premier League titles in 2015 – when he topped both the PFA and Football Writers' Player of the Year polls – and 2017, and the FA Cup in 2018 when he scored the only goal of the game from the penalty spot against Manchester United in the final at Wembley.

• Hazard was first capped by Belgium, aged 17, against Luxembourg in 2008 and has gone on to win over 90 caps. He captained his country at Euro 2016 and the 2018 World Cup, where he was awarded the Silver Ball as the tournament's second best player behind Croatia's Luka Modric.

HEADERS

In September 2011 Jone Samuelsen of Odd Grenland scored with a header from 58.13 metres in a Norwegian top-flight match against Tromso to set a record for the longest distance headed goal. He was helped, though, by the fact that the Tromso goalkeeper had gone upfield for a corner, leaving his goal unguarded.

• Huddersfield striker Jordan Rhodes scored the fastest

"On me head, son!" Norwich's Todd Cantwell goes airborne

headed hat-trick in Football League history in 2009, nodding in three goals against Exeter City in eight minutes and 23 seconds to smash a record previously held by Everton legend Dixie Dean.

• Giraffe-like striker Peter Crouch holds the record for the most headed goals in Premier League history, with 53. In the 1995/96 Premier League season Wimbledon scored a record 22 headers.

• **Cristiano Ronaldo has scored a record 24 headed goals in the Champions League for Manchester United, Real Madrid and his current club, Juventus.**

• Only two players have scored headed hat-tricks in the Premier League: Duncan Ferguson for Everton against Bolton in 1997, and Salomon Rondon for West Brom against Swansea in 2016.

HEART OF MIDLOTHIAN

Year founded: 1874
Ground: Tynecastle (20,099)
Nickname: Hearts
Biggest win: 21-0 v Anchor (1880)
Heaviest defeat: 1-8 v Vale of Leven (1883)

Hearts were founded in 1874, taking their unusual name from a popular local dance hall which, in turn, was named after the famous novel *The Heart of the Midlothian* by Sir Walter Scott. The club were founder members of the Scottish League in 1890, winning their first title just five years later.

• **The club enjoyed a golden era in the late 1950s and early 1960s, when they won two league championships and five cups. In the first of those title triumphs in 1958 Hearts scored 132 goals, many of them coming from the so-called 'Terrible Trio' of Alfie Conn, Willie Bauld and Jimmy Wardhaugh. The total is still a record for the top flight in Scotland. In the same year Hearts conceded just 29 goals, giving them the best ever goal difference in British football, an incredible +103.**

• In 1965 Hearts came agonisingly close to winning the championship again when they were pipped by Kilmarnock on goal average after losing 2-0 at home to their

Hearts have won the Scottish Cup eight times, but lost 2-1 to Celtic in the 2019 final

title rivals on the last day of the season. Twenty-one years later they suffered a similar fate, losing the title on goal difference to Celtic after a surprise last-day defeat against Dundee. Annoyingly for their fans, on both occasions Hearts would have won the title if the alternative method for separating teams level on points had been in use.

• **The club's record goalscorer is John Robertson with 214 goals between 1983 and 1998. Midfielder Gary Mackay made a record 640 appearances for Hearts between 1980 and 1997.**

• Hearts won the Scottish Cup in 2012, thrashing local rivals Hibs 5-1

TOP 10

GOALS IN SCOTTISH TOP FLIGHT SEASON

1.	Hearts (1957/58)	132
2.	Motherwell (1931/32)	119
3.	Rangers (1931/32)	118
	Rangers (1933/34)	118
5.	Celtic (1915/16)	116
6.	Celtic (1935/36)	115
7.	Motherwell (1932/33)	114
	Celtic (1937/38)	114
9.	Rangers (1932/33)	113
10.	Rangers (1938/39)	112

in the final at Hampden Park – the biggest victory in the final since Hearts themselves were hammered by the same score by Rangers in 1996. It was the eighth time that Hearts had won the Scottish Cup, making them the fourth most successful club in the competition after Celtic, Rangers and Queen's Park.

• **Hearts made their best showing in European competition in 1988/89, reaching the quarter-finals of the UEFA Cup before losing 2-1 on aggregate to German titans Bayern Munich. In 2006 the Edinburgh outfit became the first club outside the 'Old Firm' to qualify for the Champions League but they failed to reach the group stages.**

• Relegated from the Premiership in 2014, Hearts bounced back by winning the Championship in fine style the following season with a second-tier record 91 points.

HONOURS

Division 1 champions 1895, 1897, 1958, 1960
Championship champions 2015
First Division champions 1980
Scottish Cup 1891, 1896, 1901, 1906, 1956, 1998, 2006, 2012
League Cup 1955, 1959, 1960, 1963

JORDAN HENDERSON

Born: Sunderland, 17th June 1990
Position: Midfielder
Club career:
2008-11 Sunderland 71 (4)
2009 Coventry City (loan) 10 (1)
2011- Liverpool 239 (22)
International record:
2010- England 51 (0)

A dynamic, energetic and tenacious midfielder, Liverpool skipper Jordan Henderson led his club to victory in the 2019 Champions League final, when the Reds beat Tottenham 2-0 in Madrid. The previous year he finished on the losing side in the final after a 3-1 defeat to Real Madrid in Kiev.

• **A product of the Black Cats' academy, Henderson was twice voted Sunderland Young Player of the Year after making his debut for his hometown club in a forgettable 5-0 defeat at Chelsea in November 2008. He joined Liverpool for around £20 million in 2011.**

• Henderson helped Liverpool win the League Cup in 2012, although he was substituted before the Reds' penalty shoot-out victory over Cardiff City in the final, and later that year played in Liverpool's 2-1 defeat by Chelsea in the

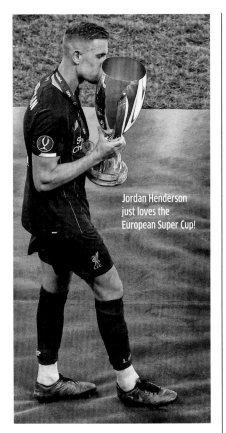
Jordan Henderson just loves the European Super Cup!

FA Cup final. After being made Liverpool captain in 2015, he led the Reds to the League Cup final the following year, but they lost on penalties to Manchester City.

• First capped by England in 2010, Henderson was named his country's Under-21 Player of the Year in 2012. He has since represented his country at four major tournaments, earning particular praise for his performances at the 2018 World Cup. However, despite accumulating 51 caps, Henderson is yet to register his first international goal – only five England outfield players, all of them defenders, have played more often for their country without once finding the net.

HIBERNIAN

Year founded: 1875
Ground: Easter Road (20,421)
Previous name: Hibernians
Nickname: Hibs
Biggest win: 22-1 v 42nd Highlanders (1881)
Heaviest defeat: 0-10 v Rangers (1898)

Founded in 1875 by Irish immigrants, the club took its name from the Roman word for Ireland, Hibernia. After losing many players to Celtic the club disbanded in 1891, but reformed and joined the Scottish League two years later.

• Hibs won the Scottish Cup for the first time in 1887 and lifted the same trophy again in 1902. However, they then had to wait 114 years before winning the cup again, beating Rangers 3-2 in a thrilling final in 2016 – the first ever between two clubs from outside the top flight.

• The club enjoyed a golden era after the Second World War, winning the league championship in three out of five seasons between 1948 and 1952 with a side managed by Hugh Shaw that included the 'Famous Five' forward line of Bobby Johnstone, Willie Ormond, Lawrie Reilly, Gordon Smith and Willie Turnbull. Reilly went on to score a record 187 league goals for the club, and is also Hibs' most decorated international, winning 38 caps for Scotland.

• In 1955 Hibs became the first British side to enter the European Cup, having been invited to participate in the new competition partly because their Easter Road ground had floodlights. They certainly did Scotland proud, reaching the semi-finals of the competition before falling 3-0 on aggregate to French side Reims.

• Hibs hold the British record for the biggest away win, thrashing Airdrie 11-1 on their own patch on 24th October 1959. As if to prove that the astonishing result was no fluke, they also hit double figures at Partick later that season, winning 10-2.

• When Hibs striker Joe Baker made his international debut against Northern Ireland in 1959 he became the first man to represent England while playing for a Scottish club. In the same season Baker scored an incredible 42 goals in just 33 league games to set a club record.

• Winger Arthur Duncan played in a club record record 446 league games for Hibs between 1969 and 1984.

HONOURS
Division 1 champions 1903, 1948, 1951, 1952
Championship champions 2017
First Division champions 1981, 1999
Division 2 champions 1894, 1895, 1933
Scottish Cup 1887, 1902, 2016
League Cup 1972, 1991, 2007

HOME AND AWAY

Brentford hold the all-time record for home wins in a season. In 1929/30 the Bees won all 21 of their home games at Griffin Park in Division Three (South). However, their away form was so poor that they missed out on promotion to champions Plymouth.

Happy Easter! Another goal for Hibs, this time by Christian Doidge

TOP 10

PREMIER LEAGUE HOME GOALS CONCEDED

1.	Swindon Town (1993/94)	45
2.	Derby County (2007/08)	43
	Wolves (2011/12)	43
4.	Bolton Wanderers (2011/12)	39
	Crystal Palace (1997/98)	39
	Wigan Athletic (2012/13)	39
7.	Cardiff City (2018/19)	38
	Fulham (2013/14)	38
9.	Blackpool (2010/11)	37
	Leicester City (1994/95)	37
	Sunderland (2005/06)	37

• The highest number of straight home wins is 25, a record set by Bradford Park Avenue in the Third Division (North) in 1926/27. Meanwhile, Manchester City won a record 20 home Premier League games on the trot between March 2011 and March 2012.

• Stockport's 13-0 win over Halifax in 1934 is the biggest home win in Football League history (equalled by Newcastle against Newport in 1946). Sheffield United hold the record for the most emphatic away win, thrashing Port Vale 10-0 way back in 1892.

• On their way to winning the title in 2009/10, Chelsea scored a record 68 Premier League goals at home. Liverpool hold the away record with an impressive 48 in 2013/14.

• Manchester City are the only club to have won 18 out of 19 home Premier League games on two occasions, in 2011/12 and 2018/19. City also racked up a record 16 away wins in 2017/18. Less impressively, Sunderland (2005/06) and Derby County (2007/08) hold the record for fewest home wins in a Premier League season, with just one. In the same dismal campaign Derby joined a list of six clubs who have failed to win on their travels.

STEPH HOUGHTON

Born: Durham, 23rd April 1988
Position: Defender
Club career:
2002-07 Sunderland Women
2007-10 Leeds United Ladies 45 (9)
2010-13 Arsenal Ladies 74 (11)
2014- Manchester City 81 (10)
International record:
2007- England 106 (12)

Girl Power: England captain Steph Houghton shows her skills at the 2019 World Cup

A central defender who carries a big threat at set pieces, Steph Houghton has been captain of the England Women's team since 2014. She has twice led England to the semi-finals of the World Cup, in 2015 and 2019, although her tournament ended in anguish on the second occasion when she missed a late penalty in the 2-1 defeat to the USA.

• Houghton started out with Sunderland Women, initially as a striker and then a midfielder before moving into defence, and was voted the Women's FA Young Player of the Year in 2007. In the same year she signed for Leeds United Ladies, with whom she won the FA Women's Premier League Cup in 2010.

• Greater success followed with Arsenal Ladies, including two Women's Super League titles and the Women's FA Cup in 2011 and 2013, Houghton scoring in the latter final after just two minutes in a 3-0 win against Bristol Academy.

• In 2014 she joined Manchester City, leading them to the league title in 2016 and the Women's FA Cup in both 2017 and 2019.

• The first woman ever to appear on the cover of *Shoot* magazine, Houghton has played for England since 2007 and also represented Great Britain at the 2012 London Olympic Games where she scored three goals in four games, including winners against both New Zealand and Brazil.

HUDDERSFIELD TOWN

Year founded: 1908
Ground: John Smith's Stadium (24,121)
Nickname: The Terriers
Biggest win: 11-0 v Heckmondwike (1909)
Heaviest defeat: 1-10 v Manchester City (1987)

Huddersfield Town were founded in 1908 following a meeting held at the local Imperial Hotel some two years earlier

– it took the club that long to find a ground to play at! The club were elected to the Second Division of the Football League two years later.

• The Terriers enjoyed a golden era in the 1920s when, under the shrewd management of the legendary Herbert Chapman, they won three consecutive league titles between 1924 and 1926 – no other club had matched this feat at the time and only three have done so since. The Terriers also won the FA Cup in 1922, beating Preston 1-0 at Stamford Bridge.

• Huddersfield won the first of their league titles in 1924 by pipping Cardiff on goal average, the first time ever the champions had been decided by this method.

• After 45 years outside the top flight Huddersfield finally returned to the big time when they beat Reading on penalties in the 2017 Championship play-off final. Huddersfield's unlikely promotion – they were the first club to go up to the Premier League despite having a negative goal difference (-2) – meant that they became only the second club (after Blackpool) to win three different divisional play-offs.

• However, the Terriers' stay lasted just two seasons, after they finished rock bottom of the Premier League in 2018/19 while setting unwanted club records for fewest points won (16), fewest goals scored (22) and fewest games won (three).

• Outside left Billy Smith made a record 521 appearances, scoring 114 goals, for Huddersfield between 1913 and 1934. Smith and his son, Conway, who started out with the Terriers before playing for QPR and Halifax, were the first father and son combination to both hit a century of goals in league football.

• Huddersfield's record scorer is England international George Brown, who notched 159 goals in all competitions between 1921 and 1929.

• The Terriers smashed their transfer record in June 2018 when they paid Monaco £17.5 million for Dutch defender Terence Kongolo, following a successful loan spell in Yorkshire. The club's coffers were boosted by a record £10 million in July 2018 when midfielder Tom Ince joined Stoke City.

> HONOURS
> **Division 1 champions** *1924, 1925, 1926*
> **Division 2 champions** *1970*
> **Division 4 champions** *1980*
> **FA Cup** *1922*

CALLUM HUDSON-ODOI

> **Born:** Wandsworth, 7th November 2000
> **Position:** Winger
> **Club career:**
> 2017- Chelsea 12 (0)
> **International record:**
> 2019- England 2 (0)

When he came on as a sub against the Czech Republic in a Euro 2020 qualifier aged 18 and 135 days in March 2019 Callum Hudson-Odoi became the youngest player to make his England debut in a competitive match.

• Hudson-Odoi joined Chelsea at the age of six and progressed through the club's academy to win two FA Youth Cups with the Blues. In January 2018 he made his first-team debut, featuring as a sub in a 3-0 victory over Newcastle in the FA Cup.

• In the January 2019 transfer window Hudson-Odoi was linked with a £30 million move to German giants Bayern Munich, but stayed with Chelsea and gradually started to play more regularly for the Blues until injury ruled him out of the final weeks of the season.

• In 2017 Hudson-Odoi played and scored for England in the final of the

Huddersfield, and their furry mascot Terry the Terrier, are rightly proud of their magnificent John Smith's Stadium

Callum Hudson-Odoi is an emerging star at Stamford Bridge

European Under-17 Championships, although opponents Spain eventually won the match on penalties. Later that year he was part of the much-heralded England team which won the Under-17 World Cup after a memorable 5-2 defeat of Spain in the final in Kolkata, India.

HULL CITY

Year founded: 1904
Ground: KC Stadium (25, 586)
Nickname: The Tigers
Biggest win: 11-1 v Carlisle United (1939)
Heaviest defeat: 0-8 v Wolves (1911)

Hull City were formed in 1904, originally sharing a ground with the local rugby league club. The Tigers joined the Football League in 1905 but failed to achieve promotion to the top flight until 2008.

• Hull enjoyed their best ever moment when they reached their first ever FA Cup final in 2014. The Tigers roared into a shock 2-0 lead against massive favourites Arsenal at Wembley, but eventually went down 3-2 after extra-time.

• In 2008 Hull first made it into the top flight thanks to a play-off final victory over Bristol City, with Dean Windass scoring the vital goal. The triumph meant that the Tigers had climbed from the bottom tier to the top in just five seasons – a meteoric rise only bettered in the past by Fulham, Swansea City and Wimbledon.

• The club's record goalscorer is Chris Chilton, who banged in 193 league goals in the 1960s and 1970s. His sometime team-mate Andy Davidson has pulled on a Hull shirt more than any other player at the club, making 520 league appearances between 1952 and 1968.

• In his first spell at Hull between 1991 and 1996, goalkeeper Alan Fettis played a number of games as a striker during an injury crisis. He did pretty well too, scoring two goals!

• In August 2016 Hull spent a club record £13 million on midfielder Ryan Mason. The Tigers received a club record £17 million when Harry Maguire moved to Leicester in June 2017.

IS THAT A FACT?

Hull were the first English team to ever lose a penalty shoot-out, Manchester United beating the Tigers 4-3 on spot-kicks in the semi-final of the Watney Cup in 1970.

• Hull have qualified for Europe just once, reaching the play-off round of the Europa League in 2014 before losing on the away goals rule to Lokeren.

• Goalkeeper Steve Harper became Hull's oldest ever player when he turned out in a 0-0 draw against Manchester United on 24th May 2015, aged 40 years and 60 days.

HONOURS
Division 3 champions 1966
Division 3 (North) champions 1933, 1949

Hull players, like Kevin Stewart here, are renowned for their 'Tiger-ish' tackling!

ZLATAN IBRAHIMOVIC

Born: Malmo, Sweden, 3rd October 1981
Position: Striker
Club career:
1999-2001 Malmo 40 (16)
2001-04 Ajax 74 (35)
2004-06 Juventus 70 (23)
2006-09 Inter Milan 88 (57)
2009-11 Barcelona 29 (16)
2010-11 AC Milan (loan) 29 (14)
2011-12 AC Milan 32 (28)
2012-16 Paris Saint-Germain 122 (113)
2016-18 Manchester United 33 (17)
2018- LA Galaxy 44 (38)
International record:
2001-16 Sweden 116 (62)

A tremendously gifted striker with a uniquely individualistic style of play, LA Galaxy superstar Zlatan Ibrahimovic is the only player to have won league titles with six different European clubs.

• His incredible run began with Ajax, who he had joined from his first club Malmo in 2001, when the Amsterdam giants won the Dutch league in 2004. Ibrahimovic's golden touch continued with his next club, Juventus, where he won back-to-back Serie A titles, although these were later scrubbed from the record books following Juve's involvement in a match-fixing scandal.
• At his next club, Inter Milan, Ibrahimovic fared even better, helping the Nerazzuri win a hat-trick of titles in 2007, 2008 and 2009. He then moved to Barcelona and, despite failing to see eye-to-eye with boss Pep Guardiola, won a La Liga title medal in 2010. Returning to Italy, his astonishing run of success continued with AC Milan, who were crowned Serie A champions in 2011.
• In the summer of 2012 Ibrahimovic was transferred to newly moneyed Paris Saint-Germain for £31 million,

"You know, you're incredibly lucky to be playing with me, the great Zlatan!"

taking his combined transfer fee up to a then world record £150 million. In four years with PSG, he won four league titles, two French cups, was voted Ligue 1 Player of the Year three times, topped the Ligue 1 scoring charts three times and became the club's all-time leading scorer after banging in 156 goals in all competitions, including a season's best 50 in 2015/16.
• Ibrahimovic enjoyed yet more success with Manchester United in 2016/17. He scored twice in the Red Devils' 3-2 defeat of Southampton in the League Cup

final and helped his new club reach the Europa League final, although he sadly missed their win over Ajax through injury.

INTER MILAN

Year founded: 1908
Ground: San Siro (80,018)
Nickname: Nerazzurri (The black and blues)
League titles: 18
Domestic cups: 7
European cups: 6
International cups: 3

Founded in 1908 as a breakaway club from AC Milan, Internazionale (as they are known locally) are the only Italian team never to have been relegated from Serie A and have spent more seasons in the top flight, 89, than any other club.
• **Inter were the first Italian club to win the European Cup twice, beating the mighty Real Madrid 3-1 in the 1964 final before recording a 1-0 defeat of Benfica the following year. They had to wait 45 years, though, before making it a hat-trick with a 2-0 defeat of Bayern Munich in Madrid in 2010 – a victory that, with the domestic league and cup already in the bag, secured Inter the first ever Treble by an Italian club.**
• Under legendary manager Helenio Herrera, Inter introduced the 'catenaccio' defensive system to world football in the 1960s. Playing with a sweeper behind two man-markers, Inter conceded very few goals as they powered to three league titles between 1963 and 1966.

All Inter Milan's league goals, like this one by Stefano Sensi, have come in Serie A

Can the Tractor Boys plough their way out of League One?

• The club endured a barren period domestically until they were awarded their first Serie A title for 17 years in 2006 after Juventus and AC Milan, who had both finished above them in the league table, had points deducted for their roles in a match-fixing scandal. Inter went on to win the championship in more conventional style in the following four years – the last two of these triumphs coming under Jose Mourinho – winning an Italian record 17 consecutive league games in 2006/07.

• Inter's San Siro stadium, which they share with city rivals AC Milan, is the largest in Italy, with a capacity of over 80,000. The stadium has hosted the European Cup/Champions League final on four occasions, a record only surpassed by Wembley.

HONOURS
Italian champions 1910, 1920, 1930, 1938, 1940, 1953, 1954, 1963, 1965, 1966, 1971, 1980, 1989, 2006, 2007, 2008, 2009, 2010
Italian Cup 1939, 1978, 1982, 2005, 2006, 2010, 2011
European Cup/Champions League 1964, 1965, 2010
UEFA Cup 1991, 1994, 1998
Intercontinental Cup/Club World Cup 1964, 1965, 2010

IPSWICH TOWN

Year founded: 1878
Ground: Portman Road (30,311)
Nickname: The Blues, The Tractor Boys
Biggest win: 10-0 v Floriana (1962)
Heaviest defeat: 1-10 v Fulham (1963)

The club was founded at a meeting at the town hall in 1878 but did not join the Football League until 1938, two years after turning professional.

• Ipswich were the last of just four clubs to win the old Second and First Division titles in consecutive seasons, pulling off this remarkable feat in 1962 under future England manager Sir Alf Ramsey. The team's success owed much to the strike partnership of Ray Crawford and Ted Phillips, who together scored 61 of the club's 93 goals during the title-winning campaign.

• Two years after that title win, though, Ipswich were relegated after conceding 121 goals – only Blackpool in 1930/31 (125 goals against) have had a worse defensive record in the top flight. The Blues' worst defeat in a season to forget was a 10-1 hammering at Fulham, the last time a team has conceded double figures in a top-flight match.

• However, the club enjoyed more success under their longest serving boss Bobby Robson, another man who went on to manage England, in the following two decades. In 1978 Ipswich won the FA Cup, beating favourites Arsenal 1-0 in the final at Wembley, and three years later they won the UEFA Cup with midfielder John Wark contributing a then record 14 goals during the club's continental campaign.

• Ipswich have the best home record in European competition of any club, remaining undefeated at Portman Road in 31 games (25 wins and six draws) since making their debut in the European Cup in 1962 with a 10-0 hammering of Maltese side Floriana – the Blues' biggest win in their history.

• With 203 goals for the Tractor Boys between 1958 and 1969, Ray Crawford is the club's record goalscorer. Mick Mills is the club's record appearance maker, turning out 591 times between 1966 and 1982.

• Relegated from the Championship after a 17-year stay in 2019, Ipswich hold the record for the worst ever defeat in the Premier League, suffering a 9-0 mauling at Manchester United in 1995.

HONOURS
Division 1 champions 1962
Division 2 champions 1961
Division 3 (South) champions 1954, 1957
FA Cup 1978
UEFA Cup 1981

ITALY

First international: Italy 6 France 2, 1910
Most capped player: Gianluigi Buffon, 176 caps (1997-2018)
Leading goalscorer: Luigi Riva, 35 goals (1965-74)
First World Cup appearance: Italy 7 USA 1, 1934
Biggest win: Italy 11 Egypt 3, 1928
Heaviest defeat: Hungary 7 Italy 1, 1924

Italy have the joint best record of any European nation at the World Cup, having won the tournament four times (in 1934, 1938, 1982 and 2006). Only Brazil, with five wins, have done better in the competition.

• The Azzurri, as they are known to their passionate fans, are the only

RAUL JIMENEZ

Born: Tepeji, Mexico, 5th May 1991
Position: Striker
Club career:
2011-14 Club America 96 (36)
2014-15 Atletico Madrid 21 (1)
2015-19 Benfica 80 (18)
2018-19 Wolverhampton Wanderers (loan) 38 (13)
2019- Wolverhampton Wanderers
International record:
2013- Mexico 77 (22)

Mamma mia! Italy's fans certainly are crazy about the Azzurri

country to have been involved in two World Cup final penalty shoot-outs. In 1994 they lost out to Brazil, but in 2006 they beat France on penalties after a 1-1 draw in the final in Berlin.

• Legendary Italy goalkeeper Dino Zoff is the oldest man to play in a World Cup final, helping the Azzurri win in 1982 against West Germany when aged 40 and 133 days.

• **The most humiliating moment in Italy's sporting history came in 1966 when they lost 1-0 to unsung minnows North Korea at the World Cup in England. The Italians had a remarkably similar embarrassment at the 2002 tournament when they were knocked out by hosts South Korea after a 2-1 defeat.**

• With 176 appearances for Italy before he retired from international football in 2018, goalkeeper Gianluigi Buffon is the highest-capped European player ever and the fourth highest in football history.

• Italy have won the European Championship just once, beating Yugoslavia 2-0 in a replayed final in Rome in 1968 after a 1-1 draw. They reached the final again in 2000 but lost 2-1 to France on the 'golden goal' rule in Rotterdam, and endured more disappointment in 2012 when they

were hammered 4-0 by Spain in the final in Kiev.

HONOURS
World Cup winners 1934, *1938, 1982, 2006*
European Championship winners
1968
World Cup Record
1930 Did not enter
1934 Winners
1938 Winners
1950 Round 1
1954 Round 1
1958 Did not qualify
1962 Round 1
1966 Round 1
1970 Runners-up
1974 Round 1
1978 Fourth place
1982 Winners
1986 Round 2
1990 Third place
1994 Runners-up
1998 Quarter-finals
2002 Round 2
2006 Winners
2010 Round 1
2014 Round 1
2018 Did not qualify

Raul Jimenez has added some Mexican spice to Wolves' attack

During a season-long loan from Benfica in 2018/19, Wolves striker Raul Jimenez scored 13 league goals – the most ever in a single Premier League season by a player for the Black Country club. Small wonder, then, that boss Nuno Espirito Santo was eager to sign up the tall and powerful Mexican on a permanent basis, eventually securing the deal for a club record £30 million.

• Jimenez began his career with Mexico City-based outfit Club America, with whom he won the league in 2013. The following year he moved to Atletico Madrid for around £9 million, but in a frustrating season with the Spanish side only managed a solitary goal.

• In an attempt to revive his fortunes he joined Benfica in August 2015, helping the Portuguese giants win consecutive league titles in 2016 and 2017. In the second of those years he was part of the Benfica which also won the domestic cup, beating Vitoria Guimaraes 2-1 in the final.

• At the 2012 London Olympics Jiminez collected a Gold medal after coming on as a sub in Mexico's 2-1 defeat of Brazil in the final of the football tournament Wembley. The following year he made his senior debut against Denmark and in 2019 he starred as Mexico won the Gold Cup with a 1-0 victory over the USA in the final, scoring five goals in total and collecting the Golden Ball for the tournament's best player.

JUVENTUS

Year founded: 1897
Ground: Juventus Stadium (41,507)
Nickname: The Zebras
League titles: 35
Domestic cups: 13
European cups: 8
International cups: 2

The most famous and successful club in Italy, Juventus were founded in 1897 by pupils at a school in Turin – hence the team's name, which means 'youth' in Latin. Six years later the club binned their original pink shirts and adopted their distinctive black-and-white-striped kit after an English member of the team had a set of Notts County shirts shipped out to Italy.

• Juventus emerged as the dominant force in Italian football in the 1930s when they won a then best ever five titles in a row. They have a record 35 titles to their name and are the only team in Italy allowed to wear two gold stars on their shirts, signifying 20 Serie A victories. In 2018/19 Juve became the first Italian club to win the Serie A title eight times on the trot, while the previous season they became the first ever to win four consecutive Doubles. The club's tally of 13 victories in the Coppa Italia is also a record.

• When, thanks to a single goal by their star player, French playmaker Michel Platini, Juventus beat Liverpool in the European Cup final in 1985 they became the first ever club to win all three European trophies. However, their triumph at the Heysel Stadium in Brussels was overshadowed by the death of 39 of their fans, who were crushed to death as they tried to flee from crowd trouble before the kick-off.

• Juventus won the trophy again in 1996, beating Ajax on penalties in Rome, but since then have lost five Champions League finals, most recently going down 4-1 to Real Madrid in Cardiff in 2017. The club's total of seven defeats in the final is a record for the competition.

• In July 2018 Juventus splashed out £88 million on Real Madrid striker Cristiano Ronaldo, a record fee for an Italian club.

• In 2014 Juventus won the Serie A title with a record 102 points, winning a record 33 league games including all 19 of their home matches.

HONOURS
Italian champions 1905, 1926, 1931, 1932, 1933, 1934, 1935, 1950, 1952, 1958, 1960, 1961, 1967, 1972, 1973, 1975, 1977, 1978, 1981, 1982, 1984, 1986, 1995, 1997, 1998, 2002, 2003, 2012, 2013, 2014, 2015, 2016, 2017, 2018, 2019
Italian Cup 1938, 1942, 1959, 1960,

Top-class players like Cristiano Ronaldo have made Juventus the most successful club in Italy

Will the prolific Harry Kane win a third Premier League Golden Boot in 2020?

1965, 1979, 1983, 1990, 1995, 2015, 2016, 2017, 2018
European Cup/Champions League 1985, 1996
UEFA Cup 1977, 1990, 1993
European Cup Winners' Cup 1984
European Super Cup 1984, 1996
Club World Cup 1985, 1996

HARRY KANE

Born: Chingford, 28th July 1993
Position: Striker
Club career:
2011- Tottenham Hotspur 178 (125)
2011 Leyton Orient (loan) 18 (5)
2012 Millwall (loan) 22 (7)
2012-13 Norwich City (loan) 3 (0)
2013 Leicester City (loan) 13 (2)
International record:
2015- England 39 (22)

England captain Harry Kane is the only player to have scored against every Premier League club he has faced, Cardiff City becoming his 28th victims when he netted the opener in Tottenham's 3-0 away win on 1st January 2019. At the end of the campaign he returned from injury to lead Spurs' frontline in the Champions League final, but was powerless to prevent Liverpool securing a 2-0 victory. However, after hitting the winner against Borussia Dortmund earlier in the tournament he became Tottenham's all-time top scorer in European matches with 24 goals.

• Premier League Golden Boot winner in 2016 and 2017, Kane also holds the record for the most goals in the competition in a calendar year, with 39 in 2017. His total of 56 goals in all competitions was the best in the whole of Europe, breaking the seven-year domination of La Liga's Cristiano Ronaldo and Lionel Messi.

• A clever player who can create as well as score goals, Kane came through the Tottenham youth system and spent time on loan with Leyton Orient, Millwall, Norwich and Leicester before finally establishing himself in the Spurs first team in 2014. The following year his fine form saw him voted PFA Young Player of the Year.

• An England international at Under-17, Under-19, Under-20 and Under-21 level, Kane made his senior debut against Lithuania in a Euro 2016 qualifier at Wembley in March 2015. His international career got off to a dream start, too, as he came off the bench to score with a header after just 78 seconds – the third fastest goal by an England player on debut.

• After a disappointing Euro 2016, Kane showed his best form at the 2018 World Cup in Russia. His total of six goals at the tournament won him the Golden Boot – only the second Englishman (after Gary Lineker in 1986) to win the award – and he was also voted into the FIFA World Cup Dream Team. In November 2018 he banged in the winner against Croatia at Wembley to enable England to qualify for the last four of the inaugural UEFA Nations League.

N'GOLO KANTE

Born: Paris, France, 29th March 1991
Position: Midfielder
Club career:
2011-13 Boulogne 38 (3)
2013-15 Caen 75 (4)
2015-16 Leicester City 37 (1)
2016- Chelsea 105 (6)
International record:
2016- France 38 (1)

After helping Chelsea win the Premier League title in 2017, N'Golo Kante became the first outfield player to lift the trophy in consecutive seasons with two different clubs, having starred in the

Leicester City team which surprisingly claimed the top spot the previous year. Kante's unstinting efforts for the Blues also saw him win both the PFA Player of the Year award and the Footballer of the Year gong. Two years later he was part of the Chelsea side which become the first from England to win the Europa League twice, following a convincing 4-1 victory over Arsenal in Baku.

• A tenacious midfielder who loves to make surging forward runs from deep, Kante started out with Boulogne in the third tier of French football, before moving to Caen in 2013. In his first season with his new club he played in every match as Caen won promotion to Ligue 1.

• After a £5.6 million transfer to Leicester in the summer of 2015, Kante was soon gaining plaudits for his hard-working, unselfish style of play which helped propel the Foxes to the top of the table. His excellent campaign, which saw him make a season best 175 tackles, ended with him being nominated for the PFA Player of the Year award and named in the PFA Team of the Year before he moved to Stamford Bridge for £32 million, then a record for a player leaving the King Power Stadium.

• Kante was rewarded with his first French cap in March 2016, coming on as a half-time sub in a 3-2 win against the Netherlands in Amsterdam. Later that month he made his first start for Les Bleus, scoring in a 4-2 win against Russia in Paris. In 2018 he was a key part of the France side which won the World Cup, starting all seven of his country's matches.

KICK-OFF

Scottish club Queen's Park claim to have been the first to adopt the traditional kick-off time of 3pm on a Saturday,

IS THAT A FACT?
Southampton striker Shane Long scored the fastest goal in Premier League history on 23rd April 2019 when he netted against Watford at Vicarage Road just 7.69 seconds after kick-off, beating Ledley King's previous record by more than two seconds.

which allowed those people who worked in the morning sufficient time to get to the match.

• The fastest ever goal from a kick-off was scored in just two seconds by Nawaf Al Abed, a 21-year-old striker for Saudi Arabian side Al Hilal in a cup match against Al Shoalah in 2009. After a team-mate tapped the ball to him, Al Abed struck a fierce left-foot shot from the halfway line which sailed over the opposition keeper and into the net.

• The fastest goal in the FA Cup was scored by Gareth Morris for Ashton United, who struck from 60 yards just four seconds after the kick-off against Skelmersdale United in the first qualifying round of the competition in September 2001.

• The first ever league match to be played on a Sunday kicked-off at 11.30am on 20th January 1974, a London derby between Millwall and Fulham. To get around the law at the time, admission to The Den was by 'programme only' – the cost of a programme cunningly being the same as a match ticket.

• The earliest ever kick-off for a Premier League match was 11am for the Manchester derby on 20th March 1993. The latest start saw West Ham and Manchester United kick-off at 8.30pm in the last ever match at Upton Park on 10th May 2016.

KILMARNOCK

Year founded: 1869
Ground: Rugby Park (17,889)
Nickname: Killie
Biggest win: 13-2 v Saltcoats Victoria (1896)
Heaviest defeat: 1-9 v Celtic (1938)

The oldest professional club in Scotland, Kilmarnock were founded in 1869 by a group of local cricketers who were keen to play another sport during the winter months. Originally, the club played rugby (hence the name of Kilmarnock's stadium, Rugby Park) before switching to football in 1873.

• That same year Kilmarnock entered the inaugural Scottish Cup and on 18th October 1873 the club took

part in the first ever match in the competition, losing 2-0 in the first round to Renton.

• Kilmarnock's greatest moment was back in 1965 when they travelled to championship rivals Hearts on the last day of the season requiring a two-goal win to pip the Edinburgh side to the title on goal average. To the joy of their travelling fans, Killie won 2-0 to claim the title by 0.04 of a goal.

• Two years later Kilmarnock had their best ever run in Europe, when they reached the semi-finals of the Fairs Cup before losing 4-2 on aggregate to Leeds United.

• Alan Robertson played in a club record 607 games for Kilmarnock between 1972 and 1989. Killie's top scorer is Willie Culley, who notched 149 goals between 1911 and 1923.

• Kilmarnock have won the Scottish Cup three times, most recently defeating Falkirk 1-0 in the 1997 final. The club won the League Cup for the first time in 2012, after a 1-0 win against Celtic in the final.

• Under boss Steve Clarke, who left to manage Scotland soon afterwards, KIllie finished third in the Scottish Premiership in 2018/19 and racked up a club record 67 points.

HONOURS
Division 1 champions 1965
Division 2 champions 1898, 1899
Scottish Cup 1920, 1929, 1997
Scottish League Cup 2012

FRAN KIRBY

Born: Reading, 19th June 1993
Position: Striker
Club career:
2012-15 Reading Women 42 (67)
2015- Chelsea Women 50 (32)
International record:
2014- England 40 (12)

Nippy Chelsea Women striker Fran Kirby became the most expensive female player in Britain when she joined the Blues from Reading for £60,000 in July 2015, shortly after being dubbed 'the mini Messi' by then England boss Mark Sampson for her impressive performances at the Women's World Cup in Canada.

• In 2018 Kirby was named the PFA Player of the Year and the Football Writers' Women's Footballer of the

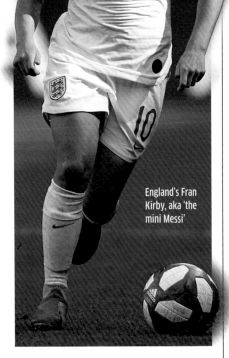

England's Fran Kirby, aka 'the mini Messi'

Year following a great season with the Blues, which culminated in her scoring with a delightfully placed curling shot in the 3-1 defeat of Arsenal Ladies in the Women's FA Cup final at Wembley.

• After joining Reading as a seven-year-old and progressing through the Royals' youth system, Kirby became the first woman to be offered a professional contract by the club. A prolific goal poacher, she was top scorer in the Women's Super League 2 in 2014 with 24 goals in just 16 appearances.

• Kirby made her England debut in August 2014, scoring in a 4-0 thrashing of Sweden at Victoria Park, Hartlepool. She was part of the England squad which came fourth at the 2019 Women's World Cup in France but failed to reproduce her 2015 form and was dropped to the bench for the semi-final defeat by the USA.

KIT DEALS

In May 2016 Barcelona signed the biggest ever kit deal in football history with American company Nike. The deal, which started at the beginning of the 2018/19 campaign, sees Barcelona being paid £1 billion over 10 seasons in return for wearing Nike supplied training and playing kit. Real Madrid's 10-year deal with Adidas signed in 2015 is not far behind, being worth around £980 million.

• Manchester United's £75 million per year kit deal with Adidas is the most lucrative in the Premier League, followed by Manchester City's £65 million per year deal with Puma.

• Nike were the most popular kit suppliers at the 2019 Women's World Cup in France, providing home and away strips for 14 of the 24 countries including eventual winners USA.

JURGEN KLOPP

Born: Stuttgart, Germany, 16th June 1967
Managerial career:
2001-08 Mainz 05
2008-15 Borussia Dortmund
2015- Liverpool

After losing six major cup finals on the trot with Borussia Dortmund and Liverpool, Jurgen Klopp finally broke the hoodoo when he led the Reds to Champions League glory with a 2-0 victory over Tottenham in the Champions League final. He also steered the Merseysiders to second place in the Premier League with an impressive 97 points – the most ever by a team failing to lift the title.

• Klopp took his first steps in management in 2001 with Mainz 05, the club he had previously turned out for more than 300 times as a striker-turned-defender. By the time he left Mainz in 2008 he was the club's longest serving manager.

• An engaging character who is rarely seen without a big smile on his face, Klopp made his reputation with Borussia Dortmund, who he led to consecutive Bundesliga titles in 2011 and 2012. In the second of those years Dortmund also claimed their first ever domestic Double after thrashing Bayern Munich 5-2 in the final of the German Cup.

• The following year Klopp took Dortmund to the final of the Champions League after they overcame Jose Mourinho's Real Madrid in the semi-finals. Again, their opponents in the final were Bayern, but this time the Bavarian side exacted revenge with a 2-1 victory at Wembley. Klopp then endured more agony when Dortmund lost the 2014 and 2015 German Cup finals to Bayern and Wolfsburg, respectively. After replacing the sacked Brendan Rodgers as Liverpool boss in October 2015 he lost another three finals in the League Cup (2016), Europa League (2016) and the Champions League (2018).

• Klopp was named German Manager of the Year in 2011 and 2012, the first man ever to win this award in two consecutive years.

Life at Liverpool is 'wunderbar' for Jurgen the German

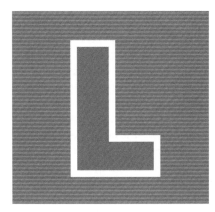

ALEXANDRE LACAZETTE

Born: Lyon, France, 28th May 1991
Position: Striker
Club career:
2008-11 Lyon B 53 (23)
2010-17 Lyon 203 (100)
2017- Arsenal 67 (27)
International record:
2013- France 16 (3)

After scoring 19 goals in all competitions and helping the Gunners reach the Europa League final, Alexandre Lacazette was voted Arsenal Player of the Season by the club's fans in 2018/19. The French striker was signed by the north Londoners from Lyon for a then club record fee of £46.5 million in July 2017 and got off to a great start, scoring after

Alexandre Lacazette has always been pretty good in the air!

just 94 seconds of his Premier League debut against Leicester City.

• A lively two-footed striker who possesses pace and dribbling ability, Lacazette came through the academy of his hometown club, Lyon, making his senior debut aged 19. In 2012 he helped Lyon win the French cup, thanks to a 1-0 win against third-tier semi-professional Quevilly in the final at the Stade de France.

• His best season with Lyon was in 2014/15 when he was voted Ligue 1 PLayer of the Year after topping the division's goalscoring charts with an impressive 27 goals.

• Lacazette has represented France from Under-16 level onwards, and in 2010 scored the winning goal in the European Under-19 Championship final when hosts France beat Spain 2-1. He made his senior debut in June 2013 in a 1-0 friendly loss to Uruguay in Montevideo but missed the cut for the 2018 World Cup.

FRANK LAMPARD

Born: Romford, 20th June 1978
Managerial career:
2018-19 Derby County
2019- Chelsea

In July 2019 Frank Lampard was appointed Chelsea manager on a three-year contract as successor to Maurizio Sarri, becoming the club's first English boss since Glenn Hoddle in the mid-1990s. The previous season Lampard had started his managerial career with Derby County, taking the Rams to the Championship play-off final, which they lost 2-1 to Aston Villa.

• A true Chelsea legend, Lampard joined the Blues from West Ham for £11 million in 2001 and over the next 13 years went on to score 211 goals in all competitions to become the club's highest ever scorer. His total of 177 Premier League goals makes him the highest-scoring midfielder in the league's history while his total of 609 appearances in the competition is only bettered by Gareth Barry and Ryan Giggs.

• Lampard won the league three times with the Blues and the FA Cup on four

Chelsea boss Frank Lampard has still got it!

occasions, scoring the winner against Everton in the 2009 final at Wembley with a typical long-range shot from outside the box. After numerous near misses, he finally won the Champions League with Chelsea in 2012, scoring one of his team's penalties in the shoot-out against Bayern Munich in the final, and the following year he skippered the Blues to victory in the Europa League.

• One of just nine England players to win a century of international caps, Lampard represented the Three Lions at three World Cups, famously having a legitimate goal against Germany at the 2010 tournament in South Africa ruled out when the officials failed to spot that his shot had clearly crossed the line after bouncing down off the crossbar. The incident was later cited by then FIFA President Sepp Blatter when goal-line technology was finally introduced at the next World Cup in Brazil.

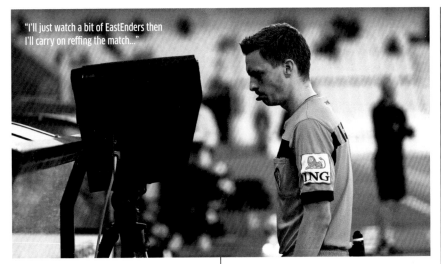

"I'll just watch a bit of EastEnders then I'll carry on reffing the match..."

LAWS

Thirteen original laws of association football were adopted at a meeting of the Football Association in 1863, although these had their roots in the eponymous 'Cambridge Rules' established at Cambridge University as far back as 1848.

• No copy of those 1848 rules now exist, but they are thought to have included laws relating to throw-ins, goal-kicks, fouls and offside. They even allowed for a length of string to be used as a crossbar.

• Perhaps the most significant rule change occurred in 1925 when the offside law was altered so that an attacking player receiving the ball would need to be behind two opponents, rather than three. The effect of this rule change was dramatic, with the average number of goals per game in the Football League rising from 2.55 in 1924/25 to 3.44 in 1925/26.

• The laws of the game are governed by the International Football Association Board, which was founded in 1886 by the four football associations of the United Kingdom. Each of these associations still has one vote on the IFAB, with FIFA having four votes. Any changes to the laws of the game require a minimum of six votes.

• Important changes to the laws of the game in recent decades include the introduction of the 'back pass' rule in 1992, which prevented goalkeepers from handling passes from their own team-mates; goals being permitted direct from the kick off (1997); and the introduction of goal-line technology (2012) and video assistant referees (2018).

LEAGUE CUP

With eight wins to their name, Liverpool are the most successful club in League Cup history. The Reds have also appeared in a record number of finals, 12. However, Manchester City have dominated the competition in recent years with four triumphs in the last six seasons, most recently beating Chelsea on penalties in the 2019 final.

• The competition has been known by more names than any other in British football. Originally called the Football League Cup (1960-81), it has subsequently been rebranded through sponsorship deals as the Milk Cup (1981-86), Littlewoods Cup (1986-90), Rumbelows Cup (1990-92), Coca-Cola Cup (1992-98), Worthington Cup (1998-2003), Carling Cup (2003-12), the Capital One Cup (2012-16) and the Carabao Cup (from 2017).

• Ian Rush won a record five winner's medals in the competition with Liverpool (1981-84 and 1995) and, along with Geoff Hurst, is also the leading scorer in the history of the League Cup with 49 goals. In the 1986/87 season Tottenham's Clive Allen scored a record 12 goals in the competition.

• Oldham's Frankie Bunn scored a record six goals in a League Cup match when Oldham thrashed Scarborough 7-0 on 25th October 1989.

• Liverpool won the competition a record four times in a row between 1981 and 1984, going undefeated for an unprecedented 25 League Cup matches.

• In 1983 West Ham walloped Bury 10-0 to record the biggest ever victory in the history of the League Cup. Three years later Liverpool equalled the Hammers' tally with an identical thrashing of Fulham.

• On 25th September 2018 Fulham midfielder Harvey Elliott became the youngest player ever to appear in the competition when he came on as a sub in a win at Millwall aged 15 and 174 days.

• Swansea City recorded the biggest ever win in the final, thrashing Bradford City 5-0 in 2013, although the Bantams were the first side from the fourth tier of English football to reach a major Wembley final.

• The first League Cup final to be played at Wembley was between West Brom and QPR in 1967. QPR were then a Third Division side and pulled off a major shock by winning 3-2. Prior to 1967, the final was played over two legs.

• On two occasions a League Cup match has featured a record 12 goals: Arsenal's 7-5 win at Reading in 2012, and Dagenham's 6-6 draw with Brentford two years later.

• Manchester City hold the record for the biggest ever win at the semi-final stage in 2019, trouncing Burton Albion 9-0 at the Etihad before making it a 10-0 record aggregate score in the second leg at the Pirelli Stadium.

TOP 10

TOTAL LEAGUE CUP FINAL GOALS

1.	Liverpool	20
2.	Aston Villa	16
3.	Chelsea	14
4.	Manchester City	12
	Manchester United	12
6.	Leicester City	10
7.	Arsenal	9
8.	Nottingham Forest	8
	Tottenham Hotspur	8
	West Bromwich Albion	8

LEEDS UNITED

32Red

Year founded: 1919
Ground: Elland Road (37,890)
Nickname: United
Biggest win: 10-0 v Lyn Oslo (1969)
Heaviest defeat: 1-8 v Stoke City (1934)

Leeds United were formed in 1919 as successors to Leeds City, who had been expelled from the Football League after making illegal payments to their players. United initially joined the Midland League before being elected to the Second Division in 1920.

Can Eddie Nketiah and co. finally fire Leeds back to the top flight?

Year founded: 1884
Ground: King Power Stadium (32,312)
Previous name: Leicester Fosse
Nickname: The Foxes
Biggest win: 13-0 v Notts Olympic (1894)
Heaviest defeat: 0-12 v Nottingham Forest (1909)

• Leeds' greatest years were in the 1960s and early 1970s under legendary manager Don Revie. The club were struggling in the Second Division when he arrived at Elland Road in 1961 but, building his side around the likes of Jack Charlton, Billy Bremner and Johnny Giles, Revie soon turned Leeds into a formidable force.

• During the Revie years Leeds won two league titles in 1969 and 1974, the FA Cup in 1972, the League Cup in 1968, and two Fairs Cup in 1968 and 1971. In the last of those triumphs Leeds became the first ever club to win a European trophy on the away goals rule after they drew 2-2 on aggregate with Italian giants Juventus.

• Leeds also reached the final of the European Cup in 1975, losing 2-0 to Bayern Munich. Sadly, rioting by the club's fans resulted in Leeds becoming the first English club to be suspended from European competition. The ban lasted three years.

• Peter Lorimer, another Revie-era stalwart, is the club's leading scorer, hitting 168 league goals in two spells at Elland Road (1962-79 and 1983-86). England World Cup winner Jack Charlton holds the club appearance record, turning out in 773 games in total between 1952 and 1973.

• In 1992 Leeds pipped Manchester United to the title to make history as the last club to win the old First Division before it became the Premiership. Ironically, Leeds' star player at the time, Eric Cantona, joined the Red Devils the following season. The club remained a force over the next decade, even reaching the Champions League semi-final in 2001, but financial mismanagement saw them plummet to League One in 2007 – a season in which Leeds used a club record 44 players – before they climbed back into the Championship three years later.

• Leeds' record signing is Rio Ferdinand, who they bought from West Ham for £18 million in July 2000. Two years later the stylish England defender moved on to Manchester United for £30.8 million, making him the Yorkshire side's most expensive sale too.

• Under charismatic Argentinian boss Marcelo Bielsa Leeds reached the Championship play-offs in 2019. In the semi-finals, United won the first game at Derby County 1-0 but then became the first team ever not to reach the second-tier final after holding the lead from the away leg when they lost 4-2 to the Rams at Elland Road.

HONOURS
Division 1 champions 1969, 1974, 1992
Division 2 champions 1924, 1964, 1990
FA Cup 1972
League Cup 1968
Fairs Cup 1968, 1971

Founded in 1884 as Leicester Fosse by old boys from Wyggeston School, the club were elected to the Second Division a decade later. In 1919 they changed their name to Leicester City, shortly after Leicester was given city status.

• Leicester enjoyed their greatest success in 2016 when, under the leadership of popular manager Claudio Ranieri, they won the Premier League title in one of the greatest upsets in sporting history. The Foxes were 5,000-1 outsiders at the start of the campaign, but defied the odds thanks in part to the goals of striker Jamie Vardy, who set a new Premier League record by scoring in 11 consecutive matches.

• The following season Leicester enjoyed their best ever European campaign, reaching the quarter-finals of the Champions League before losing 2-1 on aggregate to Atletico Madrid.

• Leicester have won the second-tier championship seven times – a record only matched by Manchester City. On the last of these occasions in 2013/14 the Foxes set a number of significant club records, including highest number of points (102) and most league games won (33).

• The Foxes are the only club to have played in four FA Cup finals and lost them all. Beaten in 1949, 1961 and 1963, they were defeated again by Manchester City in 1969 – the same season they were relegated from the top flight. Previously, only Manchester City (in 1926) had suffered this double blow.

• Leicester's only cup success has come in the League Cup, the Foxes winning the competition in 1964, 1997 and 2000 – when skipper Matt Elliott scored both goals in a 2-1 defeat of Tranmere Rovers at Wembley.

• Leicester made their record signing in July 2019, when Belgian midfielder Youri Tielemans joined the club from Monaco

"Listen carefully Jamie, to get hair this cool all you need to do is..."

for £40 million after a successful loan spell at the King Power. The following month the Foxes received a club record £80 million when defender Harry Maguire signed for Manchester United in the biggest deal ever between two Premier League clubs.

• **Arthur Chandler holds the club goalscoring record, netting 259 times between 1923 and 1935, while Arthur Rowley hit a record 44 of Leicester's seasonal best 109 league goals in 1956/57. The club's appearance record is held by defender and ex-Leicestershire county cricketer Graham Cross, who turned out 599 times in all competitions for the Foxes between 1960 and 1976.**

• Goalkeeper Mark Wallington played in a club record 331 consecutive games between 1975 and 1982.

• **Long-serving midfielder Andy King has won a club record 50 caps for Wales since making his international debut in 2009.**

HONOURS
Premier League champions 2016
Championship champions 2014
Division 2 champions 1925, 1937, 1954, 1957, 1971, 1980
League One champions 2009
League Cup 1964, 1997, 2000

NEIL LENNON

Born: Lurgan, 25th June 1971
Managerial career:
2010-14 Celtic
2014-16 Bolton Wanderers
2016-19 Hibernian
2019- Celtic

After taking over as Celtic boss from Brendan Rodgers in February 2019, initially on a caretaker basis, Neil Lennon led the Bhoys to an historic 'treble Treble' when they added the Scottish Cup to their League Cup and Scottish Premiership titles with a 2-1 defeat of Hearts in the final at Hampden Park.

• **Lennon is in his second spell in the Parkhead hotseat, having won three league titles and two Scottish Cups in his first stint in charge between 2010 and 2014. However, his tenure was marked by numerous controversies, including two touchline bans during the 2010/11 season and an incident at Hearts when he was attacked in his technical area by a crazed home fan. Even worse, a parcel bomb was sent to Lennon in April 2011 but, fortunately, the package was intercepted by the Royal Mail before it was delivered to his house.**

• After leaving Celtic, Lennon took over as Bolton manager in October 2014

but struggled to make an impact at a club plagued by financial problems. He fared better at Hibs, who he joined in June 2016, guiding them to the Scottish Championship in his first season at the helm and then a respectable fourth-place finish in the Premiership in the following campaign. However, a heated exchange with players and club officials in January 2019 led to Lennon's departure from the Edinburgh outfit.

• **A hard-working midfielder in his playing days, Lennon twice won the League Cup with Leicester before joining Celtic in 2000, where he won five league titles and three Scottish Cups. Capped 40 times by Northern Ireland he quit international football in 2002 after receiving death threats from Protestant extremists for suggesting he would be happy to play for a United Ireland team.**

ROBERT LEWANDOWSKI

Born: Warsaw, Poland, 21st August 1988
Position: Striker
Club career:
2005 Delta Warsaw 10 (4)
2005-06 Legia Warsaw II 5 (2)
2006-08 Znicz Pruszkow 59 (36)
2008-10 Lech Poznan 58 (32)
2010-14 Borussia Dortmund 131 (74)
2014- Bayern Munich 159 (128)
International record:
2008- Poland 106 (57)

On 22nd September 2015 Robert Lewandowski scored five goals for Bayern Munich against Wolfsburg in just eight minutes and 59 seconds – the fastest five-goal haul ever in any major European league. Incredibly, the pacy Polish striker had begun the match on the bench!

• **After starting out in the Polish lower leagues, Lewandowski made his name at Lech Poznan. In only his second season in the top flight, in 2009/10, he led the scoring charts with 18 goals as Poznan won the title.**

• In the summer of 2010 Lewandowski moved on to Dortmund for around £4 million. The fee proved to be a bargain as Lewandowski's goals helped his club win two league titles and the German Cup in 2012, the Pole scoring a hat-trick in Dortmund's 5-2 demolition of Bayern Munich in the final. The following season

Bayern Munich goal machine Robert Lewandowski

Lewandowski set a new club record when he scored in 12 consecutive league games, and he also became the first player to score four goals in a Champions League semi-final, achieving this record in Dortmund's shock 4-1 defeat of competition heavyweights Real Madrid.

• After topping the Bundesliga scoring charts in 2013/14 he moved on to Bayern Munich, with whom he has since won five titles. In 2015/16 Lewandowski became the first player for 39 years to score 30 goals in a Bundesliga campaign and the following season he was even more prolific, hitting a career-best 54 goals in total for club and country. He was the Bundesliga's top scorer again in 2017/18 and 2018/19 and his total of 202 goals in the German league is a record for a foreign player. Lewandowski's brace for Bayern in their 3-0 win over RB Leipzig in 2019 made him the all-time top scorer in German Cup finals with six goals.

• Polish Player of the Year a record seven times, Lewandowski first played for Poland aged 20 in 2008, coming off the bench to score in a World Cup qualifier against San Marino to become his country's second ever youngest goalscorer on his debut. During the qualifiers for Russia 2018 he scored a European record 16 goals and he is now his country's highest scorer ever with 57 goals.

LEYTON ORIENT

Year founded: 1881
Ground: Brisbane Road (9,271)
Previous name: Eagle FC, Clapton Road, Orient
Nickname: The O's
Biggest win: 9-2 v Aldershot (1934) and Chester (1962)
Heaviest defeat: 0-8 v Aston Villa (1929)

Originally founded by members of a local cricket team, the club chose the name 'Orient' in 1888 following a suggestion by one of the players who worked for the Orient Shipping Company. The club's 112-year stay in the Football League ended in 2017 but the O's bounced back two years later after topping the National League. Tragically, the man who led them up, former Spurs defender Justin Edinburgh, died after suffering cardiac arrest in June 2019.

• Over 40 Orient players and staff fought in World War I, three of them dying in the conflict. In recognition of this sacrifice, the Prince of Wales (later King Edward VIII) watched an Orient match in 1921 – the first time a member of the Royal Family had attended a Football League match.

• Orient are the only club to have played home league matches at the old Wembley Stadium. During the 1931/32 season, the club played two games at 'the home of football' after their own Lea Bridge ground was temporarily closed for failing to meet official standards.

• Orient's record scorer is Tommy Johnston, who notched 121 goals for the O's in two spells at the club between 1956 and 1961. Following his death in 2008 the South Stand at Brisbane Road was named after the prolific striker.

• In 2001 O's striker Chris Tate scored the fastest goal in a play-off final, netting after just 27 seconds in the fourth tier promotion decider against Blackpool at the Millennium Stadium, Cardiff. Despite this great start Orient ended up losing 4-2.

HONOURS
Division 3 champions 1970
Division 3 (South) champions 1956
National League champions 2019

LINCOLN CITY

Year founded: 1884
Ground: Sincil Bank (10,120)
Nickname: The Imps
Biggest win: 13-0 v Peterborough United (1895)
Heaviest defeat: 3-11 v Manchester City (1895)

Lincoln City were founded in 1884 as the successors to Lincoln Rovers and are the oldest club never to have played in the top flight. The Imps have endured a fair amount of misery over the years, suffering a record five demotions from the Football League but always bouncing back, most recently winning the National League championship in 2017. Two years later Lincoln were crowned League Two champs after topping the table for virtually the entire season.

• Lincoln made headline news in 2017 when they became the first non-league club for 103 years to reach the quarter-finals of the FA Cup after thrilling wins against Championship duo Ipswich and Brighton, and Premier League Burnley. However, with Wembley in their sights the Imps' cup dreams

After winning promotion in 2019 Lincoln are in Imp-ish mood!

were cruelly crushed by Arsenal, who beat them 5-0 at the Emirates.

• In 1976, under the stewardship of future England boss Graham Taylor, Lincoln won the old Fourth Division title with a record 74 points (the highest ever total until 1981/82 when wins earned an additional point).

• Stalwart defender Grant Brown made a record 407 league appearances for the Imps between 1989 and 2002. Lincoln's record scorer is Andy Graver, who banged in 143 goals in three spells at Sincil bank between 1950 and 1961.

• Strangely, Lincoln enjoyed their biggest win and suffered their heaviest defeat in the same year, 1895, going down 11-3 to Manchester City in the old Second Division before thrashing Peterborough 13-0 in the first qualifying round of the FA Cup a few months later.

HONOURS
Division 3 (North) champions 1932, 1948, 1952
Division 4 champions 1976
National League champions 2017
Conference champions 1988
Football League Trophy 2018

JESSE LINGARD

Born: Warrington, 15th December 1992
Position: Midfielder
Club career:
2011- Manchester United 111 (17)
2012-13 Leicester City (loan) 5 (0)
2013-14 Birmingham City (loan) 13 (6)
2014 Brighton and Hove Albion 15 (3)
2015 Derby County (loan) 14 (2)
International record:
2016- England 24 (4)

A lively and enterprising attacking midfielder, Jesse Lingard has played a central role in Manchester United's successes since the departure of legendary boss Sir Alex Ferguson in 2013. He came off the bench to hit the winner in extra-time against Crystal Palace in the 2016 FA Cup final and the following year was on target again at Wembley, scoring for the Red Devils in their 3-2 defeat of Southampton in the League Cup final.

• **Lingard joined United as a seven-year-old and graduated through the ranks to help the Red Devils win the**

Jesse Lingard's knack of scoring important goals makes him an Old Trafford favourite

FA Youth Cup in 2011, getting on the scoresheet in a 6-3 aggregate win in the final against Sheffield United. He then had a number of loans away from Old Trafford, most notably at Birmingham City where he scored four goals on his debut in August 2013 against Sheffield Wednesday in a 4-1 win at St Andrew's.

• Lingard made his England debut in a 2-0 victory against Malta at Wembley in October 2016, and he notched his first goal for the Three Lions in a 1-0 friendly win away to the Netherlands in March 2018. At the World Cup finals in Russia later that year he scored one of the goals of the tournament with a delicious curler in England's 6-1 rout of Panama.

• **He continued his good form at international level with a goal in England's 2-1 defeat of Croatia at Wembley in November 2018, which took the Three Lions through to the finals of the inaugural UEFA Nations League in Portugal.**

LIVERPOOL

Year founded: 1892
Ground: Anfield (54,074)
Nickname: The Reds
Biggest win: 11-0 v Stromsgodset (1974)
Heaviest defeat: 1-9 v Birmingham City (1954)

Liverpool were founded as a splinter club from local rivals Everton following a dispute between the Toffees and the landlord of their original ground at Anfield, John Houlding. When the

majority of Evertonians decided to decamp to Goodison Park in 1892, Houlding set up Liverpool FC after his attempts to retain the name 'Everton' had failed.

• **With 18 league titles to their name, including the Double in 1986, Liverpool are the second most successful club in the history of English football behind deadly rivals Manchester United – although their last championship success came way back in 1990. The Reds' total of 105 seasons in the top flight is only surpassed by Aston Villa (106) and Everton (117).**

• Liverpool dominated English football in the 1970s and 1980s after the foundations of the club's success were laid by legendary manager Bill Shankly in the previous decade. Under Shankly's successor, Bob Paisley, the Reds won 13 major trophies – a haul only surpassed by Manchester United's Sir Alex Ferguson.

• **As their fans love to remind their rivals Liverpool are the most successful English side in Europe, having won the European Cup/ Champions League on six occasions. The Reds first won the trophy in 1977, beating Borussia Monchengladbach 3-1 in Rome, and the following year became the first British team to retain the cup (after a 1-0 win in the final against Bruges at Wembley, club legend Kenny Dalglish grabbing the all-important goal). After claiming the trophy again in 1981, 1984 and 2005 Liverpool made it six in 2019 when they beat Tottenham 2-0 in Madrid in only the second ever all-English Champions League final. The Reds have also won the UEFA Cup three times, giving them a total of nine major European triumphs – a tally only surpassed by Real Madrid.**

• Liverpool have won the League Cup a record eight times, including an unmatched four times in a row between 1981 and 1984. Reds striker Ian Rush is the joint-leading scorer in the history of the competition with 49 goals, hitting all but one of these for Liverpool in two spells at the club in the 1980s and 1990s.

• **Rush also scored a record five goals in three FA Cup finals for Liverpool in 1986, 1989 and 1992 – all of which were won by the Reds. In all, the Merseysiders have won the trophy seven times, most recently in 2006 when they became only the second team (after Arsenal the previous year) to claim the cup on penalties.**

Liverpool's numerous European successes are certainly 'unbearable' for Everton fans!

• When Liverpool recorded their biggest ever victory, 11-0 against Norwegian no-hopers Stromsgodset in the Cup Winners' Cup in 1974, no fewer than nine different players got on the scoresheet to set a British record for the most scoring players in a competitive match.

• England international striker Roger Hunt is the club's leading scorer in league games, with 245 goals between 1958 and 1969. His team-mate Ian Callaghan holds the Liverpool appearance record, turning out in 640 league games between 1960 and 1978.

• Powerful centre-back Virgil van Dijk is the club's record signing, joining the Reds from Southampton in January 2018 for £75 million, a world record fee for a defender. In the same month hugely popular Brazilian midfielder Philippe Coutinho left Anfield for Barcelona for £142 million, in the most expensive deal ever involving a British club.

• Between 1976 and 1983 Liverpool full-back Phil Neal played in 365 consecutive league games – a record for the top flight of English football.

• Kop legend Steven Gerrard won a club record 114 international caps for England between 2000 and 2014, and scored a British record 41 goals in European competition.

• Liverpool utility man James Milner holds the record for scoring in the most Premier League matches, 52, without once finishing on the losing side.

• Under charismatic manager Jurgen Klopp Liverpool finished second in the Premier League in 2019 behind Manchester City despite accumulating an incredible 97 points – a record for the club and the most ever by a team not winning the title.

HONOURS

Division 1 champions *1901, 1906, 1922, 1923, 1947, 1964, 1966, 1973, 1976, 1977, 1979, 1980, 1982, 1983, 1984, 1986, 1988,1990*
Division 2 champions *1894, 1896, 1905, 1962*
FA Cup *1965, 1974, 1986, 1989,1992, 2001, 2006*
League Cup *1981, 1982, 1983, 1984, 1995, 2001, 2003, 2012*
Double *1986*
European Cup/Champions League *1977, 1978, 1981, 1984, 2005, 2019*
UEFA Cup *1973, 1976, 2001*
European Super Cup *1977, 2001, 2005, 2019*

LIVINGSTON

Year founded: 1943
Ground: Almondvale Stadium (8,716)
Previous names: Ferranti Thistle, Meadowbank Thistle
Nickname: The Lions
Biggest win: 8-0 v Stranraer (2012)
Heaviest defeat: 0-8 v Hamilton Academical (1974)

Founded in 1943 as the works team Ferranti Thistle, the club changed its name on joining the Scottish League in 1974 to Meadowbank Thistle after moving to the council-owned Meadowbank Stadium in Edinburgh. In 1995 the club moved west to Livingston and adopted the town's name.

• Livingston's best season in the old SPL was in 2002 when the club finished third in the league behind Celtic and Rangers. The following campaign the Lions competed in the UEFA Cup for the first time, but were knocked out in the first round by Austrian outfit SK Sturm Graz.

• The club's greatest day, though, came in 2004 when they beat Hibs 2-0 in the final of the Scottish League Cup at Hampden Park.

• Since joining the club in 2007 South African midfielder Keaghan Jacobs has made a record 232 league appearances for Livingston.

• Livingston received a club record £1 million when Spanish striker David Fernandez joined Celtic in 2002. The Lions' record signing cost an altogether more modest £60,000, when midfielder Barry Wilson signed from Inverness Caledonian Thistle in 2000.

HONOURS

First Division champions *2001*
League One champions *2017*
Second Division champions *1987, 1999, 2011*
Third Division champions *1996, 2010*
League Cup *2004*

HUGO LLORIS

Born: Nice, France, 26th December 1986
Position: Goalkeeper
Club career:
2004-06 Nice B 20
2005-08 Nice 72
2008-12 Lyon 146
2012- Tottenham Hotspur 239
International record:
2008- France 110

Tottenham's Hugo Lloris has won more caps for France than any other goalkeeper and has also captained his country a record 85 times. His greatest moment for Les Bleus came in 2018 when he led them to victory in the World Cup final against Croatia.

• After starting out with his hometown club Nice, Lloris made his name with Lyon. During a four-year stint with the

Hugo Lloris' King Kong impersonation was spot on!

French giants, Lloris was voted Ligue 1 Goalkeeper of the Year three times, but only managed to win one piece of silverware – the French Cup in 2012, following a 1-0 victory in the final over third-tier US Quevilly. He joined Tottenham that summer, and in 2019 skippered the north Londoners in their first ever Champions League final, a 2-0 defeat to Liverpool in Madrid.

• Famed for his superb reflexes, his fast and accurate distribution and his ability to rush out to the edge of the box to snuff out dangerous opposition attacks, Lloris won the European Under-19 Championship with France in 2005. He was awarded his first senior cap in 2008, keeping a clean sheet in a 0-0 draw with Uruguay, and he led his country for the first time in a 2-1 friendly win against England at Wembley in November 2010.

• At Euro 2016 Lloris was in fine form, especially in France's 2-0 win against Germany in the semi-final. However, in the final he was beaten by a long-range low shot from Portugal's Eder in extra-time and finished on the losing side.

RUBEN LOFTUS-CHEEK

Born: Lewisham, 23rd January 1996
Position: Midfielder
Club career:
2014- Chelsea 46 (7)
2017-18 Crystal Palace (loan) 24 (2)
International record:
2017- England 10 (0)

A powerful central midfielder with a deft touch, Ruben Loftus-Cheek enjoyed his best season yet with Chelsea in 2018/19, chipping in with 10 goals in all competitions, including a hat-trick against BATE Borisov in the group stages of the Europa League. However, just when he seemed to have cemented a starting place in the Blues team a serious achilles injury ruled him out of the final against Arsenal in Baku.

• The south Londoner joined Chelsea when aged eight, and progressed through the club's academy to help the Blues win the FA Youth Cup in 2012 and 2014 and the UEFA Youth League in 2015.

• Loftus-Cheek made his senior bow for Chelsea as a sub in a Champions League match against Sporting Lisbon in December 2014, but found it difficult to pin down a first-team place at Stamford Bridge before joining Crystal Palace on a season-long loan in July 2017.

• Capped by England from Under-16 level onwards, Loftus-Cheek scored in the final against France at the Under-21 Toulon Tournament in 2016 and was named Player of the Tournament. The following year he made his senior debut, putting in a Man of the Match display in a 0-0 draw with Germany at Wembley and he was a surprise selection in Gareth Southgate's squad for the World Cup in Russia.

DAVID LUIZ

Born: Diadema, Brazil, 22nd April 1987
Position: Defender
Club career:
2006-07 Vitoria 26 (1)
2015 Benfica (loan) 10 (0)
2007-11 Benfica 72 (4)
2011-14 Chelsea 81 (6)
2014-16 Paris Saint-Germain 53 (3)
2016-19 Chelsea 79 (5)
2019- Arsenal
International record:
2010- Brazil 56 (3)

Along with his former Chelsea team-mate Cesar Azpilicueta, David Luiz is one of just two players to win the Europa League twice with an English club. The hugely-experienced Brazilian defender first won the competition with the Blues in 2013, and repeated the feat in 2019 when Chelsea beat London rivals Arsenal 4-1 in the final in Baku. Ironically, Luiz then joined the Gunners for £8 million on the August transfer deadline day.

• The frizzy-haired centre-back had two spells at Stamford Bridge, returning to London from Paris Saint-Germain for £32 million on transfer deadline day in August 2016. In his first season back he helped the Blues win the Premier League title, his consistent performances in a back three under then boss Antonio Conte earning him a place in the PFA Team of the Year.

Unfortunately, David Luiz's 'bad hair days' have followed him across London from Chelsea to Arsenal...

• Luiz initially joined Chelsea from Benfica in January 2011, and the following year starred in Chelsea's successful Champions League campaign, bravely stepping up to score one of his team's penalties in the shoot-out victory over Bayern Munich which brought the trophy to London for the first – and, so far, only – time.

• In 2010 Luiz made his debut for Brazil in a 2-0 friendly win over the USA, and two years later he captained his country for the first time in a 1-0 win against South Africa. He had mixed fortunes at the 2014 World Cup, scoring a thunderous free kick in the quarter-final against Colombia but ending the tournament in tears when the hosts were hammered 7-1 by Germany in the semi-final.

ROMELU LUKAKU

Born: Antwerp, Belgium, 13th May 1993
Position: Striker
Club career:
2009-11 Anderlecht 73 (33)
2011-14 Chelsea 10 (0)
2012-13 West Bromwich Albion (loan) 35 (17)
2013-14 Everton (loan) 31 (15)
2017-19 Manchester United 66 (28)
2019- Inter Milan
International record:
2010- Belgium 81 (48)

In August 2019 Romelu Lukaku became only the second player (after a certain Cristiano Ronaldo) to be sold for a second time for a fee in excess of £70 million when he joined Inter Milan from Manchester United for £74 million. Two years earlier he had arrived at Old Trafford from Everton for £75 million, in the most expensive

Belgium star Lukaku made a goal-scoring debut for Inter Milan

TOP 10

BELGIAN PREMIER LEAGUE GOALSCORERS

1.	Romelu Lukaku (2011-19)	113
2.	Eden Hazard (2012-19)	85
3.	Christian Benteke (2012-)	70
4.	Marouane Fellaini (2008-19)	37
5.	Kevin Mirallas (2012-)	29
6.	Kevin De Bruyne (2013-)	23
7.	Nacer Chadli (2013-18)	21
8.	Vincent Kompany (2008-19)	18
9.	Divock Origi (2014-)	15
	Branko Strupar (1999-2002)	15

ever transfer between two English clubs at the time.

• Lukaku's 25 goals in 2016/17 put him second behind Harry Kane in the race for the Golden Boot and was the best ever haul by an Everton player in the Premier League era – as is his total of 53 league goals for the Toffees. During the campaign Lukaku scored in nine consecutive home games to equal a club record set by the legendary Dixie Dean in 1934.

• Quick and athletic, Lukaku enjoyed a great first season with his original club, Anderlecht, scoring 15 league goals as they won the Belgian championship in 2010. The following campaign he was the top scorer in Belgium with 20 goals across all competitions.

• Chelsea snapped up Lukaku for £10 million in 2011 but he struggled to make an impact at Stamford Bridge and the following season was loaned out to West Brom. The young striker thrived at the Hawthorns, netting 17 goals – the most ever in a single season by a Baggies player in the Premier League era. After another successful loan season at Everton, Lukaku joined the Toffees in a permanent deal for £28 million in July 2014, making him the club's most expensive ever player at the time.

• The son of a former Zaire (now DR Congo) international, Lukaku made his bow for Belgium in March 2010 while still only 16. He is now his country's all-time top scorer and enjoyed a good World Cup in Russia in 2018, scoring four goals to help Belgium finish third.

LUTON TOWN

Year founded: 1885
Ground: Kenilworth Road (10,356)
Nickname: The Hatters
Biggest win: 15-0 v Great Yarmouth Town (1914)
Heaviest defeat: 0-9 v Small Heath (1898)

Founded in 1885 following the merger of two local sides, Luton Town Wanderers and Excelsior, Luton Town became the first professional club in the south of England five years later.

• The club's greatest moment came in 1988 when they beat Arsenal 3-2 in the League Cup final. The Hatters returned to Wembley for the final the following year, but lost to Nottingham Forest – the same club which beat them in their only FA Cup final appearance in 1959.

• In 1936 Luton striker Joe Payne scored a Football League record 10 goals in a Third Division (South) fixture against Bristol Rovers. The Hatters won the match 12-0 to record their biggest ever league victory.

• Midfielder Bob Morton made a record 495 league appearances for the Hatters between 1946 and 1964, while his team-mate Gordon Turner scored a record 243 goals for the club.

• In January 2013, while they were languishing in the Football Conference, Luton became the first non-league team to beat a Premier League outfit in the FA Cup when they won 1-0 at Norwich City in a fourth round tie. The following season the Hatters won the Conference title with a club record 101 points.

• Defender Mal Donaghy won a club record 58 caps for Northern Ireland while with the Hatters between 1980 and 1988.

• After winning promotion from League Two in 2018, Luton won the League One championship the following year while remaining unbeaten for a club record 28 consecutive league matches.

HONOURS

Division 2 champions 1982
League One champions 2005, 2019
Division 3 (South) champions 1937
Division 4 champions 1968
Conference champions 2014
League Cup 1988
Football League Trophy 2009

MICK MCCARTHY

Born: Barnsley, 7th February 1959
Managerial career:
1992-96 Millwall
1996-2002 Republic of Ireland
2003-06 Sunderland
2006-2012 Wolverhampton Wanderers
2012-18 Ipswich Town
2018- Republic of Ireland

In November 2018 Mick McCarthy became the first man to manage the Republic of Ireland twice on a permanent basis when he succeeded Martin O'Neill. The straight-talking Yorkshireman had previously been in charge of the Republic between 1996 and 2002.

• In McCarthy's first spell at the helm he led his country to the 2002 World Cup finals in Japan and Korea, but his plans for the tournament were thrown into turmoil when a blazing row with his star player Roy Keane ended with the midfielder returning home before a ball had been kicked. Despite this unfortunate start, the Irish made it through to the second round where they were beaten by Spain on penalties. However, McCarthy was widely criticised in the Irish media for his handling of the Keane affair and he resigned from the job later that year.

• In a long managerial career McCarthy has guided both Sunderland and Wolves into the Premier League, but was unable to perform the same feat with his last club, Ipswich Town. He did manage to take the Tractor Boys to the Championship play-offs in 2015 but they lost out in the semi-finals to local rivals Norwich City.

• McCarthy spent most of his playing career with Barnsley, his hometown club, and Manchester City, before moving on to Celtic, with whom he won the Double in 1988. A rugged centre-back, he won 57 caps for the Republic of Ireland, helping his country reach the quarter-finals of the 1990 World Cup in Italy.

MACCLESFIELD TOWN

Year founded: 1874
Ground: Moss Rose (5,908)
Nickname: The Silkmen
Biggest win: 9-0 v Hartford St Johns (1884)
Heaviest defeat: 0-8 v West Ham United (2018)

Previously a rugby union club, Macclesfield switched to football in 1874 but had to wait until 1997 before finally achieving league status. Relegated from League Two in 2012, the Silkmen returned to the big time as National League champions in 2018 and the following season narrowly avoided the drop under their new boss, former England defender Sol Campbell, who has since left the club.

• Stalwart defender Darren Tinson played in a record 263 Football League games for Macclesfield between 1997 and 2003, while his team-mate Matthew Tipton is the Silkmen's top league scorer with 50 goals between 2002 and 2010.

• On 28th December 1999 Macclesfield's Chris Priest scored the last Football League goal of the twentieth century in a 2-1 win against Carlisle United.

• In 2013 the Silkmen reached the FA Cup fourth round for the only time in their history, but their hopes of further progress were dashed by a 1-0 defeat to Wigan Athletic.

HONOURS
National League champions 2018
Conference champions 1995, 1997

HARRY MAGUIRE

Born: Sheffield, 5th March 1993
Position: Defender
Club career:
2011-14 Sheffield United 134 (9)
2014-17 Hull City 54 (2)
2015 Wigan Athletic (loan) 16 (1)
2017-19 Leicester City 69 (6)
2019- Manchester United
International record:
2017- England 20 (1)

A commanding and physically imposing centre-half, Harry Maguire became the most expensive defender in world football when he moved from Leicester City to Manchester United for £80 million in August 2019. The deal was the biggest ever between two Premier League clubs and also made Maguire the most expensive English player of all time.

• Maguire came through the youth system at Sheffield United to make his debut for the Blades against Cardiff City in April 2011. He was voted the club's 'Player of the Year' in 2012, and two years later joined Premier League outfit Hull City for £2.5 million.

Macclesfield are all smiles after putting Blackpool out of the 2019/20 Carabao Cup on penalties

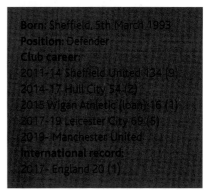

Manchester United's Harry Maguire, the world's most expensive defender

Writers' Association Manager of the Year award, after guiding her country to the finals of the Women's World Cup for the first time. However, the honour was ultimately awarded to Kilmarnock manager Steve Clarke.

MANCHESTER CITY

Year founded: 1887
Ground: Etihad Stadium (55,097)
Previous name: Ardwick
Nickname: The Citizens
Biggest win: 12-0 v Liverpool Stanley (1890)
Heaviest defeat: 2-10 v Small Heath (1894)

City have their roots in a church team which was renamed Ardwick in 1887 and became founder members of the Second Division five years later. In 1894, after suffering financial difficulties, the club was reformed under its present name.

• **Now owned by Sheikh Mansour of the Abu Dhabi Royal Family, City are one of the richest clubs in the world. In recent years the Sheikh has splashed out big money on stars like Kevin de Bruyne, Raheem Sterling and Riyad Mahrez and he has been rewarded with a stash of silverware, receiving the first return on his huge investment in 2011 when City won the FA Cup. More silverware followed the next season as City won the Premier League, their first league title since 1968, after pipping arch rivals Manchester United on goal difference. In 2014 City won the Premier League for a second time, Chilean boss Manuel Pellegrini becoming the first non-European manager to win the title.**

• Another title arrived in 2018 under the guidance of former Barcelona and Bayern Munich boss Pep Guardiola. Playing a slick and inventive brand of attacking football that thrilled fans and bewildered opponents, City smashed numerous Premier League records during a memorable campaign including most points won (100), most goals scored (106), best goal difference (+79), most wins (32), most consecutive wins (18) and biggest title-winning margin (19 points).

• However, he initially struggled to make an impact with the Tigers and was sent on loan to Wigan. He eventually became a regular with Hull in the 2016/17 season at the end of which he was voted the club's 'Player of the Year'. Following Hull's relegation he was sold to Leicester for £12 million in June 2017 and after a fine debut campaign with the Foxes in which he played every minute of the club's 38 league matches he collected another 'Player of the Year' award.

• **Capped just once at Under-21 level in November 2012, Maguire made his debut for England as a starter in a 1-0 defeat of Lithuania in August 2017. He was one of the unsung heroes of the Three Lions' run to the semi-finals of the 2018 World Cup, thwarting numerous opposition attacks and scoring with a thumping header in the quarter-final win against Sweden.**

• In 2019 he helped England claim third place at the UEFA Nations League, converting his spot-kick in the shoot-out in the play-off against Switzerland.

MANAGER OF THE SEASON

Former Manchester United boss Sir Alex Ferguson won the FA Premier League Manager of the Season award a record 11 times. He also won the old Manager of the Year award in 1993, giving him a total of 12 triumphs.

• **Arsène Wenger (in 1998, 2002 and 2004), Jose Mourinho (2005, 2006 and 2015) and Pep Guardiola (2018 and 2019) are the only other managers to win the award more than once since it was introduced in the 1993/94 season.**

• Just two English managers have won the award: Harry Redknapp (Tottenham Hotspur) in 2010 and Alan Pardew (Newcastle United) in 2012.

• **Tony Pulis topped the poll in 2014 despite his club, Crystal Palace, only finishing 11th in the Premier League – the lowest ever placing for a manager collecting the award.**

• In 2019 Scotland head coach Shelley Kerr became the first woman to be nominated for the Scottish Football

After winning four trophies in 2018/19, Manchester City decided to have a quiet little party...

• The following season City became the first English club ever to win the domestic Treble, pipping Liverpool by one point in the Premier League, beating Chelsea on penalties to win a fourth League Cup in six years and then smashing Watford 6-0 in the FA Cup final to record the joint-equal biggest win in the showpiece event.

• Prior to the modern era, the late 1960s were the most successful period in City's history, a side featuring the likes of Colin Bell, Francis Lee and Mike Summerbee winning the league title (1968), the FA Cup (1969), the League Cup (1970) and the European Cup Winners' Cup (also in 1970), and for a short time usurping Manchester United as the city's premier club.

• City also won the league title in 1937. Incredibly, the following season they were relegated to the Second Division despite scoring more goals than any other side in the division. To this day they remain the only league champions

to suffer the drop in the following campaign. Almost as bizarrely, City were agonisingly demoted from the top flight in 1983 after spending just the final four minutes of the entire season in the relegation zone.

• Argentinian striker Sergio Aguero, a key figure in City's recent triumphs, is the club's all-time leading goalscorer with 231 goals in all competitions since arriving from Atletico Madrid in 2011. The club's record appearance maker is Alan Oakes, who turned out 564 times in the sky blue shirt between 1958 and 1976.

• The club have won the League Cup six times, a record only bettered by Liverpool with eight wins. City have also won the FA Cup six times and, in 1926, were the first club to reach the final and be relegated in the same season. A 1-0 defeat by Bolton at Wembley ensured a grim campaign ended on a depressing note.

• City have won the title for the second tier of English football a joint-record seven times, most recently in 2002 when they returned to the Premiership under then manager Kevin Keegan. Four years earlier the club experienced their lowest ever moment when they dropped into the third tier of English football for the first and only time in their history – the first European trophy winners to ever sink this low.

• The club's most expensive purchase is Spanish midfielder Rodri, who signed from Atletico Madrid for £62.8 million in July 2019. The following month City

received a club record £34.1 million when they sold Brazilian defender Danilo to Juventus.

• Mercurial midfielder David Silva is the club's highest capped international, winning 77 of his 125 caps for Spain while at the Etihad.

• City hold the record for most consecutive home wins in the Premier League with 20 between March 2011 and March 2012. The club also jointly hold (with Chelsea) the record for consecutive away wins, with 11 in 2017.

HONOURS
Premier League champions 2012, 2014, 2018, 2019
Division 1 champions 1937, 1968
First Division champions 2002
Division 2 champions 1899, 1903, 1910, 1928, 1947, 1966
FA Cup 1904, 1934, 1956, 1969, 2011, 2019
League Cup 1970, 1976, 2014, 2016, 2018, 2019
Treble 2019
European Cup Winners' Cup 1970

MANCHESTER UNITED

Year founded: 1878
Ground: Old Trafford (74,879)
Previous name: Newton Heath
Nickname: Red Devils
Biggest win: 10-0 v Anderlecht (1956)
Heaviest defeat: 0-7 v Blackburn (1926), Aston Villa (1930) and Wolverhampton Wanderers (1931)

The club was founded in 1878 as Newton Heath, a works team for employees of the Lancashire and Yorkshire Railway. In 1892 Newton Heath (who played in yellow-and-green-halved shirts) were elected to the Football League but a decade later went bankrupt, only to be immediately reformed as Manchester United with the help of a local brewer, John Davies.

• United are the most successful club in the history of English football, having won the league title a record 20 times. The Red Devils have been the dominant force of the Premier League era, winning the title a record 13 times under former manager Sir Alex Ferguson.

IS THAT A FACT?
Manchester City scored 169 goals in all competitions in the 2018/19 season – a record for a top-flight English club.

Old Trafford's huge capacity means it's a noisy place come matchday

• United were the first English club to win the Double on three separate occasions, in 1994, 1996 and 1999. The last of these triumphs was particularly memorable as the club also went on to win the Champions League, famously beating Bayern Munich 2-1 in the final in Barcelona thanks to late goals by Teddy Sheringham and Ole Gunnar Solskjaer.

• Under legendary manager Sir Matt Busby United became the first ever English club to win the European Cup in 1968, when they beat Benfica 4-1 in the final at Wembley. Victory was especially sweet for Sir Matt who, a decade earlier, had narrowly survived the Munich air crash which claimed the lives of eight of his players as the team returned from a European Cup fixture in Belgrade. United also won European football's top club prize in 2008, beating Chelsea in the Champions League final on penalties in Moscow.

• When United won the Europa League in 2017 – after beating Dutch outfit Ajax 2-0 in the final in Stockholm – they became only the second British club (after Chelsea) to win all three historic European trophies, having previously won the Cup Winners' Cup in 1991.

• United won the FA Cup for the first time in 1909, beating Bristol City 1-0 in the final, and the club's total of 12 wins in the competition is only bettered by Arsenal. In 2000 the Red Devils became the first holders not to defend the cup when they played in the first FIFA Club World Cup Championship instead.

• Old Trafford has the highest capacity of any dedicated football ground bar Wembley in Britain but, strangely, when United set an all-time Football League attendance record of 83,260 for their home game against Arsenal on 17th January 1948 they were playing at Maine Road, home of local rivals Manchester City. This was because Old Trafford was badly damaged by German bombs during the Second World War, forcing United to use their neighbours' ground in the immediate post-war period.

• United's leading appearance maker is Ryan Giggs, who played in an incredible 963 games in all competitions for the club between 1991 and 2014. Winger Steve Coppell played in a club record 206 consecutive league games between 1977 and 1981.

• The club's highest goalscorer is Wayne Rooney, who banged in a total of 253 goals in all competitions between 2004 and 2017. Rooney is also United's most capped international, with 110 appearances for England in his time at Old Trafford.

• United provided seven players for the England team for a World Cup qualifier away to Albania in March 2001, equalling a record set by Arsenal in 1934. David Beckham, Nicky Butt, Andy Cole, Gary Neville and Paul Scholes all started the match, while Wes Brown and Teddy Sheringham came off the bench in England's 3-1 win.

• United hold the record for the biggest ever Premier League victory, thrashing Ipswich Town 9-0 at Old Trafford in March 1995. Andy Cole scored five goals in that game to set a record for the league that has since been matched by four other players, including United striker Dimitar Berbatov, against Blackburn in November 2010. However two United players have scored a club record six goals in a game: Harold Halse against Swindon Town in 1911, and George Best against Northampton Town in 1970.

• Known for many years as a big-spending club, United's record signing is French midfielder Paul Pogba, who cost a then world record £89.3 million when he moved from Juventus in August 2016. The club's most expensive sale is former Old Trafford hero Cristiano Ronaldo, who joined Real Madrid for a then world record £80 million in 2009.

• United legend Denis Law scored a club record 46 goals in all competitions in 1963/64, and also banged in a record 18 hat-tricks for the Red Devils.

• With around 122 million followers on Facebook, Instagram and Twitter, Manchester United have more fans worldwide than any other English club.

HONOURS
Premier League champions 1993, 1994, 1996, 1997, 1999, 2000, 2001, 2003, 2007, 2008, 2009, 2011, 2013
Division 1 champions 1908, 1911, 1952, 1956, 1957, 1965, 1967
Division 2 champions 1936, 1975
FA Cup 1909, 1948, 1963, 1977, 1983, 1985, 1990, 1994, 1996, 1999, 2004, 2016
League Cup 1992, 2006, 2009, 2010, 2017
Double 1994, 1996, 1999
European Cup/Champions League 1968, 1999, 2008
Europa League 2017
European Cup Winners' Cup 1991
European Super Cup 1991
Intercontinental Cup/Club World Cup 1999, 2008

TOP 10

TOTAL PREMIER LEAGUE POINTS

1.	Manchester United	2,168
2.	Arsenal	1,955
3.	Chelsea	1,931
4.	Liverpool	1,849
5.	Tottenham Hotspur	1,595
6.	Everton	1,427
7.	Manchester City	1,369
8.	Newcastle United	1,272
9.	Aston Villa	1,223
10.	West Ham United	1,098

SADIO MANE

Born: Sedhiou, Senegal, 10th April 1992
Position: Striker/winger
Club career:
2011-12 Metz 22 (2)
2012-14 Red Bull Salzburg 63 (31)
2014-16 Southampton 67 (21)
2016- Liverpool 92 (45)
International record:
2012- Senegal 60 (18)

Senegal international Sadio Mane was joint-top scorer in the Premier League in 2018/19 with 22 goals, a tally matched by his Liverpool team-mate Mo Salah and Arsenal's Pierre-Emerick Aubameyang. He also played a vital role in the Reds' Champions League success, winning a penalty after just 24 seconds of the final against Tottenham in Madrid when his cross hit Moussa Sissoko's arm. The previous season Mane scored himself in the Champions League final, but ended on the losing side after a 3-1 defeat to Real Madrid in Kiev.

• A speedy attacker who generally finishes with calm confidence, Mane started out with French club Metz before coming to the fore

2018/19's joint Premiership Golden Boot winner Sadio Mane

with Red Bull Salzburg, with whom he won the Austrian Double in 2014. In the same year he joined Southampton for £11.8 million.

• In May 2015 Mane made headlines when he hit the fastest Premier League hat-trick ever, scoring three times in a 6-1 rout of Aston Villa in an incredible two minutes and 56 seconds. The following season he was the Saints' top scorer in all competitions with 15 goals and in June 2016 he joined Liverpool for £34 million, then a record fee for an African player.

• Mane made his debut for Senegal in 2012, representing his country at that year's Olympics in London. In 2019 he helped Senegal reach the final of the Africa Cup of Nations for just the second time in their history, but they lost 1-0 to Algeria in Cairo.

MANSFIELD TOWN

Year founded: 1897
Ground: One Call Stadium (9,186)
Previous names: Mansfield Wesleyans, Mansfield Wesley
Nickname: The Stags
Biggest win: 9-2 v Rotherham United (1932)
Heaviest defeat: 1-7 v Reading (1932), Peterborough United (1966) and QPR (1966)

The club was founded as Mansfield Wesleyans, a boys brigade team, in 1897, before becoming Mansfield Town in 1910. The Stags eventually joined the Football League in 1931, remaining there until relegation to the Conference in 2008. Five years later the club bounced back to League Two as Conference champions with a club record 95 points.

• In 1950/51 Mansfield were the first club ever to remain unbeaten at home in a 46-game season, but just missed out on promotion to the old Second Division. The Stags finally reached the second tier in 1977, but were relegated at the end of the campaign.

• Already Sheffield United's all-time top scorer, striker Harry Johnson arrived at Mansfield in 1932 and in just three seasons scored 104 league goals to set a record for the Stags that still

Forward Omari Sterling-James will be hoping to fire the Stags into League One

stands. Goalkeeper Rod Arnold played in a club record 440 league games for the Stags between 1971 and 1984.

• Mansfield's Field Mill ground (now known as the One Call Stadium for sponsorship purposes) is the oldest in the world hosting professional football, the first match having been played there in 1861.

• Beaten in the League Two play-off semi-finals in 2019, the Stags won promotion to the third tier in 1963 after scoring a club record 108 league goals.

HONOURS
Division 3 champions 1977
Division 4 champions 1975
Conference champions 2013
EFL Trophy 1987

MASCOTS

Britain's oldest mascot is 105-year-old Preston fan Bernard Jones, who led the Lillywhites out for their first game of the 2017/18 season against Sheffield Wednesday in his wheelchair. The Premier League record is held by 102-year-old Manchester City fan Vera

Cohen, who performed mascot duties with her sister Olga Hanlon, 97, at City's home match against Fulham in September 2018.

• Swansea mascot Cyril the Swan was fined a record £1,000 in 1999 for celebrating a goal against Millwall in the FA Cup by running onto the pitch and pushing the referee. Two years later Cyril was in trouble again when he pulled off the head of Millwall's Zampa the Lion mascot and drop-kicked it into the crowd.

• West Ham United were criticised during the 2018/19 season for charging their child

mascots £700 each for accompanying the players out of the London Stadium tunnel and onto the pitch. At the other end of the scale, a number of Premier League clubs, including Arsenal, Chelsea and Manchester City, did not charge their mascots a penny.

• Charlton fan Daniel Boylett was jailed for 21 months and banned from attending football matches for six years after attempting to punch Crystal Palace's mascot, a live eagle called Kayla, during the south London rivals' League Cup tie in September 2015. Kayla, though, had the last laugh as the Eagles ran out 4-1 winners.

• The first World Cup mascot was World Cup Willie, a lion wearing a Union Jack waistcoat created by children's illustrator Reg Hoye for the 1966 tournament in England. Since then notable World Cup mascots include Naranjito (an orange sporting the colours of Spain for the 1982 tournament), Ciao! (a red-white-and green stickman for Italia '90), Footix (a massive blue cockerel for France '98) and Zabivaka (a Russian wolf for the 2018 World Cup).

• The mascot for Euro 2020 is Skillzy, a freestyling youth with a topknot.

Leganes' 'Super Pepino' – 'Super Cucumber' to you and me – is quite possibly the world's silliest mascot!

MATCH-FIXING

The first recorded incidence of match-fixing occurred in 1900 when Jack Hillman, goalkeeper with relegation-threatened Burnley, was alleged to have offered a bribe to the Nottingham Forest captain. Hillman was found guilty of the charges by a joint Football Association and Football League commission and banned for one year.

• Nine players received bans after Manchester United beat Liverpool at Old Trafford in April 1915. A Liverpool player later admitted the result had been fixed in a Manchester pub before the match. For his part in the scandal, United's Enoch West was banned for life – although the punishment was later waived... when West was 62!

• In the mid-1960s English football was rocked by a match-fixing scandal when former Everton player Jimmy Gauld revealed in a newspaper interview that a number of games had been rigged as part of a betting coup. Gauld implicated three Sheffield Wednesday players in the scam, including England internationals Tony Kay and Peter Swan. The trio were later sentenced to four months in prison and banned for life from football. Ringleader Gauld received a four-year prison term.

• In July 2018 Parma striker Emanuele Calaio was banned for two years and fined £17,800 for attempting to fix a match against Spezia on the last day of the 2017/18 season which Parma needed to win to earn automatic promotion to Serie A. Parma, who won that game 2-0, were also docked five points but allowed to keep their newly-acquired top-flight status.

• In May 2019 Spanish police investigating an alleged match-fixing ring arrested a number of people, including former Real Madrid player Raul Bravo and Huesca President Agustin Lasaoso.

• In October 2018 Belgian prosecutors charged 19 people, including referees, agents and the coach of Club Bruges, with fraud and match-fixing over allegations that at least two matches in the Belgian league in March 2018 had been subject to fixing. Then, a month later, the Belgian FA revealed that three members of the country's Under-16 women's team had been offered $50,000 each by a Turkish man to influence a match at an international tournament.

KYLIAN MBAPPE

Born: Paris, France, 20th December 1998
Position: Striker
Club career:
2015-16 Monaco B 12 (4)
2015-18 Monaco 41 (16)
2017-18 Paris St-Germain (loan) 27 (13)
2018- Paris St-Germain 29 (33)
International record:
2017- France 33 (13)

French Player of the Year in 2019, Paris Saint-Germain striker Kylian Mbappe became the second most expensive player in the world when he joined the club from Monaco, initially on a season-long loan, for £166 million in the summer of 2017. He immediately paid back some of that staggering fee by helping PSG win the Double in his first campaign in the French capital and then topped the Ligue 1 goalscoring charts with 33 goals as his club won the title again in 2019.

• A product of the famous Clairefontaine national academy, Mbappe holds the records for Monaco as the club's youngest player and goalscorer -– in both cases passing benchmarks previously set by the legendary Thierry Henry. In 2017 he helped Monaco win their first league title for 17 years, contributing 26 goals in all competitions.

• A devastatingly quick attacker, Mbappe was part of the French Under-19 team which won the European Championships in 2016, scoring five goals in the tournament in total – just one fewer than the top scorer, his team-mate Jean-Kevin Augustin.

• He made his senior debut for France against Luxembourg in March 2017 aged 18, becoming the second youngest ever player to represent his country. The following year Mbappe became the first teenager since the legendary Pele in 1958 to score in the World Cup final, rifling home from the edge of the box in France's 4-2 win against Croatia in Moscow.

LIONEL MESSI

Rated by many as the best player in the world, Lionel Messi is Barcelona's all-time leading scorer with an incredible 603 goals in all competitions. No fewer than 419 of those came in La Liga, making the diminutive Argentinian the competition's leading all-time scorer. He also holds the record for hat-tricks in La Liga (33) and, jointly with Cristiano Ronaldo, in the Champions League (8).

• Life, though, could have been very different for Messi, who suffered from a growth hormone deficiency as a child in Argentina. However, his outrageous talent was such that Barcelona were prepared to move him and his immediate family to Europe

France's Kylian Mbappe, top scorer in Ligue I in 2018/19

TOP 10

LA LIGA GOALSCORERS

1.	Lionel Messi (2004-)	419
2.	Cristiano Ronaldo (2009-18)	311
3.	Telmo Zarra (1940-55)	251
4.	Hugo Sanchez (1981-94)	234
5.	Raul (1994-2010)	228
6.	Alfredo Di Stefano (1953-66)	227
7.	Cesar Rodriguez (1939-55)	223
8.	Quini (1970-87)	219
9.	Pahino (1943-56)	210
10.	Edmundo Suarez (1939-50)	195

when he was aged just 13 and pay for his medical treatment.

• Putting these problems behind him, he has flourished to the extent that in 2009 he was named both World Player of the Year and European Player of the Year, and in 2010 he was the inaugural winner of the FIFA Ballon d'Or – an award he won a record four times before it was rebranded as the FIFA Men's Best Player.

• A brilliant dribbler and superb finisher from long or short range, in 2012 Messi became the first player to be top scorer in four consecutive Champions League campaigns (2009-12) and he also set another record for the competition when he struck five goals in a single game against Bayer Leverkusen. In 2015 he helped Barcelona become the first European club to win the Treble of league, cup and Champions League twice, scoring twice in the Copa del Rey final against Athletic Bilbao.

• Messi scored a world record 91 goals in the calendar year of 2012 for club and country, and the following year became the first player to score against every other La Liga club in consecutive matches. In 2019 he claimed the European Golden Shoe for a record sixth time after netting 36 goals in La Liga to help Barcelona win the title for a tenth time in his 15 years at the Nou Camp.

• Messi made his international debut in 2005 but it was a forgettable occasion – he was sent off after just 40 seconds for elbowing a Hungarian defender. Happier times followed in 2007 when he was voted Player of the Tournament at the Copa America and in 2008 when he won a gold medal with the Argentine football team at the Beijing Olympics.

• At the 2014 World Cup he won the Golden Ball as the tournament's

"I'd like to thank all my Barcelona team-mates – even though none of them are anyway near as good as me…"

Boro manger Jonathan Woodgate really wants Messi's microphone...

outstanding player, but had to be satisfied with a runners-up medal after Argentina's defeat by Germany in the final. The following year he turned down the Player of the Tournament award at the Copa America following Argentina's defeat to hosts Chile in the final and after his country's defeat in the final to the same opposition in 2016 he announced his retirement from international football.

• However, a huge public campaign calling for him to change his mind was successful, and he marked his return with the winning goal against old foes Uruguay in a World Cup qualifier in September 2016. With 68 goals for his country, Messi is Argentina's all-time top scorer.

MIDDLESBROUGH

Year founded: 1876
Ground: Riverside Stadium (34,742)
Nickname: Boro
Biggest win: 11-0 v Scarborough (1890)
Heaviest defeat: 0-9 v Blackburn Rovers (1954)

Founded by members of the Middlesbrough Cricket Club at the Albert Park Hotel in 1876, the club turned professional in 1889 before reverting to amateur status three years later. Winners of the FA Amateur Cup in both 1895 and

1898, the club turned pro for a second time in 1899 and was elected to the Football League in the same year.

• In 1905 Middlesbrough became the first club to sign a player for a four-figure transfer fee when they forked out £1,000 for Sunderland and England striker Alf Common. On his Boro debut Common paid back some of the fee by scoring the winner at Sheffield United... the Teesiders' first away win for two years!

• The club had to wait over a century before winning a major trophy, but finally broke their duck in 2004 with a 2-1 victory over Bolton in the League Cup final at the Millennium Stadium, Cardiff.

• Two years later Middlesbrough reached the UEFA Cup final, after twice overturning three-goal deficits earlier in the competition. There was no happy ending, though, as Boro were thrashed 4-0 by Sevilla in the final in Eindhoven.

• In 1997 the club were deducted three points by the FA for calling off a Premier League fixture at Blackburn at short notice after illness and injury ravaged their squad. The penalty resulted in Boro being relegated from the Premier League at the end of the season. To add to their supporters' disappointment the club was also beaten in the finals of the League Cup and FA Cup in the same campaign – no other club has suffered three such disappointments in one season.

• Veteran goalkeeper Mark Schwarzer is Boro's highest capped international, playing 51 times for Australia while at the Riverside between 1997 and 2008.

• In 1926/27 striker George Camsell hit an astonishing 59 league goals, including a record nine hat-tricks, as the club won the Second Division championship. His tally set a new Football League record and, although it was beaten by Everton's Dixie Dean the following season, Camsell still holds the divisional record. An ex-miner, Camsell went on to score a club record 325 league goals for Boro – a tally only surpassed by Dean's incredible 349 goals for Everton.

• **On 14th August 2018 defender Nathan Wood became Middlesbrough's youngest ever player when he came on as a sub against Notts County in a League Cup tie aged 16 and 72 days.**

HONOURS
First Division champions 1995
Division 2 champions 1927, 1929, 1974
League Cup 2006
FA Amateur Cup 1895, 1898

MILLWALL

Year founded: 1885
Ground: The Den (20,146)
Previous name: Millwall Rovers
Nickname: The Lions
Biggest win: 9-1 v Torquay (1927) and Coventry (1927)
Heaviest defeat: 1-9 v Aston Villa (1946)

The club was founded as Millwall Rovers in 1885 by workers at local jam and marmalade factory, Morton and Co. In 1920 they joined the Third Division, gaining a reputation as a club with some of the most fiercely passionate and partisan fans in the country.

• **In 1988 Millwall won the Second Division title to gain promotion to the top flight for the first time in their history. The Lions enjoyed a few brief weeks at the top of the league pyramid in the autumn of 1988 but were relegated two years later.**

• The club's greatest moment, though, came in 2004 when they reached their first FA Cup final. Despite losing 3-0 to Manchester United, the Lions made history by becoming the first club from outside the top flight to contest the final in the Premier League era, while substitute Curtis Weston set a new record for the youngest player to appear in the final (17 years and 119 days).

• **Lions boss Neil Harris is the club's all-time leading scorer with 125 goals in two spells at the Den between 1998 and 2011. Legendary central defender Barry Kitchener turned out in a club record 523 league games between 1966 and 1982.**

• On their way to winning the Division Three (South) championship in 1928 Millwall scored 87 goals at home, an all-time Football League record. Altogether, the Lions managed 127 goals that season – a figure only ever bettered by three other clubs.

• **In 1937 Millwall became the first club from the third tier to reach the semi-finals of the FA Cup after beating three teams from the old First Division along the way. The Lions have a great giant-killing history in the competition, having knocked out 25 teams from the top flight while not in the elite division themselves – a record only Southampton can match.**

HONOURS
Division 2 champions 1988
Second Division champions 2001
Division 3 (South) champions 1928, 1938
Division 4 champions 1962

MILTON KEYNES DONS

Year founded: 2004
Ground: Stadium MK (30,500)
Nickname: The Dons
Biggest win: 7-0 v Oldham (2014)
Heaviest defeat: 0-6 v Southampton (2015)

The club was effectively formed in 2004 when Wimbledon FC were controversially allowed to re-locate to Milton Keynes on the ruling of a three-man FA commission despite the passionate opposition of the club's supporters, the Football League and even the FA.

Ryan Leonard will be hoping to get the Lions roaring in 2019/20

• Despite pledging to Wimbledon fans that they would not change their name, badge or colours, within a few seasons all three of these things had happened, reinforcing the impression amongst many in the game that the MK Dons are English football's first 'franchise'. The MK Dons have since handed back to Merton Council all the honours and trophies won by Wimbledon FC and claimed by rivals AFC Wimbledon.

• Club captain Dean Lewington has made a record 619 league appearances for the Dons since making his debut in 2004. Striker Izale McLeod is the club's leading scorer, with 62 goals in two spells at the Stadium MK between 2004 and 2014.

• **Striker Simon Church won a club record nine caps for Wales during a season with MK Dons in 2015/16.**

• Promoted back to League One in 2018, MK Dons sold dynamic midfielder Dele Alli to Tottenham for a club record £5 million in January 2015. The England international is the club's youngest ever hat-trick scorer, striking three times against Notts County in March 2014 when aged 17 and 330 days.

HONOURS
League Two champions 2008
EFL Trophy 2008

LUKA MODRIC

Born: Zagreb, Croatia, 9th September 1985
Position: Midfielder
Club career:
2003-08 Dinamo Zagreb 112 (31)
2003 Zrinjski Mostar (loan) 22 (8)
2004 Inter Zapresic (loan) 18 (4)
2008-12 Tottenham Hotspur 127 (13)
2012- Real Madrid 166 (9)
International record:
2006- Croatia 113 (14)

When he was voted the Best FIFA Men's Player in 2018 midfield maestro Luka Modric broke a decade-long stranglehold of the top individual award by arch rivals Lionel Messi and Cristiano Ronaldo.

• Modric started out with Croatian side Dinamo Zagreb, winning three league titles and the national Player of the Year award with his hometown club before joining Tottenham in 2008. He recovered from a broken leg to help Spurs qualify for the Champions League for the first time in 2010, but the following summer he agitated for a move to Chelsea until being forced to honour his contract by Tottenham chairman Daniel Levy. He finally left White Hart Lane in 2012, joining Real for around £33 million and has gone on to win the Champions League four times – a record for a Croatian player.

• A gifted playmaker who is known as 'the Croatian Cruyff' in his home country, Modric made his international debut in 2006 and two years later starred at Euro 2008, where he was voted into the Team of the Tournament after some magnificent displays – only the second Croatian player ever to achieve this honour.

• At the World Cup in Russia in 2018 Modric skippered Croatia in their first ever major final. Luck was against them on the day and they went down to a 4-2 defeat against France, but there was consolation for the talented midfielder when he was voted the tournament's best player and awarded the Golden Ball.

MONEY

The Premier League is easily the richest league in world football. In the 2017/18 season the league's revenues hit a record £4.8 billion with domestic and worldwide TV rights accounting for more than half of that money.

• Barcelona's Lionel Messi is the world's richest footballer, raking in £100 million per year in earnings and endorsements. He is followed on the rich list by his old adversary, Juventus striker Cristiano Ronaldo (£86 million). However both players could one day be mere paupers compared to Brunei captain and Leicester City reserve Faiq Bolkiah, who is an heir to the Sultan of Brunei's £13 billion fortune.

• According to Forbes, Real Madrid are the most valuable club in the world, worth $4.24 billion in 2019. The Spanish giants lead the way ahead of Barcelona ($4 billion) and Manchester United ($3.8 billion), while Manchester City, Chelsea, Arsenal,

Luka Modric, the world's best player in 2018

TOP 10

CLUB REVENUES 2017/18

1.	Real Madrid	£665.2 million
2.	Barcelona	£611.6 million
3.	Manchester United	£590 million
4.	Bayern Munich	£557.4 million
5.	Manchester City	£503.5 million
6.	Paris Saint-Germain	£479.9 million
7.	Liverpool	£455.1 million
8.	Chelsea	£448 million
9.	Arsenal	£389.1 million
10.	Tottenham Hotspur	£379.4 million

Liverpool and Tottenham also feature in the top 10.

• The wealthiest manager in the world is Atletico Madrid boss Diego Simeone, who earns a staggering £35 million every year.

MORECAMBE

Year founded: 1920
Ground: Globe Arena (6,476)
Nickname: The Shrimps
Biggest win: 8-0 v Fleetwood Town (1993)
Heaviest defeat: 0-7 v Chesterfield (2016)

Founded in 1920 after a meeting at the local West View Hotel, Morecambe joined the Lancashire Combination League that same year and subsequently spent the next 87 years of their history in non-league football.

• The greatest moment in the club's history came in 2007 when the Shrimps beat Exeter 2-1 in the Conference play-off final at Wembley to win promotion to the Football League. The Shrimps have remained in League Two ever since, and are now the division's longest-serving club.

• Appointed in May 2011, Morecambe boss Jim Bentley is currently the longest-serving manager in the Football League/Premier League.

• For the second season running, Morecambe had the lowest average attendance in the Football League in 2018/19. However, the average of 2,033 fans attending the Shrimps' home games at the Globe Arena was an impressive 36% up on the figure for 2017/18.

MOTHERWELL

Year founded: 1886
Ground: Fir Park (13,677)
Nickname: The Well
Biggest win: 12-1 v Dundee United (1954)
Heaviest defeat: 0-8 v Aberdeen (1979)

Motherwell were founded in 1886 following the merger of two local factory-based sides, Alpha and Glencairn. The club turned pro in 1893 and, in the same year, joined the newly formed Scottish Second Division.

• The club enjoyed its heyday in the 1930s, winning the league title for the first and only time in 1932 and finishing as runners-up in the Scottish Cup three times in the same decade.

• Striker Willie McFadyen scored a remarkable 52 league goals for the Well when they won the title in 1931/32, a Scottish top-flight record that still stands today. His team-mate Bob Ferrier played in a Scottish record 626 league games between 1917 and 1937.

• Motherwell had to wait until 1952 before they won the Scottish Cup for the first time, and they did it in some style by thrashing Dundee 4-0 in the final. In 1991, the Well beat Dundee United 4-3 in an exciting final.

• Motherwell have won the Scottish League Cup just once, beating favourites Hibs 3-0 in the final at Hampden Park in the 1950/51 season.

HONOURS
Division 1 champions 1932
First Division champions 1982, 1985
Division 2 champions 1954, 1969
Scottish Cup 1952, 1991
League Cup 1951

LUCAS MOURA

Born: Sao Paulo, Brazil, 13th August 1992
Position: Winger
Club career:
2010-12 Sao Paulo 74 (19)
2013-18 Paris Saint-Germain 153 (34)
2018- Tottenham Hotspur 38 (10)
International record:
2011- Brazil 35 (4)

Exciting Brazilian winger Lucas Moura was the star of Tottenham's run to the 2019 Champions League final, scoring a remarkable second-half hat-trick against Ajax in the second leg of the semi-final as the north Londoners fought back from 3-0 down on aggregate to go through on the away goals rule.

• Lucas also scored the first hat-trick at his club's new Tottenham Hotspur Stadium, filling his boots in a 4-0 demolition of Huddersfield Town on 13th April 2019.

• Fast, mobile and direct, Lucas began his career with his hometown club, Sao Paulo, before moving to Paris Saint-Germain for a then club record £38 million in January 2013. In five years in the French capital he won four league titles and played in two domestic cup finals, both of them on the winning side, before joining Spurs for around £25 million in January 2018.

• Lucas was a member of the Brazil team which won the 2011 Under-20 South American Championship, scoring a hat-trick in a 6-0 thrashing of Uruguay in the final. In the same year he made his full international debut against Scotland, and in 2012 he was part of the Brazil squad which won Silver at the London Olympics.

JOSE MOURINHO

Born: Setubal, Portugal, 26th January 1963
Managerial career:
2000 Benfica
2001-02 Uniao Leiria
2002-04 Porto
2004-07 Chelsea
2008-10 Inter Milan
2010-13 Real Madrid
2013-15 Chelsea
2016-18 Manchester United

In December 2018 Jose Mourinho was sacked as manager of Manchester United after leading the Red Devils to their worst ever start to a Premier League season – just 26 points from their opening 17 games. However, the spiky Portuguese boss had reason to feel hard done by, having guided United to both the League Cup and the Europa League only the previous year.

• Mourinho started out as Bobby Robson's assistant at Sporting Lisbon, Porto and Barcelona before briefly managing Benfica in 2000. Two years

"So, you think it's funny I got the sack from Man U?"

later he returned to Porto, where he won two Portuguese league titles and the UEFA Cup before becoming Europe's most sought-after young manager when his side claimed the Champions League trophy in 2004.

• Shortly after this triumph, Mourinho replaced Claudio Ranieri as Chelsea manager, styling himself as a 'Special One' in his first press conference. He certainly lived up to his billing, as his Blues team won back-to-back Premier League titles in 2005 and 2006, the FA Cup in 2007, and the League Cup in both 2005 and 2007.

• After falling out with owner Roman Abramovich, Mourinho left Stamford Bridge in September 2007. He made a sensational return to west London in 2013 and in his second season back with the Blues guided them to both the Premier League and the League Cup, picking up a third Manager of the Year award in the process. However, after a calamitous start to the following campaign Mourinho was sacked in December 2015. Six months later he was appointed United manager, succeeding Louis van Gaal.

• In between his stints at Chelsea, Mourinho took charge of Italian giants Inter Milan and Real Madrid. He led Inter to the first ever Treble, including the Champions League, by an Italian club in 2010, and guided Real to the Spanish title two years later with record tallies for points (100) and goals (121), making him the only manager to have won the championship in England, Italy and Spain.

NAPOLI

Year founded: 1926
Ground: Stadio San Paolo (60,240)
Nickname: Azzurri
League titles: 2
Domestic cups: 5
European cups: 1

The club was formed in 1926 following the merger of Internazionale Napoli and Poths' Naples FC, a club created two decades earlier by English sailor William Poths. Three years later Napoli were founder members of Italy's first national league, Serie A.

• After a fairly undistinguished history, Napoli's fortunes were transformed by the arrival of the great Diego Maradona from Barcelona for a then world record fee of £6.9 million in July 1984. The club won their first title three years later – the first ever by a team from southern Italy – sparking massive celebrations across the city. In the same year the club also won the Coppa Italia, and another league title followed in 1990.

• Napoli's sole European success came in 1989 when they beat German side Stuttgart 5-4 on aggregate in the UEFA Cup final.

• **In the 2015/16 season Napoli striker Gonzalo Higuain scored 36 goals in Serie A, an all-time record for the Italian league.**

• Since the glory days of Maradona Napoli have struggled to compete with the big powers in the north of the country, but they did win the Coppa Italia in 2012 and 2014 and in 2019 they finished runners up to perennial title winners Juventus.

> HONOURS
> ***Italian champions*** *1987, 1990*
> ***Italian Cup*** *1962, 1976, 1987, 2012, 2014*
> ***UEFA Cup*** *1989*

NATIONAL LEAGUE

The pinnacle of the non-league system which feeds into the Football League, the fifth tier of English football was rebranded as the National League in 2015, having previously been called the Football Conference. The league was founded as the Alliance Premier League in 1979 and has been divided into three sections – National, North and South – since 2004.

• **Promotion and relegation between the Football League and the Conference became automatic in 1987, when Scarborough United replaced Lincoln City.**

• However, clubs have to satisfy the Football League's minimal ground requirements before their promotion can be confirmed and Kidderminster Harriers, Macclesfield Town and Stevenage Borough all failed on this

IS THAT A FACT?
AFC Wimbledon set a National League scoring record for the play-offs in 2011 thrashing Fleetwood 8-1 on aggregate in the semi-finals.

count in the mid-1990s after topping the Conference table.

• **Barnet (1991, 2005 and 2015) and Macclesfield Town (1995, 1997 and 2018) have both won the division a record three times.**

• In 2014 Luton Town won the league after finishing a record 19 points clear of the runners up, Cambridge United. The Hatters also set a new record for the best goal difference in the league's history, +67.

THE NETHERLANDS

First international: Belgium 1 Netherlands 4, 1905
Most capped player: Wesley Sneijder, 134 caps (2003-18)
Leading goalscorer: Robin van Persie, 50 goals (2005-17)
First World Cup appearance: Netherlands 2 Switzerland 1, 1934
Biggest win: Netherlands 11 San Marino 0, 2011
Heaviest defeat: England amateurs 9 Netherlands 1, 1909

Long associated with an entertaining style of attacking football, the Netherlands have only won one major tournament, the European Championship in 1988. In the final that year the Dutch beat Russia with goals from their two biggest stars of the time, Ruud Gullit and Marco van Basten.

• **The Netherlands are the only country to have lost all three World Cup finals they have played in. On the first two of these occasions they had the misfortune to meet the hosts in the final, losing to West Germany in 1974 and Argentina in 1978. Then, in**

Napoli captain Lorenzo Insigne

The Netherlands' players have sometimes been accused of being big-headed...

the 2010 final, they went down 1-0 in extra-time to Spain in Johannesburg following a negative, at times brutal, Dutch performance which was totally at odds with the country's best footballing traditions. At the next World Cup, the Netherlands again did well, coming third.

• A professional league wasn't formed in the Netherlands until 1956, and it took some years after that before the country was taken seriously as a football power. Their lowest ebb was arguably reached in 1963 when the Dutch were humiliatingly eliminated from the European Championships by perennial minnows Luxembourg.

• However, the following decade saw a renaissance in Dutch football. With exciting players like Johan Cruyff, Johan Neeskens and Ruud Krol in their side, the Netherlands were considered the best team in Europe. Pivotal to their success was the revolutionary 'Total Football' system devised by manager Rinus Michels which allowed the outfield players constantly to switch positions during the game.

• In 2011 the Netherlands strolled to their biggest ever win, 11-0 against San Marino in a Euro 2012 qualifier – just two goals shy of Germany's record European Championships qualifying victory against the same hapless opposition five years earlier.

• In 2019 the Netherlands reached the inaugural UEFA Nations League final, but were beaten 1-0 by hosts Portugal in Porto.

HONOURS
European Championship winners
1988
World Cup Record
1930 Did not enter
1934 Round 1
1938 Round 1
1950 Did not enter
1954 Did not enter
1958 Did not qualify
1962 Did not qualify
1966 Did not qualify
1970 Did not qualify
1974 Runners-up
1978 Runners-up
1982 Did not qualify
1986 Did not qualify
1990 Round 2
1994 Quarter-finals
1998 Fourth place
2002 Did not qualify
2006 Round 2
2010 Runners-up
2014 Third place
2018 Did not qualify

PHIL NEVILLE

Born: Bury, 21st January 1977
Managerial career:
2015 Salford City (caretaker)
2018- England Women

Appointed head coach of the England women's team in January 2018, Phil Neville led the Lionesses to victory in the SheBelieves Cup the following year

and then to fourth place at the 2019 Women's World Cup in France – one place below their best-ever showing in the tournament.

• Neville is the first former male international to lead the women's team, but his appointment was criticised by some on the grounds that he had no previous experience in the women's game. However, he had previously worked as a coach for the England Under-21 team, Manchester United and Valencia and briefly managed Salford City, the National League club he co-owns with several of his former United team-mates.

• In a long career spent mostly with Manchester United, Neville won six Premier League titles, three FA Cups and was an unused substitute when United beat Bayern Munich in the 1999 Champions League final in Barcelona to clinch a remarkable Treble.

• A steady full-back who could also play in midfield, Neville won 59 caps for England between 1996 and 2007, including a record 31 alongside his brother Gary.

Looks like Phil Neville has pinched Gareth Southgate's 'lucky' waistcoat!

£40 million striker Joelinton is Newcastle's record signing

NEWCASTLE UNITED

Year founded: 1892
Ground: St James' Park (52,354)
Nickname: The Magpies
Biggest win: 13-0 v Newport County (1946)
Heaviest defeat: 0-9 v Burton Wanderers (1895)

The club was founded in 1892 following the merger of local sides Newcastle East End and Newcastle West End, gaining election to the Football League just a year later.

• In 1895 Newcastle suffered their worst ever defeat, going down 9-0 to Burton Wanderers in a Second Division match. However, their most embarrassing loss was a 9-1 home hammering by Sunderland in December 1908. The Toon recovered, though, to win the title that season, making that defeat by their local rivals the heaviest ever suffered by the eventual league champions. The Magpies recorded their best ever win in 1946, thrashing Newport County 13-0 to equal Stockport County's record for the biggest ever victory in a Football League match. Star of the show at St James' Park was Len Shackleton, who scored six of the goals on his Newcastle debut to set a club record.

• Newcastle have a proud tradition in the FA Cup, having won the competition on six occasions. In 1908 the Magpies reached the final after smashing Fulham 6-0, the biggest ever win in the semi-final. Then, in 1924, 41-year-old defender Billy Hampson became the oldest player ever to appear in the cup final, when he turned out for the Toon in their rain-swept 2-0 defeat of Aston Villa at Wembley.

• The club's best cup era was in the 1950s when they won the trophy three times, boss Stan Seymour becoming the first man to lift the cup as a player and a manager. Legendary centre-forward Jackie Milburn was instrumental to Newcastle's success, scoring in every round in 1951 and then notching after just 45 seconds in the 1955 final against Manchester City – the fastest Wembley cup final goal ever at the time. In 1952 Chilean striker George Robledo notched the winner against Arsenal to become the first foreign player to score in the FA Cup final.

• Milburn is the club's leading goalscorer in league matches with 178 strikes between 1946 and 1957. However, Alan Shearer holds the overall club goalscoring record, finding the net 206 times in all competitions after his then world record £15 million move from Blackburn Rovers in 1996. In the 1993/94 season Magpies striker Andy Cole scored 34 goals in the Premier League — a record for a single campaign matched by Shearer the following year.

• Newcastle's only success in Europe came in 1969 when they won the Fairs Cup following a 6-2 aggregate win against Hungarian outfit Ujpest Dozsa. Skipper Bobby Moncur was the unlikely hero of that triumph, the central defender pitching in with three goals over the two legs.

• The club's leading appearance maker is goalkeeper Jimmy Lawrence, who featured in 432 league games between 1904 and 1921. Another goalkeeper, Shay Given, is easily Newcastle's most honoured international with 83 caps for the Republic of Ireland between 1997 and 2009.

• In January 2011 Newcastle sold striker Andy Carroll to Liverpool for a club record £35 million, the highest fee at the time for a British player moving from one Premier League club to another. In July 2019 the Magpies signed Brazilian striker Joelinton from

German club Hoffenheim for a club record fee of around £40 million.

• The club's youngest ever player is midfielder Steve Watson, who was aged 16 and 233 days when he made his debut against Wolves in November 1990.

HONOURS
Division 1 champions 1905, 1907, 1909, 1927
Championship champions 2010, 2017
First Division champions 1993
Division 2 champions 1965
FA Cup 1910, 1924, 1932, 1951, 1952, 1955
Fairs Cup 1969

NEWPORT COUNTY

Year founded: 1912
Ground: Rodney Parade (7,850)
Nickname: The Ironsides
Biggest win: 10-0 v Merthyr Town (1930)
Heaviest defeat: 0-13 v Newcastle United (1946)

Founded in 1912, Newport County joined the Football League eight years later. After finishing bottom of the old Fourth Division in 1988 the club dropped into the Conference, only to be expelled in February 1989 for failing to fulfil their fixtures. The club reformed later that year in the Hellenic League, four divisions below the Football League.

• **The road back for Newport was a long one, but they eventually returned to the Football League after beating Wrexham 2-0 in the Conference play-off final in 2013, in the first ever final at Wembley between two Welsh clubs.**

• The club's greatest days came in the early 1980s when, after winning the Welsh Cup for the only time, County reached the quarter-finals of the European Cup Winners' Cup in 1981 before narrowly falling 3-2 on aggregate to eventual finalists Carl Zeiss Jena of East Germany.

• **Beaten in the League Two play-off final by Tranmere Rovers in 2019, Newport also reached the fifth round of the FA Cup for just the second time in their history in the same year. However, after giving eventual**

winners Manchester City a real fright, the Ironsides went down to a rather harsh 4-1 defeat.

HONOURS
Division 3 (South) champions 1939
Welsh Cup 1980

NEYMAR

Born: Mogi das Cruzes, Brazil, 5th February 1992
Position: Striker/winger
Club career:
2009-13 Santos 103 (54)
2013-17 Barcelona 123 (68)
2017- Paris Saint-Germain 37 (34)
International record:
2010- Brazil 97 (60)

In August 2017 Brazilian superstar Neymar became the most expensive footballer ever when he moved from Barcelona to Paris Saint-Germain for an incredible £200 million – more than double the previous record. He has since helped PSG win two league titles, but his 2018/19 campaign was marred by injury and a controversial moment after his club's shock French Cup final defeat by Rennes when he appeared to hit an abusive fan in the face.

• **A superbly talented player who is stronger than his slight frame suggests, Neymar shot to fame soon after making his Santos debut in 2009 when he scored five goals in a cup match against Guarani. Two years later he helped Santos win the Copa Libertadores for the first time since 1963, scoring against Penarol in the final and earning the Man of**

IS THAT A FACT?
Despite missing PSG's Champions League last 16 tie with Manchester United through injury in 2019, Neymar still managed to pick up a three-match ban for insulting the VAR officials on Instagram after they awarded United a last-minute penalty.

the Match award. He was named South American Footballer of the Year in 2011 and 2012 before joining Barcelona in 2013 for £48.6 million – making him the most expensive ever export from South America.

• After a mediocre first season with Barcelona, Neymar was on fire throughout 2014/15, impressing as part of a three-pronged strikeforce with Lionel Messi and Luis Suarez. He scored a total of 39 goals, including one against Juventus in the Champions League final and another in the final of the Copa del Rey against Athletic Bilbao as Barcelona stormed to a superb Treble. The following season he had to be satisfied with just a domestic Double, but again he scored in the Copa del Rey final, this time against Sevilla. In 2017 Neymar equalled a record set by the great Ferenc Puskas in 1962 when he scored in a third consecutive Copa Del Rey final, a 3-1 win over Alaves.

• **First capped by Brazil in 2010, Neymar has gone on to become the pin-up boy of Brazilian football and is now his country's third highest scorer**

An incredibly rare shot of Neymar sprawled on the grass clutching his ankle...

of all time behind Pele and Ronaldo. At the 2014 World Cup he was Brazil's top scorer with four goals, despite missing his country's last two matches through injury. Two years later he scored the winning goal in the shoot-out against Germany as Brazil won Olympic Gold on home soil.

NORTHAMPTON TOWN

Year founded: 1897
Ground: Sixfields Stadium (7,724)
Nickname: The Cobblers
Biggest win: 11-1 v Southend United (1909)
Heaviest defeat: 0-11 v Southampton (1901)

The club was founded at a meeting of local school teachers at the Princess Royal Inn in Northampton in 1897. After turning professional in 1901 Northampton were founder members of the Third Division in 1920.

• The club's first full-time manager was Herbert Chapman (1907-12), who later became the first manager to win the league title with two different clubs, Huddersfield and Arsenal.

• Despite being injured fighting in France during the Second World War, winger Tommy Fowler went on to make a record 552 appearances for the Cobblers between 1946 and 1961. His team-mate Jack English is the club's record scorer with a total of 143 goals.

• The Cobblers enjoyed a rollercoaster decade in 1960s, rising from the old Fourth Division to the First in just six seasons. In the process they became the first club to rise through the three lower divisions to the top flight, before plummeting back down by 1969.

• Northampton reached the FA Cup fifth round for the only time in their history in 1970, but were hammered 8-2 on their own patch by Manchester United with the legendary George Best grabbing six of the goals.

HONOURS
Division 3 champions 1963
League Two champions 2016
Division 4 champions 1987

NORTHERN IRELAND

First international: Northern Ireland 2 England 1, 1923
Most capped player: Pat Jennings, 119 caps (1964-86)
Leading goalscorer: David Healy, 36 goals (2000-13)
First World Cup appearance: Northern Ireland 1 Czechoslovakia 0 (1958)
Biggest win: Northern Ireland 7 Wales 0, 1930
Heaviest defeat: England 9 Northern Ireland 2, 1949

Until Trinidad and Tobago appeared at the 2006 tournament, Northern Ireland were the smallest country to qualify for a World Cup finals tournament. They have made it on three occasions, reaching the quarter-finals in 1958 and beating the hosts Spain in 1982 on their way to the second round.

• **Northern Ireland's Norman Whiteside is the youngest player ever to appear at the World Cup. He was aged just 17 years and 42 days when he played at the 1982 tournament in Spain, beating the previous record set by Pelé in 1958.**

• During the Euro 2008 qualifying campaign Northern Ireland's highest ever scorer David Healy scored a competition best 13 goals.

• Under manager Michael O'Neill Northern Ireland qualified for the European Championships for the first time in 2016. They did it in fine style too, becoming the first ever country from the fifth pot in the draw to top their qualifying group. At the finals they enjoyed their first ever win, beating Ukraine 2-0, before going out to Wales in the last 16.

• Northern Ireland were the last winners of the British Home Championship in 1984, winning on goal difference ahead of Wales, England and Scotland after all four countries finished level on points.

World Cup Record
1930 Did not enter
1934 Did not enter
1938 Did not enter
1950 Did not qualify
1954 Did not qualify
1958 Quarter-finalists
1962 Did not qualify
1966 Did not qualify
1970 Did not qualify
1974 Did not qualify
1978 Did not qualify
1982 Round 2
1986 Round 1
1990 Did not qualify
1994 Did not qualify
1998 Did not qualify
2002 Did not qualify
2006 Did not qualify
2010 Did not qualify
2014 Did not qualify
2018 Did not qualify

Northern Ireland midfielder Paddy McNair

NORWICH CITY

Year founded: 1902
Ground: Carrow Road (27,244)
Nickname: The Canaries
Biggest win: 10-2 v Coventry City (1930)
Heaviest defeat: 2-10 v Swindon Town (1908)

Founded in 1902 by two school teachers, Norwich City soon found themselves in hot water with the FA and were expelled from the FA Amateur Cup in 1904 for being 'professional'. The club joined the Football League as founder members of the Third Division in 1920.

• Norwich were originally known as the Citizens, but adopted the nickname Canaries in 1907 as a nod to the longstanding popularity of canary-keeping in the city – a result of 15th-century trade links with Flemish weavers who had brought the birds over to Europe from Dutch colonies in the Caribbean. Soon afterwards, the club changed their colours from blue and white to yellow and green.

• City fans enjoyed the greatest day in their history when Norwich beat Sunderland 1-0 at Wembley in 1985 to win the League Cup. However, joy soon turned to despair when the Canaries were relegated from the top flight at the end of the season, the first club to experience this particular mix of sweet and sour.

• Ron Ashman is the club's leading appearance maker, turning out in 592 league matches between 1947 and 1964. The Canaries' leading scorer is Ashman's team-mate John Gavin, who notched 122 league goals between 1948 and 1958.

• Now under the ownership of cook and recipe book author Delia Smith, Norwich came a best ever third in the inaugural Premiership season in 1992/93 – albeit with a goal difference of -4, the worst ever by a team finishing in the top three in the top flight. The following season the Canaries played in Europe for the first and only time, famously beating Bayern Munich away in the second round of the UEFA Cup.

• In January 2016 the Canaries splashed out a club record £9.1 million to bring Everton striker Steven Naismith to Carrow Road. In July 2018

Norwich received a club record £25 million when they sold midfielder James Maddison to Leicester.

• Norwich have been relegated from the Premier League a joint-record four times, but have also been promoted a joint-record four times, most recently winning the Championship in 2019.

• Midfielder Wes Hoolahan won a club record 42 caps for the Republic of Ireland while at Carrow Road between 2008 and 2017.

• Norwich have reached the FA Cup semi-finals three times in their history, most famously as a third-tier club in 1959 when they lost 1-0 to Luton in a replay.

NOTTINGHAM FOREST

Year founded: 1865
Ground: The City Ground (30,445)
Nickname: The Reds
Biggest win: 14-0 v Clapton (1891)
Heaviest defeat: 1-9 v Blackburn Rovers (1937)

Now the oldest club in the Football League, Nottingham Forest were founded in 1865 at a meeting at the Clinton Arms in Nottingham by a group of former players of 'shinty' (a form of hockey), who decided to switch sports to football.

• Over the following years the club was at the forefront of important innovations in the game. For instance, shinguards were invented by Forest player Sam Widdowson in 1874, while four years later a referee's whistle was first used in a match between Forest and Sheffield Norfolk. In 1890, a match between Forest and Bolton Wanderers was the first to feature goal nets.

• Forest enjoyed a golden era under legendary manager Brian Clough, who sat in the City Ground hotseat from 1975 until his retirement in 1993. After winning promotion to the top flight in 1977, the club won the league championship the following season – a feat that no promoted team has achieved since. Forest also won the League Cup to become the first side to win this particular double. Even more incredibly, the Reds went on to win the European Cup in 1979 with a 1-0 victory over Malmo in the final. The next year Forest retained the trophy, beating Hamburg 1-0 in the final in Madrid, to become the first and only team to win the European Cup more times than their domestic league.

• Those glory days, however, felt very distant in 1999 when Forest became the first club to suffer the indignity of finishing rock bottom of the Premier League on three separate occasions.

• In 1959, in the days before subs, Forest won the FA Cup despite being reduced to 10 men when Roy Dwight, an uncle of pop star Elton John, was carried off with a broken leg after 33 minutes of the final

Nottingham Forest are proud to be the oldest club in the whole Football League

against Luton Town. It was the first time that a club had won the cup with fewer than 11 players.

• Defender Bobby McKinlay, a member of that 1959 team, is Forest's longest serving player, turning out in 614 league games in 19 seasons at the club. The Reds' record scorer is Grenville Morris, who fell just one short of a double century of league goals for the club in the years before the First World War.

• Hardman left-back Stuart 'Psycho' Pearce won a club record 76 caps for England while at the City Ground between 1987 and 1997.

• The first British club to spend a million pounds on a player (Birmingham City's Trevor Francis in 1979), Forest splashed out a club record £13.2 million on Benfica midfielder Joao Carvalho in June 2018. The previous summer Forest received a record £15 million when striker Britt Assombalonga moved to Middlesbrough.

> HONOURS
> **Division 1 champions** *1978*
> **First Division champions** *1998*
> **Division 2 champions** *1907, 1922*
> **Division 3 (South) champions** *1951*
> **FA Cup** *1898, 1959*
> **League Cup** *1978, 1979, 1989, 1990*
> **European Cup** *1979, 1980*
> **European Super Cup** *1979*

NOTTS COUNTY

Year founded: 1862
Ground: Meadow Lane (19,841)
Nickname: The Magpies
Biggest win: 15-0 v Rotherham (1885)
Heaviest defeat: 1-9 v Aston Villa (1888), Blackburn (1889) and Portsmouth (1927)

Notts County are the oldest professional football club in the world. Founded in 1862, the club were founder members of the Football League in 1888 and played a record 4,940 matches in the competition (losing a record 1,916 games) before dropping into the National League for the first time in 2019.

• In their long history County have swapped divisions more often than any other league club, winning 13 promotions and suffering the agony of relegation 17 times.

• The club's greatest ever day was way back in 1894 when, as a Second Division outfit, they won the FA Cup – the first time a team from outside the top flight had lifted the trophy. In the final at Goodison Park, County beat Bolton 4-1, with Jimmy Logan scoring the first ever hat-trick in the FA Cup final.

• Striker Henry Cursham scored a competition record 48 goals for Notts County in the FA Cup between 1880 and 1887, playing alongside his two brothers in the same Magpies team.

• In their long history Notts County have had 67 different managers, a record for an English club.

> HONOURS
> **Division 2 champions** *1897, 1914, 1923*
> **Division 3 (South) champions** *1931, 1950*
> **League Two champions** *2010*
> **Third Division champions** *1998*
> **Division 4 champions** *1971*
> **FA Cup** *1894*

NUMBERS

Shirt numbers were first used in a First Division match by Arsenal against Sheffield Wednesday at Hillsborough on 25th August 1928. On the same day Chelsea also wore numbers for their Second Division fixture against Swansea at Stamford Bridge.

• In 1933 teams wore numbers in the FA Cup final for the first time. Everton's players were numbered 1-11 while Manchester City's wore 12-22.

HIGHEST SHIRT NUMBERS IN 2018/19 PREMIER LEAGUE

1.	Trent Alexander-Arnold (Liverpool)	66
	Kayne Ramsay (Southampton)	66
3.	Rafael Camacho (Liverpool)	64
4.	Michael Obafemi (Southampton)	61
5.	Harvey Elliott (Fulham)	56
6.	Callum Slattery (Southampton)	55
7.	Mason Greenwood (Manchester United)	54
8.	Ben Johnson (West Ham United)	53
9.	Oliver Skipp (Tottenham Hotspur)	52
10.	Tyreke Johnson (Southampton)	51

Six years later, in 1939, the Football League made the use of shirt numbers obligatory for all teams.

• England and Scotland first wore numbered shirts on 17th April 1937 for the countries' Home International fixture at Hampden Park. Scotland won 3-1. The following year numbers were introduced for the World Cup tournament in France.

• Squad numbers were adopted by Premier League clubs at the start of the 1993/94 season. The highest number worn to date by a Premier League player is 78 by Manchester City's Spanish midfielder Jose Angel Pozo in the 2014/15 season.

• Between 1997 and 2000 Chilean striker Ivan Zamorano wore '1+8' for Inter Milan after Brazil legend Ronaldo arrived from Barcelona and took his number nine shirt.

• In 2010 Australia's Thomas Oar set a world record for a high shirt number

Ivan Zamorano (right) shows off his famous 1+8 Inter Milan shirt

in an international match when he sported '121' on his back for an Asian Cup qualifier against Indonesia.

• In July 2015 Atletico Mineiro goalkeeper Victor wore the highest ever shirt number in football history, 2019, against Sao Paulo to commemorate the fact that he had signed a new contract with the club until 2019.

• At the Soccer Aid match at Stamford Bridge in 2019 between England and a World XI sprinter Usain Bolt wore 9.58 on the back of his shirt, alluding to his world record time in the 100 metres.

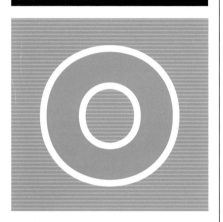

OLDHAM ATHLETIC

Year founded: 1895
Ground: Boundary Park (13,512)
Previous name: Pine Villa
Nickname: The Latics
Biggest win: 11-0 v Southport (1962)
Heaviest defeat: 4-13 v Tranmere Rovers (1935)

Originally known as Pine Villa, the club was founded by the landlord of the Featherstone and Junction Hotel in 1895. Four years later the club changed to its present name of Oldham Athletic and in 1907 they joined the Second Division, winning promotion to the top flight after three seasons.

• Relegated from League One in 2018 after a 21-year stint in the third tier, the Latics enjoyed a golden era in the early 1990s under manager Joe Royle, reaching the League Cup final (in 1990), two FA Cup semi-finals (1990 and 1994) and earning promotion to the top flight (1991). The club were founder members of the Premier League in 1992 but were relegated two years later.

• Defender Ian Wood played in a club record 525 league games for the Latics between 1966 and 1980. The club's record scorer is winger Roger Palmer with 141 goals between 1980 and 1994.

• In 1989 Oldham striker Frankie Bunn scored a remarkable six of his side's goals in a 7-0 hammering of Scarborough in the third round of the League Cup. He remains the only player to have notched a double hat-trick in the competition.

• On Boxing Day 1935 Oldham were hammered 13-4 at Tranmere in the highest-scoring Football League match ever. Remarkably, just the day before the Latics had beaten Rovers 4-1 at home!

> **HONOURS**
> **Division 2 champions** 1991
> **Division 3 champions** 1974
> **Division 3 (North) champions** 1953

MICHAEL O'NEILL

Born: Portadown, 5th July 1969
Managerial career:
2006-08 Brechin City
2009-11 Shamrock Rovers
2011- Northern Ireland

A surprise choice as his country's manager in December 2011, Michael O'Neill led Northern Ireland to their first ever European Championships when they topped their Euro 2016 qualifying

Michael O'Neill has grabbed his opportunity with Northern Ireland

group – the first time a country from the fifth pot of seeds had achieved this feat.

• To the delight of their fans, O'Neill took his side into the last 16 of the competition where they narrowly lost 1-0 to Chris Coleman's Wales in the first ever meeting between two British nations at the knock-out stage of a major tournament.

• He subsequently guided Northern Ireland to their first ever World Cup play-off, but they were deeply unfortunate to lose 1-0 to Switzerland after conceding a controversial penalty. In January 2018 O'Neill turned down the chance of becoming Scotland manager following discussions with the Scottish Football Association and he has since led Northern Ireland to their best ever start to a qualifying campaign, with four straight wins in their bid to reach the finals of Euro 2020.

• A former Northern Ireland international midfielder, O'Neill began his managerial career with Brechin City before rising to prominence as manager of Shamrock Rovers, who he guided to the League of Ireland title in 2010 and the Setanta Sports Cup the following year. In 2011 he became the first manager to lead a League of Ireland side into the group stage of a European competition when Rovers beat Serbia's Partizan Belgrade in the final qualifying round of the Europa League.

OWN GOALS

The first ever own goal in the Football League was scored on the opening day of the inaugural 1888/89 season, the unfortunate George Cox of Aston Villa putting through his own net in his team's 1-1 draw with Wolves.

• The record number of own goals in a single match is, incredibly, 149. In 2002 Madagascan team

Stade Olympique l'Emyrne staged a predetermined protest against alleged refereeing bias by constantly whacking the ball into their own net, their match against AS Adema finishing in a 149-0 win for their opponents. The Madagascan FA took a dim view of the incident and promptly handed out long suspensions to four SOE players.

• The hapless Richard Dunne, formerly of QPR, holds the overall individual Premier League own goal record, with an amazing 10 strikes at the wrong end. Everton are ahead of the pack for total own goals in the Premier League with 50.

• During the 1934/35 season Middlesbrough's Bobby Stuart scored five own goals – a record for a single campaign. Former Liverpool defender Martin Skrtel scored a Premier League record four own goals in 2013/14, a tally matched by Brighton's Lewis Dunk in 2017/18.

• A record 18 own goals were scored in the Champions League in 2017/18. In the whole history of the tournament, Barcelona and Sporting Lisbon have conceded the most own goals (nine), while the Catalan clubs have benefitted from a record 14 strikes at the wrong end – a tally also matched by Chelsea and Real Madrid.

• A record 12 own goals were scored at the World Cup in 2018, including one in the final for the first time ever by Croatia's Mario Mandzukic.

OXFORD UNITED

Year founded: 1893
Ground: Kassam Stadium (12,500)
Previous name: Headington, Headington United
Nickname: The U's
Biggest win: 9-1 v Dorchester Town (1995)
Heaviest defeat: 0-7 v Sunderland (1998) and Wigan Athletic (2017)

The club was founded by a local vicar and doctor in 1893 as Headington, primarily as a way of allowing the cricketers of Headington CC to keep fit during the winter months. The name Oxford United was adopted in 1960, six years before Oxford were elected to the Football League.

• In 1964 Oxford became the first Fourth Division side to reach the quarter-finals of the FA Cup. However, despite being backed by a record crowd of 22,750 at their old Manor Ground, the U's went down 2-1 to eventual finalists Preston.

• The club enjoyed a golden era under controversial owner Robert Maxwell in the 1980s, although the decade began badly when the newspaper proprietor proposed that Oxford and Reading should merge as the 'Thames Valley Royals'. The fans' well-organised campaign against the idea was successful, and their loyalty was rewarded when Oxford became the first club to win consecutive third and second-tier titles to reach the top flight in 1985.

• The greatest day in the club's history, though, came in 1986 when Oxford defeated QPR 3-0 at Wembley to win the League Cup. The following two decades saw a period of decline, however, and by 2006 Oxford had become the English game's first major trophy winners to sink down into the Conference.

• In July 2016 Oxford sold striker Kemar Roofe to Leeds United for a club record £3 million.

HONOURS
Division 2 champions 1985
Division 3 champions 1968, 1984
League Cup 1986

MESUT OZIL

Born: Gelsenkirchen, Germany, 15th October 1988
Position: Midfielder
Club career:
2006-08 Schalke 30 (0)
2008-10 Werder Bremen 71 (13)
2010-13 Real Madrid 102 (19)
2013- Arsenal 166 (32)
International record:
2009-18 Germany 92 (23)

One of the most creative midfielders in the game, Ozil set a new Premier League record in the 2015/16 season when he provided an assist for a goal in seven consecutive matches. In the same season Ozil was credited with 19 assists in total, just one short of Thierry Henry's record of 20 set in 2002/03. In March 2018 he reached 50 Premier League assists in just 141 games, beating the old record set by Manchester United legend Eric Cantona.

• When he won the FA Cup with Arsenal in 2014 Mesut Ozil became the first player to win the major domestic cup competition in England, Germany and Spain having previously triumphed with Werder Bremen (2009) and Real Madrid (2011). Following Arsenal's win in the final against Chelsea in 2017, Ozil became

Ben Woodburn goes charging forward from midfield for Oxford

Mesut Ozil, looking to create yet another assist for Arsenal

the first German (along with his team-mate Per Mertesacker) to win the cup three times.

• Ozil became Arsenal's record signing at the time when he joined the Gunners for £42.4 million from Real Madrid in September 2013. He had previously won the Copa del Rey (2011) and La Liga (2012) with the Spanish titans after starting his career in his native Germany with Schalke and Werder Bremen.

• A third generation Turkish-German, Ozil first captured global attention in the summer of 2009 when was named as Man of the Match after the German Under-21 side smashed their English counterparts 4-0 in the European Championships final, prompting the manager of the team to hail him as 'the German Messi'.

• German national team Player of the Year a record five times, Ozil played a full part in his country's World Cup success in Brazil in 2014 but, like many of his team-mates, was under par four years later in Russia as the reigning world champions slumped out of the tournament at the group stage.

• Before the tournament began Ozil was criticised by some German fans after posing for a photo with Turkey's controversial leader, President Erdogan. Feeling that he had come under fire unfairly, the midfielder announced his retirement from international football in July 2018, alleging that he had been the victim of racism by the German football authorities – a claim strongly denied by Germany boss Joachim Low.

PARIS SAINT-GERMAIN

Year founded: 1970
Ground: Parc des Princes (47,929)
Nickname: PSG
League titles: 8
Domestic cups: 12
European cups: 1

Founded as recently as 1970 following a merger between Paris FC and Stade Saint-Germain, Paris Saint-Germain are now one of the richest clubs in the world after being bought by the Qatar Investment Authority in 2011. Their investment has paid off with PSG winning six French league titles and four French cups in the years since thanks to the arrival of some expensively-assembled talent, led by £200 million superstar Neymar.

• In 1996 PSG became only the second French club to win a European trophy when they beat Rapid Vienna 1-0 in the final of the Cup Winners' Cup. The Paris outfit had a good chance to become the only club to retain the trophy the following year, but lost in the final to Barcelona.

• In running away with the French title in 2015/16 PSG set numerous Ligue 1 records, including most points (96), best ever goal difference (+83), most wins (30), fewest goals conceded (19) and longest unbeaten run (36 matches).

• PSG have won the French Cup a record 12 times, but were surprisingly beaten on penalties in the 2019 final by Rennes.

> **HONOURS**
> **French League champions** 1986, 1994, 2013, 2014, 2015, 2016, 2018, 2019
> **French Cup** 1982, 1983, 1993, 1995, 1998, 2004, 2006, 2010, 2015, 2016, 2017, 2018
> **European Cup Winners' Cup** 1996

NIKITA PARRIS

> **Born:** Liverpool, 10th March 1994
> **Position:** Striker
> **Club career:**
> 2011-15 Everton Ladies 37 (12)
> 2015 Manchester City (loan) 13 (4)
> 2016-19 Manchester City 59 (33)
> 2019- Olympique Lyon Feminine
> **International record:**
> 2016- England 39 (13)

After being named the Football Writers' Association Women's Player of the Year in 2019, Nikita Parris went on to perform well for England at the Women's World Cup in France, helping the Lionesses claim fourth place.

• A lively and quick-witted striker who possesses excellent ball control, Parris came through the Everton School of Excellence to make her first-team debut aged 16 in August 2010. In 2015, shortly after joining Manchester City on loan, she was shortlisted for the PFA Women's Young Player, but lost out to Arsenal's Leah Williamson.

• After moving on a permanent basis to City, Parris helped the club win the league title in 2016. She added two FA Cup winner's medals to her growing collection of silverware before joining French club Lyon when her contract ran out in May 2019.

Nikita Parris was one of England's breakout stars at the 2019 World Cup

• The sister of boxer Natasha Jones, Parris made her senior England debut in a 7-0 thrashing of Serbia in June 2016. She was England's top scorer in the qualifiers for the 2019 World Cup with six goals.

PENALTIES

Penalty kicks were first proposed by goalkeeper William McCrum of the Irish FA in 1890 and adopted the following year. Wolves' John Heath was the first player to take and score a penalty in a Football League match, in a 5-0 win against Accrington at Molineux on 14th September 1891.

• Francis Lee holds the British record for the most penalties in a league season, scoring 15 for Manchester City in Division One in 1971/72. He earned many of the penalties himself, leading fans to dub him 'Lee Won Pen'. In the Premier League era, Andy Johnson scored a record 11 penalties for Crystal Palace in 2004/05, but to no avail as the Eagles were still relegated at the end of the season.

• A record 29 penalties were awarded at the 2018 World Cup in Russia, smashing the previous benchmark of 18 set in 2002. The spectacular rise in the number of spot-kicks was attributed to the new

video assistant referee (VAR) system, which allowed referees to change their decision after reviewing a possible penalty incident.

• Alan Shearer is the most prolific penalty-taker in the Premier League era, scoring 56 times from the spot. A record 106 penalties were awarded in the Premier League in both 2009/10 and 2016/17.

• The most penalties ever awarded in a British match is five in the game between Crystal Palace and Brighton at Selhurst Park in 1989. Palace were awarded four penalties (one scored, three missed) while Brighton's consolation goal in a 2-1 defeat also came from the spot.

• Argentina's Martin Palermo missed a record three penalties in a Copa America match against Colombia in 1999. His first effort struck the crossbar, his second penalty sailed over, but remarkably Palermo still insisted on taking his side's third spot-kick of the match. Perhaps he shouldn't have bothered, as his shot was saved by the goalkeeper.

• Cristiano Ronaldo has scored a record 15 penalties in the Champions League, while his former Real Madrid team-mate Iker Casillas has saved a record seven spot-kicks in the competition.

• A record 26 penalties were awarded at the 2019 Women's World Cup in France, the tally being bolstered by the use of VAR at the competition for the first time.

PENALTY SHOOT-OUTS

Penalty shoot-outs were first used in England as a way to settle drawn matches in the Watney Cup in 1970. In the first ever shoot-out Manchester United beat Hull City in the semi-final of the competition, United legend George Best being the first player to take a penalty while his team-mate Denis Law was the first to miss.

• The third/fourth place play-off between Birmingham and Stoke in 1972 was the first FA Cup match to be decided by penalties, Birmingham winning 4-3 after a 0-0 draw. However, spot-kicks weren't used to settle normal FA Cup ties until the 1991/92 season, Rotherham United becoming the first team to progress by this method when they beat Scunthorpe United 7-6 in the shoot-

Manchester City celebrate their penalty shoot-out triumph in the 2019 Community Shield

out after their first-round replay finished 3-3. In 2005 Arsenal became the first team to win the final on penalties, defeating Manchester United 5-4 after a 0-0 draw.

• The first World Cup match to be settled by penalties was the 1982 semi-final between France and West Germany. The Germans won 5-4 on spot-kicks and have the best overall record in the competition with four wins out of four. In 1994 the final was settled by penalties for the first time, Brazil defeating Italy 3-2 on spot-kicks after a dull 0-0 draw. The 2006 final also went to penalties, Italy beating France 5-3 after a 1-1 draw.

• **The first major international tournament to be settled on penalties was the 1976 European Championships final between Czechoslovakia and West Germany in Belgrade. Following a 2-2 draw, the Czechs won 5-3 in the shoot-out, Antonin Panenka scoring the decisive penalty with a cheeky dinked shot down the middle. The longest shoot-out in the final of a major international tournament saw Ivory Coast finally beat Ghana 11-10 after a total of 24 penalties had been taken in the 1992 Africa Cup of Nations final in 1992.**

• The longest FA Cup shoot-out saw Scunthorpe defeat Worcester City 14-13 after 32 penalties had been taken in their second-round tie in December 2014.

• **The longest ever penalty shoot-out was between fifth-tier Czech sides SK Batov and FC Frystak in a regional championship match in June 2016.**

After an incredible total of 52 kicks, SK Batov emerged victorious 22-21.

• A world record 29 consecutive penalties were scored in the shoot-out between Brockenhurst and Andover Town in the Hampshire Senior Cup on 9th October 2013. Andover missed the 30th, allowing Brockenhurst to win 15-14.

• **Five League Cup finals have been decided on penalties, with Liverpool and Manchester City winning two each, City most recently edging past Chelsea in the 2019 final at Wembley.**

• Two finals of the Women's World Cup have gone to penalties. In 1999 the USA beat China on spot-kicks after a 0-0 draw, but in 2011 the Americans lost to Japan following a 2-2 draw.

NICOLAS PEPE

Born:	Mantes-la-Jolie, France, 29th May 1995
Position:	Winger/striker
Club career:	
2012-13	Poitiers 9 (2)
2013-15	Angers II 41 (9)
2013-17	Angers 40 (3)
2015-16	Orleans (loan) 29 (7)
2017-19	Lille 74 (35)
2019-	Arsenal
International record:	
2016-	Ivory Coast 13 (4)

Pacy winger Nicolas Pepe became Arsenal's record signing when he moved from Lille to north London for £72 million in August 2019. The Ivory Coast international had tempted the Gunners

to splash out after an impressive 2018/19 season in which he scored 22 league goals – a tally only bettered by PSG superstar Kylian Mbappe – and was voted into the Ligue 1 Team of the Year.

• **Pepe actually started out as a goalkeeper with his local side in Paris, before switching to an attacking role with his first professional club, fifth-tier Poitiers. In 2013 he moved on to Angers, playing initially for the club's reserve team.**

• After helping Orleans win promotion from the third tier during a season-long loan in 2015/16, Pepe returned to Angers and in 2017 started in the French Cup final, although he finished on the losing side following a 1-0 loss to PSG. That summer he moved on to Lille for around £9 million.

• **Pepe made his international debut for the Ivory Coast as a sub in a 0-0 draw with France in November 2016, and 18 months later scored his first goals for his country with a brace in a 2-2 draw with Togo. He was part of the Ivory Coast squad which reached the quarter-finals of the 2019 Africa Cup of Nations before losing on penalties to eventual winners Algeria.**

PETERBOROUGH UNITED

Year founded:	1934
Ground:	London Road (15,314)
Nickname:	The Posh
Biggest win:	9-1 v Barnet (1998)
Heaviest defeat:	1-8 v Northampton Town (1946)

Peterborough were founded in 1934 at a meeting at the Angel Hotel to fill the void left by the collapse of local club Peterborough and Fletton United two years earlier.

• **The club's unusual nickname, The Posh, stemmed from Peterborough and Fletton manager Pat Tirrel's remark in 1921 that the club wanted "Posh players for a Posh team". When the new club played its first game against Gainsborough Trinity in 1934 there were shouts of "Up the Posh!" and the nickname stuck.**

• Peterborough were finally elected to the Football League in 1960 after

Nicolas Pepe, Arsenal's record signing

numerous failed attempts. The fans' long wait was rewarded when Peterborough stormed to the Fourth Division title in their first season, scoring a league record 134 goals. Striker Terry Bly notched an amazing 52 of the goals to set a record for the fourth tier.

• **After famously beating Arsenal 2-1 in the fourth round, Peterborough reached the quarter-finals of the FA Cup for the first and only time in 1965 only for their Wembley dreams to be shattered by a 5-1 defeat at Chelsea. The following season the Posh went a stage further in the League Cup, but were beaten 6-3 on aggregate in the semi-finals by eventual winners West Bromwich Albion.**

• In June 2019 Peterborough made their record signing, buying striker Mo Eisa from Bristol City for £1.25 million.

• **Winger Terry Robson played in a record 482 games for the Posh between 1969 and 1981.**

> HONOURS
> **Division 4 champions** 1961, 1974
> **EFL Trophy** 2014

JORDAN PICKFORD

> **Born:** Washington, 7th March 1994
> **Position:** Goalkeeper
> **Club career:**
> 2011-17 Sunderland 31
> 2012 Darlington (loan) 17
> 2013 Alfreton Town (loan) 12
> 2013 Burton Albion (loan) 12
> 2014 Carlisle United (loan) 18
> 2014-15 Bradford City (loan) 33
> 2015 Preston North End (loan) 24
> 2017- Everton 76
> **International record:**
> 2017- England 19

When he helped England beat Colombia in the last 16 at Russia 2018 Jordan Pickford became the first England goalkeeper ever to take part in a victorious World Cup penalty shoot-out. The following year he became the first ever England goalkeeper to take (and score) a penalty as England beat Switzerland in the third/fourth place shoot-out at the inaugural UEFA Nations League finals in Portugal.

• **After joining the Sunderland academy aged eight and signing his first pro contract in 2011, Pickford learned his trade with a number of loans to clubs lower down the football pyramid. His**

After his goal for England, Jordan Pickford would just love to be Everton's penalty taker!

final loan with Championship outfit Preston North End in 2015 saw him keep six consecutive clean sheets to equal the club record.

• An excellent shot-stopper, Pickford enjoyed a breakthrough season with the Black Cats in 2016/17, his impressive performances earning him a nomination for the PFA Young Player of the Year award – the first player from a relegated club to appear on the shortlist since West Ham's Jermain Defoe in 2003. In the summer of 2017 he joined Everton for £25 million, a record transfer fee for a British goalkeeper.

• **Pickford was part of the England Under-21 team that won the Toulon Tournament in 2016 and the following year he helped the Young Lions reach the semi-finals of the European Under-21 Championships in Poland where they lost on penalties to eventual winners Germany. He made his senior debut against Germany in November 2017 and kept a clean sheet in a 0-0 draw.**

PITCHES

According to FIFA rules, a football pitch must measure between 100 and 130 yards in length and 50 and 100 yards in breadth. It's no surprise, then, that different pitches vary hugely in size.

• **Among Premier League clubs, Bournemouth have the largest pitch at 8,190 square metres. Wolves have the smallest pitch, the Molineux surface covering just 6,400 square metres.**

• The highest national stadium is the Estadio Hernando Siles in La Paz. Used

by Bolivia for home matches, it is 2,500 metres above sea level. In Europe the highest stadium is the Ottmar Hitzfeld Stadium, home of FC Gspon, in Switzerland. At 2,000 metres above sea level players and fans need to take a cable car to reach the three-quarter-size artificial turf pitch.

• **The world's largest floating football pitch is the full-size 'The Float' in Marina Bay, Singapore. Owned by the Singapore Sports Council, the stadium can seat 30,000 spectators.**

• At the start of the 1981/82 season QPR became the first English club to install an artificial pitch, with Oldham, Luton Town and Preston soon following suit. By 1994, however, Preston were the last club still playing on 'plastic' and at the start of the 1994/95 season the Football League banned all artificial surfaces on the grounds that they gave home clubs an unfair advantage.

• **In February 2019 the Scottish PFA circulated a petition calling for the artificial pitches at Premiership clubs Hamilton, Kilmarnock and Livingston to be replaced with grass.**

PLAY-OFFS

The play-off system was introduced by the Football League in the 1986/87 season. Initially, one club from the higher division competed with three from the lower division at the semi-final stage but this was changed to four teams from the same division in the 1988/89 season. The following season a one-off final at Wembley replaced the original two-legged final.

IS THAT A FACT?

Remarkably, Blackpool won a record 10 consecutive play-off matches between 2001 and 2010, earning three promotions.

• Blackpool have been promoted from the play-offs a record five times, and share with Huddersfield Town the distinction of having won all three divisional play-off finals. The Seasiders have also scored a record total of 47 goals in the play-offs.

• Preston have participated in the play-offs a record 10 times, but have only once won promotion – in 2015 when they beat Swindon 4-0 in the League One final. Brentford and Sheffield United have reached the play-offs a record eight times without once gaining promotion. In addition, the Blades have played in four finals and lost them all – a painful record shared with Reading. Meanwhile, Nottingham Forest and MK Dons have competed in the play-offs on a record four occasions without once reaching the final.

• The Championship play-off final is the most financially rewarding sporting event in the world, its worth to the winners in prize money, TV and advertising revenue, and increased gate receipts, being estimated at around £160-200 million.

PLYMOUTH ARGYLE

Year founded: 1886
Ground: Home Park (17,800)
Previous name: Argyle FC
Nickname: The Pilgrims
Biggest win: 8-1 v Millwall (1932) and Hartlepool (1994)
Heaviest defeat: 0-9 v Stoke City (1960)

The club was founded as Argyle FC in 1886 in a Plymouth coffee house, the name deriving from the Argyll and Sutherland Highlanders who were stationed in the city at the time. The current name was adopted in 1903, when the club became fully professional and entered the Southern League.

• After joining the Football League in 1920, Plymouth just missed out on promotion from the Third Division (South) between 1922 and 1927, finishing in second place in six consecutive seasons – a record of misfortune no other club can match.

• Wilf Carter is the only player to score five goals in a match for Plymouth, filling his boots in a 6-4 win against Charlton on 27th December 1960.

• The largest city in England never to have hosted top-flight football, Plymouth have won the third tier of English football a joint-record four times, most recently topping the Second Division in 2004.

• Relegated from League One in 2019, Plymouth thrashed Chesterfield 7-0 in January 2004, scoring five times in the first 17 minutes to set a Football League record for the fastest ever five-goal haul.

> **HONOURS**
> **Second Division champions** 2004
> **Division 3 champions** 1959
> **Division 3 (South) champions** 1930, 1952
> **Third Division champions** 2002

MAURICIO POCHETTINO

Born: Murphy, Argentina, 2nd March 1972
Managerial career:
2009-12 Espanyol
2013-14 Southampton
2014- Tottenham Hotspur

Following a dramatic comeback against Ajax in the semi-final, Tottenham boss Mauricio Pochettino wept tears of joy after leading his club to their first ever Champions League final in 2019. However, there was to be no happy ending for the Argentinian as Spurs put in a lacklustre performance in Madrid against Liverpool and went down to a 2-0 defeat.

• Pochettino began his managerial career with Spanish side Espanyol in 2009, but was sacked three years later when the Barcelona-based club slipped to the bottom of La Liga.

• Later that season, however, he was a surprise choice to replace Nigel Adkins at Southampton. Despite never speaking to the press in English, Pochettino soon won over the Saints fans by introducing a vibrant and entertaining attacking style of play. In his only full season at St Mary's in 2013/14, Pochettino guided Southampton to a then best ever eighth

Mauricio Pochettino is simply baffled by Tottenham's recent lack of trophies place finish in the Premier League. In May 2014 he was appointed Tottenham boss, and he has since led the north Londoners to four consecutive top-four finishes – the best record of any Spurs boss since the legendary Bill Nicholson in the early 1960s.

• A central defender in his playing days, Pochettino twice won the Copa del Rey with Espanyol. He also represented Argentina at the 2002 World Cup, famously fouling Michael Owen in the penalty area to allow England captain David Beckham to score the only goal of the group game between the sides from the spot.

PAUL POGBA

Born: Lagny-sur-Marne, France, 15th March 1993
Position: Midfielder
Club career:
2011-12 Manchester United 3 (0)
2012-16 Juventus 124 (28)
2016- Manchester United 92 (24)
International record:
2013- France 69 (10)

Although his form dipped somewhat towards the end of the campaign, Manchester United midfielder Paul Pogba enjoyed his best season yet with the Red Devils in 2018/19, scoring 13 Premier League goals and earning a place in the PFA Team of the Year – the only player not from champions Manchester City or runners-up Liverpool to make the cut.

• In August 2016 Pogba became the most expensive player in football at the time when he rejoined United from Juventus for £89.3 million. In his first season at Old Trafford he paid back some of that fee by helping United win the League Cup and then scoring in the Red Devils' 2-0 comfortable defeat of Ajax in the Europa League final in Stockholm.

• Pogba won four successive Scudetto titles with Juve after joining the Turin giants from Manchester United in 2012. His best season was in 2015/16 when he scored a personal best eight goals and topped the Serie A assists chart with 12. His outstanding performances for both club and country saw him win the 2013 Golden Boy award for the best young player in Europe.

• Pogba started out with Le Havre before moving to England in 2009 aged just 16. However, he only made a handful of appearances for United and frustrated with his lack of progress at Old Trafford decided to move to Italy.

• A midfielder whose tentacle-like long legs have earned him the nickname 'Paul the Octopus', Pogba made his debut for France in 2013 and three years later was part of the French team that lost to Portugal in the final of Euro 2016.

He had better luck at the 2018 World Cup, scoring in the final in France's 4-2 win against Croatia in Moscow.

PORT VALE

Year founded: 1876
Ground: Vale Park (19,052)
Previous name: Burslem Port Vale
Nickname: The Valiants
Biggest win: 9-1 v Chesterfield (1932)
Heaviest defeat: 0-10 v Sheffield United (1892) and Notts County (1895)

Port Vale's name derives from the house where the club was founded in 1876. Initially, the club was known as Burslem Port Vale – Burslem being the Stoke-on-Trent town where the Valiants are based – but the prefix was dropped in 1911.

• In their first season as a league club, in 1892/93, Port Vale suffered the worst ever home defeat in Football League history when Sheffield United hammered them 10-0. However, Vale's defence was in significantly better nick in 1953/54 when they kept a league record 30 clean sheets on their way to claiming the Third Division (North) championship.

• In the same season the Valiants came desperately close to being the first third-tier club to reach the FA Cup final. Having knocked out holders Blackpool in the fifth round, Vale took the lead against West Brom in the semi-final at Villa Park but eventually lost 2-1.

• Port Vale's longest-serving player is loyal defender Roy Sproson, appearing in a phenomenal 761 league games between 1950 and 1972. Only two other players in the history of league football have made more appearances for the same club.

• Vale's top scorer is Wilf Kirkham with 153 league goals, including a club seasonal best of 38 in 1926/27. The hotshot striker also scored a club record 13 hat-tricks for the Valiants in two spells at Vale Park.

HONOURS
Division 3 (North) champions 1930, 1954
Division 4 champions 1959
EFL Trophy 1993, 2001

Paul Pogba was shocked to see an orb-shaped alien floating towards him!

Porto's Pepe is a keen fan of martial arts!

PORTSMOUTH

Year founded: 1898
Ground: Fratton Park
(19,669)
Nickname: Pompey
Biggest win: 9-1 v
Notts County (1927)
Heaviest defeat: 0-10
v Leicester City (1928)

Portsmouth were founded in 1898 by a group of sportsmen and businessmen at a meeting in the city's High Street. After starting out in the Southern League the club joined the Third Division in 1920.

• **In 1949 the club became the first team to rise from the third tier to claim the league championship, and the following year became the first of just six clubs to retain the title since the end of the Second World War.**

• The most influential player in that team was half-back Jimmy Dickinson, who went on to play a record 764 times for Pompey, the second highest number of Football League appearances with any single club. Dickinson is also comfortably Portsmouth's most decorated international, winning 48 caps for England.

• **The club won the FA Cup for the first time in 1939, when Pompey thrashed favourites Wolves 4-1 in the final at Wembley. In 2008 they lifted the cup for a second time when a single goal from Nigerian striker Kanu was enough to beat Cardiff City in only the second final at the new Wembley.**

• In 2019 Portsmouth won the EFL Trophy for the first time, defeating Sunderland on penalties at Wembley in front of a competition record crowd of 85,021. However, the Black Cats got their revenge when they later beat Pompey in the League One play-off semi-finals.

FC PORTO

Year founded: 1893
Ground: Estadio do
Dragao (50,033)
Nickname: The
Dragons
League titles: 28
Domestic cups: 20
European cups: 5
International cups: 2

One of the giants of Portuguese football, Porto were founded in 1893 by a local wine salesman who had been introduced to football on his regular trips to England.

• Porto's total of 28 domestic championships is second only to arch rivals Benfica, who have 37 to their name. The club's most successful decade was in the 1990s when they won an impressive eight titles, while they have since twice gone through a whole season unbeaten in the league – in 2010/11 and 2012/13. In the first of those campaigns Porto won the league by a record 21 points.

• Porto have the best record in Europe of any Portuguese side, with two victories in the European Cup/ Champions League (in 1987 and 2004) and two in the UEFA Cup (in 2003 and 2011), the latter of these triumphs coming under former Chelsea and Tottenham boss Andre Villas-Boas – at 33, the youngest coach ever to win a European competition.

• **Porto were undefeated at home in the league for a Portuguese record 119 games between January 1982 and April 1989.**

HONOURS
Portuguese champions 1935, 1939, 1940, 1956, 1959, 1978, 1979, 1985, 1986, 1988, 1990, 1992, 1993, 1995, 1996, 1997, 1998, 1999, 2003, 2004, 2006, 2007, 2008, 2009, 2011, 2012, 2013, 2018
Portuguese Cup 1922, 1925, 1932, 1937, 1956, 1958, 1968, 1977, 1984, 1988, 1991, 1994, 1998, 2000, 2001, 2003, 2006, 2009, 2010, 2011
European Cup/Champions League 1987, 2004
UEFA Cup/Europa League 2003, 2011
European Super Cup 1987
Intercontinental Cup 1987, 2004

IS THAT A FACT?
Portsmouth were involved in the highest-scoring Premier League match ever, thrashing Reading 7-4 at Fratton Park on 29th September 2007.

- Pompey's record goalscorer is Peter Harris who banged in 194 goals between 1946 and 1960. In the 1992/93 season striker Guy Whittingham hit a club record 42 league goals.
- An ongoing financial crisis saw Portsmouth slide all the way down to the fourth tier in 2013, but there was better news for their long-suffering fans in 2017 when Pompey won the League Two title to become only the fifth club to win all four divisions of English football. Incredibly, the south coast club only topped the table for the final 32 minutes of the season – the shortest length of time of any champions of any division ever.

HONOURS
Division 1 champions 1949, 1950
First Division champions 2003
Division 3 champions 1962, 1983
Division 3 (South) champions 1924
League Two champions 2017
FA Cup 1939, 2008
EFL Trophy 2019

PORTUGAL

First international: Spain 3 Portugal 1, 1921
Most capped player: Cristiano Ronaldo, 158 caps (2003-)
Leading goalscorer: Cristiano Ronaldo, 88 goals (2003-)
First World Cup appearance: Portugal 3 Hungary 1, 1966
Biggest win: Portugal 8 Liechtenstein 0, 1994 and 1999
Heaviest defeat: Portugal 0 England 10, 1947

After a number of near misses, Portugal won their first major trophy in 2016 when a goal from Lille striker Eder in extra-time secured them a 1-0 win over hosts France in the final of the European Championship. The Portuguese had reached the final of the same competition on home soil 12 years earlier, but went down to a surprise 1-0 defeat to Greece.
- **Portugal's best showing at the World Cup was in 1966 when they finished third after going out to hosts England in the semi-finals. Much of their success was down to legendary striker**

Portugal's record scorer, the brilliant Cristiano Ronaldo

Eusebio, who topped the goalscoring charts with nine goals.
- The southern Europeans also reached the semi-finals of the World Cup in 2006, after beating Holland in 'The Battle of Nuremberg' in the last 16 and England on penalties in the quarter-finals. A 1-0 defeat to France, though, ended their hopes of appearing in the final.
- **With 88 goals to his name Portugal captain Cristiano Ronaldo is the highest scoring European international ever – only Iran's Ali Daei with an incredible 109 goals has scored more.**
- In 2019 Portugal won the inaugural UEFA Nations League, beating Netherlands 1-0 in the final in Porto.

HONOURS
European Championship winners 2016
UEFA Nations League winners 2019
World Cup Record
1930-38 Did not enter
1950-62 Did not qualify
1966 Third place
1970-82 Did not qualify
1986 Round 1
1990-98 Did not qualify
2002 Round 1
2006 Fourth place
2010 Round 2
2014 Round 1
2018 Round 2

TOP 10

PREMIER LEAGUE GOALSCORERS

1.	Alan Shearer (1992-2006)	260
2.	Wayne Rooney (2002-18)	208
3.	Andy Cole (1993-2007)	187
4.	Frank Lampard (1997-2015)	177
5.	Thierry Henry (1999-2012)	175
6.	Sergio Aguero (2011-)	164
7.	Robbie Fowler (1993-2007)	163
8.	Jermain Defoe (2001-18)	162
9.	Michael Owen (1996-2013)	150
10.	Les Ferdinand (1992-2005)	149

PREMIER LEAGUE

The Premier League was founded in 1992 and is now the most watched and most lucrative sporting league in the world, boasting record revenues of £4.8 billion in the 2017/18 season.
- **Initially composed of 22 clubs, the Premier League was reduced to 20 teams in 1995. A total of 49 clubs have played in the league but just six – Manchester United, Blackburn Rovers, Arsenal, Chelsea, Manchester City and Leicester City – have won the title. Of this group, United are easily the most successful, having won the league 13 times.**
- Alan Shearer scored a Premier League record 260 goals for Blackburn and

Newcastle. The former England captain also holds the record for the most goals in a season (34) along with Newcastle's Andy Cole. In the 2015/16 season Jamie Vardy scored in a record 11 consecutive Premier League games for Leicester City.

• Manchester City hold the record for most points in a Premier League season with 100 in 2017/18, and in the same campaign they scored a record 106 goals, won a best ever 32 games and had a record 19-point winning margin over the runners up, Manchester United.

• Between 1998 and 2018 midfielder Gareth Barry played in a record 653 Premier League games for Aston Villa (365), Manchester City (132), Everton (131) and West Brom (25).

• Before retiring from football in 2019, Czech goalkeeper Petr Cech kept a record 202 Premier League clean sheets including a seasonal best of 24 in 2004/05.

PRESTON NORTH END

Year founded: 1879
Ground: Deepdale (23,404)
Nickname: The Lilywhites
Biggest win: 26-0 v Hyde (1887)
Heaviest defeat: 0-7 v Blackpool (1948)

Preston were founded in 1879 as a branch of the North End Cricket and Rugby Club, playing football exclusively from 1881.

• Founder members of the Football League in 1888, Preston won the inaugural league title the following year, going through the entire 22-game season undefeated and conceding just 15 goals (a league record). For good measure the club also won the FA Cup, beating Wolves 3-0 in the final, to become the first club to win the Double. The previous season, Preston demolished Hyde 26-0 to record the biggest ever win in any English competition, striker Jimmy Ross scoring seven of the goals to set a club record that has never been matched. Ross went on to score a record total of 19 goals in the cup that season.

Daniel Johnson goes on the attack for Preston

• Of the 12 founder members of the league, Preston are the only club still playing at the same ground, making Deepdale the oldest league football stadium anywhere in the world.

• The legendary Tom Finney is Preston's most capped international, turning out for England in 76 games. The flying winger is also the club's highest scorer, with 187 strikes between 1946 and 1960. North End's leading appearance maker is Alan Kelly, who played in goal for the club in 447 league games between 1958 and 1973.

• Preston are one of just five clubs to have won all four divisions of English football, achieving this feat in 1996 when they topped the Third Division (now League Two).

• Uniquely, Preston have been managed by two members of England's 1966 World Cup-winning team: Bobby Charlton (1973-75) and Nobby Stiles (1977-81).

• In 1922 Preston goalkeeper James Mitchell became the first (and last) player to wear spectacles in the FA Cup final. Perhaps it wasn't the greatest idea as the Lilywhites went down 1-0 to Huddersfield at Stamford Bridge.

HONOURS
Division 1 champions 1889, 1890
Division 2 champions 1904, 1913, 1951
Second Division champions 2000
Division 3 champions 1971
Third Division champions 1996
FA Cup 1889, 1938
Double 1889

PROMOTION

Automatic promotion from the Second to First Division was introduced in the 1898/99 season, replacing the 'test match' play-off-style system. The first two clubs to go up automatically were Glossop North End and Manchester City.

• Birmingham City, Leicester City and Notts County have gained a record 13 promotions, while the Foxes have gone up to the top flight on a record 12 occasions – most recently in 2014, after winning the Championship.

• Crystal Palace, Leicester, Norwich, Sunderland and West Brom have all been promoted to the Premier League a record four times.

• Reading won promotion to the Premier League in 2006 with a record 106 points. Since three points for a win were introduced in 1981, two clubs have been promoted to the top flight with a record low 70 points: Leicester City in 1983 and Blackpool (via the play-offs) in 2010.

• Between 2010 and 2014 SV Rodinghausen won a world record five consecutive promotions in German regional football. This feat was matched by Italian lower league outfit ASD Varesina between 2011 and 2015.

TEEMU PUKKI

Born: Kotka, Finland, 29th March 1990
Position: Striker
Club career:
2006-08 KTP 29 (3)
2008-10 Sevilla Atletico 17 (3)
2009-10 Sevilla 1 (0)
2010-11 HJK 25 (13)
2011-13 Schalke 04 37 (8)
2013-14 Celtic 26 (7)
2014-18 Brondby 130 (55)
2018- Norwich City 43 (29)
International record:
2009- Finland 74 (18)

Finnish striker Teemu Pukki was named EFL Championship Player of the Season in 2019 after his impressive haul of 29 goals helped power Norwich City to the second-tier title in his first campaign with the Canaries after joining on a free transfer from Danish side Brondby.

• A lively and clever forward who times his darting runs to perfection and finishes with aplomb, Pukki started out with his hometown club KTP. After a disappointing spell in Spain with Sevilla, he returned to Finland to play for HJK, with whom he won the Double in 2011.

• Pukki then spent two years with Schalke before joining Celtic in 2013. However, he struggled to adjust to the speed and physical nature of Scottish

Teemu Pukki was the Championship Player of the Season in 2019

football, before he revived his career with Brøndy, where he scored regularly and won the Danish Cup in 2018.

• First capped by Finland in 2009 in a friendly against Japan, Pukki starred in his country's 2018 UEFA Nations League campaign, scoring the only goal of the game in three matches to help the Finns top their group.

QUEENS PARK RANGERS

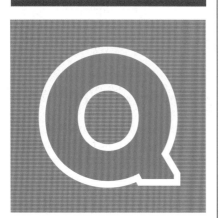

Year founded: 1882
Ground: The Kiyan Prince Foundation Stadium (18,489)
Nickname: The R's
Biggest win: 9-2 v Tranmere Rovers (1960)
Heaviest defeat: 1-8 v Mansfield Town (1965) and Manchester United (1969)

Founded in 1882 following the merger of St Jude's and Christchurch Rangers, the club was called Queens Park Rangers because the majority of the players came from the Queens Park area of north-west London.

• A nomadic outfit in their early days, QPR have staged home matches at no fewer than 19 different venues, a record for a Football League club.

• The club enjoyed its finest moment in 1967 when Rangers sensationally came back from two goals down to defeat favourites West Bromwich Albion 3-2 in the first ever League Cup final to be played at Wembley. In the same season the R's also won the Third Division title to pull off a unique double.

• Fans' favourite Rodney Marsh hit a club record 44 goals that season, 11 of them coming in the League Cup. George Goddard, though, holds the club record for league goals with 37 in 1929/30. Goddard is also the club's leading scorer, notching 174 league goals between 1926 and 1934. Meanwhile, no other player has pulled on Rangers' famous hoops more often than Tony Ingham, who made 519 league appearances between 1950 and 1963.

• In 1976 QPR finished second in the old First Division, being pipped to the league championship by Liverpool. The following season Rangers enjoyed their best-ever European campaign, reaching the quarter-finals of the UEFA Cup before losing on penalties to Greece's AEK Athens.

• In 1982 Rangers reached the FA Cup final for the only time in their history but went down 1-0 to Tottenham in a replay after the original match finished 1-1.

• Striker Charlie Austin scored 18 Premier League goals in QPR's relegation season of 2014/15 – the best return ever for a player at a club finishing at the bottom of the league.

• In 2019 the club's ground, previously known as Loftus Road, was renamed the Kiyan Prince Foundation Stadium, after a charity set up in honour of former QPR youth player Kiyan Prince, who was stabbed to death in May 2006 while trying to stop another boy from being bullied.

HONOURS
Championship champions 2011
Division 2 champions 1983
Division Three champions 1967
Division 3 (South) champions 1948
League Cup 1967

QPR's Yoann Barbet suggests the ref should have gone to Specsavers!

SERGIO RAMOS

Born: Camas, Spain, 30th March 1986
Position: Defender
Club career:
2003-04 Sevilla B 26 (2)
2004-05 Sevilla 39 (2)
2005- Real Madrid 419 (59)
International record:
2005- Spain 165 (20)

In 2018, following Real Madrid's 3-1 defeat of Liverpool in Kiev, Sergio Ramos became the first player to captain a side to three consecutive Champions League titles. Previously, Ramos had scored in two other Champions League finals: in 2014 he headed a last-minute equaliser against city rivals Atletico Madrid which enabled Real to go on and win the cup; then, in 2016, he put Real ahead against the same opposition and also scored in his team's ultimately successful penalty shoot-out.

IS THAT A FACT? Sergio Ramos has been shown more cards than any other player in the Champions League, a total of 42 (39 yellows and three reds).

• A strong tackler who can play either in central defence or at right-back, Ramos started out at Sevilla before joining Real for around £20 million in 2005 – aged 19 at the time, he was the most expensive teenager in Spanish football history at the time.
• As well as his four Champions League triumphs, Ramos has won four La Liga titles and two Spanish cups and been voted the 'Best Defender' in La Liga a record five times. Along with Lionel Messi, he is the only player to have scored in 15 consecutive La Liga seasons. Less impressively, he has been sent off in the Spanish league a record 21 times.
• **Ramos has also enjoyed huge success at international level, winning two European Championships (2008 and 2012) and the World Cup in South Africa in 2010. Ramos is also the highest-capped outfield player in Spain's history and he has played in more victories at international level (123) than any other player ever.**

Aaron Ramsey earned £41.65 just while controlling this ball!

AARON RAMSEY

Born: Caerphilly, 13th December 1990
Position: Midfielder
Club career:
2007-08 Cardiff City 16 (1)
2008-19 Arsenal 262 (40)
2010-11 Nottingham Forest (loan) 5 (0)
2019- Juventus
International record:
2008- Wales 58 (14)

In February 2019 box-to-box midfielder Aaron Ramsey became the highest paid British footballer ever when he signed a four-year contract with Italian giants Juventus worth £400,000 per week.
• **Earlier in the campaign Ramsey had turned down a new contract with Arsenal, his employers of 11 years following a £4.8 million move from Cardiff City in June 2008. During his time with the Gunners Ramsey won the FA Cup three times, scoring the winning goal for the north Londoners in both their 3-2 win over Hull City in 2014 and the 2-1 victory over London rivals Chelsea three years later.**
• A product of the Cardiff youth system, Ramsey became the club's youngest ever player when he made his debut as a sub against Hull City on the last day of the 2006/07 season aged 16 and 124 days. The following season he played in the 2008 FA Cup final against Portsmouth – aged 17, he was the second youngest player ever to appear in the final after Millwall's Curtis Weston four years earlier.

"Vamos! Quick, we need to score again before I get sent off again!"

• Ramsey is also the youngest player ever to captain Wales, wearing the armband for the first time in a Euro 2012 qualifier against England in March 2011 when he was aged just 20 and 90 days. At Euro 2016 he was one of his country's outstanding performers as Wales surprisingly reached the semi-finals, his vibrant displays earning him a place in the Team of the Tournament.

RANGERS

Year founded: 1873
Ground: Ibrox Stadium (50,817)
Nickname: The Gers
Biggest win: 14-2 v Blairgowrie (1934)
Heaviest defeat: 2-10 v Airdrieonians (1886)

The most decorated club in the history of world football, Rangers were founded by a group of rowing enthusiasts in 1873. The club were founder members of the Scottish League in 1890, sharing the inaugural title with Dumbarton.

• Rangers have won the league title 54 times, a record of domestic success which is unmatched by any club on the planet. Between 1989 and 1997 the Gers topped the league in nine consecutive seasons, initially under Graeme Souness and then under Walter Smith, to equal a record previously set by arch rivals Celtic.

• In 2000 Rangers became the first club in the world to win 100 major trophies. The Glasgow giants have since extended their tally to 115, most recently adding the League Cup and SPL title in 2011. The club's tally of seven domestic Trebles is unequalled anywhere in the world.

• Way back in 1898/99 Rangers enjoyed their best ever league season, winning all 18 of their matches to establish yet another world record.

• The club's record goalscorer is former Rangers manager Ally McCoist. In a 15-year Ibrox career between 1983 and 1998 McCoist banged in an incredible 251 goals (355 in all competitions), including a record 28 hat-tricks. McCoist is also the club's most capped international, winning 59 of his 61 Scotland caps while with the Gers.

• Rangers also hold two important records in the Scottish League Cup, with more wins (27) and more appearances in the final (34) than any other club. The Gers' first win in the competition came in its inaugural year when they thrashed Aberdeen 4-0 in the final in 1947.

• The club's record in the Scottish Cup is not quite as impressive, the Gers' 33 triumphs in the competition being bettered by Celtic's 38. However, it was in the Scottish Cup that Rangers recorded their biggest ever victory, thrashing Blairgowrie 14-2 in 1934. Striker Jimmy Fleming scored nine of the goals on the day to set a club record. Way back in 1887 Rangers reached the semi-final of the English FA Cup, but were beaten 3-1 by eventual winners Aston Villa.

• Rangers made their record signing in November 2000, buying Norwegian striker Tore Andre Flo from Chelsea for £12 million. In January 2008 defender Alan Hutton left Ibrox for Tottenham for a record £9 million.

• No player has turned out in the royal blue shirt of Rangers more often than former captain John Greig, who made 755 appearances in all competitions between 1961 and 1978. Famously, Greig led the Gers to their one success in continental competition, the European Cup Winners' Cup in 1972 when they beat Dynamo Moscow in the final.

• Rangers are the only club to have won four different Scottish divisional titles, completing this feat in 2016 when the Gers topped the Championship table – the last stage of their return to the top flight after they were forced into liquidation in 2012 and made to start from scratch in the bottom tier.

Rangers full-back James Tavernier

HONOURS
SPL champions *1999, 2000, 2003, 2005, 2009, 2010, 2011*
Premier League champions *1976, 1978, 1987, 1989, 1990, 1991, 1992, 1993, 1994, 1995, 1996, 1997*
Division 1 champions *1891 (shared), 1899, 1900, 1901, 1902, 1911, 1912, 1913, 1918, 1920, 1921, 1923, 1924, 1925, 1927, 1928, 1929, 1930, 1931, 1933, 1934, 1935, 1937, 1939, 1947, 1949, 1950, 1953, 1956, 1957, 1959, 1961, 1963, 1964, 1975*
Championship champions *2016*
League One champions *2014*
Third Division champions *2013*
Scottish Cup *1894, 1897, 1898, 1903, 1928, 1930, 1932, 1934, 1935, 1936, 1948, 1949, 1950, 1953, 1960, 1962, 1963, 1964, 1966, 1973, 1976, 1978, 1979, 1981, 1992, 1993, 1996, 1999, 2000, 2002, 2003, 2008, 2009*
League Cup *1947, 1949, 1961, 1962, 1964, 1965, 1971, 1976, 1978, 1979, 1982, 1984, 1985, 1987, 1988, 1989, 1991, 1993, 1994, 1997, 1999, 2002, 2003, 2005, 2008, 2010, 2011*
Double *1928, 1930, 1934, 1935, 1950, 1953, 1963, 1992, 1996, 2000, 2009*
Treble *1949, 1964, 1976, 1978, 1993, 1999, 2003*
European Cup Winners' Cup *1972*

MEGAN RAPINOE

Born: Redding, USA, 5th July 1985
Position: Winger
Club career:
2009-10 Chicago Red Stars 38 (3)
2011 Philadelphia Independence 4 (1)
2011 magicJack 10 (3)
2011 Sydney FC 2 (1)
2012 Sydney Sounders Women 2 (0)
2013-14 Lyon 28 (8)
2013- Seattle Reign/Reign FC 75 (37)
International record:
2006- USA 158 (50)

When, aged 34 and two days, Megan Rapinoe slotted home a penalty for the USA in the 2019 Women's World Cup final against the Netherlands she became the oldest ever player to score in the final. Her six goals in the tournament won her the Golden Boot and she also collected the Golden Ball after being voted the best player at the finals in France.

It's fair to say Megan Rapinoe was quite pleased when the USA won the 2019 Women's World Cup

• A World Cup winner in both 2015 and 2019, Rapinoe also played in the 2011 final which the USA lost on penalties to Japan, and along with Germany's Birgit Prinz is one of just two players to start in three women's finals.

• A tremendous crosser of the ball from wide areas who finishes with calm authority when given the chance, Rapinoe was also part of the USA team which won the 2012 Olympics thanks to a 2-1 victory against Japan in the final at Wembley. At club level, Rapinoe helped Lyon reach the Champions League final in 2013 but the French side lost 1-0 to Wolfsburg at Stamford Bridge.

• **One of the most outspoken figures in the women's game, Rapinoe has attracted headlines for refusing to stand during the playing of the US national anthem in protest against racial and social injustice and for demanding equal pay for the US women's team with their much less successful male counterparts. During the 2019 World Cup she also became embroiled in a much-publicised Twitter spat with US President**

Donald Trump after saying she would refuse to accept an invitation from the White House if the USA went on to win the competition.

MARCUS RASHFORD

Born: Manchester, 31st October 1997
Position: Striker
Club career:
2016- Manchester United 111 (27)
International record:
2016- England 32 (7)

When, aged 18 and 208 days, Marcus Rashford opened the scoring for England in a 2-1 friendly win over Australia at the Stadium of Light in May 2016 he became the youngest ever scorer for his country on his debut, beating the record previously set by Tommy Lawton way back in 1938.

• On the books of Manchester United since the age of seven, Rashford enjoyed a sensational start to his Old Trafford career, scoring twice in a 5-1 thrashing of Danish side Midtjylland

in the Europa League on 25th February 2016 to become the club's youngest ever scorer in European competition, eclipsing a record previously held by the legendary George Best.

• Three days later Rashford scored twice in a 3-2 home win over Arsenal, putting himself in third place in the list of United's youngest ever Premier League scorers behind Federico Macheda and Danny Welbeck. He then set another record by notching the winner away to Manchester City to become the youngest ever scorer in the Manchester derby. In 2017 he helped United win the Europa League and came third in the 'Golden Boy' poll for the best young player in Europe.

• **Fast, strong and a composed finisher in front of goal, Rashford was a surprise choice by then England manager Roy Hodgson for the 2016 European Championships, and when he came on in a 2-1 win against Wales became his country's youngest ever player at the finals, aged 18 and 229 days. In 2019 he scored England's only goal at the finals of the inaugural UEFA Nations League in a 3-1 semi-final defeat to the Netherlands.**

Marcus Rashford has made his mark at Old Trafford

READING

Year founded: 1871
Ground: Madejski Stadium (24,161)
Nickname: The Royals
Biggest win: 10-2 v Crystal Palace (1946)
Heaviest defeat: 0-18 v Preston (1894)

Reading were founded in 1871, making them the oldest Football League club south of Nottingham. After amalgamating with local clubs Reading Hornets (in 1877) and Earley FC (in 1889), the club was eventually elected to the new Third Division in 1920.

• The oldest club still competing in the FA Cup never to have won the trophy, Reading have got as far as the semi-finals just twice, losing to Cardiff City in 1927 and Arsène Wenger's Arsenal in 2015.

• In the 1985/86 season Reading set a Football League record by winning their opening 13 matches, an outstanding start which provided the launch pad for the Royals to go on to top the old Third Division at the end of the campaign.

• Reading's greatest moment, though, came in 2006 when, under manager Steve Coppell, they won promotion to the top flight for the first time in their history. They went up in fine style, too, claiming the Championship title with a Football League record 106 points and going 33 matches unbeaten (a record for the second tier) between 9th August 2005 and 17th February 2006.

• Prolific marksman Ronnie Blackman holds two scoring records for the club, with a total of 158 goals between 1947 and 1954 and a seasonal best of 39 goals in the 1951/52 campaign. Defender Martin Hicks played in a record 500 league games for the Royals between 1978 and 1991.

• Reading were involved in the highest-scoring Premier League match ever, losing 7-4 to Portsmouth in 2007. Five years later the Royals lost 7-5 to Arsenal in the joint-highest scoring League Cup match ever.

• The Royals paid out a club record £10 million to Inter Milan for Romanian striker George Puscas in August 2019. The club's bank balance was boosted by a record £6.6 million in August 2010 when stylish Icelandic midfielder Gylfi Sigurdsson joined German outfit Hoffenheim.

• Striker Kevin Doyle played in a club record 26 matches for the Republic of Ireland while with Reading between 2006 and 2009.

HONOURS
Championship champions 2006, 2012
Second Division champions 1994
Division 3 champions 1986
Division 3 (South) champions 1926
Division 4 champions 1979

REAL MADRID

Year founded: 1902
Ground: Estadio Bernabeu (81,044)
Previous name: Madrid
Nickname: Los Meringues
League titles: 33
Domestic cups: 18
European cups: 19
International cups: 7

Founded by students as Madrid FC in 1902, the title 'Real' (meaning 'Royal') was bestowed on the club by King Alfonso XIII in 1920.

• One of the most famous names in world football, Real Madrid won the first ever European Cup in 1956 and went on to a claim a record five consecutive victories in the competition with a side featuring greats such as Alfredo Di Stefano, Ferenc Puskas and Francisco Gento. Real's total of 13 victories in the European Cup/Champions League is also a record, and following their most recent success – a 3-1 defeat of Liverpool in the final in Kiev in 2018 – Real became the first club to win the trophy three times on the trot in the Champions League era.

• The club have dominated Spanish football over the years, winning a record 33 league titles (seven more than nearest rivals Barcelona), including a record five on the trot on two occasions (1961-65 and 1986-90).

• Real were unbeaten at home for a Spanish record 121 matches between February 1957 and March 1965.

• After beating Al Ain 4-1 in the final of the Club World Cup in Abu Dhabi in 2018 Real won the competition for a record fourth time.

HONOURS
Spanish League 1932, 1933, 1954, 1955, 1957, 1958, 1961, 1962, 1963, 1964, 1965, 1967, 1968, 1969, 1972, 1975, 1976, 1978, 1979, 1980, 1986, 1987, 1988, 1989, 1990, 1995, 1997, 2001, 2003, 2007, 2008, 2012, 2017
Spanish Cup 1905, 1906, 1907, 1908, 1917, 1934, 1936, 1946, 1947, 1962, 1970, 1974, 1975, 1980, 1982, 1989, 1993, 2011, 2014
European Cup/Champions League 1956, 1957, 1958, 1959, 1960, 1966, 1998, 2000, 2002, 2014, 2016, 2017, 2018
UEFA Cup 1985, 1986
European Super Cup 2002, 2014, 2016, 2017
Intercontinental Cup/Club World Cup 1960, 1998, 2002, 2014, 2016, 2017, 2018

Brazil's Vinicius Junior is a 'Real' rising star at the Bernabeu

Millie Bright cut a forlorn figure after the ref sent her off during the 2019 Women's World Cup

REFEREES

In the 19th century Colonel Francis Marindin was the referee at a record nine FA Cup finals, including eight on the trot between 1883 and 1990. His record will never be beaten as the FA now appoints a different referee for the FA Cup final every year.

• **The first referee to send off a player in the FA Cup final was Peter Willis, who dismissed Manchester United defender Kevin Moran in the 1985 final for a foul on Everton's Peter Reid. Video replays showed that it was a harsh decision.**

• Uzbek referee Ravshan Irmatov has taken charge of a record 11 World Cup matches across the 2010, 2014 and 2018 tournaments.

• **On 14th August 2019 French referee Stephanie Frappart became the first woman to take charge of a major European men's game when she officiated at the European Super Cup clash between Chelsea and Liverpool in Istanbul.**

• In the 2003/04 season Rob Styles brandished a record 12 red cards in Premier League matches. Meanwhile, Mike Dean showed a record 129 yellows in the 2018/19 campaign. In the same season Dean became the first ref to send off 100 players in the Premier League when he dismissed Manchester United defender Ashley Young in a match at Wolves.

• **In one of the most bizarre incidents ever in the history of football, a referee scored in a Dutch fourth tier match between Harkemase Boys and Hoek on 25th May 2019 when a cross from a Hoek player deflected off his leg and slowly bobbled over the line. However, a rule change made in the summer of 2019 means that similar incidents in future will result in a drop ball rather than a goal being awarded.**

RELEGATION

Birmingham City boast the unwanted record of having been relegated from the top flight more often than any other club, having taken the drop 12 times. However, the Blues have not experienced that sinking feeling as often as Notts County, who have suffered 17 relegations in total, most recently falling out of the Football League entirely in 2018/19. Meanwhile, Bristol City were the first club to suffer three consecutive relegations, dropping from Division One to Division Four between 1979/80 and 1981/82 – a fate matched by Wolves between 1983/84 and 1985/86.

• **In the Premier League era Crystal Palace, Middlesbrough, Norwich City, Sunderland and West Brom have dropped out of the top flight on a joint-record four occasions. In 1993 the Eagles were desperately unlucky to go down with a record 49 points, a tally matched by Norwich in 1985 in the old First Division. Southend in 1988/89 and Peterborough in 2012/13 were even more unfortunate, being relegated from the old Third Division and the Championship respectively despite amassing 54 points.**

• Manchester City are the only club to be relegated a year after winning the league title. Following their championship success in 1937 City went down in 1938 despite being top scorers in the First Division with 80 goals.

• **When Derby County went down from the Premier League in 2008, they did so with the lowest points total of any club in the history of English league football. The Rams accumulated only 11 points in a miserable campaign, during which they managed to win just one match out of 38. Derby's relegation was confirmed on 29th March, the earliest ever date for a Premier League club to know its grisly fate.**

• SV Lohhof (2000-2003) and FC Kempton (2008-2011) have both suffered a record four consecutive relegations in German regional football.

REPLAYS

In the days before penalty shoot-outs, the FA Cup fourth qualifying round tie between Alvechurch and Oxford City went to a record five replays before Alvechurch reached the first round proper with a 1-0 win in the sixth match between the two clubs.

• **The first FA Cup final to go to a replay was the 1875 match between Royal Engineers and Old Etonians, Engineers winning 2-0 in the second** match. The last FA Cup final to require a replay was the 1993 match between Arsenal and Sheffield Wednesday, the Gunners triumphing 2-1 in the second game. In 1999 the FA elected to scrap final replays, ruling that any drawn match would be settled on the day by a penalty shoot-out.

• In 1912 Barnsley required a record six replays in total before getting their hands on the FA Cup. Fulham also played six replays in their run to the FA Cup final in 1975, but the extra games appeared to have taken their toll on the team as they lost limply 2-0 to West Ham at Wembley.

• No World Cup final has gone to a replay but in 1968 Italy beat Yugoslavia 2-0 in Rome in the final of the European Championships after the original match finished 1-1 two days earlier.

REPUBLIC OF IRELAND

First international: Republic of Ireland 1 Bulgaria 0, 1924
Most capped player: Robbie Keane, 146 caps (1998-2016)
Leading goalscorer: Robbie Keane, 68 goals (1998-2016)
First World Cup appearance: Republic of Ireland 1 England 1, 1990
Biggest win: 8-0 v Malta (1983)
Heaviest defeat: 0-7 v Brazil (1982)

The Republic of Ireland enjoyed their most successful period under English manager Jack Charlton in the late 1980s and early 1990s. 'Big Jack' became a legend on the Emerald Isle after guiding the Republic to their first ever World Cup in 1990, taking the team to the quarter-finals of the tournament – despite not winning a single match – before they were eliminated by hosts Italy.

• Ireland have since appeared at two more World Cups in 1994 and 2002, reaching the second round on both occasions before losing to the Netherlands and Spain respectively.

• In 2009, in a World Cup play-off against France, the Republic were on the wrong end of one of the worst refereeing decisions of all time when Thierry Henry's blatant handball went unpunished before he crossed for William

Gallas to score the goal that ended Ireland's hopes of reaching the 2010 finals in South Africa. The incident was later cited by FIFA officials as an example of the type of decision which would be overturned by the VAR system.

• **The Republic have qualified for the European Championships on three occasions, reaching the knock-out stages for the first time at Euro 2016 thanks to a famous 1-0 win over Italy. However, a 2-1 defeat against hosts France ended their hopes of any further progress.**

• The Republic have been a bogey team for England in recent decades, remaining undefeated in six matches between the sides dating back to 1988.

• Republic of Ireland striker Robbie Keane has won more caps (146) and scored more international goals (68) than any other player from the British Isles.

World Cup Record
1930 *Did not enter*
1934 *Did not qualify*
1938 *Did not qualify*
1950 *Did not enter*
1954-86 *Did not qualify*
1990 *Quarter-finals*
1994 *Round 2*
1998 *Did not qualify*
2002 *Round 2*
2006 *Did not qualify*
2010 *Did not qualify*
2014 *Did not qualify*
2018 *Did not qualify*

DECLAN RICE

Born: Kingston upon Thames, 14th January 1999
Position: Midfielder
Club career:
2017- West Ham United 61 (2)
International record:
2018 Republic of Ireland 3 (0)
2019- England 3 (0)

In March 2019 West Ham midfielder Declan Rice joined a small club of England dual internationals when he made his debut for the Three Lions against the Czech Republic at Wembley having previously played three games for the Republic of Ireland.

• **A composed passer of the ball who excels in a deep-lying position just ahead of the back four, Rice started out in the Chelsea academy aged seven. When he was released by the Blues aged 14 he moved across London to West Ham, making his debut for the Hammers on the final day of the 2016/17 season.**

• The following season he became a mainstay of the West Ham side, his mature performances earning the appreciation of the fans who voted him runner-up in their 'Hammer of the Year' poll. He continued to progress in the 2018/19 campaign, and was nominated for the PFA Young Player of the Year award which was won by Manchester City's Raheem Sterling.

• **Although born and raised in Kingston upon Thames, Rice qualified for**

Declan Rice has played for more countries than clubs!

the Republic of Ireland through his grandparents and played for the Republic from Under-16 level onwards, making his full debut against Turkey in March 2018. However, after much soul-searching over a number of months, he finally pledged his international future to England in February 2019.

RICHARLISON

Born: Nova Venecia, Brazil, 10th May 1997
Position: Winger/striker
Club career:
2015-16 America Mineiro 24 (9)
2016-17 Fluminense 42 (9)
2017-18 Watford 38 (5)
2018- Everton 35 (13)
International record:
2018- Brazil 13 (6)

Following his £35 million move from Watford in the summer, Brazilian forward Richarlison paid back a good slice of that fee by scoring 13 goals for Everton in the 2018/19 Premier League season to make him the club's joint-top scorer for the campaign.

• A strong, pacy and determined player who can operate either on the wing or in a more central attacking role, Richarlison started out with Belo Horizonte-based outfit America Mineiro before switching to Fluminense in 2016. The following year he helped the Rio de Janeiro side reach the quarter-finals of the Copa Sudamericana, South America's equivalent of the Europa League.

• In August 2017 Richarlison joined Watford for £11.2 million, and his consistent performances for the Hornets ensured he was the only member of their squad to feature in every Premier League in the 2017/18 season.
• After playing for Brazil's Under-20 side, Richarlison made his full international debut in a friendly against the USA in September 2018. The following year he scored from the penalty spot in Brazil's 3-1 defeat of Peru in the final of the Copa America in Rio de Janeiro.

ROCHDALE

Year founded: 1907
Ground: Spotland Stadium (10,249)
Nickname: The Dale
Biggest win: 8-1 v Chesterfield (1926)
Heaviest defeat: 1-9 v Tranmere Rovers (1931)

Founded at a meeting at the town's Central Council Office in 1907, Rochdale were elected to the Third Division (North) as founder members in 1921.
• The proudest day in the club's history came in 1962 when they reached the League Cup final. Rochdale lost 4-0 on aggregate to Norwich City, then in the Second Division, but took pride in becoming the first team from the bottom tier to reach a major cup final. The Dale's manager at the time was

Tony Collins, the first ever black boss of a league club.
• Rochdale failed to win a single game in the FA Cup for 18 years from 1927 – the longest period of time any club has gone without victory in the competition. The appalling run finally came to an end in 1945 when the Dale beat Stockport 2-1 in a first-round replay.
• There was more misery for fans of the Dale in 1973/74 when their heroes won just two league games in the old Third Division – the worst ever return in a 46-match campaign.
• There were happier days, though, for the club's longsuffering fans in 2018 when the Dale reached the fifth round of the FA Cup for just the second time in their history. The Lancashire side earned a creditable 2-2 draw with Totttenham, before losing 6-1 in the replay at Wembley.

CRISTIANO RONALDO

Born: Madeira, Portugal, 5th February 1985
Position: Winger/striker
Club career:
2001-03 Sporting Lisbon 25 (3)
2003-09 Manchester United 196 (84)
2009-18 Real Madrid 292 (311)
2018- Juventus 31 (21)
International record:
2003- Portugal 158 (88)

In July 2018 Cristiano Ronaldo moved from Real Madrid to Juventus for £99.2 million to become the most expensive player in Italian football history. He immediately paid back much of that fee by contributing 21 goals as Juve won Serie A for a record eighth consecutive season – in the process becoming the first player ever to win the domestic title in England, Spain and Italy – and collecting the inaugural Serie A Most Valuable Player award.

Richarlison has been finding life pretty sweet with the Toffees

• Born on the Portuguese island of Madeira, Ronaldo began his career with Sporting Lisbon before joining Manchester United in a £12.25 million deal in 2003. The following year he won his first trophy with the Red Devils, opening the scoring as United beat Millwall 3-0 in the FA Cup final. He later helped United win a host of major honours, including three Premiership titles and the Champions League in 2008 before signing for Real for a then world record £80 million in 2009.

• In 2007 Ronaldo was voted PFA Player of the Year and Young Player of the Year, the first man to achieve this double since Andy Gray in 1977. The following season he scored a remarkable 42 goals for United in all competitions, and won the European Golden Boot. Three years later, in his second season with Real, he became the first player ever to win the award in two different countries. He went on to win two La Liga titles and the Champions League four times with Real, in 2014, 2016, 2017 and 2018, and is the only player in the modern era to score in three finals.

• **Ronaldo is also the leading scorer in the history of the Champions League with a total of 126 goals, including a** record 63 in the knock-out stages and a record 17 in the 2013/14 season, and has played in a record 101 wins in the competition. Additionally, he is Real's all-time leading scorer with an incredible 450 goals in all competitions, a total which includes a record 34 hat-tricks in La Liga.

• Arguably the most exciting talent in world football today, Ronaldo is the only player from the Premier League to have been voted World Footballer of the Year, having collected this most prestigious of awards in 2008. After playing second fiddle for some years to his great rival Lionel Messi, he equalled the Barcelona magician's five awards after collecting the FIFA Best Men's Player gong in 2016 and 2017.

• Captain of Portugal since 2008, Ronaldo has played for his country a record 158 times and scored an incredible 88 goals – a tally unmatched by any European player in history. After coming close a number of times, he finally led his nation to glory at Euro 2016, although he had to limp off in the first half of Portugal's eventual 1-0 defeat of hosts France in the final in Paris. His tally of nine goals at the European Championships is a joint record, and he has also made a record 21 appearances at the finals.

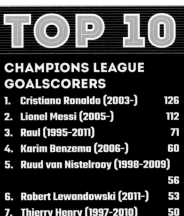

TOP 10		
CHAMPIONS LEAGUE GOALSCORERS		
1.	Cristiano Ronaldo (2003-)	126
2.	Lionel Messi (2005-)	112
3.	Raul (1995-2011)	71
4.	Karim Benzema (2006-)	60
5.	Ruud van Nistelrooy (1998-2009)	56
6.	Robert Lewandowski (2011-)	53
7.	Thierry Henry (1997-2010)	50
8.	Alfredo Di Stefano (1955-64)	49
9.	Zlatan Ibrahimovic (2001-17)	48
10.	Andriy Shevchenko (1994-2012)	48

WAYNE ROONEY

Born: Liverpool, 24th October 1985
Position: Striker/midfielder
Club career:
2002-04 Everton 67 (15)
2004-17 Manchester United 393 (183)
2017-18 Everton 31 (10)
2018- DC United 43 (23)
International record:
2003-18 England 120 (53)
2020- Derby

With 53 goals for England and 253 in all competitions for Manchester United, Wayne Rooney is the leading all-time scorer for both the Red Devils and the Three Lions. In both cases, he passed longstanding benchmarks set in the early 1970s by another United and England legend, Sir Bobby Charlton. Rooney's total of 120 England caps, meanwhile, is a record for an outfield player and only surpassed by goalkeeper Peter Shilton.

• **Rooney burst onto the scene with Everton in 2002, scoring his first league goal for the Toffees with a magnificent 20-yarder against reigning champions Arsenal at Goodison Park just five days before his 17th birthday. At the time he was the youngest ever Premiership scorer, but his record has since been surpassed by both James Milner and James Vaughan.**

• After starring for England at Euro 2004 Rooney signed for Manchester United later that summer for £25.6 million, to become the world's most expensive

"You've got to admit, I'm just so much cooler than little Lionel!"

teenage footballer. He started his Old Trafford career in sensational style with a hat-trick against Fenerbahce and until he returned on a free transfer to Everton in July 2017 played a pivotal role for the Red Devils, winning five Premier League titles, three League Cups, the FA Cup, the Champions League and, in his last match for United, the Europa League.

• Rooney's total of 208 Premier League goals is only bettered by Alan Shearer and his tally of 30 goals in the Champions League is a record for a British player. In June 2018 he joined DC United, and a year later announced that he would become player-coach at Derby County in January 2020.

• Rooney is the youngest ever England player to play 100 times for his country, reaching the landmark against Slovenia on 15th November 2014 aged 29 and 22 days. He fittingly marked the occasion with a goal from the penalty spot in a 3-1 Wembley win.

• When Wayne Rooney scored his first goal for England, against Macedonia in a Euro 2004 qualifier on 6th September

Wayne Rooney, England's all-time top scorer

2003, he was aged just 17 years and 317 days – the youngest player ever to find the net for the Three Lions.

ROSS COUNTY

	Year founded: 1929
	Ground: Victoria Park (6,541)
	Nickname: The Staggies
	Biggest win: 11-0 v St Cuthbert Wanderers (1993)
	Heaviest defeat: 0-7 v Kilmarnock (1962)

Founded in 1929, Ross County played in the Highland League until 1994 when they were elected to the Scottish Third Division with Inverness Caledonian Thistle.

• **The club enjoyed the greatest day in their history in 2016 when they beat Hibs 2-1 in the final of the Scottish League Cup thanks to a late winner by Dutch striker Alex Schalk.** Six years earlier the Staggies reached the Scottish Cup final for the first and only time, after sensationally beating Celtic in the semi-final. However, they had to settle for second best on their big day, after going down 3-0 to Dundee United in the final at Hampden Park.

• In 2012 the club won promotion to the top flight for the first time in their history, after a magnificent campaign which saw them go 34 matches undefeated – a joint record for the Scottish second tier – and finish a record 24 points clear at the top of the Scottish First Division. After a six-year stay in the Premiership the club were relegated in 2018 but bounced back the following season as Championship winners.

• Veteran midfielder Michael Gardyne is the Staggies' top appearance maker and all-time leading scorer with 71 goals in all competitions in 392 games since making his debut in 2006.

ROTHERHAM UNITED

	Year founded: 1925
	Ground: New York Stadium (12,021)
	Nickname: The Millers
	Biggest win: 8-0 v Oldham Athletic (1947)
	Heaviest defeat: 1-11 v Bradford City (1928)

The club had its origins in Thornhill FC (founded in 1878, later becoming Rotherham County) and Rotherham Town, who merged with County to form Rotherham United in 1925.

• **The club's greatest moment came in 1961 when they reached the first ever League Cup final, losing 3-2 on aggregate to Aston Villa.** Six years earlier Rotherham had missed out on goal average on securing promotion to the First Division – the closest they've ever been to playing top-flight football.

• Gladstone Guest scored a record 130 goals for the Millers between 1946 and 1956, while his team-mate Danny Williams played a club best 459 games in midfield.

• **Centre back Kari Arnason played in a club record 36 matches for Iceland while with the Millers between 2012 and 2015.**

• Relegated from the Championship for a second time in three seasons in 2019, Rotherham scored a club record 114 goals in Division Three (North) in 1946/47, a campaign in which they won all but one of their 21 home games.

SACKINGS

The stats show that the Southampton job is by far the riskiest in the Premier League. Not counting the period 2005 to 2012 when they were out of the top flight, the Saints have had 19 managers in the elite division.

• In 1959 Bill Lambton got the boot from Scunthorpe United after just three days in the managerial hotseat, an English league record. His reign at the Old Showground took in just one match – a 3-0 defeat at Liverpool in a Second Division fixture.

• In May 2007 Leroy Rosenior was sacked as manager of Conference side Torquay United after just 10 minutes in charge! No sooner had the former West Ham and QPR striker been unveiled as the Gulls' new boss when he was told that the club had been bought by a business consortium and his services were no longer required.

• Notts County have sacked more managers than any other Football League club. When Neal Ardley took over at Meadow Lane in November 2018 he was the Magpies' 67th boss in their 149-year history. Unfortunately, it didn't prove to be the greatest of appointments as Ardley became

the first manager to lead County to relegation from the Football League.

• The shortest reign of any Premier League manager is that of Dutchman Frank de Boer, who was in charge of Crystal Palace for just five matches at the start of the 2017/18 season before he got the chop.

• Among the home nations Scotland have been the most trigger-happy, with current boss Steve Clarke being the 24th man to lead the Tartan Army.

ST JOHNSTONE

Year founded: 1884
Ground: McDiarmid Park (10,696)
Nickname: The Saints
Biggest win: 13-0 v Tulloch (1887)
Heaviest defeat: 0-12 v Cowdenbeath (1928)

St Johnstone were founded in 1884 by a group of local cricketers in Perth who wanted to keep fit in winter.

• **The Saints enjoyed their best ever day in 2014, when they beat Dundee United 2-0 in the Scottish Cup final at Celtic Park. Previously, the club had appeared in two League Cup finals, but lost in 1969 to Celtic and again in 1998 to Rangers.**

• Stalwart defender Steven Anderson made a record 362 appearances for the Saints between 2004 and 2019. The club's leading scorer is John Brogan who rifled in 140 goals in all competitions between 1977 and 1984.

• **Along with Falkirk, St Johnstone have won the Scottish second tier a record**

seven times, most recently claiming the First Division title in 2009 while going on a club record unbeaten run of 21 games.

• In 1946 Saints striker Willie McIntosh scored a club record six goals in a 9-0 hammering of Albion Rovers in a Scottish League Cup tie.

HONOURS
First Division champions 1983, 1990, 1997, 2009
Division 2 champions 1924, 1960, 1963
Scottish Cup 2014

ST MIRREN

Year founded: 1877
Ground: St Mirren Park (7,937)
Nickname: The Buddies
Biggest win: 15-0 v Glasgow University (1960)
Heaviest defeat: 0-9 v Rangers (1897)

Named after the patron saint of Paisley, St Mirren were founded in 1877 by a group of local cricketers and rugby players. The club were founder members of the Scottish League in 1890, but have never finished higher than third in the top flight.

• **Winners of the Premiership play-off final in 2019 after a shoot-out victory against Dundee United, the Buddies have triumphed in the Scottish Cup three times, most recently in 1987 when they beat Dundee United 1-0 in the final after extra-time – the last time that the winners have fielded an all-Scottish line-up.**

• St Mirren have won the League Cup just once, beating Hearts 3-2 in an exciting final at Hampden Park in 2013. Three years earlier the Buddies lost 1-0 to Rangers in the final despite playing the last 20 minutes of the match against just nine men.

• **Midfielder Hugh Murray played in a club record 424 games for the Buddies between 1996 and 2012. The club's top scorer is David McCrae who notched an impressive 221 goals between 1923 and 1934.**

• St Mirren defender Andy Millen holds the record for the oldest player ever to appear in the SPL, turning out for the

Austria's Ralph Hasenhüttl is the latest of Southampton's 19 top-flight managers

Buddies for the last time in a 1-1 draw with Hearts aged 42 and 279 days on 15th March 2008.

HONOURS
Championship champions 2018
First Division champions 1977, 2000, 2006
Division 2 champions 1968
Scottish Cup 1926, 1959, 1987
League Cup 2013

MOHAMED SALAH

Born: Basyoun, Egypt, 15th June 1992
Position: Winger/striker
Club career:
2010-12 El Mokawloon 38 (11)
2012-14 Basel 47 (9)
2014-16 Chelsea 13 (2)
2015 Fiorentina (loan) 16 (6)
2015-16 Roma (loan) 34 (14)
2016-17 Roma 31 (15)
2017- Liverpool 74 (54)
International record:
2011- Egypt 67 (41)

In two glorious seasons with Liverpool following a bargain £36.9 million move from Roma, Egypt international Mohamed Salah has won the Golden Boot twice: leading the way with 32 Premier League goals – a record for a 38-match campaign – in 2017/18 and then hitting 22 in 2018/19 to share the award with team-mate Sadio Mane and Arsenal's Pierre-Emerick Aubameyang.

• Salah also won both Player of the Year awards in 2018, but his biggest achievement came a year later when he scored a penalty against Tottenham in the Champions League final in Madrid to help the Reds win the trophy for a sixth time. The goal came after just 106 seconds, making it the second-fastest in the final of Europe's elite club competition after Paolo Maldini's for AC Milan against Liverpool (52 seconds) in 2005.

• A speedy and direct striker who began his career as a winger, Salah started out with Cairo club El Mokawloon before moving to Basel in 2012. After winning consecutive Swiss championships, Salah joined Chelsea in 2014, having impressed the Londoners' hierarchy by scoring in three European matches against the Blues. He failed to establish himself at Stamford Bridge, however, and was subsequently loaned out to Fiorentina and Roma before joining the club from the Italian capital for a cut-price £16 million in 2016.

• First capped by Egypt in 2011, Salah was joint-top scorer in the African section of the 2014 World

Cup qualifiers with six goals. In 2017 he was part of the Egypt team which reached the final of the Africa Cup of Nations, losing 2-1 to Cameroon. Despite not being fully fit at the 2018 World Cup in Russia, he became the first Egyptian to score twice at the tournament since 1934 with strikes against Russia and Saudi Arabia.

SALFORD CITY

Year founded: 1940
Ground: Moor Lane (5,106)
Previous name: Salford Central, Salford Amateurs
Nickname: The Ammies
Biggest win: 7-0 v Barwell (2016)
Heaviest defeat: 1-7 v St Helens Town (1994)

Founded as Salford Central in 1940, the club became Salford Amateurs in 1963, giving rise to the nickname 'the Ammies' which survives to this day, before adopting its current name in 1989. In 2014 five former members of Manchester United's 'Class of 92', including Ryan Giggs and Gary Neville, bought the club before selling half their shares to Singaporean businessman Peter Lim, the billionaire owner of Valencia. In February 2019 former England captain David Beckham also bought a 10% share in the club.

• Investment from the new owners helped propel the club to the National League North title in 2018. The following season the Ammies enjoyed a club record 20-game unbeaten run in the National League on their way to the play-off final against Fylde at Wembley, which they won

Mohamed Salah points out how many Premier League Golden Boots he's won

3-0 to become the first club to reach the Football League after successive promotions.

• In 2015 Salford made it through to the FA Cup second round for the first time in their history, but were beaten 2-0 by Hartlepool United in a replay after extra-time.

• With a capacity of just 5,106, Salford's tiny Moor Lane stadium is the smallest in League Two.

JADON SANCHO

Born: Camberwell, 25th March 2000
Position: Winger
Club career:
2017 Borussia Dortmund II 3 (0)
2017- Borussia Dortmund 46 (13)
International record:
2018- England 6 (0)

One of the most exciting young English players of his generation, Borussia Dortmund's Jadon Sancho scored 12 league goals in the 2018/19 season to become the youngest-ever player to hit double figures in a single Bundesliga campaign.

• An inventive winger who possesses lots of eye-catching tricks, Sancho joined Watford's academy aged seven before switching to Manchester

No 'Sane' City fan would want to see Leroy leave the Etihad!

Jadon Sancho is a happy expat in Dortmund

City when he was 14 for an initial fee of £66,000. However, after failing to break into City's multi-talented squad he joined Dortmund for around £8 million in August 2017.

• In October 2018 Sancho was named Bundesliga Player of the Month after scoring three goals in three games, and at the end of the campaign he was voted into the Bundesliga Team of the Year.

• Sancho was named Player of the Tournament at the European Under-17 Championships in 2017, but had to be satisfied with a runners-up medal after England lost the final to Spain on penalties. In October 2018 he made his senior bow in a 0-0 draw away to Croatia in the UEFA Nations league, a match that was played behind closed doors after the hosts were punished by UEFA for an incident before a previous international when a swastika was marked on the pitch.

LEROY SANE

Born: Essen, Germany, 11th January 1996
Position: Winger
Club career:
2014-16 Schalke 47 (11)
2016- Manchester City 89 (25)
International record:
2015- Germany 20 (5)

A talented winger who can race past defenders with a sudden blistering burst of acceleration, Leroy Sane enjoyed his most prolific season to date with Treble winners Manchester City in 2018/19, contributing 16 goals in all competitions. Perhaps, though, he didn't quite hit the heights of the previous campaign when he was voted PFA Young Player of the Year.

• Sane joined City from Schalke for £37 million in August 2016. After a relatively slow start at the Etihad, Sane's form improved to such an extent that he was nominated for the PFA Young Player of the Year award in 2017, although he was pipped in the final poll by Tottenham's Dele Alli.

• Sane can thank both his parents for providing him with excellent sporting genes. His father was an international footballer for Senegal, while his mother was a gymnast who competed for West Germany at the 1984 Olympics.

• After representing Germany at both Under-19 and Under-21 level, Sane made his full international debut in a 2-0 friendly defeat by France in Paris in November 2015 – a match which was overshadowed by a series of terrorist attacks in the French capital on the same night. To the surprise of many pundits, he was left out of Germany's squad for the 2018 World Cup but he returned in the autumn to score his first international goal in a 3-0 defeat of Russia.

KASPER SCHMEICHEL

Born: Copenhagen, Denmark, 5th November 1986
Position: Goalkeeper
Club career:
2005-09 Manchester City 8
2006 Darlington (loan) 4
2006 Bury (loan) 29
2007 Falkirk (loan) 15
2007-08 Cardiff City (loan) 14
2008 Coventry City (loan) 9
2009-10 Notts County 43
2010-11 Leeds United 37
2011- Leicester City 301
International record:
2013- Denmark 47

Kasper Schmeichel became the first biological son of a Premier League-winning father to also lift the trophy when he helped surprise package Leicester City top the table in 2016, playing every minute of the campaign.

His father, Peter, had previously won the title five times with Manchester United, a record for a goalkeeper. The following season he became the first goalkeeper in Champions League history to save a penalty in both legs of a knock-out tie when he twice denied Sevilla from the spot during the Foxes' 3-2 aggregate last-16 win.

• Schmeichel started out with Manchester City but failed to hold down a first-team place and was loaned out to five other clubs before moving to Notts Country in 2009, with whom he won the League Two title the following year.

• After spending a season with Leeds United in 2010/11, Schmeichel joined Leicester and began to impress with some tremendous performances between the goalposts. He was voted into the Championship Team of the Year in 2013 and the next season was in fine form again as the Foxes won the Championship at a canter with a club record 102 points.

• During the 2017/18 season Schmeichel went 571 minutes without conceding a goal for Denmark, breaking a record previously held by his father. At the World Cup in Russia he saved a penalty from Luka Modric in extra-time during Denmark's last 16 tie with Croatia but, despite making two more saves in the shoot-out that followed the two teams' 1-1 draw, couldn't prevent his country losing on spot-kicks. His total of 47 caps makes him Leicester's second-highest capped player ever, behind Wales' Andy King.

SCOTLAND

First international: Scotland 0 England 0, 1872
Most capped player: Kenny Dalglish, 102 caps (1971-86)
Leading goalscorer: Denis Law (1958-74) and Kenny Dalglish (1971-86), 30 goals
First World Cup appearance: Scotland 0 Austria 1, 1954
Biggest win: Scotland 11 Ireland 0, 1901
Heaviest defeat: Scotland 0 Uruguay 7, 1954

Along with England, Scotland are the oldest international team in the world. The two countries played the first official international way back in 1872, the match at Hamilton Crescent, Partick, finishing 0-0. Scotland were by far the dominant team in Britain in those early years, losing just two of their first 43 internationals.

• It took the Scots a while to make an impression on the world scene, however. After withdrawing from the 1950 World Cup, Scotland competed in the finals for the first time in 1954 but were eliminated in the first round after suffering their worst ever defeat, 7-0 to reigning champions Uruguay.

• Scotland have taken part in the World Cup finals on eight occasions but have never got beyond the group stage – a record for the tournament. They have been unlucky, though, going out in 1974, 1978 and 1982 only on goal difference.

• Scotland have a pretty poor record in the European Championships, only qualifying for the finals on two occasions, in 1992 and 1996. Again, they failed to reach the knockout stage both times, although they were unfortunate to lose out on the 'goals scored' rule to Holland at Euro '96.

• Scotland had a good record in the Home Championships until the tournament was scrapped in 1984, winning the competition 24 times and sharing the title another 17 times. Only England (34 outright wins and 20 shared) have a better overall record.

• A European record crowd of 149,415 watched Scotland beat England 3-1 at Hampden Park in the Home Championships in 1937.

"Just for a change, I fancy playing up front today!"

"You've scored for Scotland, Burkie – not many people can say that in recent years!"

• Scotland have the worst recent record of any of the four home nations, having failed to qualify for any international tournament since they were eliminated at the group stage of the 1998 World Cup in France.

World Cup Record	
1930-38	*Did not enter*
1950	*Withdrew*
1954	*Round 1*
1958	*Round 1*
1962-70	*Did not qualify*
1974	*Round 1*
1978	*Round 1*
1982	*Round 1*
1986	*Round 1*
1990	*Round 1*
1994	*Did not qualify*
1998	*Round 1*
2002	*Did not qualify*
2006	*Did not qualify*
2010	*Did not qualify*
2014	*Did not qualify*
2018	*Did not qualify*

SCOTTISH CUP

The Scottish Cup was first played for in 1873/74, shortly after the formation of the Scottish FA. Queen's Park, who the previous year had competed in the English FA Cup, were the first winners, beating Clydesdale 2-0 in the final in front of a crowd of 3,000 at the original Hampden Park.

• Queen's Park were the dominant force in the early years of the competition, winning 10 of the first 20 finals, including one in 1884 when their opponents, Vale of Leven, failed to turn up! Since then, Celtic have been the most successful side in the

TOP 10

SCOTTISH CUP WINNERS	
1. Celtic	39
2. Rangers	33
3. Queen's Park	10
4. Hearts	8
5. Aberdeen	7
6. Clyde	3
Hibernian	3
Kilmarnock	3
St Mirren	3
Vale of Leven	3

competition, winning the trophy for a 39th time in 2019 with a 2-1 victory over Hearts at Hampden Park.
• Celtic winger Bobby Lennox is the most successful player in the history of the competition, with eight wins in the final between 1965 and 1980. Celtic boss Willie Maley did even better, with an incredible 14 wins in the competition between 1899 and 1937.
• Incredibly, the biggest ever victories in the history of British football took place in the Scottish Cup on the same day, 12th September 1885. Dundee Harp beat Aberdeen Rovers 35-0 and were confident that they had set a new record. Yet, no doubt to their utter amazement, they soon discovered that Arbroath had thrashed Bon Accord, a cricket club who had been invited to take part by mistake, 36-0!
• In 1909 the trophy was not awarded after Celtic and Rangers fans rioted at the end of the replay at Hampden Park after it was announced that extra-time would not be played following the teams' 1-1 draw.

SCOTTISH LEAGUE CUP

The Scottish League Cup came into being in 1946, some 14 years before the English version. The following April, Rangers won the first final by thrashing Aberdeen 4-0 at Hampden Park.
• Surprisingly, minnows East Fife were the first club to win the trophy three times (in 1947, 1949 and 1953) but since those early years the Glasgow giants have predictably dominated the competition, Rangers leading the way with 27 triumphs to Celtic's 18.
• Ayr United (1952) and Partick Thistle (1993) jointly hold the record for the biggest win in the competition, with 11-1 hammerings of Dumbarton and Albion Rovers respectively. Celtic hold the record for the most emphatic win in the final, demolishing Rangers 7-1 at Hampden Park in 1957 in the biggest ever margin of victory in a major British final.
• Celtic won the trophy for a record five years on the trot between 1966 and 1970 before subsequently losing a record four consecutive finals between 1971 and 1974.
• Prolific striker Joe Harper is the top scorer in the competition with 74 goals for Morton, Aberdeen and Hibs between 1963 and 1981.

SCUNTHORPE UNITED

Year founded: 1899
Ground: Glanford Park (9,088)
Previous name: Scunthorpe & Lindsey United
Nickname: The Iron
Biggest win: 9-0 v Boston United (1953)
Heaviest defeat: 0-8 v Carlisle United (1952)

The club was founded in 1899 when Brumby Hall linked up with some other local teams. Between 1910 and 1958 they were known as Scunthorpe and Lindsey United after amalgamating with the latter team.
• Elected to the Third Division (North) when the league expanded in 1950, Scunthorpe won the division eight years later. In 1962 the Iron finished a best ever fourth in the old Second Division, missing out on promotion to the top flight by just five points.

- In that same 1961/62 season striker Barrie Thomas set a club record by scoring 31 league goals. Incredibly, he had reached that tally by the end of January when, to the dismay of United's fans, he was sold to Newcastle.
- In the 2013/14 season Scunthorpe boss Russ Wilcox made the best ever start of a manager in Football League history, remaining unbeaten in his first 28 matches in charge as the Iron secured promotion to League One.
- Relegated from League One in 2019, Scunthorpe have reached the fifth round of the FA Cup on just two occasions: in 1958 when they lost 1-0 to Liverpool, and in 1970 when they were beaten 3-1 by Swindon Town.

HONOURS
League One champions 2007
Division 3 (North) champions 1958

SHEFFIELD UNITED

Year founded: 1889
Ground: Bramall Lane (32,609)
Nickname: The Blades
Biggest win: 10-0 v Port Vale (1892) and Burnley (1929)
Heaviest defeat: 0-13 v Bolton (1890)

The club was founded at a meeting at the city's Adelphi Hotel in 1899 by the members of the Sheffield United Cricket Club, partly to make greater use of the facilities at Bramall Lane.
- **The Blades enjoyed their heyday in the late Victorian era, winning the** title in 1898, and lifting the FA Cup in both 1899 and 1902. The club won the FA Cup again in 1915, beating Chelsea 3-0 at Old Trafford, in what was to be the last final to be played before the First World War brought a halt to the sporting calendar. They also chalked up another victory in 1925, beating Cardiff City 1-0 in the final at Wembley.
- The club's leading scorer is Harry Johnson, who bagged 201 league goals between 1919 and 1930. During an 18-year career with the club between 1948 and 1966, Joe Shaw made a record 631 appearances for the Blades. Goalkeeper Jack Smith made a record 203 consecutive appearances for the Blades between 1936 and 1947, and also saved 11 penalties to establish another club record.
- **The Blades' home, Bramall Lane, is one of the oldest sporting arenas in the world. It first hosted cricket in 1855, before football was introduced to the ground in 1862. Sixteen years later, in 1878, the world's first ever floodlit match was played at the stadium between two sides picked from the Sheffield Football Association, the lights being provided by two generators.**
- To the dismay of their fans, United have appeared in four play-off finals and lost them all – a miserable record only matched by Reading. Most recently, the Blades lost the 2012 League One play-off final to Huddersfield on penalties after all 22 players on the pitch had been required to take a spot-kick – the first time this had ever happened in a Wembley final.
- **One of just five clubs to top all four English divisions, Sheffield United**

IS THAT A FACT?
In the 1931/32 season Sheffield United striker Jimmy Dunne scored in 12 consecutive league matches – a record for the English top flight.

hold the record for the most number of points, 90 in 2011/12, for a team failing to win promotion from the third tier.
- Promoted to the Premier League in 2019, the Blades broke their transfer record four times in the summer window, with Scotland striker Oli McBurnie ultimately topping the list following his £20 million move from Swansea.
- **Striker Peter Ndlovu won a club record 26 of his 100 caps for Zimbabwe while at Bramall Lane between 2001 and 2004.**
- United striker Billy Sharp is the leading scorer in English football in the twentieth century with a total of 227 league goals, 95 of them for the Blades.

HONOURS
Division 1 champions 1898
Division 2 champions 1953
League One champions 2017
Division 4 champions 1982
FA Cup 1899, 1902, 1915, 1925

SHEFFIELD WEDNESDAY

Year founded: 1867
Ground: Hillsborough (39,732)
Previous name: The Wednesday
Nickname: The Owls
Biggest win: 12-0 v Halliwell (1891)
Heaviest defeat: 0-10 v Aston Villa (1912)

The club was formed as The Wednesday in 1867 at the Adelphi Hotel in Sheffield by members of the Wednesday Cricket Club, who originally met on that particular day of the week. In 1929 the club added 'Sheffield' to their name, but are still often referred to by their fans as simply 'Wednesday'.

Fans at Bramall Lane are delighted to be watching Premier League football again

The Owls' Morgan Fox is on the hunt for promotion from the Championship

• In 1904 the Owls became the first club in the 20th century to win consecutive league championships, despite scoring just 48 goals in 34 matches – the lowest total ever by a title-winning side. Wednesday won back-to-back titles again in 1929 and 1930 but have not lifted the league trophy since.

• In 1935 Wednesday won the FA Cup for the third and last time beating Arsenal 1-0 in the final at Wembley, striker Ellis Rimmer scoring in every round of the competition.

• Scottish international striker Andrew Wilson made a club record 560 appearances and scored a record 199 league goals while with Wednesday between 1900 and 1920.

• In 1991, while residing in the old Second Division, the Owls won the League Cup for the first and only time in their history, beating Manchester United 1-0 at Wembley. It was the last time that a club from outside the top flight has lifted a major domestic cup.

• The Owls enjoyed their best campaign in Europe in the 1961/62 season when they reached the quarter-finals of the Fairs Cup before losing 4-3 on aggregate to Barcelona.

• On the opening day of the 2000/01 season Wednesday goalkeeper Kevin Pressman was sent off after just 13 seconds at Molineux for handling a Wolves shot while outside the penalty area – the fastest dismissal ever in elite British football.

HONOURS
Division 1 champions *1903, 1904, 1929, 1930*
Division 2 champions *1900, 1926, 1952, 1956, 1959*
FA Cup *1896, 1907, 1935*
League Cup *1991*

SHREWSBURY TOWN

Year founded: 1886
Ground: Montgomery Waters Meadow (9,875)
Nickname: The Shrews
Biggest win: 11-2 v Marine (1995)
Heaviest defeat: 1-8 v Norwich City (1952) and Coventry City (1963)

Founded at the Lion Hotel in Shrewsbury in 1886, the club played in regional football for many years until being elected to the Football League in 1950.

• Prolific striker Arthur Rowley is the club's record scorer, hitting 152 goals between 1958 and 1965 to complete his all-time league record of 434 goals (he also turned out for West Bromwich Albion, Fulham and Leicester City). His best season for the Shrews was in 1958/59 when he banged in a club best 38 goals.

• Defender Mickey Brown played in a club record 418 league games in three spells with the Shrews between 1986 and 2001, and famously scored the decisive goal in a 2-1 win at Exeter in 2000 that saved the club from relegation from the Football League.

• In 1971 Shrews striker Alf Wood became the first player in the post-war era to score four headers in a Football League match. He ended the game with five goals in a 7-1 drubbing of Blackburn Rovers.

• Shrewsbury have won the Welsh Cup six times – a record for an English club.

• The Shrews enjoyed their best ever cup run in English football in 1961 when they reached the semi-finals of the first ever edition of the League Cup before losing 4-3 on aggregate to Rotherham United.

HONOURS
Division 3 champions *1979*
Third Division champions *1994*
Welsh Cup *1891, 1938, 1977, 1979, 1984, 1985*

GYLFI SIGURDSSON

Born: Reykjavik, Iceland, 8th September 1989
Position: Midfielder
Club career:
2008-10 Reading 42 (18)
2008 Shrewsbury Town (loan) 5 (1)
2009 Crewe Alexandra (loan) 15 (3)
2010-12 1899 Hoffenheim 36 (9)
2012 Swansea City (loan) 18 (7)
2012-14 Tottenham Hotspur 58 (8)
2014-17 Swansea City 106 (27)
2017- Everton 67 (17)
International record:
2010- Iceland 68 (20)

After a relatively quiet first season at Goodison Park, Everton's record signing Gylfi Sigurdsson paid back a significant slice of his £45 million transfer fee by scoring 13 Premier League goals in 2018/19 to finish as the Toffees' joint-top leading goalscorer.

Playmaker Gylfi Sigurdsson is Everton's record signing

• An elegant attacking midfielder who is renowned for his superb delivery at set-pieces, Sigurdsson has spent the vast majority of his career in Britain, making his name initially as a teenager with Reading. In 2010 he moved on to German outfit Hoffenheim, before signing for Tottenham for £8.8 million two years later after an impressive loan spell at Swansea City.

• Sigurdsson returned to South Wales in 2014, twice winning the club's 'Player of the Season' award as his goals and assists helped keep the struggling Swans in the Premier League. He finally moved on to longtime admirers Everton in August 2017, marking his full debut with an extraordinary 50-yard goal against Hajduk Split in the Europa League.

• First capped in 2010, Sigurdsson was part of the Iceland team which reached the last eight of Euro 2016 after sensationally knocking out England. He is now his country's third top scorer of all time with 20 goals.

BERNARDO SILVA

Born: Lisbon, Portugal, 10th August 1994
Position: Midfielder
Club career:
2013-15 Benfica B 38 (7)
2013-15 Benfica 1 (0)
2014-15 Monaco (loan) 15 (2)
2015-17 Monaco 86 (22)
2017- Manchester City 71 (13)
International record:
2015- Portugal 38 (3)

In his second season with Manchester City in 2018/19 Portuguese midfielder Bernardo Silva enjoyed his most prolific campaign of his career to date, contributing 13 goals in all competitions to help the Citizens win an historic domestic Treble. His consistent performances also saw him voted into the PFA Team of the Year.

• A skilful, creative midfielder who is adept at making quick, incisive passes around the opponents' box, Silva came through the prolific Benfica youth system to be named the second tier Breakthrough Player of the Year in 2014 while representing the club's B team.

• In the same year he joined Monaco on loan, and six months later completed a £13 million move to the principality. In

Bernardo Silva will be pleased to get a bigger pic than namesake David

2017 he helped Monaco win the French league title at a canter before joining City for £43.5 million.

• Silva made his senior debut for Portugal in a 2-0 friendly defeat against Cape Verde in March 2015. The following year he missed his country's surprise triumph at Euro 2016 through injury but he played a key role in his country's 2019 UEFA Nations League victory, winning the Player of the Tournament award.

DAVID SILVA

Born: Las Palmas, Spain, 8th January 1986
Position: Midfielder
Club career:
2003-04 Valencia B 14 (1)
2004-10 Valencia 119 (21)
2004-05 Eibar (loan) 35 (5)
2005-06 Celta (loan) 34 (4)
2010- Manchester City 284 (54)
International record:
2006-18 Spain 125 (35)

A tricky midfielder who can wriggle out of the tightest of situations before delivering an astute pass, David Silva starred for Treble winners Manchester City in the 2018/19 season, his total of 10 goals in all competitions including the opener in his side's 6-0 demolition of Watford in the FA Cup final.

• Prior to moving to the Etihad stadium, Silva was an outstanding

TOP 10

SPANISH PREMIER LEAGUE GOALSCORERS

1.	Fernando Torres (2007-14)	85
2.	David Silva (2010-)	54
3.	Diego Costa (2014-17)	52
4.	Juan Mata (2011-)	51
5.	Cesc Fabregas (2003-19)	50
6.	Mikel Arteta (2005-16)	41
7.	Ayoze Perez (2014-)	33
8.	Pedro (2015-)	28
9.	Santi Cazorla (2012-18)	25
10.	Michu (2012-15)	20

David Silva, aka 'El Mago'

player in the Valencia side that regularly managed to upset Real Madrid and Barcelona. His best moment with the Spanish outfit came in 2008, when Valencia won the Copa del Rey after beating Getafe 3-1 in the final.

• Nicknamed 'El Mago' (The Magician) for his sublime skills on the ball, Silva joined City for £24 million in 2010 and in his first season in Manchester helped the Sky Blues win their first trophy for 35 years when they beat Stoke City 1-0 in the FA Cup final at Wembley. In the same campaign he topped the Premier League assists chart with 15 and he is now seventh on the all-time list with 83.

• **First capped by his country in 2006, Silva was an integral figure in the Spain side that won Euro 2008, but was restricted to just two appearances as the Spanish became world champions in South Africa two years later. However, he returned to the starting line-up at Euro 2012, heading the first goal in Spain's 4-0 thrashing of Italy in the final. Before retiring from international football in 2018 Silva won 77 of his 125 caps with Manchester City, making him the club's most decorated international.**

SIZE

The heaviest player in the history of the professional game was Willie 'Fatty' Foulke, who played in goal for Sheffield United, Chelsea and Bradford City. By the end of his career, the tubby custodian weighed in at an incredible 24 stone.

• **At just 5ft tall, Fred Le May is the shortest player ever to have appeared in the Football League. He played for Thames, Clapton Orient and Watford between 1930 and 1933. The shortest England international ever was Frederick 'Fanny' Walden, a 5ft 2in winger with Tottenham who won the first of his two caps in 1914.**

IS THAT A FACT?
At just 5ft 3in (161cm), Manchester United midfielder Angel Gomes is the shortest player in the Premier League.

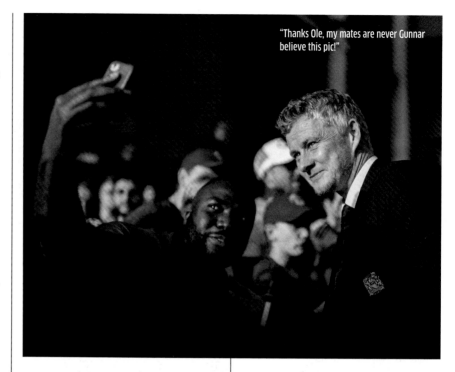

"Thanks Ole, my mates are never Gunnar believe this pic!"

• No prizes for guessing who the tallest ever England international is. It is, of course, towering striker Peter Crouch, who stands 6ft 7in in his socks. Crouch, though, is a full inch shorter than goalkeeper Costel Pantilimon — now playing in the Championship with Nottingham Forest — who claims the record as the tallest ever Premier League player.

• **The world's tallest player is Danish goalkeeper Simon Bloch Jorgensen, once a trialist with Everton, who towers over opposition strikers at a lofty 6ft 10 inches. Two players share the distinction of being the world's smallest player at just barely over five feet: Marcin Garuch of Polish fourth tier side Miedz Legnica II and Elton Jose Xavier Gomes of Saudi outfit Al-Qadisiyah.**

OLE GUNNAR SOLSKJAER

Born: Kristiansund, Norway, 26th February 1973
Managerial career:
2011-14 Molde
2014 Cardiff City
2015-19 Molde
2018-19 Manchester United (caretaker)
2019- Manchester United

Appointed caretaker manager of Manchester United in December 2018 following the sacking of Jose Mourinho, Ole Gunnar Solskjaer enjoyed a sensational start in the Old Trafford hotseat, winning 14 of his first 19 matches in charge before landing the job on a permanent basis in March 2019. However, a dip in the Red Devils' form saw them miss out on a place in the top four of the Premier League, ending their hopes of Champions League qualification.

• **A huge favourite with the United fans, Solskjaer won six Premier League titles, two FA Cups and, most famously, the Champions League with the club as a player, scoring a never-to-be-forgotten late winner in the 1999 final against Bayern Munich in Barcelona to secure his team a magnificent Treble. In the same season he also set a record for the most goals by a substitute in a single Premier League match, with four in United's 8-1 demolition of Nottingham Forest at the City Ground.**

• After hanging up his boots in 2007, Solskjaer began his managerial career at Old Trafford, serving as the club's reserve team manager under the watchful eye of his old boss Sir Alex Ferguson. He returned to his native Norway in 2011, guiding another of his former clubs, Molde, to two league titles and the domestic cup in 2013.

• **In January 2014 Solskjaer took over as Cardiff City manager but was unable to prevent the Welsh outfit from dropping out of the Premier League at the end of the campaign. After being sacked by the Bluebirds he rejoined Molde in 2015, where he remained until the surprise call came from United three years later.**

Son Heung-Min, the highest-scoring Asian player in Premier League history

SON HEUNG-MIN

Born: Chuncheon, South Korea, 8th July 1992
Position: Winger/striker
Club career:
2010 Hamburg II 6 (1)
2010-13 Hamburg 73 (20)
2013-15 Bayer Leverkusen 62 (21)
2015- Tottenham Hotspur 130 (42)
International record:
2010- South Korea 81 (24)

A hard-working frontman who loves to run at defenders before unleashing a powerful shot, Tottenham's Son Heung-min is the highest-scoring Asian player in the history of both the Premier League (42 goals) and the Champions League (12 goals).

• Son began his career in Germany, setting a record as the youngest player to score a league goal for Hamburg when he was on target against Cologne, aged 18, in 2010. Three years later he moved on to Bayer Leverkusen for a club record fee of around £8 million.

• In 2015 Son became the most expensive Asian player ever when he signed for Tottenham for £22 million, and in the same year he was named Asian International Footballer of the Year – the first South Korean to win this award. In 2018 he was named Premier League Player of the Year at the London Football

Awards and the following year he scored an historic goal: the first ever at the new Tottenham Hotspur Stadium in the home side's 2-0 win against Crystal Palace.

• First capped in 2010, Son was on the scoresheet in the 2015 Asian Cup final but had to settle for a runners-up medal after Australia won 2-1 in extra-time. He scored twice at the 2018 World Cup in Russia, including a memorable goal in South Korea's shock 2-0 victory against reigning champions Germany, and later that year helped his country win the Asian Games after a 2-1 victory against Japan in the final.

SOUTHAMPTON

Year founded: 1885
Ground: St Mary's (32,384)
Previous name: Southampton St Mary's
Nickname: The Saints
Biggest win: 14-0 v Newbury Town (1894)
Heaviest defeat: 0-8 v Tottenham (1936) and Everton (1971)

Founded as Southampton St Mary's by members of St Mary's Church Young Men's Association in 1885, the club joined the Southern League in 1894 and became simply 'Southampton' the following year.

• The Saints won the Southern League six times in the decade up to 1904 and also appeared in two FA Cup finals during that period, losing to Bury in 1900 and to Sheffield United two years later.

• The club finally won the cup in 1976. Manchester United were hot favourites to beat the Saints, then in the Second Division, but the south coast side claimed the trophy thanks to Bobby Stokes' late strike. As scorer of the first (and only) goal in the final, Stokes was rewarded with a free car... unfortunately, he still hadn't passed his driving test!

• Mick Channon, a member of that cup-winning team and now a successful racehorse trainer, is the Saints' leading scorer with a total of 185 goals in two spells at The Dell, the club's old ground. Incredibly, Channon was top scorer in the old First Division in the 1973/74 season with 21 goals but Southampton were still relegated – the first club to go down after finishing third bottom under the then new 'three up, three down' system.

• Winger Terry Paine, a member of England's 1966 World Cup-winning squad, is Southampton's longest serving player. Between 1956 and 1974 he wore the club's colours in no fewer than 713

You don't need to be old to be a Saint!

league games before moving to Hereford United. Paine's amazing total of 824 league games puts him fourth in the all-time list, behind Peter Shilton, Tony Ford and Graham Alexander.

• **England goalkeeper Shilton is the club's most capped player, winning 49 of his record 125 caps during his time at The Dell.**

• In January 2018 the Saints forked out a record £19 million to buy Argentinian striker Guido Carillo from Monaco. In the same month Southampton received £75 million from Liverpool for Dutch centre-back Virgil van Dijk in a world record deal for a defender.

• **In the 1959/60 season striker Derek Reeves scored 39 league goals in the old Division Three – a record both for the Saints and the third tier. The only player to score seven goals in a match for the Saints is Albert Brown, who achieved the feat in an 11-0 thrashing of Northampton Town in the Southern League in 1901.**

• Southampton are the only English club to have had three Dutch managers: Jan Poortvliet (2008-09), Mark Woote (2009) and Ronald Koeman (2014-16).

SOUTHEND UNITED

Year founded: 1906
Ground: Roots Hall (12,392)
Nickname: The Shrimpers
Biggest win: 10-1 v Golders Green (1934), Brentwood (1968) and Aldershot (1990)
Heaviest defeat: 1-9 v Brighton and Hove Albion (1965)

Southend United were founded in 1906 at the Blue Boar pub, just 50 yards away from the club's home, Roots Hall.

• **After joining the Football League in 1920 the Shrimpers remained in the third tier for a record 46 years, before finally dropping into the Fourth Division in 1966.**

• The club's top appearance maker is Sandy Anderson, who turned out in 452 league games between 1950 and 1962. His team-mate Roger Hollis is Southend's leading marksman, rifling in 120 league goals in just six years at the club between 1954 and 1960.

• Southend were relegated from the third tier in 1988/89 despite amassing a record points total for a demoted team (54). In all, the Shrimpers have dropped down to the fourth tier a record seven times.

• Along with Brentford, Southend hold the record for appearing in the most finals of the Football League Trophy without winning the cup once, losing to Blackpool (2004), Wrexham (2005) and Crewe (2013).

• **Southend have reached the fifth round of the FA Cup on three occasions but have lost every time, most recently going down 2-0 to Sheffield Wednesday in 1993.**

GARETH SOUTHGATE

Born: Watford, 3rd September 1970
Managerial career:
2006-09 Middlesbrough
2013-16 England Under-21
2016- England

In 2018 Gareth Southgate became the first England manager since Bobby Robson at Italia '90 to lead the Three Lions to the semi-finals of the World Cup. However, his dreams of glory were shattered by Croatia, who beat his young team 2-1 after extra-time in a pulsating tie in Moscow. The following year he took England to the semi-finals of the UEFA Nations League, but they were beaten 3-1 by the Netherlands after extra-time.

• **Southgate became England manager, initially on a four-match temporary**

"Yes! At last I've got my 'lucky' waistcoat back from Phil Neville!"

basis, following the sudden resignation of Sam Allardyce in September 2016. Two months later he was appointed full-time boss of the Three Lions on a four-year contract. He had previously been in charge of the England Under-21 team for three years.

• Southgate began his managerial career with Middlesbrough in 2006. Two years earlier he had become the first Boro captain to lift a major trophy when the Teesiders beat Bolton 2-1 in the League Cup final. However Southgate's long association with the club ended in the sack in October 2009, a few months after Boro' lost their Premier League place.

• A ball-playing centre-back, Southgate started out with Crystal Palace before moving to Aston Villa in 1995. The following year he helped Villa win the League Cup for a then joint-record fifth time and in 2000 he captained the Birmingham outfit in their 1-0 FA Cup final defeat to Chelsea. During a six-year spell at Villa Park he won a club record 42 caps for England, but his international career is best remembered for a penalty shoot-out miss against Germany which cost the Three Lions a possible place in the final of Euro 96.

SPAIN

First international: Spain 1 Denmark 0, 1920
Most capped player: Iker Casillas, 167 caps (2000-15)
Leading goalscorer: David Villa, 59 goals (2005-17)
First World Cup appearance: Spain 3 Brazil 1, 1934
Biggest win: Spain 13 Bulgaria 0, 1933
Heaviest defeat: Italy 7 Spain 1, 1928 and England 7 Spain 1, 1931

Spain are the first country in football history to win three major international titles on the trot following their successes at Euro 2008, the 2010 World Cup in South Africa and Euro 2012 in Poland and Ukraine.

• Spain secured their first ever World Cup triumph with a 1-0 victory over Holland at Soccer City Stadium in Johannesburg, midfielder Andres

Iniesta drilling home the all-important goal four minutes from the end of extra-time. Despite their entertaining close passing style of play, Spain only managed to score eight goals in the tournament – the lowest total ever by the winning nation at a World Cup.

• Along with Germany, Spain have won the European Championships a record three times. Their first success came in 1964 when they had the advantage of playing the semi-final and final, the latter against holders the Soviet Union, on home soil at Real Madrid's Bernabeu Stadium. Then, in 2008, a single Fernando Torres goal was enough to see off Germany in the final in Vienna. Finally, in 2012, Spain made it a hat-trick of victories after annihilating Italy 4-0 in the final in Kiev.

• Between 2007 and 2009 Spain went 35 matches without defeat (winning 32 and drawing just three) to equal the world record set by Brazil in the 1990s. The run came to an end when Spain lost 2-0 to USA at the 2009 Confederations Cup, but the Spanish were soon back on form, going into the 2010 World Cup on the back of 18 consecutive victories – including a record 10 in qualification – before they surprisingly lost their opening match at the finals against Switzerland. That setback, though, was soon forgotten as Vicente del Bosque's men went on to lift the trophy, sparking jubilant scenes across Spain from Santander to Seville.

• No fewer than 13 players have won 100 or more caps for the Spanish national side – a tally only matched by Estonia among European nations.

HONOURS
World Cup winners 2010
European Championships winners
1964, 2008, 2012
World Cup Record
1930 Did not enter
1934 Quarter-finals
1938 Did not enter
1950 Fourth place
1954 Did not qualify
1958 Did not qualify
1962 Round 1
1966 Round 1
1970 Did not qualify
1974 Did not qualify
1978 Round 1
1982 Round 2
1986 Quarter-finals
1990 Round 2
1994 Quarter-finals
1998 Round 1
2002 Quarter-finals
2006 Round 2
2010 Winners
2014 Round 1
2018 Round 2

Valencia's Rodrigo and three-times winners Spain will take some stopping at the 2020 European Championships

SPONSORSHIP

Manchester United's £53 million-a-year shirt sponsorship deal with US car manufacturers Chevrolet, which started in 2014, is a record for the Premier League. In European football, Real Madrid's deal with Dubai-owned airline Emirates is the most lucrative, being worth around £64 million a year.

• On 24th January 1976 Kettering Town became the first senior football club in the UK to feature a sponsor's logo on their shirts, Kettering Tyres, for their Southern League Premier Division match against Bath City. The Football Association ordered the removal of the logo, but finally accepted shirt sponsorship in June 1977. Two years later Liverpool became the first top-flight club to sport a sponsor's logo after signing a two-year deal worth £100,000 with Hitachi.

• The first FA Cup final to feature sponsored shirts was in 1984 between Everton and Watford. The Toffees wore the logo of canned meat company Hania, while the Hornets advertised industrial vehicles manufacturer Iveco.

• **The League Cup was the first major English competition to be sponsored, being renamed the Milk Cup after receiving backing from the Milk Marketing Board in 1982. It has since been rebranded as the Littlewoods Cup, the Rumbelows Cup, the Coca-Cola Cup, the Worthington Cup, the Carling Cup, the Capital One Cup, the EFL Cup and, from 2017, the Carabao Cup. Since 1994 the FA Cup has been sponsored by Littlewoods, AXA, E.ON, Budweiser, and from the 2015/16 season, Emirates. Meanwhile, the Premier League has been sponsored by Carling, Barclaycard and Barclays, but has had no sponsor since 2016.**

• The Women's Super League is sponsored by Barclays, the two organisations signing a three-year deal worth in excess of £10 million in 2019.

• **In the 2019/20 season 10 Premier League and 17 Championship clubs had the names of betting firms or online casinos on their shirts – a sponsorship trend described by campaigners against problem gambling as 'disturbing'.**

STADIUMS

With a capacity of 114,000 the Rungrado 1st of May Stadium in Pyongyang, North Korea is the largest football stadium anywhere in the world. As well as football matches, the stadium also hosts athletic meetings and mass displays of choreographed gymnastics. In the late 1990s a number of North Korean army generals were burned to death in the stadium after being implicated in a plot to assassinate the country's then dictator, Kim Jong-il.

• **Barcelona's Nou Camp is the largest football stadium in Europe and the second largest in the world with a capacity of 99,354. Old Trafford (74,994) has the largest capacity of any dedicated Premier League ground.**

• Built at a cost of $2.3 billion, the Yankee stadium in New York is the world's most expensive sporting venue. Opened in 2009, the stadium has been the home of MLS outfit New York City since 2015. Finally completed in the spring of 2019 at a cost of £1 billion, Tottenham Hotspur Stadium is the most expensive in Britain.

• **With a capacity of just 1,500, Bristol City Women's Stoke Gifford stadium is the smallest in the Women's Super League.**

RAHEEM STERLING

Born: Kingston, Jamaica, 8th December 1994
Position: Winger/striker
Club career:
20012-15 Liverpool 91 (18)
2015- Manchester City 131 (48)
International record:
2012- England 51 (8)

The FWA Footballer of the Year and the PFA Young Player of the Year, speedy winger Raheem Sterling enjoyed his most prolific season yet in 2018/19, pitching in with 25 goals in all competitions – including two in the FA Cup final against Watford – to help Manchester City win an unprecedented domestic Treble.

• **Jamaican-born Sterling started his career with QPR, before switching to Liverpool for a bargain £600,000 in 2010. He became the third youngest player ever to make his debut for the Reds when he came on as a sub in a 2-1 home defeat against Wigan Athletic on 24th March 2012. Seven months later he became the club's second youngest goalscorer at the time (behind England striker Michael Owen) when he notched his first goal for the Merseysiders in a 1-0 win against Reading.**

• Sterling was a star of Liverpool's magnificent 2013/14 Premier League campaign, during which he chipped in with nine league goals. At the end of the year he became only the second English player (after Wayne Rooney in 2004) to win the Golden Boy award for the most promising player aged under-21 in European football. However, Sterling's performances the following season were affected by a contract dispute with Liverpool, and in July 2015 he joined Manchester City for £49 million – then a record fee for an English player.

• Sterling rose through the England youth ranks to make his senior debut in a 4-2 friendly defeat away to Sweden in November 2012. In only his fourth game for the Three Lions

Raheem has given City Sterling service

he was sent off in a pre-2014 World Cup friendly against Ecuador to become the youngest ever England player to see red. He was a regular starter for England at the 2018 World Cup in Russia and the following year scored his first international hat-trick in a 5-0 drubbing of the Czech Republic at Wembley.

STEVENAGE

Year founded: 1976
Ground: Broadhall Way (6,722)
Previous name: Stevenage Borough
Nickname: The Boro
Biggest win: 7-0 v Merthyr (2006)
Heaviest defeat: 0-8 v Charlton Athletic (2018)

The club was founded in 1976 as Stevenage Borough, following the bankruptcy of the town's former club, Stevenage Athletic. In 2010 the club decided to become simply 'Stevenage'.
• **Stevenage rose through the football pyramid to gain promotion to the Conference in 1994. Two years later they won the title but were denied promotion to the Football League as their tiny Broadhall Way Stadium did not meet the league's standards.**
• Stevenage finally made it into the league in 2010 after topping the Conference table with an impressive 99 points. If the club's two victories against Chester City, who were expelled from the league during the season, had not been expunged then Stevenage would have set a new Conference record of 105 points. The following season Stevenage were promoted again, after beating Torquay United 1-0 in the League Two play-off final at Old Trafford, but their three-year stay in League One ended in 2014 when they finished bottom of the pile.
• **In 2007 Stevenage became the first club to lift a trophy at the new Wembley, beating Kidderminster Harriers 3-2 in the final of the FA Trophy watched by a competition record crowd of 53,262.**
• In 2012 Stevenage reached the fifth round of the FA Cup for the first and only time in their history before losing 3-1 to Tottenham in a replay.

HONOURS
Conference champions 1996, 2010

STOKE CITY

Year founded: 1863
Ground: Bet365 Stadium (30,089)
Previous name: Stoke Ramblers, Stoke
Nickname: The Potters
Biggest win: 11-0 v Stourbridge (1914)
Heaviest defeat: 0-10 v Preston (1889)

Founded in 1863 by employees of the North Staffordshire Railway Company, Stoke are the second oldest league club in the country. Between 1868 and 1870 the club was known as Stoke Ramblers, before simply becoming Stoke and then adding the suffix 'City' in 1925.
• **Stoke were founder members of the Football League in 1888 but finished bottom of the table at the end of the season. After another wooden spoon in 1890 the club dropped out of the league, but returned to the big time after just one season.**
• The club's greatest moment came in 1972 when they won the League Cup, beating favourites Chelsea 2-1 in the final at Wembley, thanks to a late winner by George Eastham – aged 35 and 161 days at the time, the oldest player ever to score

in the League Cup final. The Potters had a great chance to add to their meagre haul of silverware in 2011 when they reached the FA Cup final for the first time, but they lost 1-0 to Manchester City.
• **Freddie Steele is Stoke's leading scorer with 140 league goals between 1934 and 1949, including a club record 33 in the 1936/37 season. Stalwart defender Eric Skeels played in a record 507 league games for the Potters between 1960 and 1976.**
• Midfielder Greg Whelan is Stoke's most capped player, with 81 appearances for the Republic of Ireland between 2008 and 2017.
• **While playing in his second spell at Stoke, the legendary Stanley Matthews became the oldest ever player to appear in the top flight. On 6th February 1965 he played in his last game for the Potters, a 3-1 home win against Fulham, five days after celebrating his 50th birthday.**
• On 27th January 1974 Stoke became the first top-flight club to host Sunday football when they played Chelsea at their former home, the Victoria Ground. Ignoring the complaints of religious groups, a crowd of nearly 32,000 turned up to see Stoke win 1-0.

HONOURS
Division 2 champions 1933, 1963
Second Division champions 1993
Division 3 (North) champions 1927
League Cup 1972
EFL Trophy 1992, 2000

Stoke love playing a bit of 'Spot the Odd One Out' before a free-kick...

"Hey, Luis, the boss wants us to pass to someone other than Messi. I know, I laughed too..."

LUIS SUAREZ

Born: Salto, Uruguay, 24th January 1987

Position: Striker

Club career:

2005-06 Nacional 27 (10)

2006-07 Groningen 29 (10)

2007-11 Ajax 110 (81)

2011-14 Liverpool 110 (69)

2014- Barcelona 163 (131)

International record:

2007- Uruguay 111 (58)

A quick-witted striker who is famed for his ability to score from the tightest of angles, Luis Suarez became the third most expensive player in football history at the time when he joined Barcelona from Liverpool in July 2014 for £75 million. Since then he has helped the Catalan giants win the domestic Double in 2015, 2016 and 2018, the La Liga title in 2019 and the Champions League in 2015, scoring in the final against Juventus. In 2016 he won the European Golden Shoe after scoring a career-best league 40 goals.

• Suarez enjoyed a rollercoaster three years with Liverpool after signing for the Merseysiders from Ajax for £22.8 million in January 2011. In his first full season with the Reds he helped them win the Carling Cup but, significantly less impressively, was given an eight-match ban by the FA and fined £40,000 for racially abusing Manchester United and France defender Patrice Evra.

• The following season Suarez was in hot water again after he bit Chelsea defender Branislav Ivanovic on the arm in an unprovoked attack. The striker, who had been banned for seven games after a similar incident while playing for his previous club Ajax, was hit with a 10-game ban – the fifth longest in Premier League history.

• However, the Uruguayan appeared to turn over a new leaf in 2013/14 when he topped the Premier League scoring charts with 31 goals, won both Player of the Year awards and became the first player ever to score 10 Premier League goals in a single month in December 2013.

• The temperamental Suarez was involved in another shocking incident at the 2014 World Cup when he bit Italy defender Giorgio Chiellini, earning a four-month ban from all football activities in the stiffest ever sanction handed out by FIFA at the World Cup for on-field misconduct. In happier days with Uruguay, Suarez was named Player of the Tournament when his country won the 2011 Copa America, and two years later he became the South Americans' all-time leading scorer.

SUBSTITUTES

Substitutes were first allowed in the Football League in the 1965/66 season. The first player to come off the bench was Charlton's Keith Peacock, who replaced injured goalkeeper Mike Rose after 11 minutes of the Addicks' match away to Bolton on 21st August 1965. On the same afternoon Barrow's Bobby Knox became the first substitute to score a goal when he notched against Wrexham. The following year substitutes were permitted in Scottish football, with St Mirren's Archie Gemmill being the first to come on in a League Cup tie at Clyde.

• **The fastest ever goal scored by a substitute was by Arsenal's Nicklas Bendtner, who headed in a corner against Tottenham at the Emirates on 22nd December 2007, just 1.8 seconds after replacing Emmanuel Eboue.**

• The most goals ever scored in a Premier League game by a substitute is four by Ole Gunnar Solskjaer in Manchester United's 8-1 win at Nottingham Forest in 1999. Incredibly, the Norwegian striker was only on the pitch for 19 minutes. However, Jermain Defoe has scored the most Premier League goals as a sub with 24 for his various clubs. Burnley striker Peter Crouch has made a record 164 Premier League appearances as a sub since 2002.

• **Substitutes were first allowed at the World Cup in 1970, with Holland's Dick Nanninga becoming the first sub to score in the final eight years later. The most goals scored by a sub at the tournament in a single match is three by Hungary's Lazlo Kiss against El Salvador in 1982. Brazilian winger Denilson made a record 11 appearances as a substitute at the finals in 1998 and 2002.**

• At the 2018 World Cup Russia's Aleksandr Yerokhin became the first fourth substitute to be used at the tournament when he came on in extra-time during the host nation's last 16 tie with Spain.

PREMIER LEAGUE SUBSTITUTE APPEARANCES 2018/19

1.	Lys Mousset (Bournemouth)	23
2.	Morgan Gibbs-White (Wolves)	21
	Kelechi Iheanacho (Leicester City)	21
	Gabriel Jesus (Manchester City)	21
	Isaac Success (Watford)	21
	Adama Traore (Wolves)	21
7.	Olivier Giroud (Chelsea)	20
	Shinji Okazaki (Leicester City)	20
9.	Ruben Loftus-Cheek (Chelsea)	18
	Ademola Lookman (Everton)	18

- Jermain Defoe made a record 35 substitute appearances for England between 2004 and 2017, scoring a record seven goals for the Three Lions off the bench.
- The first substitute to score in the final of the Women's World Cup is Nia Kunzer, who notched Germany's winner in their 2-1 defeat of Sweden in Carson, California in 2003.

SUNDERLAND

Year founded: 1879
Ground: Stadium of Light (49,000)
Previous name: Sunderland and District Teachers' AFC
Nickname: The Black Cats
Biggest win: 11-1 v Fairfield (1895)
Heaviest defeat: 0-8 v Sheffield Wednesday (1911), West Ham (1968), Watford (1982) and Southampton (2014)

The club was founded as the Sunderland and District Teachers' AFC in 1879 but soon opened its ranks to other professions and became simply 'Sunderland' the following year.
- **Sunderland were the first 'new' club to join the Football League, replacing Stoke in 1890. Just two years later they won their first league championship and they retained the title the following year, in the process becoming the first club to score 100 goals in a league season. In 1895 Sunderland became the first club ever to win three championships, and their status was further enhanced when they beat Scottish champions Hearts 5-3 in a one-off 'world championship' match.**
- Sunderland were the first Second Division team in the post Second World War era to win the FA Cup, beating Leeds 1-0 at Wembley in 1973 in one of the biggest upsets of all time thanks to a goal by Ian Porterfield. Incredibly, their line-up featured not one single international player.

- Goalkeeper Jim Montgomery, a hero of that cup-winning side, is the Black Cats' record appearance maker, turning out in 537 league games between 1960 and 1977. Inside forward Charlie Buchan is Sunderland's record scorer with 209 league goals between 1911 and 1925.
- Sunderland's record victory was an 11-1 thrashing of Fairfield in the FA Cup in 1895. However, the club's best ever league win, a 9-1 demolition of eventual champions and arch rivals Newcastle at St James' Park in 1908, probably gave their fans more pleasure. To this day, it remains the biggest ever victory by an away side in the top flight.
- **Sunderland last won the league championship in 1935/36, the last time, incidentally, that a team wearing stripes has managed to top the pile. The Wearsiders' success, however, certainly wasn't based on a solid defence – the 74 goals they conceded that season is more than any other top-flight champions before or since.**
- Beaten by Charlton in the League One play-off final in 2019, Sunderland have finished rock bottom of the Premier League on three occasions – in 2003, 2006 and 2017 – to match a record first set by Nottingham Forest in the 1990s.
- **Defender Charlie Hurley is Sunderland's most-capped**

player, appearing 36 times for the Republic of Ireland between 1957 and 1969.

> HONOURS
> **Division 1 champions** 1892, 1983, 1895, 1902, 1913, 1936
> **Championship champions** 2005, 2007
> **Division 2 champions** 1976
> **Division 3 champions** 1988
> **FA Cup** 1937, 1973

SUPERSTITIONS

Many footballers, including some of the great names of the game, are highly superstitious and believe that performing the same personal routines before every game will bring them good luck. England midfielder Dele Alli, for instance, has been wearing the same 'lucky' shinpads since he was aged 11 while Three Lions skipper Harry Kane never shaves once he starts one of his scoring streaks.
- **Kolo Toure's superstition almost cost his then club Arsenal dear in their 2009 Champions League clash with Roma. Believing that it would be bad luck to walk out of the dressing room before team-mate William Gallas, who was receiving treatment, Toure failed to appear for the start of the second half, leaving the Gunners to restart the match with just nine players!**
- Juventus star Cristiano Ronaldo has a number of pre-match superstitions, including always sitting in the same spot on the team bus, insisting on being the last player out on the pitch (unless he is playing for Portugal, when he is always first) and taking a slug of water after the official team photo.
- **In 2012 Cardiff City owner Vincent Tan ruled that the club's home shirts should be changed from blue to red, as the latter was his 'lucky colour'. The Welsh club's fans were incensed and after two years of protests Tan agreed to changed the shirts back to blue.**
- In October 2008 17 players from Zimbabwe club Midland Portland Cement entered the Zambezi river in a bid to 'cleanse the spirits' after a poor run of results. Unfortunately, the superstition backfired horribly as only 16 players emerged from the crocodile-infested waters!

The Black Cats' Charlie Wyke demonstrates suitably feline agility

• Some superstitions are not entirely irrational. For example, Arsenal always make sure that a new goalkeeper's jersey is washed before it is used for the first time. The policy stems from the 1927 FA Cup final, which the Gunners lost when goalkeeper Dan Lewis let in a soft goal against Cardiff. He later blamed his mistake on the ball slipping from his grasp and over the line as it brushed against the shiny surface of his new jumper.

Swansea are super-serious about pushing for promotion in 2019/20

SWANSEA CITY

Year founded: 1912
Ground: Liberty Stadium (21,088)
Previous name: Swansea Town
Nickname: The Swans
Biggest win: 12-0 v Sliema Wanderers (1982)
Heaviest defeat: 0-8 v Liverpool (1990) and Monaco (1991)

The club was founded as Swansea Town in 1912 and entered the Football League eight years later. The present name was adopted in 1970.

• Under former Liverpool striker John Toshack the Swans climbed from the old Fourth Division to the top flight in just four seasons between 1978 and 1981, the fastest ever ascent through the Football League. The glory days soon faded, though, and by 1986 Swansea were back in the basement division once again.

• In 2011, though, Swansea beat Reading 4-2 in the Championship play-off final at Wembley to become the first Welsh club to reach the Premier League. Again, their rise was a rapid one as they had been in the basement tier just six years earlier.

• The club's greatest day came in 2013 when they won their first major trophy, the League Cup. The Swans triumphed in fine style, too, demolishing League Two outfit Bradford City 5-0 at Wembley in the biggest ever victory in the final.

• Ivor Allchurch is the Swans' leading scorer, banging in 166 goals in two spells at the club between 1949 and 1968. One-club man Wilfred Milne is the Swans' leading appearance maker, turning out in 586 league games between 1920 and 1937.

• Former Wales captain Ashley Williams won a club record 50 caps for his country while with the Swans between 2008 and 2016.

• Iceland midfielder Gylfi Sigurdsson is the most expensive player to leave the Swans, signing for Everton for £45 million in August 2017. In January 2018 striker Andre Ayew re-signed for the club from West Ham for a record £18 million.

HONOURS
League One champions 2008
Division 3 (South) champions 1925, 1949
Third Division champions 2000
League Cup 2013
EFL Trophy 1994, 2006
Welsh Cup 1913, 1932, 1950, 1961, 1966, 1981, 1982, 1983, 1989, 1991

SWINDON TOWN

Year founded: 1879
Ground: The County Ground (15,728)
Previous name: Swindon Spartans
Nickname: The Robins
Biggest win: 10-1 v Farnham United Breweries (1925)
Heaviest defeat: 1-10 v Manchester City (1930)

The club was founded by the Reverend William Pitt in 1879, becoming Swindon Spartans two years later before adopting the name Swindon Town in 1883. In 1920 Swindon were founder members of

the Third Division, kicking off their league career with a 9-1 thrashing of Luton.

• The Robins' finest moment came in 1969 when, as a Third Division club, they beat mighty Arsenal 3-1 in the League Cup final on a mud-clogged Wembley pitch. Legendary winger Don Rogers was the star of the show, scoring two of Swindon's goals.

• Defender Rod Thomas, a member of that cup-winning side, won a club record 30 caps for Wales between 1967 and 1973.

• In 1993, three years after being denied promotion to the top flight for the first time because of a financial scandal, Swindon went up to the Premiership via the play-offs. The following campaign, though, proved to be a miserable one as the Robins finished bottom of the pile and conceded 100 goals – a record total for the Premier League that has yet to be beaten.

• Swindon won the Fourth Division title in 1985/86 with a then Football League best 102 points, a total which remains a record for the bottom tier.

• John Trollope is Swindon's longest serving player, appearing in 770 league games for the club between 1960 and 1980 – a record for a single club. Harry Morris scored a record 229 goals for the club between 1926 and 1933, including a seasonal best of 47 in the league in his first year with the Robins.

HONOURS
Second Division champions 1996
League Two champions 2012
Division 4 champions 1986
League Cup 1969

THROW-INS

Former athlete Thomas Gronnemark from Denmark holds the world record for the longest ever throw. Employing a forward hand-spring technique he hurled the ball an incredible 51.33 metres on 18th June 2010.

• During the 2008/09 season Stoke City scored a record eight goals in the Premier League from throw-ins, thanks to the remarkable ability of Rory Delap, a one-time schoolboy javelin champion, to send the ball deep into the opposition box from as far away as the halfway line.

• The most bizarre goal from a throw-in came in a derby between Birmingham City and Aston Villa in 2002. Villa defender Olof Mellberg threw the ball back to goalkeeper Peter Enckelman and it dribbled under his foot and into the net. Despite Villa's protests, referee David Elleray ruled that the goal should stand because Enckelman had made contact with the ball.

• Tottenham defender Serge Aurier became the first player ever to make three foul throws in the same Premier League match during Spurs' visit to Crystal Palace on 25th February 2018.

• Cardiff City were the most wasteful thrown in takers in the Premier League in 2018/19, gifting the ball back to the opposition an average nine times a match.

IS THAT A FACT?

In the summer of 2018 Liverpool appointed the Premier League's first ever throw-in coach – none other than long throw record-holder Thomas Gronnemark.

KIERAN TIERNEY

Born: Douglas, 5th June 1997
Position: Defender
Club career:
2015-19 Celtic 102 (5)
2019- Arsenal
International record:
2016- Scotland 12 (0)

On transfer deadline day in August 2019 Kieran Tierney became the most expensive Scottish footballer ever when he joined Arsenal from Celtic for £25 million – also a record fee for a deal involving a Scottish club.

• **Born on the Isle of Man, Tierney moved to Scotland with his family as a baby. He signed for Celtic aged just seven, progressing through the club's youth system to make his debut as a sub against Dundee in April 2015 when he was still only 17.**

• In four glorious seasons with the Glasgow giants, Tierney was a key part of the Celtic team which won the 'Treble Treble' and he also picked up both the Scottish PFA and Scottish Writers' Young Player of the Year award in 2016, 2017 and 2018.

• **An attack-minded left-back who can also fill a central defensive role, Kierney played for Scotland at Under-18 and Under-19 level before winning his first full cap in a 1-0 friendly win against Denmark at Hampden Park in March 2016. Eighteen months later he captained his country for the first time in a 1-0 defeat to the Netherlands.**

Kieran Tierney is the most expensive Scottish player ever

TOTTENHAM HOTSPUR

Year founded: 1882
Ground: Tottenham Hotspur Stadium (62,062)
Previous name: Hotspur FC
Nickname: Spurs
Biggest win: 13-2 v Crewe (1960)
Heaviest defeat: 0-8 v Cologne (1995)

The club was founded as Hotspur FC in 1882 by a group of local cricketers, most of whom were former pupils of Tottenham Grammar School. Three years later the club decided to add the area prefix 'Tottenham'.

• **Tottenham were members of the Southern League when they won the FA Cup for the first time in 1901, defeating Sheffield United 3-1 in a replay at Bolton's Burnden Park. Spurs' victory meant they were the first (and, so far, only) non-league club to win the cup since the formation of the Football League in 1888.**

• In 1961 Tottenham created history when they became the first club in the 20th century to win the fabled league and cup Double. Their title success was based on a storming start to the season, Bill Nicholson's side winning their first 11 games to set a top-flight record which has not been matched since.

• **As Arsenal fans like to point out, Tottenham have failed to win the league since those 'Glory, Glory' days of skipper Danny Blanchflower, Dave Mackay and Cliff Jones. Spurs, though, have continued to enjoy cup success, and their total of eight victories in the FA Cup is only surpassed by the Gunners and Manchester United. Remarkably, five of those triumphs came in years ending in a '1', giving rise to the legend that these seasons were particularly lucky for Spurs.**

• Tottenham have also enjoyed much success in the League Cup, winning the competition four times. The last of these triumphs, in 2008 following a 2-1 defeat of holders Chelsea in the final, saw Tottenham become the first club to win the League Cup at the new Wembley.

• **Spurs have a decent record in Europe, too. In 1963 they thrashed Atletico Madrid 5-1 in the final of the**

The new Tottenham Hotspur Stadium's South Stand is a sight to behold on matchday

European Cup Winners' Cup, striker Jimmy Greaves grabbing a brace, to become the first British club to win a European trophy. Then, in 1972, Tottenham defeated Wolves 3-2 on aggregate in the first ever UEFA Cup final and the first European final to feature two English clubs. A third European triumph followed in 1984 when Tottenham beat Anderlecht in the first UEFA Cup final to be settled by penalties. However, a first ever Champions League success just eluded Spurs in 2019 when they lost 2-0 to Liverpool in the final in Madrid.

• Ace marksman Jimmy Greaves holds two goalscoring records for Tottenham. His total of 220 league goals between 1961 and 1970 is a club best, as is his impressive tally of 37 league goals in 1962/63. Clive Allen, though, struck an incredible total of 49 goals in all competitions in 1986/87, including a record 12 in the League Cup.

• Stalwart defender Steve Perryman is the club's longest serving player, pulling on the famous white shirt in 655 league games between 1969 and 1986, including 613 in the old First Division – a top-flight record for a player at a single club. His team-mate Pat Jennings is the club's most decorated international, winning 74 of his record 119 caps for Northern Ireland while at the Lane.

• In August 2013 Spurs received a then world record transfer fee of £86 million from Real Madrid for Welsh winger Gareth Bale. The club's record buy is French midfielder Tanguy Ndombele, who cost £55 million from Lyon in July 2019. The previous year Spurs became the first Premier League club ever not to buy a single player in the summer transfer window.

• Tottenham's first title success was in 1950/51 when Arthur Rowe's stylish 'Push and Run' team topped the table just one year after winning the Second Division championship. In the years since, only Ipswich Town (in 1961 and 1962) have managed to claim the top two titles in consecutive seasons.

• On 24th August 2014 midfielder Nacer Chadli scored a goal for Tottenham in a 4-0 defeat of QPR after 48 passes – a record for the Premier League.

• Spurs' incredible 9-1 trouncing of Wigan on 22nd November 2009 was only the second time a club had scored nine goals in a Premier League game. Jermain Defoe struck five times after half-time to set a Premier League record for the most goals scored in a single half.

• In 2017 Tottenham moved to Wembley for a season while work continued on their new 62,062-capacity stadium at White Hart Lane, and attracted a record Premier League crowd of 83,222 for the visit of local rivals Arsenal on 10th February 2018. Finally, in April 2019 Spurs moved into their new stadium – at £1 billion, one of the most expensive ever built – and kicked off with a 2-0 win against Crystal Palace.

TRANMERE ROVERS

Year founded: 1884
Ground: Prenton Park (16,567)
Previous name: Belmont FC
Biggest win: 13-0 v Oswestry United (1914)
Heaviest defeat: 1-9 v Tottenham Hotspur (1953)

Founded as Belmont FC in 1884 by members of two local cricket clubs, the club changed its name to Tranmere Rovers the following year and joined the Football League for the first time in 1921 as members of the newly-created Third Division (North).

• Tranmere enjoyed their greatest day in 2000 when they played Leicester City in the League Cup final at Wembley, eventually going down 2-1.

"Cheer up, mate, we've been promoted in both the last two seasons!"

- Rovers' best league victory, 13-4 against Oldham on Boxing Day 1935, set a record for the highest-scoring Football League match ever. Striker Robert 'Bunny' Bell scored nine goals in the match, a league record at the time until it was beaten by Luton's Joe Payne later that same season.
- Between 1946 and 1955 Tranmere's Harold Bell appeared in 375 consecutive league games, a run unmatched by any other Football League player. He went on to make a club record 595 appearances before retiring in 1964.
- Promoted to the third tier in 2019 after back-to-back play-off final wins at National League and League Two level, Tranmere conceded the fastest ever goal in Football League history in 1964 when Bradford Park Avenue's Jim Fryatt netted against them after just four seconds.

HONOURS
Division 3 (North) champions 1938
EFL Trophy 1990
Welsh Cup 1935

TRANSFERS

The world's most expensive player is Brazilian striker Neymar, who moved from Barcelona to Paris Saint-Germain in August 2017 for an incredible £200 million, more than double the previous record set a year earlier when Paul Pogba joined Manchester United from Juventus for £89.3 million.

- **Premier League clubs spent £1.43 billion on new players during the summer of 2017, a record for a single transfer window. In the summer of** 2019 the figure was only slightly lower, coming in at £1.41 billion once all the various moves had been added up.
- In 1975 Italian international striker Giuseppe Savoldi moved from Bologna to Napoli for £1.2 million in the first ever seven-figure deal.
- **In August 2018 Spain international Kepa Arrizabalaga became the most expensive goalkeeper in football history when he moved from Athletic Bilbao to Chelsea for £71.6 million.**

TOP 10

TRANSFERS IN WORLD FOOTBALL

1. Neymar (Barcelona to PSG, 2017) £200 million
2. Kylian Mbappe (Monaco to PSG, 2017) £166 million
3. Philippe Coutinho (Liverpool to Barcelona, 2018) £142 million
4. Joao Felix (Benfica to Atletico Madrid, 2019) £114 million
5. Antoine Griezmann (Atletico Madrid to Barcelona, 2019) £107 million
6. Cristiano Ronaldo (Real Madrid to Juventus, 2018) £99.2 million
7. Ousmane Dembele (Borussia Dortmund to Barcelona, 2017) £97 million
8. Paul Pogba (Juventus to Manchester United, 2016) £89.3 million
9. Eden Hazard (Chelsea to Real Madrid, 2019) £89 million
10. Gareth Bale (Tottenham to Real Madrid, 2013) £86 million

- According to a FIFA study, women's football clubs spent just £375,000 on international transfers in 2018. The equivalent for the men's game during the same period was a staggering £5.4 billion.

TREBLES

In 2019 Celtic became the first club ever to win the 'Treble Treble' when they made a clean sweep of the Premiership, Scottish Cup and League Cup for a third successive season.

- **In the same year Manchester City won the domestic Treble for the first time in England after beating Chelsea on penalties in the League Cup final, finishing a point clear of Liverpool in the Premier League and then thrashing Watford 6-0 in the FA Cup final.**
- Rangers first won the league title, Scottish Cup and Scottish League Cup all in the same season in 1949, and have gone on to win a world record seven 'Trebles'.
- **In 1922 Northern Ireland outfit Linfield became the first club in the world to land a 'Treble', actually winning all seven trophies they competed for that season including the Irish league, Irish Cup and County Antrim Shield.**

TV AND RADIO

The first ever live radio broadcast of a football match was on 22nd January 1927 when the BBC covered the First Division encounter between Arsenal and Sheffield United at Highbury. The *Radio Times* printed a pitch marked into numbered squares, which the commentators used to describe where the ball was at any given moment (which some suggest gave rise to the phrase 'back to square one').

- **The 1937 FA Cup final between Sunderland and Preston was the first to be televised, although only parts of the match were shown by the BBC. The following year's final between Preston and Huddersfield was the first to be screened live and in full, although the audience was only around 10,000 as so few people had TV sets at the time.**
- The biggest British TV audience ever for a football match (and, indeed, the biggest ever for any TV broadcast in this country) was 32.3 million for the 1966 World Cup final between England and West Germany. The 2019 Women's World Cup

semi-final between England and the USA was watched by 11.7 million people – the biggest British TV audience for a women's game. The biggest worldwide TV audience for any football match is 3.2 billion for the 2014 World Cup final between Germany and Argentina.

• The BBC's *Match of the Day* is the longest-running football programme in the world. It was first transmitted on 22nd August 1964 when highlights of Arsenal's trip to Liverpool were broadcast to an audience estimated to be around 20,000.

• The Premier League will make a record £9.2 billion from domestic and international TV deals over the three years between 2019 and 2022. The incredible sum is made up of £5 billion from UK broadcasters Sky, BT and Amazon – who together will screen 200 of the total 380 Premier League matches per season – and another £4.2 billion from various overseas companies.

TWITTER

Cristiano Ronaldo has more followers on Twitter than any other footballer in the world, with over 79 million at the last count. Brazil star Neymar is next on the list with nearly 44 million followers.

• The 2018 World Cup in Russia attracted a record 115 billion 'Impressions' (views on Twitter), with the most tweeted match being the final between France and Croatia. Kylian Mbappe's goal for Les Bleus in that game was the most tweeted moment of the whole tournament.

• Arsenal midfielder Mesut Ozil is comfortably the most popular Premier League footballer on Twitter, with over 24 million followers.

• Chelsea defender Ashley Cole was fined a record £90,000 for a tweet in October 2012, when he posted abusive comments about the FA after the governing body had questioned the truth of his statements in the John Terry race abuse inquiry.

• England striker Toni Duggan has more Twitter followers, around 150,000, than any other British woman player. However, she is a long way behind USA striker Alex Morgan, whose four million followers make her the most popular female player on the site.

UEFA

UEFA, the Union of European Football Associations, was founded in 1954 at a meeting in Basel during the World Cup. Holding power over all the national FAs in Europe, with 55 members it is the largest and most influential of the six continental confederations of FIFA.

• UEFA club competitions include the Champions League (first won as the European Cup by Real Madrid), the Europa League (formerly the UEFA Cup) and the UEFA Super Cup.

• The longest serving UEFA President is Sweden's Lennart Johansson, who did the job for 17 years between 1990 and 2007. In 2015 the then President, former French international Michel Platini, was forced to step down after an investigation by FIFA's Ethics Committee and was replaced the following year by Slovenian lawyer Aleksander Ceferin.

• Among the international competitions run by UEFA are the European Championship (first won in 1960 by the Soviet Union) and the UEFA Nations League (first won in 2019 by hosts Portugal).

UEFA NATIONS LEAGUE

A new UEFA competition largely designed to replace international friendlies, the first edition of the Nations League ran from September 2018 to June 2019 and was won by hosts Portugal, who beat the Netherlands 1-0 in the final in Porto. England claimed third spot thanks to a penalty shoot-out victory over Switzerland.

• Fulham's Serbian striker Aleksandar Mitrovic was the top scorer in the competition with six goals.

• At the end of the mini-league format, Germany, Iceland, Poland and Croatia were relegated from League A, with League B countries Ukraine, Sweden, Denmark and Bosnia and Hercegovina taking their places. Elsewhere, Scotland were promoted from League C to League B, with both Northern Ireland and the Republic of Ireland making the opposite journey.

• The Nations League will provide a pathway into the 2020 European Championship for the four highest-finishing countries which fail to reach the finals through the normal qualification process.

MOST FOLLOWED FOOTBALLERS ON TWITTER

1.	Cristiano Ronaldo	79.1 million
2.	Neymar	43.9 million
3.	Kaka	29.7 million
4.	Andres Iniesta	24.3 million
5.	Mesut Ozil	24.2 million
6.	Gerard Pique	19.4 million
7.	James Rodriguez	18.3 million
8.	Gareth Bale	18.1 million
9.	Radamel Falcao	17.1 million
	Wayne Rooney	17.1 million

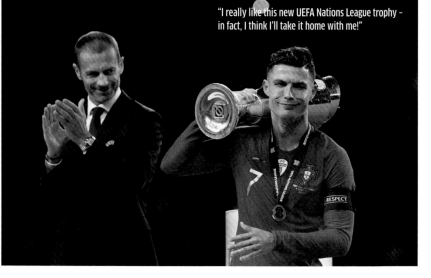

"I really like this new UEFA Nations League trophy – in fact, I think I'll take it home with me!"

URUGUAY

First international:
Uruguay 2 Argentina 3, 1901
Most capped player:
Diego Godin, 131 caps (2005-)
Leading goalscorer:
Luis Suarez, 58 goals (2007-)
First World Cup appearance: Uruguay 1 Peru 0, 1930
Biggest win: Uruguay 9 Bolivia 0, 1927
Heaviest defeat: Uruguay 0 Argentina 6, 1902

HONOURS
World Cup winners 1930, 1950
Copa America winners 1916, 1917, 1920, 1923, 1924, 1926, 1935, 1942, 1956, 1959, 1967, 1983, 1987, 1995, 2011
World Cup Record
1930 Winners
1934 Did not enter
1938 Did not enter
1950 Winners
1954 Fourth place
1958 Did not qualify
1962 Round 1
1966 Quarter-finals
1970 Fourth place
1974 Round 1
1978 Did not qualify
1982 Did not qualify
1986 Round 2
1990 Round 2
1994 Did not qualify
1998 Did not qualify
2002 Round 1
2006 Did not qualify
2010 Fourth place
2014 Round 2
2018 Quarter-finals

In 1930 Uruguay became the first winners of the World Cup, beating arch rivals Argentina 4-2 in the final on home soil in Montevideo. The match was a repeat of the Olympic final of 1928, which Uruguay had also won. In terms of population size, Uruguay is easily the smallest nation ever to lift the World Cup.

• **In 1950 Uruguay won the World Cup for a second time, defeating hosts Brazil 2-1 in 'the final' (it was actually the last and decisive match in a four-team final group). The match was watched by a massive crowd of 199,854 in the Maracana Stadium in Rio de Janeiro, the largest ever to attend a football match anywhere in the world.**

• Uruguay set a record at the 1970 World Cup when they started their group game with Italy with no fewer than eight players from the same club, Montevideo outfit Nacional. Although they only managed to draw 0-0 the South Americans went on to reach the semi-finals before losing 3-1 to Brazil.

• **At the 2010 World Cup in South Africa Uruguay again finished fourth. However, their campaign is mostly remembered for a blatant handball on the line by striker Luis Suarez, which denied their opponents Ghana a certain winning goal in the teams' quarter-final clash.**

• Uruguay are – slightly surprisingly – the most successful team in the history of the Copa America. Winners of the inaugural tournament in 1916, Uruguay have won the competition a grand total of 15 times, most recently lifting the trophy in 2011 after beating Paraguay 3-0 in the final.

VIRGIL VAN DIJK

Born: Breda, Netherlands, 8th July 1991
Position: Defender
Club career:
2011-13 Groningen 62 (7)
2013-15 Celtic 76 (9)
2015-18 Southampton 67 (4)
2018- Liverpool 52 (4)
International record:
2015- Netherlands 28 (4)

In his first full season with Liverpool Virgil van Dijk was named PFA Player of the year, while his composed and powerful performance for the Reds in their 2-0 defeat of Tottenham in the 2019 Champions League final in Madrid saw him pick up UEFA's Man of the Match award. Then, in August 2019, he was named UEFA Men's Player of the Year.

• **A strong, powerful and commanding centre-back, Virgil van Dijk became the world's most expensive defender at the time when he moved from Southampton to Liverpool in 2018 for £75 million. He helped the Reds reach the final of the Champions League in his first half-season at Anfield, but finished on the losing side after a 3-1 defeat to Real Madrid in Kiev.**

• Van Dijk began his career with Groningen before moving to Celtic for £2.6 million in 2013. In two successful seasons in Glasgow he won two league titles and was twice voted into the PFA Scotland Team of the Year. He moved on to Southampton for £13 million in September 2015, and was named Saints captain a little over a year later. However, after missing the final of the 2017 League Cup through injury

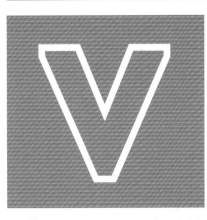

Liverpool fans are worried Virgil van Dijk is sometimes just a bit too relaxed!

he became increasingly unhappy at St Mary's as speculation mounted about Liverpool's interest in him.

• In October 2015 van Dijk made his debut for the Netherlands in a Euro 2016 qualifier against Kazakhstan. He was made captain of his country by new boss Ronald Koeman in March 2018, wearing the captain's armband for the first time in a 1-0 friendly defeat by England.

JAMIE VARDY

Born: Sheffield, 11th January 1987
Position: Striker
Club career:
2007-10 Stocksbridge Park Steels 107 (66)
2010-11 Halifax Town 37 (27)
2011-12 Fleetwood Town 36 (31)
2012- Leicester City 239 (100)
International record:
2015- England 28 (4)

The prolific Jamie Vardy is in the pink

In April 2019 Jamie Vardy became only the sixth Leicester player – and the first for 58 years – to score 100 league goals for the Foxes when he bagged a brace in a 3-0 defeat of Arsenal at the King Power stadium.

• In 2016 Vardy was voted Footballer of the Year by the football writers – the first Leicester player to be honoured in this way – after his 24 goals helped fire the Foxes to the Premier League title. He also scored in 11 consecutive Premier League games to set a new record for the league.

Then, in 2017/18, he scored 20 goals to finish the season as the fourth best marksman in the Premier League behind Mohamed Salah, Harry Kane and Sergio Aguero.

• Vardy started out on £30 per week with non-league Stocksbridge Park Steels after being rejected by Sheffield Wednesday for being too short. Following spells with Halifax Town and Fleetwood Town, with whom he was top scorer in the Conference in 2011/12 with 31 goals, the Sheffield-born striker moved to Leicester City in the summer of 2012 for £1.7 million – a record fee for a non-league player. After initially struggling to adjust to higher level football, Vardy enjoyed a superb season in 2013/14, scoring 16 league goals as the Foxes claimed the Championship title at a canter.

• A hard-working, pacy and clinical striker who loves chasing after long balls, Vardy made his England debut as a sub in a 0-0 friendly draw with the Republic of Ireland in June 2015. The following year he scored his first goal for his country with a clever backheel flick in a 3-2 win against Germany in Berlin, and he was also on the scoresheet in England's 2-1 victory over Wales at Euro 2016. He announced his retirement from international football in August 2018, although said he would still make himself available in the event of an injury crisis.

JAN VERTONGHEN

Born: Saint-Niklaas, Belgium, 24th April 1987
Position: Defender
Club career:
2006-12 Ajax 155 (23)
2012 RKC Waalwijk (loan) 12 (3)
2011- Tottenham Hotspur 209 (5)
International record:
2007- Belgium 114 (9)

A composed and consistent central defender, Jan Vertonghen was a mainstay of the Tottenham team which reached the Champions League final in 2019, picking up the competition's 'Player of the Week'

award for his outstanding performance in an unfamiliar left wing-back role against Borussia Dortmund in the last 16.

• Vertonghen started out at Ajax, with whom he won two league titles and two Dutch Cups before moving to Tottenham in the summer of 2012. In the same year he was named the Dutch game's Footballer of the Year.

• Although he has yet to win silverware with Spurs, Vertonghen did help the north Londoners reach the League Cup final in 2015 and he has twice been voted into the PFA Team of the Season.

• Vertonghen made his debut for Belgium against Portugal in 2007 and is now comfortably his country's most decorated player with well over 100 caps to his name.

VIDEO ASSISTANT REFEREE

In March 2016 the International Football Association Board approved trials of the Video Assistant Referee (VAR) system allowing referees to review decisions with the help of video replays in four categories: potential penalties, red-card offences, goals scored and cases of possible mistaken identity.

• The first trial of the VAR system was in August 2016 in a match between

"Add a nice pinch of sugar, and you've got perfect Belgian waffles!"

New York Red Bulls II and Orlando City B in the third division of the United Soccer League. In the 35th minute referee Ismail Elfath decided to review a foul just outside the penalty area and sent off Orlando defender Conor Donovan for unfairly denying his opponent a clear goalscoring opportunity.

• The VAR system was first used in an international match in September 2016 when France beat Italy 3-1 in Bari. The experiment was judged to be a success, and the VAR system was later approved by FIFA for use at the 2018 World Cup. It was also used at the 2019 Women's World Cup in France, with the most controversial incident coming in the England-Cameroon last 16 tie when a 'goal' for the African side was ruled out for offside after being referred to the VAR officials.

• For the first time VAR was used in England for FA Cup matches shown live on TV in 2018. The first ever goal to be awarded after a video review was scored by Leicester City striker Kelechi Iheanacho against Fleetwood Town. Referee Jon Moss originally disallowed the goal for offside but after consulting with his video assistant, Mike Jones, decided that the goal should stand. Leicester would go on to win the match 2-0.

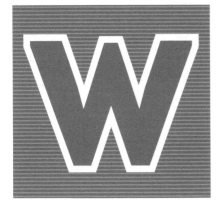

Defender Chris Gunter is Wales' highest-capped player

WALES

First international: Scotland 4 Wales 0, 1876
Most capped player: Chris Gunter, 97 caps (2007-)
Leading goalscorer: Gareth Bale, 31 goals (2006-)
First World Cup appearance: Wales 1 Hungary 1, 1958
Biggest win: Wales 11 Ireland 0, 1888
Heaviest defeat: Scotland 9 Wales 0, 1878

Wales have only qualified for two major international tournaments, but on both occasions did their loyal fans more than proud. The country's finest moment came at Euro 2016 in France when a Welsh side including the likes of Gareth Bale, Aaron Ramsey and skipper Ashley Williams defied the odds to reach the last four.

• Despite losing to England in their second match, Wales topped their group after impressive victories against Slovakia and Russia. Following a narrow 1-0 win over Northern Ireland in the last 16, Wales produced a superb performance against Belgium in the quarter-finals, coming from a goal down to triumph 3-1. However, they were unable to repeat those heroics in the semi-final, losing 2-0 to eventual winners Portugal.

• Wales' only other tournament experience came in 1958 when a side including such great names as John Charles, Ivor Allchurch, Cliff Jones and Jack Kelsey qualified for the World Cup finals in Sweden after beating Israel in a two-legged play-off. After drawing all three of their group matches, Wales then beat Hungary in a play-off to reach the quarter-finals where they lost 1-0 to eventual winners Brazil.

• **Wales winger Billy Meredith is the oldest international in the history of British football. He was aged 45 years and 229 days when he won the last of his 48 caps against England in 1920, a quarter of a century after making his international debut. Six months earlier he scored in a 2-1 win against England, to set a record for the oldest scorer in an international match (45 years and 73 days) which still stands today.**

• Wales' most-capped player is Reading defender Chris Gunter who passed goalkeeper Neville Southall's old benchmark of 92 appearances when he skippered the Dragons in a 1-0 friendly loss to Albania in November 2018.

World Cup Record
1930-38 Did not enter
1950-54 Did not qualify
1958 Quarter-finals
1962-2018 Did not qualify

KYLE WALKER

Born: Sheffield, 28th May 1990
Position: Defender
Club career:
2008-09 Sheffield United 2 (0)
2008 Northampton Town (loan) 9 (0)
2009-17 Tottenham Hotspur 183 (4)
2009-10 Sheffield United (loan) 26 (0)
2010-11 QPR (loan) 20 (0)
2011 Aston Villa (loan) 15 (1)
2017- Manchester City 65 (1)
International record:
2011- England 48 (0)

An athletic right-back who enjoys surging forward from deep, Kyle Walker became the second most expensive British defender ever (after John Stones) when he moved from Tottenham to Manchester City for an initial £45 million in July 2017. After being sent off on his home debut against Everton he went on to enjoy a great first season at the Etihad, helping City win the Premier League and the League Cup. The following season he went one better, being part of the City side which won a unique domestic Treble.

• Walker joined Sheffield United, his local club, when he was aged just seven, eventually going on to make his first-team debut in an FA Cup tie against Leyton Orient in January 2009. Later that year he became the youngest ever Blades player to appear at Wembley, when he turned out for United in their Championship play-off final defeat against Burnley three days short of his 19th birthday.

• That summer he joined Tottenham along with team-mate Kyle Naughton for a combined fee of £9 million, but was immediately loaned back to the Yorkshire outfit. Further loans at QPR and Aston Villa followed before Walker cemented his place in the Tottenham line-up at the start of the 2011/12 season. At the end of the campaign he was voted PFA Young Player of the Year.

• While representing England at Under-21 level Walker was named in the Team of the Tournament at the 2011 European Under-21 Championships. Later that year he made his senior debut as a sub in a 1-0 friendly win over Spain at Wembley. After establishing himself at right-back, he was successfully switched by England manager Gareth Southgate to a central defensive position at the 2018 World Cup in Russia.

• Walker has yet to score for England in nearly 50 appearances for the Three Lions, but he unfortunately netted at the wrong end in his country's 3-1 defeat by the Netherlands in the semi-finals of the UEFA Nations League in June 2019.

WALSALL

Year founded: 1888
Ground: Banks's Stadium (11,300)
Previous name: Walsall Town Swifts
Nickname: The Saddlers
Biggest win: 10-0 v Darwen (1899)
Heaviest defeat: 0-12 v Small Heath (1892) and Darwen (1896)

The club was founded in 1888 as Walsall Town Swifts, following an amalgamation of Walsall Swifts and Walsall Town. Founder members of the Second Division in 1892, the club changed to its present name three years later.

• Walsall have never played in the top flight, but they have a history of producing momentous cup shocks, the most famous coming back in 1933 when they sensationally beat eventual league champions Arsenal 2-0 in the FA Cup. The Saddlers' opening goal on that historic afternoon was scored by prolific striker Gilbert Alsop, who went on to score a record 22 hat-tricks for the club. 50 years later the Saddlers beat Arsenal again in the League Cup on their way to the semi-finals, where they lost 4-2 on aggregate to Liverpool.

• Walsall's all-time leading scorer is Tony Richards, who notched 184 league goals for the club between 1954 and 1963. Loyal defender Colin Harrison played in a club record 473 league games for Walsall between 1964 and 1982.

• **Relegated to League Two in 2019,** Walsall finally made it to Wembley in 2015 when they reached the final of the EFL Trophy. Sadly for their fans, the day did not end happily as the Saddlers lost 2-0 to Bristol City.

> HONOURS
> *League Two champions* 2007
> *Division 4 champions* 1960

WATFORD

Year founded: 1881
Ground: Vicarage Road (21,577)
Previous name: Watford Rovers, West Herts
Nickname: The Hornets
Biggest win: 10-1 v Lowestoft Town (1926)
Heaviest defeat: 0-10 v Wolves (1912)

Founded as Watford Rovers in 1881, the club changed its name to West Herts in 1893. Five years later, following a merger with Watford St Mary's, the club became Watford FC.

• **The club's history was fairly nondescript until pop star Elton John became chairman in 1976 and** invested a large part of his personal wealth in the team. With future England manager Graham Taylor at the helm, the Hornets rose from the Fourth to the First Division in just five years, and reached the FA Cup final in 1984, losing 2-0 to Everton. Watford matched that feat in 2019, but were hammered 6-0 by Manchester City to equal the worst ever defeat suffered by a team in the final.

• After finishing second in the old First Division in 1983, Watford made their one foray into Europe, reaching the third round of the UEFA Cup before losing 7-2 on aggregate to Sparta Prague.

• Luther Blissett, one of the star players of that period, is the club's record appearance maker. In three spells at Vicarage Road the energetic striker notched up 415 league appearances and scored 148 league goals (also a club record).

• In the 1959/60 season striker Cliff Holton scored a club record 42 league goals for the Hornets, helping them gain promotion from the third tier.

• **England winger John Barnes and Wales defender Kenny Jackett made a club record 31 appearances each for their respective countries while with Watford in the 1980s.**

• In August 2019 the Hornets paid French side Rennes £25 million for Senegal winger Ismaila Sarr, their most expensive signing ever. In July 2018 the Hertfordshire side received a record £35 million when Brazilian winger Richarlison joined Everton.

• **In May 2007 Watford goalkeeper Alec Chamberlain became the second oldest player in Premier League**

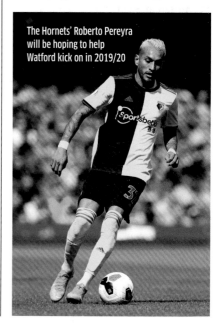

The Hornets' Roberto Pereyra will be hoping to help Watford kick on in 2019/20

history when he came off the bench against Newcastle aged 42 years and 327 days.

• Striker Keith Mercer became Watford's youngest ever player when he came on as a sub in a 1-0 defeat at Tranmere aged 16 and 125 days in February 1973.

HONOURS
Second Division champions 1998
Division 3 champions 1969
Division 4 champions 1978

WEMBLEY STADIUM

Built at a cost of £798 million and with a capacity of 90,000, the new Wembley Stadium is the second largest in Europe and the largest in the world to have every seat under cover.

• The stadium's most spectacular feature is a 315m-wide arch, the world's longest unsupported roof structure. Wembley also boasts a staggering 2,618 toilets, more than any other venue in the world.

• Originally scheduled to open in 2003, the stadium was not completed until 2007 due to a variety of financial and legal difficulties. The first professional match was played at the new venue on 17th March 2007 when England Under-21s met their Italian counterparts, with the first goal arriving after just 28 seconds when Giampaolo Pazzini struck for the visitors. Half an hour later, David Bentley became the first Englishman to score at the new stadium.

• The first Wembley Stadium was opened in 1923, having been constructed in just 300 days at a cost of £750,000. The first match played at the venue was the 1923 FA Cup final between Bolton and West Ham, although the kick-off was delayed for nearly an hour when thousands of fans spilled onto the pitch because of overcrowding in the stands.

• Tottenham moved into Wembley for the 2017/18 season on a full-time basis while construction work continued on their new stadium at White Hart Lane and stayed for most of the 2018/19 campaign as well. Spurs had previously played four European games at Wembley during the 2016/17 campaign, and have now played a record 58 games at the new national stadium.

• England captain Harry Kane has scored a record 37 goals at the new Wembley, with 31 for Tottenham and another half dozen for the Three Lions.

WEST BROMWICH ALBION

Year founded: 1878
Ground: The Hawthorns (26,688)
Previous name: West Bromwich Strollers
Nickname: The Baggies
Biggest win: 12-0 v Darwen (1892)
Heaviest defeat: 3-10 v Stoke City (1937)

Founded as West Bromwich Strollers in 1878 by workers at the local Salter's Spring Works, the club adopted the suffix 'Albion' two years later and were founder members of the Football League in 1888.

• The Baggies were the first club to lose two consecutive FA Cup finals, going down to Blackburn Rovers in 1886 and Aston Villa the following year. In 1888, though, West Brom recorded the first of their five triumphs in the cup, beating favourites Preston 2-1 in the final.

• In 1931 West Brom became the first and only club to win promotion and the FA Cup in the same season, when they beat local rivals Birmingham City 2-1 in the final. The Baggies came close to repeating this particular double in 2008 when they topped the Championship, but they were beaten in the FA Cup semi-final by eventual winners Portsmouth.

• West Brom claimed their only league title in 1920, in the first post-First World War season. The 60 points they amassed that season and the 104 goals they scored were both records at the time. The club's then manager, Fred Everiss, was in charge at the Hawthorns from 1902-48, his 46-year stint being the longest in European football history.

• In 1966 West Brom won the last League Cup final to be played over two legs, overcoming West Ham 5-3 on aggregate. The next year they appeared in the first one-off final at Wembley, but surprisingly lost 3-2 to Third Division QPR after leading 2-0 at half-time.

• The Baggies, though, returned to Wembley the following season and beat Everton 1-0 in the FA Cup final. West Brom's winning goal was scored in extra-time by club legend Jeff Astle, who in the process became one of just 12 players to have scored in every round of the competition. Astle also found the target in his side's 2-1 defeat by Manchester City in the 1970 League Cup final to become the first player to score in both domestic cup finals at Wembley.

• In 1892 West Brom thrashed Darwen 12-0 to record their biggest ever win. The score set a record for the top flight which has never been beaten, although Nottingham Forest equalled it in 1909.

• Cult hero Tony 'Bomber' Brown is West Brom's record scorer with 218 league goals to his name. The attacking midfielder is also the club's longest serving player, turning out in 574 league games between 1963 and 1980.

• West Brom's record purchase is winger Oliver Burke who joined the club from Leipzig in August 2017 for £15 million, making him the

West Brom's Darnell Furlong shows off his keepy-uppy skills

most expensive Scottish player ever at the time. The club's bank balance was boosted by a record £15 million when striker Saido Berahino joined Stoke City in January 2017.

• **West Brom Have twice reached the quarter-finals of a European competition, losing to Dunfermline in the Cup Winners' Cup in 1969 and to Red Star Belgrade in the UEFA Cup a decade later.**

> HONOURS
> *Division 1 champions* 1920
> *Championship champions* 2008
> *Division 2 champions* 1902, 1911
> *FA Cup* 1888, 1892, 1931, 1954, 1968
> *League Cup* 1966

WEST HAM UNITED

Year founded: 1895
Ground: London Stadium (60,000)
Previous name: Thames Ironworks
Nickname: The Hammers
Biggest win: 10-0 v Bury (1983)
Heaviest defeat: 2-8 v Blackburn (1963)

The club was founded in 1895 as Thames Ironworks by shipyard workers employed by a company of the same name. In 1900 the club was disbanded but immediately reformed under its present name.

• **The biggest and best supported club in east London, West Ham have a proud tradition in the FA Cup. In 1923 they reached the first final to** be played at the original Wembley Stadium, eventually losing 2-0 to Bolton Wanderers.

• The Hammers experienced a more enjoyable Wembley 'first' in 1965 when they became the first English side to win a European trophy on home soil, defeating Munich 1860 2-0 in the final of the Cup Winners' Cup.

• **The following year West Ham were the only club to provide three members – Bobby Moore, Geoff Hurst and Martin Peters – of England's World Cup-winning team. Between them Hurst and Peters scored all four of England's goals in the final against West Germany while Moore, as captain, collected the trophy.**

• West Ham's leading scorer is Vic Watson, with an impressive 298 league goals between 1920 and 1935, including a record 42 goals in the 1929/30 season.

• **No West Ham player has turned out more often for the club than former manager Billy Bonds. Between 1967 and 1988 the tireless 'Bonzo', as he was dubbed by fans and team-mates alike, appeared in 663 league games.**

• FA Cup winners in 1964, West Ham lifted the trophy again in 1975 after a 2-0 victory against Fulham – the last time the winners have fielded an entirely English line-up. When the east Londoners triumphed for a third time in 1980 they became the last club from outside the top flight to win the FA Cup. The Hammers, then residing in the old Second Division, beat hot favourites Arsenal 1-0 thanks to a rare headed goal by England midfielder Trevor Brooking.

• **The legendary Bobby Moore is the club's most capped international. He played 108 times for England to set a record that has since only been passed** by Peter Shilton, David Beckham, Wayne Rooney and Steven Gerrard.

• On 19th October 1968 Geoff Hurst scored a club record six goals in a 8-0 drubbing of Sunderland – a feat unmatched in the top flight since. Hurst later admitted that his first goal should have been disallowed as he had punched the ball into the net.

• **On Boxing Day 2006 Teddy Sheringham became the oldest player ever to score in the Premier League when he netted for West Ham against Portsmouth aged 40 years and 266 days. Four days later he made his last appearance for the Hammers at Manchester City, stretching his own record as the oldest outfield player in the league's history.**

• The Hammers smashed their transfer record in July 2019, buying French striker Sebastien Haller from Eintracht Frankfurt for £45 million. In January 2017 they sold former fans' favourite Dimitri Payet to Marseille for a record £25 million.

> HONOURS
> *Division 2 champions* 1958, 1981
> *FA Cup* 1964, 1975, 1980
> *European Cup Winners' Cup* 1965

ELLEN WHITE

Born: Aylesbury, 9th May 1989
Position: Striker
Club career:
2005-08 Chelsea 48 (21)
2008-10 Leeds Carnegie 19 (21)
2010-13 Arsenal 38 (11)
2014-16 Notts County 24 (6)
2017-19 Birmingham City 26 (23)
2019- Manchester City
International record:
2011- England 88 (35)

One of the stars of the 2019 Women's World Cup in France, Ellen White's total of six goals made her joint-top scorer at the tournament along with the USA duo Alex Morgan and Megan Rapinoe and represented the best ever return at the finals by an England player.

• **A penalty box predator who specialises in slotting the ball neatly into the corner of the net, White played for England at Under-17 level onwards before making her senior debut in March 2010, scoring in a 3-0 defeat of Austria. The following year she was voted England Women's Player of the Year.**

West Ham boss Manuel Pellegrini is a stickler for punctuality

Ellen White had an eye-catching goal celebration at the 2019 Women's World Cup

• Spotted by an Arsenal ladies scout aged eight, White went on to play for Chelsea, Leeds Carnegie, Arsenal, Notts County and Birmingham City before moving to Manchester City in May 2019. She enjoyed most success with Arsenal, winning two Women's Super League titles with the Gunners and two FA Cups, scoring in the 2013 final against Bristol Academy at the Keepmoat Stadium, Doncaster.

• While with Birmingham, White was top scorer in the Women's Super League in 2018 with 15 goals – a WSL record for a single season until Arsenal's Vivianne Miedama banged in 22 goals the following year.

WIGAN ATHLETIC

Year founded: 1932
Ground: DW Stadium (25,138)
Nickname: The Latics
Biggest win: 7-0 v Oxford United (2017)
Heaviest defeat: 1-9 v Tottenham Hotspur (2009)

The club was founded at a public meeting at the Queen's Hotel in 1932 as successors to Wigan Borough, who the previous year had become the first ever club to resign from the Football League. After 34 failed attempts, including a bizarre application to join the Scottish Second Division in 1972, Wigan were finally elected to the old Fourth Division in 1978 in place of Southport.

• **The greatest day in the club's history came in 2013 when Wigan won their first major trophy, the FA Cup, after beating hot favourites Manchester City 1-0 in the final at Wembley thanks to a last-minute header by Ben Watson. Sadly for their fans, Wigan's eight-year stay in the Premier League ended just three days after that triumph, meaning that they became** the first club ever to win the FA Cup and be relegated in the same season.

"I'll just hide the ball under my shirt, then run all the way into the goal!"

• In November 2009 Wigan were hammered 9-1 at Tottenham, only the second time in Premier League history that a side had conceded nine goals. The eight goals the Latics let in after the break was a record for a Premier League half.

• **The club's record goalscorer is Andy Liddell, who hit 70 league goals between 1998 and 2003. No player has pulled on Wigan's blue-and-white stripes more often than Kevin Langley, who made 317 league appearances in two spells at the club between 1981 and 1994.**

• Midfielder Jimmy Bullard made a club record 123 consecutive league appearances for Wigan between January 2003 and December 2005.

• **Wigan's most decorated international is flamboyant goalkeeper Ali Al Habsi who played 42 times for Oman between 2010 and 2015.**

• Winger Antonio Valencia boosted Wigan's coffers by a record £16 million in 2009 when he joined Manchester United. In the same year the Latics bought Newcastle winger Charles N'Zogbia for a club record £7 million.

HONOURS
League One champions 2016, 2018
Second Division champions 2003
Third Division champions 1997
FA Cup 2013
EFL Trophy 1985, 1999

WOLVERHAMPTON WANDERERS

Year founded: 1877
Ground: Molineux (32,050)
Previous name: St Luke's
Nickname: Wolves
Biggest win: 14-0 v Cresswell's Brewery
Heaviest defeat: 1-10 v Newton Heath

Founded as St Luke's by pupils at a local school of that name in 1877, the club adopted its present name after merging with Blakenhall Wanderers two years later. Wolves were founder members of the Football League in 1888, finishing the first season in third place behind champions Preston and Aston Villa.

After decades in the doldrums, Wolves are hungry for success

- The Black Country club enjoyed their heyday in the 1950s under manager Stan Cullis, a pioneer of long ball 'kick and rush' tactics. After a number of near misses, Wolves were crowned league champions for the first time in their history in 1954 and won two more titles later in the decade to cement their reputation as the top English club of the era. Incredibly, the Black Country outfit scored a century of league goals in four consecutive seasons between 1958 and 1961 – a feat unmatched by any other club before or since. In the same period, Wolves won the last of their FA Cups in 1960.
- When Wolves won a number of high-profile friendlies against foreign opposition in the 1950s in some of the first ever televised matches they were hailed as 'champions of the world' by the national press, a claim which helped inspire the creation of the European Cup. In 1958 Wolves became only the second English team to compete in the competition, following in the footsteps of trailblazers Manchester United. However,

they fared rather poorly, going out in the first round to German side Schalke.
- The skipper of that great Wolves team, centre-half Billy Wright, is the club's most capped international. Between 1946 and 1959 he won a then record 105 caps for England, captaining his country in 90 of those games (another record).
- Steve Bull is Wolves' record scorer with an incredible haul of 250 league goals between 1986 and 1999. His impressive total of 306 goals in all competitions included a record 18 hat-tricks for the club. Stalwart defender Derek Parkin pulled on the famous gold shirt more often than any other player, making 501 appearances in the league between 1967 and 1982.
- Wolves were the first team in the country to win all four divisions of the Football League, finally completing the 'full house' in 1989 when they won the old Third Division title a year after claiming the Fourth Division championship.
- On their way back to the big time, Wolves won the League One title in 2014 after amassing a third-tier record 103 points.
- Wolves striker Tom Phillipson scored in a Football League record 13 consecutive games in the Second Division in 1926/27.
- On 14th September 1891 Wolves' John Heath took and scored the first ever penalty in the Football League in a 5-0 drubbing of Acrrington at Molineux.
- Wolves made their record signing in April 2019 when they splashed out £30 million on Benfica striker Raul

Jimenez. The club received a record £14 million in August 2012 when Scottish international striker Steven Fletcher joined Sunderland.

> **HONOURS**
> **Division 1 champions** 1954, 1958, 1959
> **Championship champions** 2009, 2018
> **Division 2 champions** 1932, 1977
> **League One champions** 2014
> **Division 3 champions** 1989
> **Division 3 (North) champions** 1924
> **Division 4 champions** 1988
> **FA Cup** 1893, 1908, 1949, 1960
> **League Cup** 1974, 1980
> **EFL Trophy** 1988

WOMEN'S CHAMPIONS LEAGUE

Known as the UEFA Women's Cup until 2009, the Women's Champions League was set up in 2001 as the premier club competition for women's clubs in countries affiliated to UEFA.
- The most successful club in the tournament's history are Lyon, who have won the trophy six times. The French outfit are also the current holders, after beating Barcelona 4-1 in the 2019 final in Budapest.
- The only English club to win the competition are Arsenal, who defeated Sweden's Umea IK 1-0 over two legs in 2007, Alex Scott scoring the winning goal for the Gunners. Three years later the first one-off final was played between Turbine Potsdam and Lyon at the Coliseum Alfonso Perez, home of Getafe, with the German side lifting the trophy after a penalty shoot-out.
- In the 207/18 season Norwegian striker Ada Hegerberg of Lyon scored 15 goals in the competition, a record for a single campaign.
- An enthusiastic, competition record crowd of 50,212 watched the 2012 final between Lyon and four-times winners Frankfurt at the Olympic stadium in Munich. Lyon won 2-0.

WOMEN'S FA CUP

The first Women's FA Cup final took place in 1971, two years after the Women's FA was founded. A total of 71 teams, including some from Scotland and Wales, entered the competition which was won by Southampton who beat Scottish outfit Stewarton and Thistle

IS THAT A FACT?
Wolves defender Conor Coady was one of just three outfield players to play every minute of the 2018/19 Premier League season.

Steph Houghton lifts the Women's FA Cup – Man City must need a pretty big trophy cabinet these days...

TOP 10

WOMEN'S WORLD CUP GOALSCORERS

1.	Marta (Brazil, 2003-)	17
2.	Birgit Prinz (Germany, 1995-2007)	14
	Abby Wambach (USA, 2003-15)	14
4.	Michelle Akers (USA, 1991-99)	12
5.	Cristiane (Brazil, 2007-)	11
	Sun Wen (China, 1991-2003)	11
	Bettina Wiegmann (Germany, 1991-2003)	11
8.	Ann Kristin Aarones (Norway, 1995-99)	10
	Carli Lloyd (USA, 2011-)	10
	Heidi Mohr (Germany, 1991-95)	10
	Christine Sinclair (Canada, 2003-)	10

4-1 in the final. Manchester City are the current holders after beating West Ham 3-0 in the 2019 final.

• **The most successful side in the competition are Arsenal with 14 victories, including a record four on the trot between 2006 and 2009.**

• Former England midfielder Katie Chapman has won the cup a record 10 times with Millwall Lionesses (1997), Fulham (2002 and 2003), Charlton (2005), Arsenal (2007, 2008, 2009 and 2011) and Chelsea (2015 and 2018).

• **Since 2015 the final has been played at Wembley, with a record crowd of 45,423 watching Chelsea beat Arsenal 3-1 in the 2018 showpiece.**

WOMEN'S LEAGUE CUP

The first Women's League Cup final took place in 2011, Arsenal beating Birmingham City 4-1. The Gunners have gone on to win the competition a record five times. The only other club to lift the trophy are current holders Manchester City with three triumphs.

• **In 2014 Chelsea recorded the biggest win in the competition's history with a 13-0 hammering of London Bees.**

• In 2019 the final went to penalties for the first time after a 0-0 draw between Arsenal and Manchester City at Bramwell Lane. The Citizens got the better of the Gunners in the shoot-out, winning 4-2.

WOMEN'S SUPER LEAGUE

In a bid to attract more fans to games, the top flight of women's football in England was reorganised in 2011 as a semi-professional summer league consisting of eight clubs (now expanded to 10 clubs), the FA Women's Super League. However, the FA ultimately decided to return to a winter league in 2017 with Chelsea finishing top of that year's one-off bridging competition, the Spring Series.

• **Arsenal have won the league a record three times (2011, 2012 and 2019) while Liverpool and Chelsea both have two titles to their name. The only other club to top the table are Manchester City in 2016.**

• A number of important records were set in the WSL in the 2018/19 season: Arsenal won the league with a record 54 points and scored a record 70 goals, Yeovil finished bottom with an all-time low of minus three points after entering administration and Arsenal's Dutch international striker Vivianne Miedema was the league's top scorer with a record 22 goals.

WOMEN'S WORLD CUP

Since it was first competed for in China in 1991 there have been eight Women's World Cup tournaments. The USA won the first World Cup and have gone on to lift the trophy a record four times, most recently beating the Netherlands 2-0 in the 2019 final in Paris. Germany have won the tournament twice, while Norway (1995) and Japan (2011) are the only two other nations to take the trophy home.

• **The top scorer in the World Cup is Marta (Brazil) with 17 goals between 2003 and 2019. Michelle Akers of the USA scored a record 10 goals at the 1991 tournament, including a record five in one game against minnows Chinese Taipei.**

• The USA's Kristine Lilly played in a record 30 games at the World Cup between 1991 and 2007.

• **The USA hold the record for the biggest win at the Women's World Cup, thrashing Thailand 13-0 in 2019.**

• Brazil midfielder Formiga played in a record seven World Cup tournaments between 1995 and 2019 and is the oldest player to figure in the competition, turning out for the south Americans in their 2-1 loss to hosts France in 2019 aged 41 and 112 days.

WORLD CUP FINALS

1991 USA 2 Norway 1 (China)
1995 Norway 2 Germany 0 (Sweden)
1999 USA 0 China 0 (USA)*
2003 Germany 2 Sweden 1 (USA)
2007 Germany 2 Brazil 0 (China)
2011 Japan 2 USA 2 (Germany)*
2015 USA 5 Japan 2 (Canada)
2019 USA 2 Netherlands 0 (France)
* Won on penalties

WORLD CUP

The most successful country in the history of the World Cup is Brazil, who have won the competition a record five times. Germany and Italy are Europe's leading nation with four wins each, the Germans becoming the first European nation to triumph in South America when they beat Argentina 1-0 in the 2014 final in Brazil. Neighbours Argentina and Uruguay have both won the competition twice, the Uruguayans emerging victorious when the pair met in the first ever World Cup final in Montevideo in 1930. France can also boast two triumphs, on home soil in 1998 and in 2018 in Russia, when they beat Croatia 4-2 in the final in Moscow. The only other countries to have claimed the trophy are England (1966) and Spain (2010).

• Including both Japan and South Korea, who were joint hosts for the 2002 edition, the World Cup has been held in 16 different countries. The first nation to stage the tournament twice was Mexico (in 1970 and 1986), while Italy (1934 and 1990), France (1938 and 1998), Germany (1974 and 2006) and Brazil (1950 and 2014) have also welcomed the world to the planet's biggest football festival on two occasions each.

• Brazil are the only country to have played at all 21 tournaments and have recorded the most wins (73) and scored the most goals (229).

• However, Hungary hold the record for the most goals scored in a single tournament, banging in 27 in just five games at the 1954 finals in Switzerland. Even this incredible tally, though, was not quite sufficient for the 'Magical Magyars' to lift the trophy as they went down to a 3-2 defeat in the final against West Germany, a team they had beaten 8-3 earlier in the tournament.

• Hungary also hold the record for the biggest ever victory at the finals, demolishing El Salvador 10-1 in 1982. That, though, was a desperately close encounter compared to the biggest win in qualifying, Australia's 31-0 annihilation of American Samoa in 2001, a game in which Aussie striker Archie Thompson helped himself to a record 13 goals.

• The legendary Pele is the only player in World Cup history to have been presented with three winner's medals. The Brazilian superstar enjoyed his first success in 1958 when he scored twice in a 5-2 rout of hosts Sweden in the final, and was a winner again four

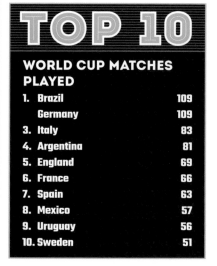

TOP 10

WORLD CUP MATCHES PLAYED

1.	Brazil	109
	Germany	109
3.	Italy	83
4.	Argentina	81
5.	England	69
6.	France	66
7.	Spain	63
8.	Mexico	57
9.	Uruguay	56
10.	Sweden	51

years later in Chile despite hobbling out of the tournament with a torn leg muscle in the second match. He then made it a hat-trick in 1970, setting a sparkling Brazil side on the road to an emphatic 4-1 victory against Italy in the final with a fearsome trademark bullet header.

• The leading overall scorer in the World Cup is Germany's Miroslav Klose with 16 goals between 2002 and 2014. He is followed by Brazil legend Ronaldo with 15, including two in the 2002 final against Germany.

• England's Geoff Hurst had previously gone one better in 1966, scoring a hat-trick as the hosts beat West Germany 4-2 in the final at Wembley. His second goal, which gave England a decisive 3-2 lead in extra-time, was the most controversial in World Cup history and German fans still argue to this day that his shot bounced on the line after striking the crossbar, rather than over it. Naturally, England fans generally agree with the eagle-eyed Russian linesman, Tofik Bahramov, who awarded the goal.

• Germany midfielder Lothar Matthaus made a record 25 World Cup appearances for his country between 1982 and 1998. Mexico's Rafael Marquez captained his country in a record 17 matches between 2002 and 2018.

• Argentina have featured in a record five penalty shoot-outs, winning four of them – a tally matched by Germany, who have triumphed in all four of their shoot-outs.

• Turkey striker Hakan Sukur scored the fastest goal at the finals after just 11

Kylian Mbappe just loved winning the World Cup in 2018

seconds of the play-off for third place against South Korea in 2002. The fastest goal in the final itself was scored by Netherlands midfielder Johan Neeskens from the penalty spot after 90 seconds against hosts West Germany in 1974.

• The oldest player to appear at the finals is Egypt goalkeeper Essam El-Hadary who played in a 2-1 defeat by Saudi Arabia in 2018 aged 45 and 161 days. The youngest player is Northern Ireland's Norman Whiteside, who was aged 17 and 41 days when he lined up against Yugoslavia in 1982.

• Carlos Ruiz of Guatemala scored a record 39 goals in qualifiers between 2002 and 2016 but his country never actually made it to the finals.

• Oleg Salenko scored a record five goals for Russia in their 6-1 hammering of Cameroon in 1994. Meanwhile, the unfortunate Ernest Wilimowski is the only player to score four goals in a World Cup match and still finish on the losing side, in Poland's 6-5 defeat by Brazil in 1938.

• Spain have been awarded a record 18 penalties at the finals, scoring 15.

WORLD CUP FINALS

1930 Uruguay 4 Argentina 2 (Uruguay)
1934 Italy 2 Czechoslovakia 1 (Italy)
1938 Italy 4 Hungary 2 (France)
1950 Uruguay 2 Brazil 1 (Brazil)
1954 West Germany 3 Hungary 2 (Switzerland)
1958 Brazil 5 Sweden 2 (Sweden)
1962 Brazil 3 Czechoslovakia 1 (Chile)
1966 England 4 West Germany 2 (England)
1970 Brazil 4 Italy 1 (Mexico)
1974 West Germany 2 Netherlands 1 (West Germany)
1978 Argentina 3 Netherlands 1 (Argentina)
1982 Italy 3 West Germany 1 (Spain)
1986 Argentina 3 West Germany 2 (Mexico)
1990 West Germany 1 Argentina 0 (Italy)
1994 Brazil 0* Italy 0 (USA)
1998 France 3 Brazil 0 (France)
2002 Brazil 2 Germany 0 (Japan/South Korea)
2006 Italy 1* France 1 (Germany)
2010 Spain 1 Netherlands 0 (South Africa)
2014 Germany 1 Argentina 0 (Brazil)
2018 France 4 Croatia 2 (Russia)
* Won on penalties

WORLD CUP GOLDEN BALL

The Golden Ball is awarded to the best player at the World Cup following a poll of members of the global media. The first winner was Italian striker Paolo Rossi, whose six goals at the 1982 World Cup helped the Azzurri win that year's tournament in Spain.

• Rossi was followed in 1986 by another World Cup winner, Argentina captain Diego Maradona, but since then only one player has claimed the Golden Ball and a winner's medal at the same tournament, Brazilian striker Romario in 1994.

• The only goalkeeper to win the award to date is Germany's Oliver Kahn, who finished on the losing side in the final against Brazil in 2002. The most controversial winner, meanwhile, was France's mercurial midfielder Zinedine Zidane, who was named as the outstanding performer at the 2006 World Cup before the final – a game which ended in disgrace for Zidane after he was sent off for headbutting Italian defender Marco Materazzi.

• Croatia's Luka Modric won the Golden Ball at Russia 2018, the fourth time in five tournaments that a losing finalist collected the award.

WORLD CUP GOLDEN BALL WINNERS

1982 Paolo Rossi (Italy)
1986 Diego Maradona (Argentina)
1990 Salvatore Schillaci (Italy)
1994 Romario (Brazil)
1998 Ronaldo (Brazil)
2002 Oliver Kahn (Germany)
2006 Zinedine Zidane (France)
2010 Diego Forlan (Uruguay)
2014 Lionel Messi (Argentina)
2018 Luka Modric (Croatia)

WORLD CUP GOLDEN BOOT

Now officially known as the 'Adidas Golden Shoe', the Golden Boot is awarded to the player who scores most goals in the World Cup finals. The first winner was Guillermo Stabile, whose eight goals helped Argentina reach the final in 1930.

• French striker Just Fontaine scored a record 13 goals at the 1958 tournament in Sweden. At the other end of the scale, nobody managed more than four goals at the 1962 World Cup in Chile, so the award was shared between six players.

• Surprisingly, it wasn't until 1978 that the Golden Boot was won outright by a player, Argentina's Mario Kempes, whose country also won the tournament. Since then only Italy's Paolo Rossi in 1982 and Brazil's Ronaldo in 2002 have won both the Golden Boot and a World Cup winner's medal in the same year.

• At the 2010 World Cup in South Africa Germany's Thomas Muller was one of four players to top the scoring charts with five goals, but FIFA's new rules gave him the Golden Boot because he had more assists than his three rivals for the award, David Villa, Wesley Sneijder and Diego Forlan.

• At the 2018 World Cup in Russia England captain Harry Kane's six goals, including a hat-trick against Panama, won him the Golden Boot outright. Previously, the only other England player to win the award was Gary Lineker back in 1986.

WYCOMBE WANDERERS

Year founded: 1887
Ground: Adams Park (9,617)
Nickname: The Chairboys
Biggest win: 15-1 v Witney Town (1955)
Heaviest defeat: 0-8 v Reading (1899)

Wycombe Wanderers were founded in 1887 by a group of young furniture-makers (hence the club's nickname, The Chairboys) but had to wait until 1993 before earning promotion to the Football League.

• In 2001 the Chairboys caused a sensation by reaching the semi-finals of the FA Cup where they lost 2-1 to eventual winners Liverpool at Villa Park. Wycombe also reached the semi-finals of the League Cup in 2007, but were beaten 5-1 on aggregate by eventual winners Chelsea.

• On 23rd September 2000 Wycombe's Jamie Bates and Jermaine McSporran set a new Football League record for the shortest time between two goals when they both scored against Peterborough within nine seconds of each other either side of half-time.

• Stalwart midfielder Matt Bloomfield has played in a record 444 league games for Wycombe since making his debut in 2003. In two spells at Adams Park between 2004 and 2019 striker Nathan Tyson scored a club record 50 league goals.

• Wycombe were promoted to League One in 2018 after winning a club record 24 league games. The Chairboys' top scorer with 17 goals was burly striker Adebayo Akinfenwa, at 103 kgs the heaviest player in the whole of the Football League.

HONOURS
Conference champions 1993
FA Amateur Cup 1931

WILFRIED ZAHA

Born: Abidjan, Ivory Coast, 10th November 1992
Position: Winger
Club career:
2010-13 Crystal Palace 110 (12)
2013-15 Manchester United 2 (0)
2013 Crystal Palace (loan) 16 (1)
2014 Cardiff City (loan) 12 (0)
2014-15 Crystal Palace (loan) 16 (1)
2015- Crystal Palace 147 (31)
International record:
2012-13 England 2 (0)
2017- Ivory Coast 14 (4)

Pacy Crystal Palace winger Wilfried Zaha is the Eagles' record scorer in the Premier League with 31 goals. The stats also show that he is one of the most targeted players in the league, with only former Chelsea star Eden Hazard being fouled more often in the last five seasons.

• **Zaha moved from Africa to London with his family aged four. He came through the ranks of the Crystal Palace academy to make his debut, aged 17, in April 2010, and the following year gained national prominence when he starred in the Eagles' shock 2-1 victory away to Manchester United in the League Cup quarter-final. At the end of**

Wilfried Zaha flies like an Eagle at Selhurst Park

the 2011/12 campaign he was voted the Football League's Young Player of the Year.

• A £15 million move to Manchester United followed in January 2013, making Zaha the most expensive player to leave Selhurst Park at the time. However, he was immediately loaned back to the Eagles, helping them gain promotion to the Premier League via the play-offs. When he eventually pitched up at Old Trafford Zaha soon fell out of favour with then United boss David Moyes and was loaned out to Cardiff City. A further loan to Palace resulted in a permanent move back to Selhurst Park, and he was a key figure in Palace's run to the 2016 FA Cup final – which they lost to United.

• After making two non-competitive appearances for England back in the 2012/13 season, Zaha disappointed Three Lions boss Gareth Southgate by switching his allegiance to his birth nation, Ivory Coast, ahead of the 2017 Africa Cup of Nations. Zaha went on to figure in all three of the reigning champions' group matches at the tournament but couldn't prevent Ivory Coast from being dumped out at the first stage.

ZINEDINE ZIDANE

Born: Marseille, France, 23rd June 1972
Managerial career:
2014-16 Real Madrid Castilla
2016-18 Real Madrid
2019- Real Madrid

In 2018 Real Madrid boss became the first manager in the Champions League era to win the trophy three years on the trot, following his side's 3-1 defeat of

Liverpool in Kiev. However, he resigned just five days after that triumph, only to return to the club for a second spell in March 2019.

• **After learning his trade with Real's reserve team, Castilla, Zidane enjoyed huge success in charge of the first team following his initial appointment in January 2016 as the successor to Rafa Benitez, also winning the La Liga title in 2017 and two Club World Cups.**

• An extravagantly gifted midfielder in his playing days, Zidane won two Serie A titles with Juventus before moving to Real Madrid for a then world record fee of £46 million in 2001. The following year he scored with a spectacular volley in his new club's 2-1 defeat of Bayer Leverkusen in the Champions League final and the next season he won his only league title with Real.

• Although of Algerian descent, Zidane chose to play for his native France and in 1998 scored with two headers in his country's 3-0 defeat of Brazil in the World Cup final in Paris. Two years later 'Zizou', as he was known to his team-mates, was voted Player of the Tournament as France beat Italy 2-1 in the final of the European Championships in Rotterdam.

• Zidane came out of international retirement to help a struggling French team qualify for the 2006 World Cup. However, his magnificent career ended on a sour note when he was sent off in the final for headbutting Italian defender Marco Materazzi in the chest after his opponent had made derogatory comments about Zidane's family. Nonetheless, Zidane's sublime performances at the tournament in Germany ensured that he was awarded the Golden Ball as the outstanding player of the finals.